D1301297

e-business

A Canadian Perspective for a Networked World

Gerald Trites
St. Francis Xavier University

David Pugsley
St. Francis Xavier University

Prentice Hall

TORONTO

This book is dedicated to:
Sue—GT   Lori-Anne—DP

Canadian Cataloguing in Publication Data

E-Business: a Canadian perspective for a networked world

Includes index.
ISBN 0-13-093122-5

1. Electronic commerce. I. Pugsley, David 1973- II. Title.

HF5548.32.T748   2003   658'.054678   C2001-903860-7

ISBN 0-13-093122-5

Vice President, Editorial Director: Michael J. Young
Acquisitions Editor: James Bosma
Executive Marketing Manager: Cas Shields
Developmental Editor: Toni Chahley
Production Editor: Julia Hubble
Copy Editor: Valerie Adams
Production Coordinator: Janette Lush
Page Layout: Hermia Chung
Permissions Research: Beth McAuley
Art Director: Mary Opper
Interior Design: Lisa LaPointe
Cover Design: Lisa LaPointe
Cover Image: Eyewire

1 2 3 4 5   07 06 05 04 03
Printed and bound in the USA.

Prentice Hall

Contents

Preface

Although e-business is a global phenomenon, Canadian businesses face legal and cultural issues that are unique to this country. *E-business: A Canadian Perspective for a Networked World* is the first text to address e-business in a Canadian context.

E-business: A Canadian Perspective for a Networked World is not simply a printed textbook. It is a combined textbook/website that reflects a Canadian perspective on the growing and exciting field of e-business. Although only a few years old, e-business has already been accepted by a wide variety of business and educational professionals as one of the most significant events to have taken place in business and in the wider world for several hundred years. Educational institutions are developing new courses, programs and research efforts in an attempt to embrace this area.

The essential rationale of this combined textbook/website is to provide a dual vehicle for educational delivery—a core textbook and a dynamic website. The two interact with each other to deliver both the core concepts of e-business and recent developments that impact upon its evolution. The textbook sets out the concepts that guide e-business, and deals fully with the business strategies and models that have emerged. The website extends these core areas to deal with new developments and emerging trends. While there is nothing new about linking textbooks to websites, this textbook/website has a much more tightly knit and dynamic relationship than is the norm. For example, our website offers the unique feature of interactivity with instructors, allowing instructors to add their comments and suggestions for content for the website, and discuss with other instructors issues related to teaching e-business.

There is absolutely no doubt that e-business is changing and evolving fast. Conventional textbooks alone cannot fill the need to reflect current events in e-business courses. Many texts attempt to fill this gap by simply adding press reports and new website links, and this approach is often lacking in pedagogical merit and can be time consuming for the instructor. The motivation behind this project is to overcome these issues and provide a dynamic tool for teaching e-business.

We have also provided a Canadian perspective, which we believe is important for Canadian students, despite the fact that e-business is often considered as an international or global phenomenon. While e-business is international, at least to the extent that various parts of the world have technologies and infrastructures that can support e-business, there are distinctly Canadian elements and issues that Canadian students need to learn. In addition, students can relate more closely to cases and examples that are Canadian.

Our legal structures and new statutes such as the Canadian Privacy Legislation are central to the Canadian experience with e-business. They are influenced by the activities of the Canadian government in establishing infrastructure, such as the Strategis initiatives of Industry Canada and the digitization of Canada Post. E-business in Canada is also influenced by the activities of Canadian business enterprises, such as the banks' efforts to develop a comprehensive Internet billing and payment system, the ventures of Rogers Cablesystems and others into Web TV, the movement of the banks to virtual banking, and the Canadian capitalists that experienced the rise and subsequent decline of the dot-coms in Canada. Books that are not Canadian simply do not discuss these important aspects of Canadian e-business.

The Combined Text/Website Approach

The textbook is similar to most textbooks in content in that it includes chapters that fully cover the major elements of e-business and case studies. This offers the instructor greater flexibility in crafting course curricula. The book addresses major contemporary trends that have emerged so far, such as trading exchanges, e-procurement, and customer relationship management. Where it differs from other conventional textbooks is in the extent to which it interfaces with the website.

While the emphasis of the textbook is on the macro issues—those that change less frequently—the emphasis of the Website is on the micro issues that are in a constant state of flux. Accordingly, the website presents new case studies, exercises and problems based on current events. Presentation/discussion materials on new developments are added during the year and tied into the textbook, so that any course can easily encompass them and remain current. This will be accomplished by doing more than adding links to the website, although links will be added. Descriptive and contextual material will be added to amplify the events and place them in the context of the course. Therefore, courses developed using this textbook/website will be dynamic courses, changing to reflect the most recent developments in this very fast-moving area.

We believe this to be a critical aspect of this project. E-business is simply moving too fast to be able to rely completely on conventional educational resources and techniques.

Combined Text/Website Approach

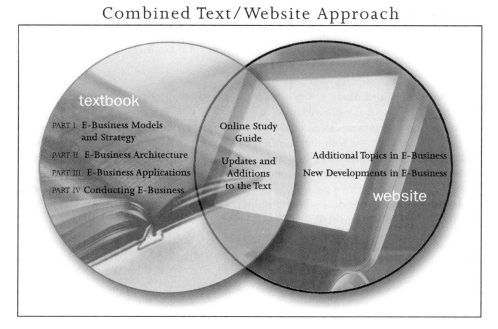

textbook

PART I E-Business Models and Strategy

PART II E-Business Architecture

PART III E-Business Applications

PART IV Conducting E-Business

Online Study Guide

Updates and Additions to the Text

Additional Topics in E-Business

New Developments in E-Business

website

Organization of the Text

The book is divided into four parts comprising 13 chapters, an Appendix of Cases, and a Glossary.

Part I   E-Business Models and Strategy

This part places electronic business into an entire business perspective beginning with an introductory chapter (Chapter 1) aimed at discussing some of the basics of e-business. Chapter 2 addresses strategic planning and business models to ensure that a business mindset is maintained throughout the book.

Part II   E-Business Architecture

This part reviews the architecture of e-business (Chapter 3), and explores the required technologies (Chapter 4) and the impacts on business and management (Chapter 5).

Part III   E-Business Applications

Starting with supply chain management (Chapter 7), this part examines some of the crucial technologies in e-business (Chapter 8), and explores how these technologies are applied for success in e-business (Chapter 9).

Part IV   Conducting E-Business

This part explores the materials needed to integrate the operation of e-business within the broader business context, including marketing issues (Chapter 11), small business operations (Chapter 12), and legal issues (Chapter 13).

Features of the Text

A special effort has been made with this book to incorporate features that will facilitate learning and enhance an understanding of e-business.

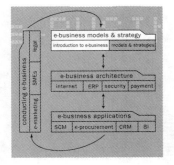

- **E-Business Mind Maps** at the beginning of each chapter provide students with a visual overview of the organization of the text, and where each chapter fits into the dynamic of e-business as a whole. The Mind Map illustrates the dynamic relationship between the foundation of e-business (models and strategies), the tools of e-business (architecture), how these tools are used (application), and the environment that they are used in (conducting e-business).

- **Learning Objectives** at the beginning of each chapter summarize the skills and knowledge to be learned in that chapter.

- **Chapter Introductions** provide an overview of the material discussed in each chapter.

- **Key terms** are boldfaced in the text, listed and defined in the margin of the text, and found at the end of each chapter. For easy reference, all the key terms and their definitions are collated in a **Glossary** at the end of the text.

- **Weblink icons** appear in the margin, providing URLs for the companies discussed in the text.

- **E-Strategy Boxes** emphasize the importance of the strategic employment of e-business in each chapter.

- **New Business Models Boxes** highlight how technology has impacted business models and illustrate how rapid changes in e-business require that business models be flexible and adaptable to remain competitive.

- **Canadian Snapshots Boxes** highlight Canadian businesses to demonstrate how competition and the Canadian marketplace are changing. These boxes demonstrate how e-businesses have developed within the Canadian context and some of the difficulties they have faced.

- **E-business in Global Perspective Boxes** address global issues and opportunities in e-business. These boxes provide examples of either international companies, or companies competing globally and discuss issues of technology related to the management of e-business.

- **Chapter Summaries** recap the issues discussed in the chapter.

- **Tools for Online Learning Boxes** direct students to our website for self-testing material, updates to the text, streaming CBC videos and accompanying cases, and up-to-date information on new developments in e-business.

- The **Appendix of Cases** includes five decision-based case studies with discussion questions to be used in the classroom or for assignments. These cases provide a mechanism for many of the topics in the text to be applied to current and interesting situations facing e-business managers today.

Organization of the Website

While the textbook provides students with a core resource for their studies, the website ensures that the text content is up-to-date and integrated with the Internet for improved learning. The website also provides additional material that complements the text so that instructors and students interested in a particular area may expand the learning experience related to particular topics of interest.

Online Study Guide

Students can develop their knowledge of text material on this portion of the website. With Internet Exercises, Chapter Summaries, Review Questions and Exercises, Problems for Discussion, and Quizzes, students can review chapter content and study for exams.

Updates and Additions to the Text

This portion of the website provides updates to cases and boxes in the text, international comparative studies, and learning modules providing more in-depth information on key topic areas in the text.

Additional Topics in E-business

This portion of the website contains continuously updated online learning modules covering topics such as e-business in specific industries and infrastructure.

New Developments in E-business

This portion of the website keeps students and instructors up-to-date with the evolution of e-business with the latest Internet and e-commerce statistics, commentaries on current trends in e-business, and current new items.

Features of the Website

In keeping with our desire to provide a website that is both dynamic and fully integrated with the textbook, we have provided web resources that are linked directly to the text, and other web resources that complement the material in the text. Our website will be updated regularly to keep pace with new developments in e-business.

Online Study Guide

- Learning Objectives
- Web Links
- Internet Exercises
- CBC Videos and Cases
- Chapter Summary
- Key Terms and Definitions
- Review Questions and Exercises
- Problems for Discussion
- Chapter Quiz—Multiple Choice Questions
- Chapter Quiz—Short Answer Questions

Updates and Additions to the Text

- Updates to Boxes
- Comparative Studies
- Recommended Readings
- Security Issues—for further study
- Business Intelligence—for further study

Additional Topics in E-business

- Start-Ups
- E-business in Specific Industries
- Mobile Business
- Infrastructure
- MySAP
- Starting an E-business

New Developments in E-business

- Internet and E-Commerce Statistics
- Commentaries on Current Trends
- E-business in the News
- Links to White Papers

Instructor's Resources Area

- Instructor's Discussion Area
- Instructor's Manual
- PowerPoint Slides

Course Design

A major purpose of this text is to facilitate a dynamic course design. The topic is so fast moving that from the time of course design to delivery there are often significant changes. While the course design can focus on the textbook as a core, the use of the website can vary to reflect current needs.

This text/website is intended primarily for undergraduate courses, or first courses in e-business at the Masters level. Essentially, it is for survey courses provided to students who have minimal previous exposure to the subject. There is sufficient material to support a one-semester course.

Potential course designs can include

1. A chapter-by-chapter textbook driven course, with occasional references to the website, lectures and discussion of problems in class;

2. A topic-driven course, with blended use of the text and the website materials, lectures and discussion of problems in class;

3. A case driven seminar course, focusing on particular topics;

4. A web survey that is directed by the organization of the course, but with an emphasis on selected websites.

Accordingly, the text/website can be used to support conventional, lecture/discussion based courses as well as seminars using cases and/or web materials.

The authors have found that for undergraduates, a combined lecture (maximum half-hour) and discussion-based course (with a variety of other tools) provides the best approach for engaging students. Some classes can focus on problems, others on cases, and others on website materials. Of course, combinations of these resources can be used in many classes.

The result is that the resource offers a variety of potential course designs and considerable flexibility in their delivery.

Supplements

The following supplements have been carefully prepared to accompany this new book:

- The *Website* (detailed above) contains an online study guide, updates and additions to the text, additional topics in e-business, current news in e-business, and instructor's resources, including an instructor's discussion board for faculty to share information.

- An *Instructor's Manual,* which includes additional background material for cases and exercises as well as a solutions manual.

- A *Test Item File* of over 300 questions, organized by chapter, with the level of difficulty (i.e.: easy, moderate, or difficult) indicated for each question.

- *PowerPoint Slides* which includes customizable slides for lectures.

- *CBC/Pearson Education Canada Video Library for E-Business,* which is a special compilation of video segments from news magazines of the Canadian Broadcasting Corporation. Each video segment has been carefully selected to illustrate topics relevant to e-business. These video segments are accompanied by case studies on the website, and can be viewed online.

Acknowledgments

We wish to acknowledge the help of many people during the preparation of this work. In particular, we wish to thank our colleagues at the Gerald Schwartz School of Business and Information Systems at St Francis Xavier University for their advice and support. We also wish to express a hearty thank you to our development editor, Toni Chahley, for her cheerful and always helpful prompting and encouragement. We also express our gratitude to the other tremendous Pearson staff who helped us, including, James Bosma, Cas Shields, Julia Hubble, Valerie Adams, Susan Wallace-Cox, Lisa LaPointe, Janette Lush, Robin Blair, Laura Canning, Bhavin Desai, and Larry Sulky. We would also like to thank our students who have provided us with a great deal of feedback in our courses and assisted in the development of case studies and supporting materials. Among our students, we owe a particular debt of gratitude to Christian Schmuck, BBA, a 2000 graduate of the Gerald Schwartz School.

Finally, and certainly no less important, we wish to thank the people who took the time to review and provide commentary on various chapters. They included:

John Pliniussen, Queen's University
Gina Grandy, Mount Allison University
Michael Barrett, University of Alberta
Craig Fleisher, University of New Brunswick
Dianne Cyr, Technical University of British Columbia
Stéphanie Gagnon, University of Quebec at Montreal
Ron Murch, University of Calgary
Ken Sekhon, Camosun College
Albert Ersser, Mohawk College
Ron George, University of Calgary
Lilly Buchwitz, University of New Brunswick
Vivian W. Lee, Simon Fraser University/BCIT
Devi Ambati, Durham College of Science and Technology
Ernie Love, Simon Fraser University

Professor Gerald Trites and Professor David Pugsley
Gerald Schwartz School of Business and Information Systems
St Francis Xavier University

Introduction to E-Business

learning objectives

When you complete this chapter you should be able to:

1. Identify the components of e-business.

2. Describe how e-business fits into the traditional business environment.

3. Explain the more significant reasons why businesses enter into e-business.

4. Identify and evaluate the major strategies followed by enterprises that adopt e-business.

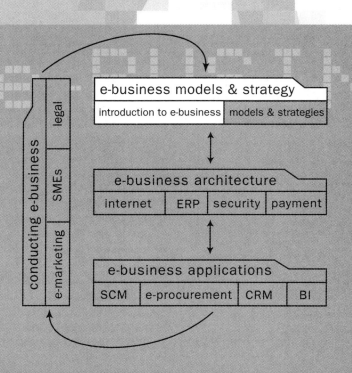

Introduction

The invasion of the Internet into so many aspects of our lives is truly revolutionizing our world. What we have seen so far, however, is only the beginning of a fundamental change that many people have compared to the Industrial Revolution in its scope and potential impact. New types of business have started that we wouldn't have even thought of only five years ago. Businesses that have been around for decades have found they need to use the Internet in order to remain competitive. Ultimately, business and a great deal else in society will be changed forever.

Over the past five years, the media has reported phenomenal success stories about the "new economy." With new dot-com companies arriving daily, it seemed that upstart companies could launch directly into global markets through the Internet and could raise billions on the stock markets with little or nothing in the way of hard assets. They made billionaires of their owners, many of whom had yet to see their thirtieth birthday. Stories abounded of Amazon.com, eBay, and E*TRADE Canada, and Canadian phenomena like PhotoPoint and Research In Motion. The idea of being able to launch a successful business on the Web without needing large amounts of capital to finance hard assets was an appealing one. The cost of entry seemed minimal; the rewards grand.

Reality has presented a harsher picture. By 2001 Amazon has yet to make money (see the E-Strategy box). Research In Motion went through a reality check when tech stocks took a nosedive in 2000 and then suffered further declines in 2001. The financial community and investors generally confirmed what they really knew all along:

1. a business still needs to make profits to survive and grow, and

2. many of the traditional business fundamentals continue to make sense in this new electronic world, even though the specific business models are changing and evolving.

Some of the business models of the dot-com companies did not include any plans on how they would make money on a long-term basis. Napster, the challenged utility for exchanging music over the Internet completely free of charge, was a case in point. The company offered the service free of charge to the users, and did not have any other plans, such as advertising, that would generate money to keep it going. Only after Napster had been in operation for some time, and had been challenged in the courts, did it begin to discuss charging some fees. It is quite possible that if the courts had not curtailed the company's activities, Napster would not have survived for economic reasons.

Increasingly, the mystique of the Internet is fading and business is simply embracing it as a powerful and essential tool for achieving strategic goals and remaining competitive in the new economy.

This glitzy realm of "new economy" businesses is only one part of the world of e-commerce, or what more accurately should be described as e-business. While the dot-coms lost some of their lustre—not all of it, because there still are amazing success stories out there—large "old economy" companies are moving heavily into e-business. A good example is the **trading exchange** "Covisint" (see the E-Business in Global Perspective box), launched by the automobile industry to streamline its sources of supply and make it more competitive. This too is e-business,

Amazon.com
www.Amazon.com

eBay.com
www.ebay.com

eTrade.com
www.etrade.com

Research In Motion
www.rim.net

Napster
www.napster.com

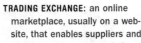

TRADING EXCHANGE: an online marketplace, usually on a website, that enables suppliers and customers to carry out their business electronically, often using auctioning techniques.

E-STRATEGY

Amazon.com: An Illustration of Changing E-Strategy—from Clicks to Bricks

Amazon.com was one of the first companies to sell books on the Web. Certainly it was the most widely noticed of the Internet start-ups and one that caused traditional bookstores like Barnes & Noble to also open websites to sell their product. Amazon started in 1995 with the idea it would be able to take orders over the Web and fill them by ordering from suppliers as demand required. Part of the strategy was to be able to supply books without incurring the infrastructure costs that other businesses had to bear, therefore enabling the company to sell at lower prices.

The reality that emerged was that it took Amazon until 1999 to get out of a loss position, and in that year it only achieved a break-even financial result. For a time, Amazon's shares rose despite its losses, but in 2000, reality began to set in with regard to the "dot-com" shares on the market and Amazon's shares declined considerably.

The reason Amazon had trouble making money was that the company had to spend far more on marketing and infrastructure than it had foreseen. The marketing expenditure had been hard to predict because Internet marketing is a new field. The infrastructure costs arose because Amazon found that it was having trouble delivering orders on a timely basis and eventually had to make the decision to develop some of its own warehousing and distribution infrastructure to address this issue. Amazon still relied heavily on order by demand, but began buffering this approach with some warehouse buying. Of course, that was completely contrary to the original strategy. To deal with the additional costs, the company had to find a strategy that would gener-ate higher revenues. Amazon began to expand its offerings on the Web by adding products, such as videos, health and beauty products, hardware, games, toys, and other items. The company also added an auctioning feature, where goods could be sold in online auctions, rather like the well-known auctioning site eBay.com.

From a strategic viewpoint, Amazon moved from a clearly defined strategy of selling books at a low price without the need for an infrastructure as outlined above to one in which the company needed to find other sources of revenue to pay for the infrastructure it had to buy. The idea of adding new products seemed a logical way to make effective use of this infrastructure by adding revenues with minimal incremental cost. It is a classic case of a changing and evolving Internet strategy.

Questions

1. What was the significance of Amazon's need to build warehouses?
2. What is the likely impact of Amazon's move to bricks and mortar on their long-term competitive advantage?

SOURCE: www.amazon.com.

of a business-to-business (or B2B) nature. B2B activity represents by far the biggest part of e-business at this stage in its evolution.

Another good example is Sears Roebuck, which has been a major player in retail for many years, but now has one of the top e-business websites on the Internet, grossing over US$18 billion per year. Sears.com (Figure 1.1) is one of the top-rated sites in North America. It has been making the transition to the world of e-business—from bricks to clicks.

Figure 1.1   **Sears Website**

The Sears.com homepage is illustrative of the variety of retail offerings.

SOURCE: www.sears.com.

A Definition of E-Business

ELECTRONIC DATA INTERCHANGE (EDI): a structured way of creating electronic "forms" that can be transmitted between trading partners to execute business transactions without the need to generate any paper.

In a very broad and general sense, electronic business has often been defined as any business carried out in electronic form. Therefore, if business transactions are carried out by using **electronic data interchange (EDI),** this is a form of e-business. If a bank transaction is carried out by electronic transfers between branches, this is a form of e-business. So e-business has been in existence for a good many years—certainly years before the Internet became an economic force.

The growth of the Internet did create a significant change, opening up new market channels and wider markets. Initially, the use of the Internet for selling goods and services was referred to as e-commerce. More recently, the term "e-business" has been used widely to reflect the fact that the effective delivery of e-commerce requires considerable organizational commitment and change. The term "e-business" therefore conveys a much broader meaning. This new meaning is illustrated by Kalakota and Robinson, who have stated, "e-Business is the complex fusion of business processes, enterprise applications, and organizational structure necessary to create a high-performance business model."[1]

This definition of e-business connects the idea of business change and structure to the creation of business models that will sustain themselves. Under this definition, the whole business is critical to e-business—how it is structured, what technology is being used, and how the business is carried out. Therefore a consideration of e-business extends well beyond the use of the Internet, although the Internet remains central. It extends into a range of management issues, from strategy to execution to supervision, and incorporates the strategic use of information technology to achieve corporate goals. If anything, it is difficult to define the boundaries of e-business, but that is what we must attempt in this chapter.

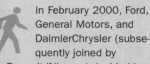

E-BUSINESS IN GLOBAL PERSPECTIVE

Covisint and the Automotive Industry

In February 2000, Ford, General Motors, and DaimlerChrysler (subsequently joined by Renault/Nissan) decided to start a trading exchange to solidify their sources of supply and make them more competitive. Covisint was initially the outcome of this initiative. A joint venture between the large automakers and their suppliers, Covisint was initially intended to become the preferred method for suppliers to sell their products to the big manufacturers, but has grown to encompass design and other areas to the point of providing a technological business infrastructure for the industry.

In the fall of 2000, the regulators approved Covisint and it began operating. The auto manufacturers plan to continue running their purchasing departments so they can conduct their procurement activities in the traditional manner as well as through the exchange. Part of their procurement operations works on an auctioning basis, under which a manufacturer places an order on the exchange, and their suppliers bid on filling that order at a particular price and time.

Covisint is a trading exchange on the Internet, located at www.covisint.com. It is expected to process as much as US$750 billion in annual business when it matures. By mid-2000, more than 25 suppliers had signed on to Covisint, including some of the world's biggest auto parts suppliers, such as Delphi Automotive Systems. Other suppliers, including Meritor Automotive, Johnson Controls, and Federal-Mogul indicated early interest in joining, and technology giants Oracle and CommerceOne also joined the exchange and hold equity positions in Covisint.

During 2000, Covisint came under scrutiny by the U.S. Federal Trade Commission and the antitrust divisions of the U.S. Department of Justice and the European Commission. These regulators feared that the major auto manufacturers would use the exchange to dictate pricing and purchasing practices suppliers must use, in effect using the exchange as a vehicle for fixing prices. Covisint executives maintained that the exchange would not violate an-

titrust laws because it is open to other manufacturers.

The regulators were concerned as to whether the exchange would be used to constrict the market by forcing the suppliers to do their business through the exchange as opposed to other means. There were reports that some of the employees of the big automakers indicated this to suppliers, but it is not clear that the companies actually followed this strategy. If the exchange is successful, then suppliers will want to use it to be part of the network and to be able to use the infrastructive and technologies it makes available.

Another issue of concern to regulators was whether the exchanges themselves could turn into monopolies. Theoretically, this could happen if buyers and sellers become interested in using only the biggest exchange(s) available. Part of their concern was that the big buyers or suppliers that own exchanges could have access to information on deals that might give them an unfair trading advantage, but these concerns were subsequently cleared.

Questions

1. Why would suppliers register with Covisint? What would be the advantages to them?
2. What are the benefits of Covisint to the big auto companies?
3. Did the regulators have legitimate concerns?

SOURCE: www.covisint.com.

WORLD WIDE WEB: the user-friendly, graphics-capable component of the Internet.

While not all e-business is carried out on the Internet, it is undeniable that the rise in the use of the Internet is the single most important enabler of e-business of any type. Even types of e-business that were carried out before the age of the Internet are moving to the Internet, or more specifically to the **World Wide Web (WWW)**. A good example of this is EDI, which started on private networks called VANs (for Value Added Networks), but have been moving to the Web because of the economies that are possible.

The Business-to-Consumer (B2C) Arena

Many kinds of business are carried out on the Internet involving interaction between businesses and consumers, referred to as business-to-consumer (B2C) e-business. In the B2C arena, companies are offering a growing range of goods and services on the Internet directly to consumers, often bypassing their traditional distributors. Besides the books that are offered on Amazon.com, early initiatives involved the sale of investments, through such sites as eTrade.com and Schwab.com. These sites are particularly interesting in that the former is an Internet upstart and the latter is an old-economy entrant into e-business, but both have been successful in their efforts.

Charles Schwab
www.schwab.com

The Internet also ushered in the idea of online auctioning and other bidding-related retail systems. A notable early success in this area was eBay.com, but auctioning sites have since proliferated considerably, and any search engine index will reveal vast numbers of them. The most important use of auctioning, however, has been in the business-to-business procurement systems and trading exchanges as described previously, where auctioning is perceived as a way in which suppliers can be made to be more competitive and responsive to their customers.

AUTOMATED TELLER MACHINES (ATMS): user-friendly computers, usually located in bank branches, that enable bank customers to carry out their own banking transactions online.

A notable aspect of consumer oriented e-business is that of the banks, who have formed their business strategies around aggressive e-business strategies. Banks have technically been involved in e-business for many years, particularly when they began to install their **automated teller machines (ATMs)** during the 1970s. The process of moving customer service to an automated format, where the customer actually performs the input activity for the bank, proved to be a lucrative strategy. The banks did not have to pay to have this input performed; the customers actually paid them for the "privilege"! The banks installed more ATMs, reduced their staffing, closed branches, and made more money. Then, during the 1990s, the banks moved their e-business to the Internet by introducing Internet banking. After some shaky starts, with concerns about security and sometimes using doubtful technology, the banks got their acts together and now all of them offer substantial Internet banking to their customers. People can log onto the bank website and view their account balances and recent transactions, make transfers of funds, pay bills, and request other services. More recently, the ability to make loan applications and handle electronic bill presentment and payment services have been added to the banks' offerings. Internet banking has been very successful and in fact offers even greater cost savings to the banks (see Figure 1.2) than do ATMs.

Figure 1.2   Cost of Banking Transactions (US Dollars)

The cost of banking transactions drops dramatically when the Internet is used for processing them.

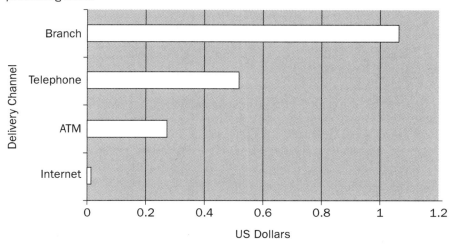

B2C has been growing and changing the business environment. E-tailing will continue to be an expanding phenomenon as the use of the Internet expands to greater numbers of people.

The Business-to-Business (B2B) Arena

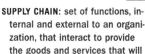

In the business-to-business (B2B) arena, activity has centred on the streamlining of the **supply chain** by establishing shared systems between suppliers and customers using the Internet or related technology. Activity in the B2B world has focused on the **buy-side**, which deals with the procurement activity of a business, and the **sell-side**, which relates to relationships with customers and the consequent marketing and selling activity. In a sense, of course, the two are simply opposite sides of the same coin (see Figure 1.3).

Finally, e-business includes the front- and back-office information system applications that form the engine for modern business. These include the applications that enable information relating to the customers to be captured and used in finding better and more efficient ways to serve them—the so-called **customer relationship management (CRM)** applications (discussed in Chapter 9)—as well as the **e-procurement** applications (discussed in Chapter 8). They also include the applications that serve to integrate the information systems of a business to streamline its value chain. The streamlining of the internal value chain and the external supply chain is a fundamental strategy of e-business that enables businesses to respond quickly to the increasingly stringent demands of e-customers.

In summary, the definition of e-business includes a wide range of business activity—a range that is widening to the point that experts including Don

SUPPLY CHAIN: set of functions, internal and external to an organization, that interact to provide the goods and services that will be sold to the customers.

BUY-SIDE: the purchasing end of the supply chain, which consists of suppliers and the processes that connect with them.

SELL-SIDE: the selling end of the supply chain, which consists of customers and the processes that connect with them.

CUSTOMER RELATIONSHIP MANAGEMENT: the set of strategies, technologies, and processes that enable the business to continuously improve offerings to customers.

E-PROCUREMENT: the use of technology to improve the process of acquiring those goods and services that are needed as raw materials or to support the operation of the business.

Figure 1.3   Essential Structure of E-Business

E-business encompasses the full range of business activity, from suppliers to customers.

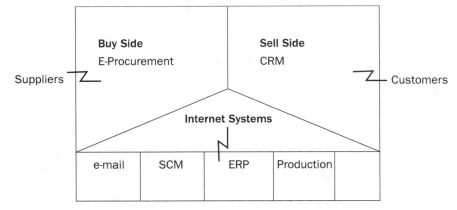

Tapscott, author of *Paradigm Shift* and *The Digital Economy*, are saying that ultimately all business will be e-business.[2] The Canadian Snapshots box illustrates how some companies are using e-business.

Forces of Change

With the tremendous growth in e-business over the past few years, it is important to consider why this has taken place. Clearly, there has been a strong interest in the Internet, as well as considerable hype, but in order for it to be adopted by businesses, there must be solid business justification for its use. Put simply, the benefits of using the Internet must be greater than the costs, such that it will result in a satisfactory contribution to profits.

These solid business reasons generally involve the quest for improved profitability, but more specifically include:

- increasing sales;
- reducing costs;
- improving customer service;
- competitive pressure;
- increased market reach; and
- progress in addressing user concerns.

Increasing Sales

The Internet offers the possibility of increasing sales through various means. It represents a new sales channel, one that can be used to support and augment the more traditional channels, like stores, mail-order catalogues, and field sales personnel. This new sales channel also may reach new people, particularly those who use the Internet most frequently and are comfortable buying online. Finally, the Internet offers the possibility of reaching new geographical areas around the globe, many of which would not have been economically accessible before the advent of the Internet. This aspect of increasing sales, of course, relates to the matter of increased market reach, which will be discussed shortly.

CANADIAN SNAPSHOTS

Research In Motion, Sierra Wireless Inc., and Certicom Corp.

Research In Motion Ltd. (RIM) is a high-tech start-up company based in Waterloo, Ontario, and listed on the NASDAQ Stock Exchange and the Toronto Stock Exchange. The company, which started in 1984, specializes in producing handheld wireless products, such as the BlackBerry wireless e-mail unit, various pagers and wireless personal computer adapters, and radio modems. (Its major competition is the popular PalmPilot, produced by Palm Inc., an American company owned by US Robotics Corporation.)

By 1999, RIM had begun to make its mark in the U.S. market with its BlackBerry unit and its shares climbed from $12.95 in 1998 to more than $260 in early 1999. At this amount, RIM was worth a total of $17.7 billion. Although the shares fell back during the high-tech sell-off of 2000, its value has held well. In 2000, the company announced a technology and marketing agreement with Nortel Networks for the development of new wireless Internet technologies and international wireless Internet market opportunities. This deal solidified RIM's place in the global high-tech market.

The company has a website at www.rim.net, where one can view and purchase its products online.

RIM is now a world leader in small handheld Internet-based technology. Other companies in the same business include Sierra Wireless Inc., a manufacturer of wireless devices that enable laptops to connect with corporate networks and the Internet. Sierra has made some high-profile deals with U.S. companies. Another is Certicom Corp., which develops encryption technology designed to make wireless e-commerce secure and keep hackers from eavesdropping.

Wireless devices are allowing managers and business owners to have more flexible control over organizations. For example, a manager travelling to the airport could be notified of an inventory shortage in a particular product line that required immediate attention. The wireless device may allow the manager to authorize a rush order to ensure customer satisfaction and monitor production progress while at a conference. The emergence of wireless devices adds convenience and flexibility to existing information systems.

Companies like RIM are leaders in the global wireless market, and are establishing Canada as a major presence in this emerging aspect of e-business.

Questions

1. What would have been the advantage to RIM of the alliance with Nortel?
2. What would have been the advantage to Nortel?
3. How would wireless devices add to the value of existing information systems from a management and strategic perspective?

SOURCE: www.rim.net.

Reducing Costs

One of the clear advantages of e-business is the lower cost of executing transactions, as illustrated so well by the banking business. This lower cost comes from several sources, in addition to the fact that the input process can be moved from the staff to the customers and outside users. Another example is that of airline travel. Under the old reservation systems, the customer would call or visit the airline and state his or her requests to an employee, who would then enter those requests into the computer system and generate confirmations and tickets.

Now all the major airlines have Internet reservation systems, which require the customer to log in and type all their requests into forms provided on the site. The system confirms the availability of the flights and the specific requests such as seating or special meals, then generates tickets that can be mailed from a central point or even electronic tickets that are faxed or e-mailed to the customer. All of the input has been carried out by the customer and no airline employee involvement has been required other than perhaps taking a printed ticket off a printer and inserting it into an envelope for mailing. Reduced need for customer service personnel leads to considerable and obvious cost savings. In the case of the electronic ticket sent by e-mail, the customer is even printing the ticket, which leads directly into one of the other reasons why Internet commerce is cheaper—infrastructure.

Under older traditional systems, the owners of those systems had to acquire the hardware, software, and communications capability to enable the applications to be employed. The Internet offers the opportunity for some of this infrastructure, such as printers, to be pushed out to the owner community. More importantly, it also offers a communications infrastructure that is largely cost-free to the user. Certainly, there are Internet-related costs, such as fees paid to the **Internet service providers (ISPs),** and there is still a need to establish additional infrastructure because of the Internet, such as new servers and firewalls to ensure security. However, the cost of these additional items, though sometimes considerable, pales in comparison to the cost that would be incurred if a communications infrastructure comparable to the Internet had to be acquired by the business. This is one of the major reasons why the Internet offers cost savings to business.

The use of the Internet and its applications for e-business involves many different processes carried out in the business. As technology is applied, it is necessary to rationalize and improve these processes to make efficient use of the technological and human resources required. Consequently, e-business offers an opportunity to achieve economies in the improvement of business processes, and this is one of the techniques used by businesses entering into e-business to reduce costs.

Another cost reduction measure inherent in e-business involves the costs of procurement from suppliers. Automation of these procurement activities should result in cost savings. In addition, when procurement activities are more closely tied into the processes of the suppliers, it often means improved supplier relations and the resulting opportunity to obtain better prices.

INTERNET SERVICE PROVIDERS (ISPs): companies that offer Internet access and related services to individuals and businesses for a fee. Connections are offered through telephone lines or direct connection.

Improving Customer Service

The inclusion of web pages on the World Wide Web provides an opportunity for customers and prospective customers to log in and obtain information about the company, its products and its people. The website can provide a vehicle through which users can obtain answers to their questions.

Some examples of additional services to customers offered through the Web include:

- bank sites providing the location of branches;
- websites of professional service firms detailing the specific services offered and providing contact information for the persons in charge of that area;
- news sites like CNN offering reader surveys, where users can quickly vote on an issue and read the results of the vote to date; and
- automobile sites providing working demos of particular models and details about those models.

CNN
www.cnn.com

Competitive Pressure

Finally, many companies find they simply must enter into the use of the Internet for competitive reasons. Part of this reason relates to image—if the competitors are doing it, then people will ask why the company isn't. It also relates to simple economics. If the competition is obtaining financial benefits such as increased sales and reduced costs from using the Web, then they will eventually obtain a competitive advantage from this, and it will be necessary for their competitors to use the Web in order to survive.

Increased Market Reach

The increased usage of the Internet around the world has played a major role in the increased interest of businesses in using it. One of the major implications of this increased usage is the fact it affords a business the opportunity to reach a far wider market than it previously could. Theoretically, it offers the opportunity to reach people all around the world. Therefore, if companies wish to do business in a new country, or wish to establish direct cost-effective communications links with existing business partners in other areas of the globe, they can now do so through the Internet.

Some businesses have felt that they now have the opportunity to establish a global market for their products. Of course, there are limitations to this global Internet reach. For one thing, there are significant parts of the globe that do not have any Internet access, or whose access is extremely limited. Much of the underdeveloped world falls into this category. Many of these countries do not have the communications infrastructure necessary to make the Internet available to their populace. In addition, there are many countries that simply have not yet seized the Internet challenge. Accordingly, the actual ability to reach significant numbers of people outside of North America, Western Europe, and other advanced economies is somewhat limited, as shown in Table 1.1. Over the longer term, though, we can expect that this situation will change.

Progress in Addressing User Concerns

Ever since the Internet began to be used more often for conducting commercial transactions, there has been concern about the lack of security and privacy on the Internet. Initially, it was widely acknowledged that there was little or no security available on the Internet and that it was an environment rife with hackers, viruses, and other threats to data and system integrity. As a result of this lack of security,

Table 1.1   The World Internet Population, January 2000

Although the Internet has made large inroads into North America, Europe, and parts of Asia, there are many areas of the world where it is used very little or not at all.

Geographic Area	Estimated Internet Users (in Millions)
Africa	2.1
Asia/Pacific	40.0
Europe	70.0
Middle East	1.9
Canada and United States	120.0
South America	8.0
World Total	**242.0**

SOURCE: January 2000 Table from "Worldwide Internet Population. Industry Statistics." *CommerceNet.* <http://www.commerce.net/research/stats/wwstats.html>. November 2001. Reprinted with permission.

people were reluctant to allow any of their private information to be entered into the Internet and were especially reluctant to provide information such as credit card numbers.

This latter point relates to another serious shortcoming with regard to the Internet—the lack of a satisfactory payment system. Since the Internet is an electronic medium, hard cash cannot be used to pay for goods or services purchased over the Internet. Various other methods have been tried, and for a time, the most common method was the use of credit cards through forms that were filled out offline and faxed to the vendor.

Privacy and Payment Systems

FIREWALLS: separate, highly secure computers through which access to the network from the Internet is exclusively directed.

ENCRYPTION: the use of a mathematical formula (an algorithm) that is applied to electronic data to render it illegible to anyone without the decoding key.

Since those early days of the commercial use of the Internet, considerable progress has been made in addressing these issues. Security over the Internet, at least on commercial sites, has vastly improved in recent years. Many commercial sites have installed **firewalls**, which are highly secure computers added to a corporate network, through which access to the network from the Internet is exclusively directed (see Figure 1.4 for the basic structure of a firewall). To augment security, they also have made increased use of **encryption** to prevent unauthorized persons from reading data.

While they have not been overcome, these barriers to the spread of commerce on the Internet have at least substantially improved in recent years. Nevertheless, the most recent surveys indicate that one of the most prevalent concerns of Internet users in conducting business online is the provision of their credit card information and privacy concerns generally. The issue of privacy is being addressed through legislation around the world (see Chapter 13 for further discussion).

Many of the privacy concerns of Internet users were addressed in Canadian privacy legislation, notably the Personal Information Protection and Electronic Documents Act (PIPEDA), introduced in 2000, which creates an enforceable right to privacy for individuals with respect to the collection, use, and disclosure of their personal information by the private sector in the course of commercial activities. As a result of this act, the Office of the Federal Privacy Commissioner has been established to administer it and act as something of a watchdog on matters concerning privacy of information. In addition, most provinces have established similar legislation, as has the United States, the European Union, and numerous other countries.

E-WALLETS: software that holds information about a purchaser, such as name, billing, and shipment addresses and other information needed by a seller such as credit card information, and, upon request, submits this information automatically to a website to complete a transaction.

Again, while the new legislation does not deal with all the issues that are important to e-commerce participants, it does address many of them and provides a framework for at least some of the future legislation that will surely follow.

Regarding the topic of payment systems, considerable progress has been made through the banks offering their Internet services, which include the ability to pay bills online. In addition, the banks have begun to offer **e-wallets**, which

Figure 1.4   Basic Firewall Architecture

A firewall is placed between the Internet and the networks to enable outside access to the networks to be controlled.

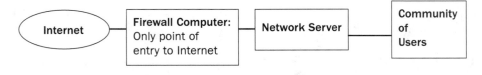

consist of software that holds necessary information about the purchaser. Such payment information enables a user to go to a site and purchase something, download the information from the e-wallet, and therefore avoid the need to input the information manually. E-wallets are considered useful by online vendors, because online sales are often abandoned while in process because the buyer refuses to take the time to input the necessary information.

Other more advanced technologies that have been tested in Canada, but not yet used widely for commercial purposes, are beginning to be used, principally by the banks. An important example is the **Mondex card**, which will be discussed more fully in Chapter 6. Essentially, Mondex offers the capability to buy something and pay for it online in a manner similar to using cash, as long as a user has the appropriate hardware. This and other payment technologies have the potential to reduce the reluctance of users to purchase online over the next few years. In April 2001, however, the banks in Canada announced they were abandoning Mondex, throwing into doubt its future in the Canadian market. Although this development will postpone the use of Mondex in Canada, the technology is by no means dead. The ability to use cash-like instruments for payment online or offline will continue to be needed for e-business to prosper.

Broad Strategic Tools

While the Internet is a central enabling technology for the rise of e-business, it is not the only one. In order to make e-business work, a great deal of activity must take place behind the web pages. The corporate systems need to be organized and integrated in such a way that there is a fast and free flow of information throughout the system. This is necessary to enable the business to be able to respond to the fast-moving pace of business in the information age and to keep the customers happy. It is also necessary to enable businesses to cope with the growing phenomenon of providing customization of their products for their customers. Quite often goods are ordered in customized form, and the first time the company finds out about it is when it gets the order. Therefore, the company needs to obtain the materials and process them in time to meet the high expectations of customers. **Systems integration** is also necessary to enable the company to provide this fast turnaround without resorting to increases in inventory.

Several tools are used by companies to enable this integration to take place. Where the Internet itself is not used, quite often other networks are used that make use of Internet technology. Where such networks are internal to the company, they are referred to as **intranets**. Where they extend outside the company, they are called **extranets**.

When we refer to Internet technology, we mean four main elements— TCP/IP, HTTP, HTML, and CGI:

- **TCP/IP**, or **Transmission Control Protocol/Internet Protocol**, is the communications protocol of the Internet. In order for any computer to use the Internet, it must be equipped with the program that enables this protocol.
- **HTTP**, or **HyperText Transfer Protocol**, is an applications protocol or set of rules that is used for exchanging files (text, graphic images, sound, video, and other multimedia) on the World Wide Web.
- **HTML**, or **HyperText Markup Language**, is the essential programming language used to create web pages. It enables the use of the familiar drill-down technique that helps make the Internet so useful and easy to use.

MONDEX CARD: card containing a computer chip that enables it to retain data that can be used for conducting transactions with stores that are equipped to read Mondex cards. Because of their memory capabilities, they are sometimes referred to as "smart cards."

SYSTEMS INTEGRATION: process of bringing together various business systems having different technologies, functions, and platforms so they can conduct business processes in such a way that the user does not see that different systems are being used.

INTRANETS: computer networks within an enterprise that make use of Internet technology.

EXTRANETS: computer networks that make use of Internet technology and include users from outside the organization as well as inside.

TRANSMISSION CONTROL PROTOCOL/INTERNET PROTOCOL (TCP/IP): the communications protocol of the Internet. In order for any computer to use the Internet, it must be equipped with the program that enables this protocol.

HYPERTEXT TRANSFER PROTOCOL (HTTP): an applications protocol or set of rules that is used for exchanging files (text, graphic images, sound, video, and other multimedia) on the World Wide Web.

HYPERTEXT MARKUP LANGUAGE (HTML): the essential programming language used to create web pages.

COMMON GATEWAY INTERFACE (CGI): a standard method by which a web server can pass a user's request over to an application program and receive data back for sending to the user.

EXTENSIBLE MARKUP LANGUAGE (XML): a tool that is similar to HTML and is compatible, but does not rely on single pre-set tags to identify information. Instead, XML provides a mechanism for any document builder to define new XML tags within any XML document.

MySap.com
www.mysap.com

- **CGI**, or **Common Gateway Interface**, is a standard method by which a web server can pass a user's request over to an application program and receive data back for sending to the user. When the user requests a web page by clicking on a link or entering a website address, the server returns the requested page.

Most recently, many Internet sites have made use of **Extensible Markup Language** (**XML**). This is a very powerful tool that is similar to HTML but does not rely on single pre-set tags to identify information. Instead, XML provides a mechanism for any document builder to define new XML tags within any XML document. This means that in addition to being a markup language, XML is a meta-language that can define new tags. Data can be tagged within a system using XML and then found quickly by an XML-enabled browser. XML is useful to locate data that might be needed by an Internet application, such as an online store.

The use of this Internet technology in intranets and extranets means that these networks have the same look, feel, and functionality as the Web. A user often cannot tell when moving from one to the other or to the Internet itself. The difference is therefore said to be transparent to the user.

Typically, websites are constructed on separate network servers, called web servers. The data on the web servers include the HTML codes for the actual web pages, as well as the software being used to construct the storefront on the Internet. Of course, the storefront software must be connected with the main system of the company, to enable orders and other requests by customers to be handled by the business. For example, the MySap.com system of SAP AG uses an approach of centring the storefront around an online catalogue. The online catalogue is linked to the main SAP systems that contain all the product and inventory records and the products that the company wishes to offer for sale at the online store. The data in the main records are located using XML.

When the online store is configured, there is the capacity to add in graphics to illustrate the products being offered and also to add in a shopping cart. Anyone who has shopped online would have seen shopping carts to which products can be added as the user browses through the store. An example can be found on Amazon.com or any number of websites that offer goods for sale. Eventually, the user will check out the purchases by going to a check-out screen that allows payment for the goods using credit cards or any other payment system that the store supports. The online catalogue and the shopping cart software would be on the web server along with the web pages.

Using a web server also facilitates security, because it enables firewalls to be strategically located so as to offer maximum security for both the customer and the company's data. Firewalls are separate, highly secure computers through which a user must go to be able to access a system. A common configuration is for a firewall to be set up between the web server and the main system. Some companies also set up firewalls outside the web server as well, leaving only the web pages available to the public. The area of security is explored in Chapter 5.

Tools for System Integration

Businesses achieve the systems integration they need by using intranets to tie together their systems internally, and by using extranets to tie their systems to those of their customers and suppliers. They also use tools like enterprise resource planning (ERP), supply chain management (SCM), customer relationship management (CRM) and e-procurement to achieve this integration both externally and internally. All of these tools are essential to e-business and are explored fully in Chapters 4, 7, 8, and 9. The purpose here is to set out how they fit into a broad perspective on e-business.

ERP systems are large software systems that are used in a business to automate its activities across their full range. Consisting of the software sold by several major vendors—including SAP, Oracle, Peoplesoft, Baan, and JD Edwards—an ERP implementation represents a major initiative for any business. Implementation of an ERP system often requires significant changes in business processes to accommodate the software, sometimes to the point of re-inventing the business. On the plus side, ERP systems offer the ability to share a common pool of data across an entire enterprise and to run their applications using a very common format. They also offer management the opportunity to have immediate access to the latest information about the organization's activities and performance.

The implementation of ERP systems predated the development of e-commerce, and many installations were prompted by the Y2K crisis that was being predicted in the late 1990s. The incredible boom in e-business, however, and the related need to integrate systems has led to a continuance of interest in ERP systems, and in many companies they are viewed as essential to delivering on e-business needs.

Customer relationship management systems also are very large information systems and present many of the issues and difficulties as ERP systems. However, CRM systems are also viewed as essential to enable the organization to be able to deliver on their customer needs on a timely basis. They accomplish this by enabling businesses to accumulate information about their customers and then use that information to offer them a product that is tailored to their needs. The idea of CRM is to be able to acquire new customers, enhance the profitability of all customers, and retain the profitable ones. CRM does not always involve integrating systems with customers, but some of the more advanced systems do.

E-procurement systems are of two main types—buy-side and sell-side systems. Buy-side procurement systems essentially involve systems within a business that fully automate purchases by staff and involve electronic contact with outside suppliers, often through the Internet or an extranet. Sell-side procurement systems, on the other hand, involve systems that are essentially trading communities, or exchanges that link directly to the systems of both suppliers and customers. Many sell-side systems are fully integrated with the systems of their participants. The existence of trading exchanges has been growing rapidly, and is a major aspect of contemporary e-business. These topics are dealt with in Chapter 8.

E-Business Models and Strategy

E-Business Models

The Internet and e-business are causing business model changes (for example, see the New Business Models box, which looks at how e-business has affected the business model of Encyclopaedia Britannica). There are several features of Internet-based business that have an impact on the business models adopted by businesses. These include:

- speed;
- convenience;

NEW BUSINESS MODELS

Encyclopaedia Britannica

Prior to the age of the Internet, *Encyclopaedia Britannica* was known widely as perhaps the world's premier encyclopedia. It was large (some 20 volumes), expensive, and aggressively sold door-to-door by its salespeople.

When technology began to creep into the encyclopedia business, the established business models of *Britannica* came under pressure for change. The first technological change that affected it was the invention of the compact disk (CD), a storage medium that could contain billions of bytes. CDs offered a way to package an entire encyclopedia in a very compact format and also included the capability to include video and sound, and—very important for a reference book—make it search-able. Another advantage of CD technology was that it was cheap to produce. There would be no need for fancy books with expensive bindings.

Microsoft Corp. saw the advantages of this new opportunity and produced its own encyclopedia, *Encarta*, which enjoyed immediate success. *Encarta* was available for approximately US$250, while the *Britannica* print version sold for over US$1500. While *Encarta* arguably lacked the content of *Britannica*, the price difference was great enough to convince many buyers. Seeing the need to respond, *Britannica* offered a CD version, but it was considerably more expensive than *Encarta* and *Britannica* couldn't catch up to the market lead that Microsoft had established.

After Internet usage began to grow, *Britannica* tried to develop a website where they would sell the product, but this too failed to take off. Then, with their very survival at stake, they implemented a radical revision of their business model. They placed the content of their encyclopedia on a website completely free of charge. In addition, they included links to other websites, the daily news, banner ads, and an online store.

The consequence of all this was that *Britannica*'s business model changed from one in which they produced and sold expensive books to another where they gave away their prime product on the Internet and made their money on advertising and selling their products through their online store. A radical change indeed!

Questions

1. What are the advantages of an electronic encyclopedia over a print version?
2. Should *Encyclopaedia Britannica* charge for their web content?

SOURCE: www.britannica.com.

- customization;
- redefinition of product value; and
- media flexibility.

Speed   Certainly, the use of technology has changed the expectations of people regarding the time it takes to satisfy their needs. We can see this impact on society generally. In the early days of technology, there was a widespread thought that it would free up a great deal of time for people, that they would be able to reduce their workweeks and take long vacations. It hasn't worked out that way, and today we see people living frantic and rushed lives—in great measure a result of the ability of technology to respond more quickly to people and enable them to get on with the next activity on their list. As a result, people expect fast turnaround to their requests, especially where technology is involved.

This means that businesses need to construct their business models so that they can deliver quickly to meet expectations. It also means that if the competition implements new technology that enables them to deliver more quickly, they may well have a competitive advantage.

Convenience   One of the reasons people use the Internet is for convenience. When they log onto banking sites, they can check their current balances without going to the bank branch and standing in line for a teller. They can pay their bills without having to write a cheque, stuff an envelope, and go to a mailbox to mail it. It's all about convenience. This fact has had a profound impact on the way in which banks offer their services to the public. They have reduced their branches, cut their staff, and set up more ATMs in partnership with retail outlets. Generally, it may be said they have been moving from "bricks to clicks." This has substantially changed their business models—by cutting their infrastructure costs, increasing their technology costs, adding new sources of revenue, and making old sources of revenue obsolete. As they find new ways to add convenience, their mix of old and new changes again, leading to modified business models.

Customization   Somewhat related to the idea of convenience is the demand for customized products and services. The use of the Internet together with integrated systems makes this possible or, to put it another way, is necessary to make it possible. One of the leaders in the provision of customized product was Dell Computer Corp., which was the first major vendor to offer computers for purchase through its website. The distinguishing feature of Dell's site was that customers could go through all the options and build a computer that most completely fit their needs. Since then, of course, other vendors have followed suit.

Dell Computer Corporation
www.dell.com

The Dell experience clearly demonstrates the impact of customization on business models. The company needed to radically change its distribution model to enable it to build and deliver the product after it had been ordered—a very different activity from filling a retail outlet with inventory or selling to retailers so they can fill their stores with inventory.

Redefinition of Product Value   The ability of the Internet to convey a variety of information, services, and other features has led to a redefinition of what is meant by a product or service. For example, when Amazon offers books online, they are including information about the book, reader reviews, sales ranking, related books, and other information. They also added to their site other services and products that they have determined their customers are likely to have an interest. In other words, they are packaging information with their prime product and the package becomes the product. This has the effect of fundamentally altering their business model, enabling them to charge for some of the additional products and, as was the case with Britannica, even giving away their main product. E-customers have come to expect packages of this type, and such packages must be kept up to consumer expectations and needs at all times.

Media Flexibility   The incredible capacity of the Internet to grow and change and to convey a variety of content (particularly multimedia such as voice, video, and music) means that business is continually challenged to keep up to date with its capabilities and to offer new features and services to customers before the customer demands them. This leads to changing product package content and consequently, changing business models.

It should be clear from these points and examples that e-business models are constantly in a state of change. They not only change when businesses enter into e-business, but also need to be constantly reviewed to keep pace with the fast-moving times. This need for continual change and improvement leads to the need for e-business strategy.

E-Business Strategy

The changes in and pressure on business models have been driving numerous strategic initiatives, some of which are unique to e-business and some of which are not. This means that strategy formulation and execution must move fast and in most cases must be tied closely to significant business processes in a way that makes them flexible and responsive. This is known as a flexible business design. More often, the desired flexibility cannot be achieved within a single business organization. The organization must look outside to be able to provide products and services or conduct particular business processes. This has led to a substantial incidence of such strategies as outsourcing, partnerships, joint ventures, liaisons, and mergers. Most recently, it has led to outright collaboration with suppliers, customers, and even competitors.

A major result of all these changes has been the creation of e-business organizations that transcend traditional business organizations—the creation of virtual corporations. A good example of this is the emergence of vertically integrated trading communities, such as verticalnet.com, where various businesses within industries integrate and collaborate to enable the ultimate industry products to remain competitive. Essentially, they join forces within an electronic environment to streamline their industries. This aptly illustrates the fundamental change being wrought by e-business.

Chapter Summary

In a very broad and general sense, electronic business is normally defined as any business carried out in electronic form. More recently, the term "e-business" has been used to refer to the process of carrying out business using the Internet as a strategic tool. The rise in the use of the Internet is the single most important enabler of e-business of any type. Even types of e-business that were carried out before the age of the Internet are moving to the Internet.

In the business-to-consumer (B2C) arena, companies are offering a wider range of goods on the Internet. The Internet also ushered in the idea of online auctioning and other bidding-related retail systems. Perhaps more importantly, the auctioning idea has extended into business-to-business procurement systems and trading exchanges where auctioning is perceived as a way in which suppliers can be made more competitive and responsive to their customers.

Activity in the B2B world has focused on the buy-side, which deals with the procurement activity of a business, and the sell-side, which relates to relationships with customers and the consequent marketing and selling activity. E-business also includes the front- and back-office information system applications that form the engine for modern business. The streamlining of the internal value chain and the external supply chain is a fundamental strategy of e-business that enables the business to respond quickly to the increasingly stringent demands of e-customers.

Businesses achieve the integration they need in their systems by using intranets to tie together their systems internally, and by using extranets to tie their systems to those of their customers and suppliers. ERP systems are used in a business to automate its activities across their full range and achieve the required integration.

KEY TERMS

trading exchange

electronic data interchange (EDI)

World Wide Web

automated teller machines (ATMs)

supply chain

buy-side

sell-side

customer relationship management (CRM)

e-procurement

Internet service providers (ISPs)

firewalls

encryption

e-wallets

Mondex card

systems integration

intranets

extranets

Transmission Control Protocol/Internet Protocol (TCP/IP)

HyperText Transfer Protocol (HTTP)

HyperText Markup Language (HTML)

Common Gateway Interface (CGI)

Extensible Markup Language (XML)

Buy-side procurement systems essentially involve systems within a business that fully automate purchases by staff and involve electronic contact with outside suppliers, often through the Internet or an extranet. Sell-side procurement systems, on the other hand, involve systems that are essentially trading communities, which link directly to the systems of both suppliers and customers.

The Internet and e-business is changing business models. This means that businesses need to construct their business models such that they can deliver quickly to meet expectations. People use the Internet for convenience and also expect a customized product.

Business models have changed substantially, by cutting infrastructure costs, increasing their technology costs, adding new sources of revenue and making old sources of revenue obsolete. Changing product package content also contributes to changing business models. The changes in and pressure on business models has been driving numerous strategic initiatives, some of which are unique to e-business and others are not.

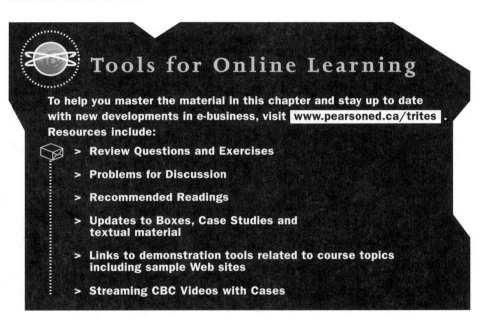

Tools for Online Learning

To help you master the material in this chapter and stay up to date with new developments in e-business, visit www.pearsoned.ca/trites . Resources include:

> Review Questions and Exercises

> Problems for Discussion

> Recommended Readings

> Updates to Boxes, Case Studies and textual material

> Links to demonstration tools related to course topics including sample Web sites

> Streaming CBC Videos with Cases

Endnotes

1. Kalakota, Ravi, and Marcia Robinson. *e-Business 2.0: Roadmap for Success. Reading, MA: Addison Wesley, 2000.*

2. As quoted in the introduction to Kalakota and Robinson, *e-Business 2.0: Roadmap for Success, Addison Wesley, 2000.*

CHAPTER 2

Business Models and Strategies

learning objectives

When you complete this chapter you should be able to:

1. **Define e-business models and strategy.**
2. **Describe how e-business models reflect strategy.**
3. **Identify the components of e-business models.**
4. **Identify and evaluate the e-business strategies followed by businesses.**
5. **Explain why e-business models and strategies are important to successful e-business.**

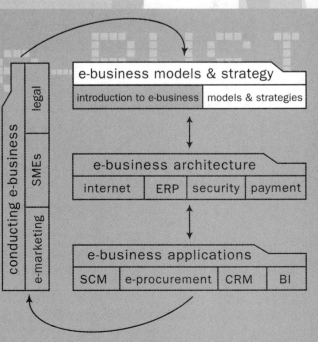

Introduction

Broadly, a business model may be defined as the manner in which a business organizes itself so as to achieve its objectives, which normally involve the generation of profits. The definition of a business model includes the way in which revenue is generated and the way in which costs are controlled or eliminated. Most often, business models are defined in terms of how a business plans to make money on a long-term basis. A major aspect of e-business strategy is how the business plans to use the Internet for these purposes.

Traditional business models have usually revolved around a central product or service. The idea was that a business would acquire or make goods, and sell them for amounts in excess of cost. Often, a business would add services or accessories to augment its profits or customer satisfaction, but the central feature of the traditional business model was the sale of a product or service at an amount in excess of its cost. This model fits the traditional industrial environment very well. Manufacturing organizations, such as Ford Motor Company, exploited this model by adopting a mass production model that enabled them to reduce unit costs and selling prices and still generate profits. Much traditional business literature has been devoted to the idea of maximizing revenues, minimizing costs, and generating competitive advantage.

During the last few decades of the 20th century, there was an increase in the numbers of organizations that sold services rather than goods. These organizations, which include various types of professional firms (such as accountants and consultants) and, increasingly, technology-related service firms, have followed a model similar to that of traditional manufacturers. They focused their efforts on a service or related package of services, hired people with the skills to provide these services, and sold their time and skills to their clients at a price in excess of the cost they had to pay. As the environment has changed, the nature and scope of the services companies have offered has changed, but they have continued to follow the same basic business model of selling something in excess of its cost.

Business literature contains various definitions of a business model that are not quite as simple as this generic traditional model. Paul Timmers has defined a business model as:

- "An architecture for the product, service and information flows, including a description of the various business actors and their roles; and
- "A description of the potential benefits for the various business actors; and
- "A description of the sources of revenues."[1]

At first glance, under this definition, a business model appears to be relatively static, as evidenced by the words *architecture* and *description*. It is, however, not entirely so, as it includes reference to information flows, roles of business actors, and potential benefits to the actors. The word *actors* refers to the various participants in the business process. The introduction into the definition of the ideas of information flows, business processes, and roles is very significant. It considerably complicates the definition of a business model, and makes it more dynamic—and more relevant to the actions a business undertakes, rather than simply how it organizes itself.

Other definitions in the literature are also broad and dynamic. For example, the definition posed by Afuah and Tucci incorporates the ideas of methods and activities. A business model is defined by them as "the method by which a firm builds and uses its resources to offer its customers better value than its competitors and to make money doing so." They go on to say that the business model is what "enables a firm to have a sustainable competitive advantage."[2]

This definition ventures into the realm of strategy, if one accepts the definition of business strategy put forward by Michael E. Porter: "The essence of strategy is choosing to perform activities differently than rivals do ... Competitive strategy is about being different. It means deliberately choosing a different set of activities to deliver a unique mix of value."[3]

One of the difficulties that these definitions present is distinguishing between business models and strategy. Some tend to think of a business model as a description of where the business is or where it wants to go, and strategy as how it plans to get there. In other words, the business model is a relatively static definition of the business approach to making profits and the strategy is a flow of activity. On the other hand, we have seen that some definitions of a business model encompass activities designed to achieve competitive advantage—or strategy. It is difficult to separate the question of strategy from the concept of the business model. However, in this chapter we will try to draw a distinction.

Types of Internet Business Models

An Internet business model involves the implementation of a business model while using the Internet as a tool for implementing it. There have been some media reports and articles by knowledgeable people that have suggested that the Internet "changes everything" so that "old economy" business models no longer apply. This view was given some credibility in the early days of the dot-com phenomenon, when companies like Amazon.com and E*TRADE Canada could go to the stock market and raise incredible amounts of capital without having ever made a profit. Some business writers pointed to the success of these ventures in raising capital and announced that the old rules didn't apply anymore.

In fact, the reason dot-com companies were able to raise money this way was that investors were lured by the possibility of future profits, and were depending on the unknown for the actual generation of these profits. The market declines in the dot-com stocks of 2000–2001 were a reality check, accompanied by a realization that a business still needs to make money in the long term. This does not seem like a radical insight, especially in hindsight, but it has often been observed that the stock markets are sometimes influenced more by emotion than logic.

Many of the businesspeople involved in e-business have recognized for some time that they need to find ways to make money, and numerous Internet-based business models have developed in recent years. The New Business Models box illustrates a situation where a new model was introduced for the music industry.

Michael Rappa has identified nine different generic business models that exist on the Web (see Table 2.1):[4]

1. brokerage;
2. advertising site;
3. infomediary;
4. merchant;
5. manufacturer;
6. affiliate;
7. community;
8. subscription; and
9. utility.

NEW BUSINESS MODELS

A Model Evolves at MusicNet

During the late 1990s, Napster turned the music industry on its head by facilitating the transfer of free music between people connected to the Web. The industry at first directed its efforts to legal battles with Napster over copyright issues, and won several of these actions. However, it was clear that the rules of the game had changed and the industry needed to find new ways to deal with the onset of Internet distribution of music in such a way that it would be economically viable for the industry and for the artists.

In 2000, RealNetworks Inc., a Seattle-based company, announced a venture under which it would work with three leading music labels— AOL Time Warner Inc., Bertelsmann AG, and EMI Group—to create an online music subscription service. Their idea was that the partners would develop a digital music distribution platform called MusicNet, incorporating a technology of RealNetworks called RealSystem iQ to enable the downloading of streaming music. Under the agreement, the downloading technology is to be licensed to distributors who wish to provide users with the ability to download music on a subscription basis.

The parties to the agreement felt that the service would make available a large amount of musical content and take advantage of AOL's large number of subscribers while building on the RealNetworks brand. It was felt that the combination of highly recognized branding and the large built-in subscriber base would be a prescription for success.

MusicNet will deal with the music labels and license the technology to distributors who meet prescribed requirements for secu-rity, copyright protection, and licensing. They will also allow the providers to package the service under their own brands.

Initially, consumers will only be able to download music to their computers, not to portable players, but presumably that potential will follow. Some observers say that such capability will be crucial to success. The president of MusicNet said that studies by Jupiter Research suggest that consumers will pay as much as US$10 a month for subscription services. Some analysts feel that consumers will be put off by the need to subscribe and that there will be a need for freedom in choice of music, easy access without the need to be a subscriber, and the ability for one-time purchases as desired. Many observers feel the market for this type of service is still vague and evolving.

Questions

1. How does the business model of MusicNet respond to the realities of music purchasing in the age of the Internet?

2. Is it likely to succeed?

SOURCE: www.Informationweek.com.

1. Brokerage

Brokers are so named because they make money by charging a fee for transactions they enable on their site. They are also often referred to as market-makers because they bring buyers and sellers together and facilitate transactions between them. There is a large number of brokerage sites and they take on a variety of specific forms, the major ones being:

- buy/sell fulfillment sites;
- market exchanges;
- business trading communities;
- buyer aggregators;
- distributors;
- virtual malls;

Table 2.1   Internet Business Models

An overview of the Internet business models proposed by Michael Rappa.

General Model Type	Specific Types	Example
1. Brokerage	(a) Buy/sell fulfillment site	Etrade.com
	(b) Market exchange	Covisint.com
	(c) Business trading community	Verticalnet.com
	(d) Buyer aggregator	Volumebuy.com
	(e) Distributor	Necx.com
	(f) Virtual mall	Yahoo.com
	(g) Metamediary	Zshops, Amazon.com
	(h) Auction broker	eBay.com
	(i) Reverse auction	Priceline.com
	(j) Classifieds	torontostarclassifieds.thestar.com
	(k) Search agent	CareerCentral.com
	(l) Bounty broker	Bountyquest.com
2. Advertising		Cybergold.com
3. Infomediary		Clickthebutton.com
4. Merchant	(a) Pure-play e-tailer	Amazon.com
	(b) Bricks-and-clicks retailer	Sears.com
5. Manufacturer		Ford.com
6. Affiliate		Affiliateworld.com
7. Community		Toronto.com
8. Subscription		Wsj.com
9. Utility		Fatbrain.com

SOURCE: Adaptation from Michael Rappa, "Business Models on the Web." *Managing the Digital Enterprise.* <http://www.digitalenterprise.org/models/models.html>. January 2002. Reprinted with permission.

- metamediaries;
- auction brokers;
- reverse auctions;
- classifieds;
- search agents; and
- bounty brokers.

Buy/Sell Fulfillment Sites A buy/sell fulfillment site can be an online financial brokerage, like Etrade.com, where customers place, buy, and sell orders for transacting financial instruments. Online travel agents also fit into this category. In this kind of site, the broker charges a transaction fee, but sometimes a lower fee than can be obtained offline because the cost of executing such transactions on the Internet is lower, enabling the savings to be passed on to the customer. Etrade.com (see Figure 2.1) is a good example of this pricing practice, where the price of executing trades is much lower than it would be if carried out by a traditional broker.

Figure 2.1   E*TRADE Canada

At eTrade.com customers place, buy, and sell orders for transacting financial instruments.

SOURCE: "Quotes and Research." *E*TRADE Canada*™. <http://www.canada.etrade.com/html/customer/ stock/shtlml>. November 2001. E*TRADE Canada is a service of E*TRADE Canada Securities Corporation (discount broker), a member of the Toronto and Montreal exchanges, the Canadian Venture Exchange, the Investment Dealers Association and the Canadian Investor Protection Fund. The E*TRADE Canada service is offered in all provinces. E*TRADE Canada, Power E*TRADE and MarketTrader are trademarks of E*TRADE Group, Inc. or its subsidiaries and are used with permission. Copyright 1998–2001 E*TRADE Securities, Incorporated and E*TRADE Canada Securities Corporation. All rights Reserved.

Market Exchanges Market exchanges are a part of the business model style often referred to as trading exchanges, which have been one of the fastest growing types of B2B business. A good example of a market exchange is the auto industry's Covisint, which was introduced in Chapter 1. In a market exchange model, a broker such as Covisint Inc., which is a separate public company in its own right, charges a transaction fee based on the value of the sale. In market exchanges, pricing of transactions can be determined by simple offers, negotiations, or auctions. Figure 2.2 illustrates the structure of a market exchange.

Business Trading Communities Sometimes referred to as a "vertical community," the concept of the business trading community was pioneered by VerticalNet.com. That site focuses on markets within designated industry groups and facilitates B2B transactions up and down the value chain within an industry. It also offers comprehensive information to assist with intra-industry trading activity. The various industry communities contain product information, buyer guides, supplier directories, industry news, job listings, and classified ads. Figure 2.3 illustrates the structure of a vertical trading community.

Buyer Aggregators The basic idea with buyer aggregation is to bring together buyers from across the Internet to act as a group and thus take advantage of the kinds of benefits that normally accrue to large buyers, such as volume discounts and favourable pricing. An example of such a site is volumebuy.com.

VolumeSoftNet Power Sales
www.volumebuy.com

Figure 2.2   **Structure of a Market Exchange**

Covisint offers a vehicle and the technology to streamline supply chain activities in the automobile industry.

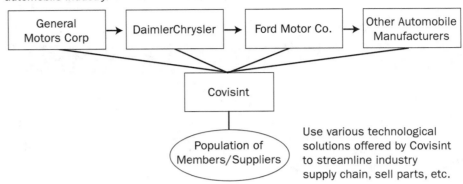

Distributors   Distributors are sites that include catalogues for a large number of product manufacturers for the benefit of volume and retail buyers. Numerous B2B sites have followed this model. The site manager acts as a broker to facilitate transactions between member distributors and their trading partners. This approach benefits both sellers and buyers: sellers by providing faster time to market and greater volume, and buyers by reducing the cost of procurement and improving access to product information.

Yahoo!
www.yahoo.com

Virtual Malls   As the name indicates, a virtual mall is a site that hosts a number of online merchants. These are used for both B2C and B2B purposes, and the mall charges fees for set-up, listings, and transactions. A good example is the Yahoo! Store, which also illustrates the combination of a mall with a popular portal site, assisting businesses to attract a large volume of visitors to the site.

Metamediaries   This is a form of virtual mall, but one that offers more services, for a fee, to ensure successful transactions and good seller–buyer relationships. Such services include transaction settlement, quality assurance, order tracking, and billing and collection.

Auction Brokers   An auction broker is a site, like eBay.com, that conducts auctions for sellers who list their products on the site. The broker charges the seller

Figure 2.3   **Illustration of a Vertical Trading Community**

A vertical trading community provides a vehicle for suppliers to connect with customers. The community provides industry information and the tools to implement transactions.

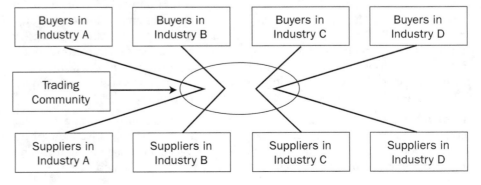

a fee, which is typically scaled to the value of the transaction. Normally the seller establishes a minimum bid and then accepts the highest offer. Specific offering and bidding rules will vary according to the site.

Reverse Auctions The most notable example of a reverse auction broker site is Priceline.com (see Figure 2.4). At this site, a prospective buyer enters an order for a particular good, such as an airline ticket for a particular destination, and states the price that he or she is willing to pay for it. The sellers on the site will be matched to the orders and if there is a fit, the order will be filled. The site manager charges a fee for registering orders and for the transactions completed.

Priceline.com
www.priceline.com

Classifieds These are simply sites that provide advertisements similar to the classified ads one finds in newspapers. The broker charges for the listings, regardless of whether a transaction ultimately takes place. An example of this kind of site would be Careerbeacon.com, which provides job advertisements for jobs in Atlantic Canada.

CareerBeacon.com
www.careerbeacon.com

Search Agents A search agent is a site that uses an intelligent software agent or "robot" to search the Internet for the best price for a good or service wanted by a buyer. Two examples of this type of site are RoboShopper.com and RUSure.com. Employment agencies use this kind of site to find jobs for people or people for jobs. An example of this type of job-related site is CareerCentral.com.

RoboShopper.com
www.roboshopper.com

Bounty Brokers These sites offer a reward, usually in the form of cash, for finding a person or a desired item. The broker charges listing fees for the desired person or item, and indicates the amount of the reward being offered. An example is BountyQuest.com.

BountyQuest.com
www.bountyquest.com

Figure 2.4   Priceline.com

Here Priceline.com shows how users can submit a price for airline tickets.

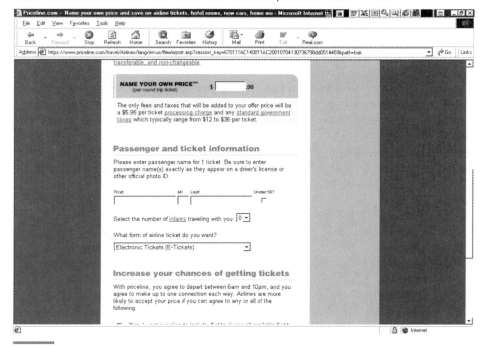

BROKERAGE SITES: sites that bring together buyers and sellers in order to facilitate business transactions on the Web.

These various types of **brokerage sites** are diverse, but it is clear that one feature they have in common is the fact they bring together buyers and sellers in order to facilitate business transactions on the Web. Largely, the different types of sites simply reflect differences in the manner in which the buyers and sellers are attracted to the sites. In addition, they reflect different ways in which the site owners can make a profit for themselves, usually by charging various kinds of fees and commissions. Chapter 8 discusses in more detail how some forms of brokerage sites operate on the Internet.

2. Advertising

From an economic point of view, advertising on the Web works similarly to the way it works in traditional media. Content is provided on the website (either free or at a bargain discount) that is intended to attract people, and advertisements are placed on the site for a fee. Quite often, the site makes its profits from the advertising revenue rather than from the content itself. On the Web, the advertising model has been prevalent, as users have become accustomed to receiving free content. The advertising messages on the Web often take the form of **banner ads**. Sometimes the fees payable on these banner ads are dependent on the **click-through count** on the banner ad. Click-through counts are done automatically by software on the website. Since a single user could click on the banner ad several times, click-through counts do not necessarily result in an accurate count of individual users who use the ad. However, they are considered a reasonable measure of volume.

BANNER ADS: small icons containing advertising messages that, when clicked, take the user to the site of the advertiser.

CLICK-THROUGH COUNTS: the number of times that users have clicked on a banner ad to take them to the website to which it refers.

The advertising model is only viable when there is a sufficiently large volume of user traffic on the site. Therefore, the strategies followed by advertising sites tend to focus on volume generation by offering diversified content and a wide array of services, like e-mail, chat, news, and message boards. Generalized portal sites like Yahoo.com and Altavista.com exemplify this approach.

Altavista.com
www.altavista.com

Yahoo also provides an example of a personalized portal—one that allows the user to customize the interface to show items of particular personal interest. This service is offered through the MyYahoo service. Numerous other generic sites offer this capability to develop user loyalty while maintaining a high volume. There is also a value-added element to personalized portals through improved access to information that may be more relevant to the user.

The idea behind a personalized portal is that users will use it as their own entry point into the Internet. Whereas ordinary portals attempt to do this as well, personalized portals seek to lure the user into using the site regularly because they allow the user to structure the site to cater to his or her particular interests. Several major portals offer this type of feature, including MyYahoo (see Figure 2.5) and Mysap.

Some portals target a defined user base, such as sports enthusiasts, investors, or homebuyers. Such specialized portals still seek large volume, but since they can't count on volumes as large as those of general portals, they often charge a premium for their advertising. The premium is supported by the claim that users with a particular interest are on the site, and since their interests are known, product advertising can be targeted to them. As users become more sophisticated in using the Web, specialized portals are likely to grow in number.

Other sites use the "incentive marketing" approach, which involves paying visitors for viewing some content or filling out forms or entering contests. Payment takes the form of some kind of point scheme similar to frequent-flyer programs offered by the airlines. An early entrant to this kind of site was

Figure 2.5   Yahoo's Personalization Screen

With MyYahoo, users can develop personalized portals.

CyberGold.com, which offered an "earn and spend community" by bringing together advertisers interested in incentive-based marketing. Advertising methods and e-marketing are discussed in more detail in Chapter 11.

3. Infomediary

Sites that build on the economic value of information about people's purchasing habits are referred to as *infomediaries*. These sites offer something free to users, and in exchange, ask them to fill out information about themselves and their buying habits. Sometimes they require a registration process for users to enter the site. The data collected this way are then sold to other businesses. Some infomediaries offer free Internet access or free access to detailed news or other content of particular interest. The site for the *New York Times* (nytimes.com) takes the registration approach, and acts as an infomediary in addition to a news service (see Figure 2.6), by selling the information it obtains.

The New York Times
www.nytimes.com

    If an infomediary site provides users with the opportunity to exchange information with each other about the quality of products and services with particular vendors, it is known as a "recommender" site. ClickTheButton.com is an example of one that takes this approach.

4. Merchant

The merchant model is simply the classic wholesaler or retailer of goods and services (online retailers are often referred to as "e-tailers"). If the business sells only

Figure 2.6 NYTimes.com

The registration screen for NYTimes.com.

SOURCE: "Help Center. Your Profile." *New York Times on the Web.* <http://www.nytimes.com/info/help/profile.html>. November 2001. Reprinted with the permission of the New York Times.

eToys.com
www.etoys.com

over the Web, such as eToys.com, it is a "pure-play" e-tailer. If it also has a traditional bricks-and-mortar presence, it is referred to as a "bricks-and-clicks" operation, or sometimes a "surf-and-turf" site. Such sites are often based on an online catalogue. A good example of a bricks-and-clicks retail operation is Sears.com. Their very successful entry into web retailing was made easier by their long history of selling through a catalogue.

5. Manufacturer Model

The use by product manufacturers of the Web to sell their products directly to their buyers is the manufacturer model. Again, there are variations of this model, depending on whom the manufacturer sells to. If it sells to end consumers, then this effectively opens a new distribution channel, which streamlines the distribution process by bypassing wholesalers and distributors. However, this situation can also create **channel conflict**, because the distributors may not approve of this system and may even rebel, as was the case with Levi's when they started selling jeans directly to customers online. Selling over the Internet is one channel that can easily be in conflict with the traditional retail stores or distributors owned by the enterprise and can take sales away from the stores. By using the Web for selling to customers, manufacturers can offer more service and can better track the buying habits and preferences of their customers—thus creating a considerable advantage.

CHANNEL CONFLICT: situation in which various sales channels for a single organization operate in competition with each other.

Levis
www.levis.com

If the Web is used by a manufacturer to sell to wholesalers and distributors, then it takes on the form of a B2B site rather than a B2C operation. Sometimes the two kinds of sites are combined, where the site is available to customers but there is a login for wholesalers or distributors where they can obtain special pricing. Either way, the use of the Web has the potential for greater efficiency than the traditional means of distribution.

6. Affiliate Model

A good example of an affiliate model is a banner ad exchange. Affiliate programs can be joined through affiliate manager sites, such as AffiliateWorld.com, which offer a point of contact for all those interested in exchanging banners. Sometimes, the arrangement includes payment of commissions to the sites hosting banner ads when sales are made to customers using them to enter the site. For example, Example.com might enter into a banner arrangement with Amazon.com under which an Amazon banner ad is placed on the Example site. Amazon tracks the entry points of people entering their site, and therefore knows which visitors have entered their site through the banner ad on Example.com. Amazon also can track when those people buy goods, and how much they spend. They can then pay a commission to Example.com for the sales.

AffiliateWorld.com
www.affiliateworld.com

For Amazon, this is a way of building sales. For Example.com, it is a way of generating some revenue from Amazon with no risk and very little cost. Amazon was a pioneer with this type of model and was granted a broad-ranging patent on the process that some observers feel may inhibit the activities of others in the field.

7. Community Model

Community sites depend on user loyalty and community identification for their viability. The sites are usually built with volunteer labour and feature a variety of content from the community, usually provided free of charge, although sometimes the site charges to host the content. The challenge for these sites is to provide adequate functionality and keep them current, given the use of volunteers. They can present an opportunity for businesses to advertise and to provide a convenient access point to their own site. A successful community site can function as a portal to local businesses, almost as a virtual shopping mall. Funding for these sites is sometimes solicited as donations from community members. An example of such a site is FamilyTreeMaker.com.

FamilyTreeMaker.com
www.familytreemaker.com

8. Subscription Model

Some businesses have users subscribe to their site in order to view some or all of the content. A good example of this approach is the *Wall Street Journal*. Other newspapers will offer some of their content for free and require subscriptions to view the full content. *The Halifax Herald*'s website provides an example of this approach. Many newspapers like the *Herald* allow subscribers to their print edition to gain access to online editions at no additional cost.

The Halifax Herald
www.herald.ns.ca

This model has been restricted because of the general reluctance of web users to pay for content. During 2000 and 2001, many businesses tried to have users pay for their content, including *Encyclopaedia Britannica* and photopoint.com, but suffered a substantial drop in visitors as a result. The viability of charging for web content is not clear. "A 1999 survey by Jupiter Communications found that 46 percent of Internet users would not pay to view content on the web."[5] It appears that the content must be of very high value to enable this model to be followed. Clearly, the model is evolving.

9. Utility Model

The utility model is a user-pay site. It offers specific services for a fee. Usually it is necessary to open an account in order to make use of the services and to facilitate the charges. An example of such a site is Fatbrain.com, which is a subsidiary of Barnes & Noble booksellers. Fatbrain offers book cataloguing, purchasing, searching, and other downloadable content. The development of good micropayment systems (discussed in Chapter 6) would be a boost to these sites, as they could charge small amounts for small services. They offer an advantage over subscription sites in that the user only has to pay for the content he or she specifically wants.

Fatbrain
www.fatbrain.com

E-BUSINESS IN GLOBAL PERSPECTIVE

E-Models at ChinaECNet

ChinaECNet is a web portal founded in 2000 by Avnet Inc., which is reported to have topped US$1 million in monthly revenue after its first six months of operations. Its chairman, Wayne Chao, reported in an interview that revenue from the site was up 400 percent in the first two months of 2001 over the final two months of the previous year.

The portal operates a unique international business by enabling small and mid-size domestic Chinese suppliers and manufacturers to easily enter into electronic business. More than 7000 Chinese companies have registered with the site, for which the portal does not charge. However, ChinaECNet does charge for several services it offers to its registrants.

These services involve a variety of benefits of e-business that would normally be available only to large or electronically sophisticated companies. They include, for example, the ability to link to foreign supply chain management networks, giving companies, through the Internet, many of the automated supply functions of more complex SCM systems.

Avnet's approach is to sell parts and integrate its own supply chain business into the Chinese Internet. The Chinese government has proved very eager to use the site to encourage automated supply management by providing registered users, through the portal, with **ISDN** lines free of charge.

Another service offered by ChinaECNet enables registrants to operate without the extensive government regulations that have been blamed for bogging down Chinese foreign business. For example, it has been the Chinese practice that most foreign vendors must use a Chinese agent through which to sell to Chinese customers, and foreign vendors are also banned from accepting Chinese currency as payment. ChinaECNet, however, can electronically send invoices directly to customers, who can pay in Chinese currency by bank transfer.

Among its other services, the portal has a generic forecasting program that allows Chinese companies to develop market projections from their own data. The program provides data that help users schedule manufacturing and also enables them to check global forecasts for any product. Chinese manufacturers can then include their forecasts in the network, which is visible to suppliers around the world.

Chinese manufacturers typically have kept two to three months of inventory on hand in order to keep production lines operating. ChinaECNet makes it possible for them to cut inventories to as little as four weeks, and thereby enjoy significant cost savings.

ISDN: integrated services digital network. This is a form of communications line that conveys data in digital rather than analogue format. Digital format means that the data is being converted into bits and bytes, similar to any computer data, while analogue format means that the data is in the form of sound waves.

Questions

1. Discuss the business model being followed by Avnet Inc., ChinaECNet, and the Chinese manufacturers using the portal.
2. How do these business models work together to result in competitive advantages for all participants?

SOURCE: www.computerworld.com.

Models and Business Strategy

While the preceding discussion makes it clear that there are many models being used on the Internet, these models are not all mutually exclusive. They can be combined in numerous ways to achieve business goals. For example, an e-tailer may make use of the simple merchant model, but also use the site to advertise its bricks-and-mortar business as well. It may enter into banner exchanges and make money through banner ad commissions, or it may enter into other affiliate programs, virtual malls, and market exchanges.

The specific model or combination of models that a business uses helps to define its Internet or e-business strategy. Will the site be used as a stand-alone initiative? Or will it be used to complement the existing business or even to launch a new type of business? What are the competitors doing? A strategist needs to answer the fundamental question—what will work for this business? The models provide a menu for the business strategist to consider when addressing these questions.

The E-Business in Global Perspective box illustrates a situation where various models are combined to achieve a strategic purpose. Although this case involves several different organizations trying to work together, nevertheless the same approach can apply to a single organization. In any event, the thrust of a great deal of contemporary e-business involves several different organizations working together in collaboration to achieve a common strategic aim or goal.

Fitting the E-Business Strategy into the Corporate Strategy

For many businesses, the procedural aspects of corporate strategic planning are a well-established feature of management. Strategic plans are developed periodically, sometimes every year, sometimes every few years with annual updates. They require employees from across the organization to be involved in determining goals, strategies, and work activities.

Most strategic planning exercises involve a process of developing broad visions, considering the constraints and assumptions that constrict or guide those visions, and defining strategic objectives for the business that come as close as possible to the visions. The strategic objectives must give recognition to the constraints, which might be based on resource restrictions, environmental constraints like legal and regulatory stipulations, and other matters. Each year, the process of strategic planning will normally involve reviewing the previous year's plans and updating those plans to reflect new trends, visions, and events. Then a plan is drafted, reviewed, and analyzed by the various stakeholders and a second draft prepared. Finally, the plan is approved and action begins. This process is illustrated in Figure 2.7.

Of course, the strategies and objectives in this kind of a plan are those that relate to the success of the business as a whole. The e-business strategy must fit into this corporate plan. See the E-Strategy box for a good example of how an e-business strategy can support the overall corporate strategy of a business.

How the e-business strategy fits into the corporate plan depends on the extent to which the business is involved in e-business. If it is a pure-play situation, where the only business is e-business, then the corporate strategic plan will be one and the same as the e-business plan. At the other end of the spectrum, where the

Figure 2.7   The Strategic Planning Process

The strategic planning for e-business must fit with the strategic planning for the enterprise as a whole.

e-business is a small part of the overall business, there may be a separate e-business strategic plan prepared. If this is the case, then there needs to be a process under which the objectives of the e-business plan are compared to the corporate objectives for consistency of purpose.

Another aspect of e-business planning originates from the critical role that information technology planning plays in any e-business initiative. This means that the IT planning must be done in conjunction with, or in a manner consistent with, the e-business plan and the corporate plan. IT planning does involve some unique elements that carry over into e-business planning. A good source of information about IT planning is found in the publication of the Canadian Institute of Chartered Accountants entitled "Information Technology Control Guidelines" (ITCG), Chapter 3.

In ITCG, the major components of an IT strategic plan are:

- *The Business Model.*
- *The Data Architecture.* This defines the **data elements** (and their location) that are necessary to meet business objectives. In e-business, the needed data will often be resident somewhere in the firm, but may not be readily available to Internet applications. This means that integration will have to take place to convey the information from other operational and legacy systems.
- *The Application Architecture,* which is the structure of applications that is necessary to process, store, retrieve, and deliver needed information in a timely and appropriate manner to users of Internet applications.

DATA ELEMENTS: those pieces of primary information used in a business, like customer name, sales invoice number, and payment amount for a transaction.

E-STRATEGY

Building an E-Business at Siemens AG

Siemens AG is a major international company that decided to use e-business to support its need to reduce inventory cycle times and streamline its supply chain. Its medical manufacturing arm, the Medical Solutions Operating Group (MED), makes medical technology systems such as ultrasound imaging and digital echocardiography systems. It began revamping its e-business strategy in December 1998 in response to the corporate vision. In step with corporate goals, the group launched a "High Speed Logistics" project with a specific aim of increasing group-wide inventory turnover by at least 25 percent within a two-year time frame.

The group began by rerouting inventory from MED's major component suppliers, which included Hewlett-Packard, Infineon Technologies, and Intel. Previously, MED would take delivery of components from these suppliers, route them to their own storage facilities, and then send the parts to the production line. Under the High Speed Logistics project, however, the components are sent directly by the suppliers to the production line for assembly, eliminating the need for factory storage. There were also other savings. Notably, the number of freight forwarders was reduced from three to one, and the group began to use its own factory experts, rather than third-party contractors to install its systems.

After two years, the delivery process was trimmed from 15 days to five, inventory turnover increased by 53 percent, and the delivery cycle was shortened by 86 percent.

One of the main challenges the project team had to overcome was motivating team members. There was a high level of complexity to the supply chain solutions, making it difficult for the team to understand. They said they had to try to motivate the teams by focusing on explaining the goals and how they would be achieved.

After the success of this program, MED began another project to focus on moving suppliers and customers to its intranet site, where orders can be placed and suppliers can see what needs are to be filled. This enabled the company's internal intranet to be used as a focal point for suppliers and customers, greatly simplifying the ordering process. Prior to this initiative, orders were taken by EDI, phone, and fax, which caused typing errors and language issues. The use of the intranet by customers enhanced the accuracy of the orders, made billing and invoicing faster, and provided greater transparency over the intranet to help speed up order fulfillment and further reduce inventory levels.

Questions

1. Discuss how the e-business initiatives of MED served the larger purposes of Siemens as a whole.
2. Do you think MED handled the issue of team motivation as well as they could have?

SOURCE: www.Informationweek.com.

- *The Technology Architecture*, which is the hardware, software, and other infrastructure components designed to deliver the services.
- *The Migration Plan*, which involves determining how the data, application, and technology architectures will be moved to the planned architectures.
- *The Tactical Plan*, which includes the funding and the detailed project management.

All of these elements need to be included in an e-business plan, or in an IT plan that is consistent with the e-business plan. It should be clear that the process of strategic planning for e-business presents numerous challenges of coordination and communication in an organization. Not only do the various types of planning—corporate, IT, and e-business—need to be consistent, but the various stakeholders in the organization need to be involved and their individual perspectives and objectives reconciled. When the business is an established one, the challenges are compounded in that they likely have had strategic plans for some years before the advent of e-business, and the introduction of the e-business must therefore take place in the context of established hierarchies and organizational structures, which will often be resistant to change. On the other hand, when the business is a new Internet startup, the whole organization depends on the e-business, and the

CANADIAN SNAPSHOTS

Old and New Dogs with New E-Tricks

The Canadian Imperial Bank of Commerce (CIBC) has been engaged in web banking through its website for several years. During 2000, CIBC and Sympatico-Lycos Inc. (SLI) joined forces to create a no-fee web bank that they would operate in conjunction with each other. Their idea represents a common view that the Web can bring about fundamental changes in the banking industry.

The new bank, to be known as Amicus Financial, comes as other online companies look at entering the banking business for the potential revenues they see there. David Marshall, CIBC's vice-chairman of electronic banking, said, "What we are seeing now is the start of the next 10 years in banking. Companies not traditionally in banking services have figured out there's not a great mystique about banking, so there really is no practical barrier to offering financial services."

The CIBC-SLI deal has been mentioned by analysts as a template for online companies trying to boost their revenue. So far, these companies have been prevented from entering retail banking, which of course involves taking customer deposits, by a lack of trust from both the public and the banking regulators. The partnership between CIBC and SLI is designed to overcome that obstacle by having the backing of the established firm, CIBC, and by offering chequing and savings accounts and other services to the Internet provider's customers. Sympatico has a monthly online audience of some seven million visitors. This provides an extensive group of potential banking customers to offer an online, no-fee, high-interest banking service.

Both partners have something different to gain from this venture. Sympatico hopes to supplement its ad revenue by selling additional services to its audience. It might also use the banking venture to bridge into other financial services, like brokerage, mortgages, and automobile sales financing. CIBC, on the other hand, wants to link with partners that have a household brand name and that are leaders in their industry to extend its banking services to new customers. It already has partnerships with Loblaw Cos. Ltd. in Canada and Winn-Dixie Stores Inc. and Safeway Inc. in the United States, along with mutual fund giant Investors Group Inc.

Other banks are getting into web-based banking. Among them is Canada's largest bank, the Royal Bank of Canada, which bought a 20-percent stake in AOL Canada Inc. in 1999 and has a marketing agreement with AOL. One difference from the CIBC-SLI deal is that the Royal Bank will promote the banking services under its own name, rather than a separate brand.

By mid-2000, Amicus had 600 000 customers in North America and was hoping to see that number reach 800 000 by year-end. The company feels there is much potential, since the low-cost service offered by Amicus can't be matched by traditional banks with their expensive infrastructure, including branches. Also, the Amicus customers will have access to CIBC's extensive network of automated banking machines.

CIBC and Sympatico are organized such that Sympatico holds no equity in Amicus Financial. It was not disclosed how the costs were split, but it is known that significant costs were absorbed by CIBC in the first quarter of 2000.

Questions

1. How does the strategy for Amicus fit with the corporate strategy of CIBC and SLI?
2. Do you think it will work? Explain.

SOURCE: www.computerworld.com.

importance of finding viable business models and developing successful strategies is not only more critical but must be built from the ground up.

Many if not most of the new dot-coms have failed because they have not been successful in finding business models and strategies that would work to make them economically viable. The problems that many businesses have experienced in venturing from their traditional spheres of activity to e-business, although they have had a lower profile, can often be traced to the same general failures. Even where a business finds a successful strategy, there is no assurance that it will continue to work for very long. The world of e-business and technology is changing so quickly that constant review and re-assessment of the strategic plans must be carried out, and the business must remain flexible in its approach to be able to adapt to the inevitable changes that will take place. The Canadian Snapshots box dealing with the Canadian Imperial Bank of Commerce and Sympatico-Lycos offers a look at the adoption of web strategies by established companies, one a "traditional" banker and the other a web-based company that has already achieved considerable success.

Chapter Summary

KEY TERMS

brokerage sites
banner ads
click-through counts
channel conflict
ISDN
data elements

Broadly, a business model may be defined as the manner in which a business organizes itself so as to achieve its objectives, which normally involve the generation of profits. Most often, business models are defined in terms of how a business plans to make money on a long-term basis. A major aspect of strategy for e-business is how the business plans to use the Internet for these purposes.

Traditional business models have usually revolved around a central product or service. Business literature contains various definitions of a business model. These definitions revolve around descriptions of the way in which the business organizes itself to conduct business and make money. They also include other factors such as a description of the potential benefits for the various participants, the information flows, business processes, and roles.

One of the difficulties that the definitions present is distinguishing between business models and strategy. Although some definitions consider a business model as a description of where the business is or where it wants to go, and strategy as how it plans to get there, other definitions are not this simple. Some include elements of business strategy and competitive advantage as part of the model. It is difficult to separate the question of strategy from the concept of the business model.

An Internet business model involves the use of the Internet as a tool for implementing a business model. Numerous Internet-based business models have developed in recent years. Notably, Michael Rappa has identified nine different generic business models that exist on the Web.

The specific model or combination of models that a business uses helps to define its Internet or e-business strategy. The models provide a menu for the business strategist to consider when addressing strategic questions.

For many businesses, the procedural aspects of corporate strategic planning are a well-established feature of management. Corporate plans are developed and e-business plans must fit into the corporate plan. The manner in which the e-business strategy fits into the corporate plan depends on the extent to which the business is involved in e-business. If it is a pure-play situation, where the only business is e-business, then the corporate strategic plan will be the same as the e-business plan. Where the e-business is a small part of the overall business, there may be a separate e-business strategic plan prepared. Because e-business includes elements of IT, an IT plan must be prepared or incorporated into the e-business plan. All of these plans must be consistent and coordinated with each other. The process of strategic planning for e-business presents numerous challenges of coordination and communication in an organization.

Tools for Online Learning

To help you master the material in this chapter and stay up to date with new developments in e-business, visit **www.pearsoned.ca/trites** . Resources include:

> **Review Questions and Exercises**

> **Problems for Discussion**

> **Recommended Readings**

> **Updates to Boxes, Case Studies and textual material**

> **Links to demonstration tools related to course topics including sample Web sites**

> **Streaming CBC Videos with Cases**

Endnotes

1. Timmers, Paul. "Business Models for Electronic Markets," *Electronic Markets,* Volume 8, No. 2, 1998.

2. Afuah, Allan, and Christopher L. Tucci. *Internet Business Models and Strategies: Text and Cases* New York, NY: McGraw-Hill Higher Education, 2001.

3. Porter, Michael E. "What Is Strategy?" *HBR OnPoint,* November–December 1996.

4. Rappa, Michael. *Business Models on the Web,* digitalenterprise.org/models/models.html.

5. Rappa, Michael. *Business Models on the Web,* ecommerce.ncsu.edu/topics/models/models.html.

The Internet, Intranets, and Extranets

learning objectives

When you complete this chapter you should be able to:

1. Describe the Internet, its history, and its overall significance.

2. Describe how the Internet is appropriate for e-business.

3. Identify the components of the Internet.

4. Identify the relationship between the Internet, extranets, and intranets.

5. Evaluate the situations in which the Internet, extranets, and intranets are used for e-business strategies.

6. Explain why the Internet, extranets, and intranets are important to successful e-business.

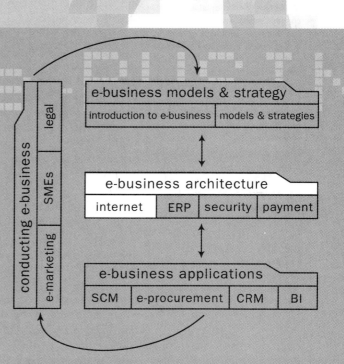

Introduction

Everyone knows what the Internet is—or do they? It is the world's largest network, connecting millions of computers from more than 100 countries. The size of the network and the number of users are growing rapidly. The popular conception is that this network just grew, with no particular planning or control. The fact is, however, the Internet isn't just a random network that grew up by accident with no planning or control. There is a very definite structure to it that is not widely known, together with specific organizations that manage it. It is useful to an understanding of e-business to know what the Internet is, how it is structured and who the major players are in its operation and governance.

History of the Internet

The Internet began as a military project in 1968 when the U.S. Defense Advanced Research Projects Agency (DARPA) formed a network intended for sharing research and development work among corporate, academic, and government researchers. They also felt a need to develop a network that would withstand a nuclear attack. On this new network, called ARPANET, each computer had a unique address. At about the same time, DARPA began the development of **packet switching**. Initially, DARPA started various programs using packet switching methods in media such as radio, satellite, and cable. After being successful with this research, the possibility arose of using these packet switching methods as a **protocol** for transmitting data between computer systems. Previously this would have been very difficult, as different computers used differing technologies. The introduction of a standard protocol made it possible to transmit data between many different types of computers, as long as they had the protocol installed on their computers.

   The new protocol could also be used by entire networks, and if two or more networks had the protocol installed, then those networks could be linked together and share data between themselves. In this way, the ARPANET became a system of linked networks.

   Dr. Vinton Cerf, the program manager for DARPA, and Dr. Robert Kahn published a paper in which they outlined a complete protocol that would work for linking networks. Further research was necessary to develop a workable system, and this led to the development of a set of protocols based on what was called the **Transmission Control Protocol (TCP)** and the **Internet Protocol (IP)**. Together, these protocols are referred to as the TCP/IP protocol.

   As the research program grew, it became necessary to form a committee to guide the work. As a result, Dr. Cerf formed the Internet Configuration Control Board (ICCB), and its first chair was Dr. David C. Clark of the Massachusetts Institute of Technology. In 1983, the ICCB was reorganized and later renamed the Internet Architecture Board (IAB). In that same year, the TCP/IP protocol was declared by the U.S. Defense Communications Agency to be the standard protocol for the ARPANET.

   As knowledge of and the role of the Internet expanded, it gained growing support from several U.S. government organizations. A coordinating committee was formed that became known as the Federal Networking Council (FNC). The FNC is the U.S. federal government's body for coordinating the agencies that support the Internet. It liaises with the Office of Science and Technology Policy, which is headed up by the President's Science Advisor, and is responsible for setting science and technology policy affecting the Internet.

PACKET SWITCHING: a method of transmitting data by breaking it up into small segments or packets and sending the packets individually in a stream. The packets are not necessarily sent together, but rather are disassembled, transmitted separately, and then reassembled when they arrive at their destination.

PROTOCOL: a special set of rules that the sending and receiving points in a telecommunication connection use when they communicate. Protocols exist at several levels, including hardware and software. Both end points must recognize and observe a protocol to be able to understand the contents of transmissions. Protocols are often described in an industry or international standard.

TRANSMISSION CONTROL PROTOCOL (TCP): protocol that uses a set of rules to exchange messages with other Internet points at the data packet level.

INTERNET PROTOCOL (IP): protocol that uses a set of rules to send and receive messages at the Internet address level. Every computer connected to the Internet has an IP address for this purpose.

The Canadian Internet

In Canada, the Internet began in earnest in 1990 when CA*net was created with support from the National Research Council. The purpose of CA*net was to provide Internet connectivity between universities and research organizations in Canada through a unified high-speed (for the time) network. CA*net linked over 20 regional networks across Canada, most of them provincially oriented, such as ONET in Ontario, BCNET in B.C., and ARNET in Alberta. CA*net, in partnership with Bell Advanced Communications, operated until March 31, 1997, when it was superseded by CA*net II.

In 1995, Canada launched into the world of **asynchronous transfer mode (ATM)** networks, which transmit data faster than previous networks, with the introduction of the National Test Network (NTN) in partnership with Bell Advanced Communications, AT&T Canada, and Teleglobe Canada. It was one of the first national ATM networks in the world, although access was initially limited to specific researchers and labs located at universities and other research facilities across the country. In 1997, NTN was upgraded to form the basis of CA*net II by linking it with international organizations using the Internet Protocol.

The core capacity of CA*net II was 155 **Megabits per second (Mbps)**. Bell Advanced Communications and AT&T Canada jointly provided the underlying ATM networks, while Teleglobe provided a connection to Europe.

CA*net II connects to individual universities, government labs, and research institutes through Regional Advanced Networks (RANs), which are operating in every province. Approved organizations can access CA*net II directly through any of the 15 Gigabit **points-of-presence**, sometimes referred to as "GigaPops," operated by Regional Advanced Networks and the three participating carriers. In 1998, the federal government began working with CANARIE Inc. (a Canadian not-for-profit corporation supported by its members, partners, and the federal government) to build a national R&D Internet network, CA*net 3, based on **fibre optic** technology. CANARIE selected a consortium led by Bell Canada as the provider of the core network. CANARIE's mission is to accelerate Canada's advanced Internet development and use by facilitating the widespread adoption of faster, more efficient networks and by enabling the next generation of advanced products, applications, and services to run on them.

CANARIE was involved during the development of CA*net and supported the upgrade of the network. CA*net was critical to the development of the Canadian Internet because it provided an east–west backbone for the Internet at a time when it would have been simpler and cheaper to connect south to the closest U.S. city. CA*net was the only **Internet backbone** in Canada for several years. While working with CA*net, CANARIE collaborated with the carriers Stentor and AT&T Canada to develop Canada's initial ATM networks.The CA*net 3 network was intended to operate at up to 40 Gigabits per second (Gbps), or 250 times the speed of the CA*net II backbone, and roughly 750 000 times the speed of the original CA*net. Ca*net 3 is built from the ground up to carry Internet traffic, unlike other advanced optical networks that are based on SONET technology, which is intended to carry voice first and Internet traffic second.

International Developments

An international Coordinating Committee for Intercontinental Research Networks (CCIRN) was formed to include the FNC of the United States, CANARIE of Canada, and its counterparts in and Europe. Co-chaired by the executive directors

ASYNCHRONOUS TRANSFER MODE (ATM): a switching technology that organizes digital data into 53-byte cell units and transmits them using digital signalling technology. A cell is processed asynchronously relative to other related cells.

MEGABITS PER SECOND (Mbps): a measure of speed for data transmission. It means a million bits per second, and states the number of data bits that are transmitted per second on a particular medium.

POINT-OF-PRESENCE (POP): an access point to the Internet that has a unique IP address. An Internet service provider (ISP), which is an organization that sells access to the Internet, has at least one point-of-presence on the Internet.

FIBRE OPTIC: the transmission of information as light impulses along a glass or plastic wire or fibre. Fibre optic media carries more data than conventional copper media and is less subject to electromagnetic interference. Most telephone company long-distance lines are now fibre optic.

INTERNET BACKBONE: an organized and managed communications system, often based on fibre-optic cables, that forms the central connection for a section of the Internet.

of the FNC and the European Association of Research Networks (RARE), the CCIRN provides a forum for cooperative planning among the principal North American and European research networking bodies.

The Internet Architecture Board (IAB) remains the coordinating committee for Internet design, engineering, and management. Today, the IAB is an independent committee of researchers and professionals with an interest in the technical strength and growth of the Internet. The entire system is evolving rapidly to deal with the changing technology, the needs of Internet users, and the concerns of the various core network providers within the system. The IAB meets quarterly to review the condition of the Internet, to approve any proposed changes or additions to the TCP/IP protocol, to set technical development priorities, to discuss policy matters that may need the attention of the Internet sponsors, and to agree on the addition or retirement of IAB members and on the addition or retirement of task forces reporting to the IAB.

The IAB has two extremely important continuing task forces:

1. the Internet Engineering Task Force (IETF), and
2. the Internet Research Task Force (IRTF).

The Internet Engineering Task Force   The IAB established the Internet Engineering Task Force (IETF) to help coordinate the operation, management, and evolution of the Internet. There was a recognition that the Internet had grown to widely geographically dispersed networks and, perhaps more importantly, had moved from experimental to commercial deployment. Of course, since that time, the commercial applications on the Internet have grown exponentially, and the importance of the IETF to e-business has also expanded tremendously.

The IETF has responsibility for specifying the short- and mid-term Internet protocols and architecture and recommending standards for IAB approval, providing a forum for the exchange of information within the Internet community, identifying relevant operational and technical problem areas, and convening working groups to explore solutions.

The IETF is a large open community of network designers, operators, vendors, and researchers concerned with the Internet and its protocols. The work of the IETF is performed by its working groups, of which there are currently more than 40. The working groups tend to have a narrow focus, such as particular security issues or encryption standards, and are normally disbanded when their project is completed.

The Internet Research Task Force   The Internet Research Task Force (IRTF) was formed to promote research in networking and the development of new technology. Since the distinction between research and engineering is not always clear, there is sometimes an overlap between the activities of the IETF and the IRTF. The IRTF is generally more concerned with understanding than with products or standard protocols. The IRTF is a community of network researchers, generally with an Internet focus, and is organized into a number of research groups, focusing on subjects such as the development of privacy-enhanced electronic mail software.

Internet Technologies

The Internet, as we have seen, is a collection of interlinked networks. In a real sense, the Internet can be viewed as a very large client-server network, and is often discussed in those terms. A client-server network can be analyzed in terms of clients and servers as illustrated in Figure 3.1. It shows a series of three "**clients**,"

CLIENT: a computer that is used by a network user to gain access to and operate applications on the network.

CANADIAN SNAPSHOTS

Internet Services at Telus

Telus Corp., the giant B.C./Alberta-based telephone and telecommunications company, recently bought Toronto Internet services company Daedalian eSolutions Inc. for around $29 million. It was the fourth in a series of such purchases. At its 2001 annual meeting, Telus said that it planned to spend $800 000 or more on ventures outside Western Canada as well as another $1.4 billion on wireless services and Internet protocols.

Telus said that Daedalian's employees had needed skills related to web design and consulting, in addition to their skills in running an ISP. Telus's strategy is to imple-ment data and Internet-related services. Earlier, it had also an-nounced the purchase of Williams Communication Canada, Inc., of Markham, Ontario, a data and voice equipment service provider. And in January 2001, Telus bought the data network and facilities management business of NorthWest Digital in Calgary.

Telus adopted this strategy because it feels there is very little margin to be earned in voice com-munications, but a lot of margin in data and related services business. So it is placing its expansion strategy squarely on the Internet. Telus has concluded that it is an extremely important market in which to establish a presence. Another reason that Telus was interested in Daedalian was its Ontario location, which Telus felt would be useful. Analysts feel that Telus's incursion into the Ontario market by buying an Ontario ISP is significant because it gives Telus access to the Ontario Internet services market.

Daedalian is expected to become part of the e-business division of Telus Client Solutions, which is focused on e-business enablement. According to an analyst, Telus paid less than what other telephone companies are paying for such a company.

Questions

1. How would you describe the strategy that Telus is following in the Internet services market?
2. Does it make sense that Telus would expand into Ontario?
3. Why does it matter where Daedalian is located?

SOURCE: Globetechnology.com.

---

which are simply the computers with which users are accessing the network, and the "**server**," which is a large central computer holding the software and perhaps the data on the network. Actual client-server networks take many different forms, depending on the strategy of the organization using them.

Figure 3.2 expands this diagram to specify some of the major characteristics of the World Wide Web as a client-server network. Again, the computer being used by the user to access the Internet is the client. Again, there are servers, owned by the company where the user works or by an Internet service provider (ISP) that the user has signed a contract with, such as Sympatico or Interlink. The ISP then connects to the regional network, or else directly to an Internet backbone, such as CA*net, and through that to a web server at the site targeted for communication. If a user logs into the WWW, for example, and wishes to shop for a General Motors car from home, he or she would dial and log into the web server of a local ISP. Then the user would enter the **Uniform Resource Locator (URL)** of General Motors (which is www.gm.com). A signal would go from the user's computer's browser to the ISP's web server and then would be forwarded through the regional networks and backbones to GM's prime web server. Since TCP/IP is being used, the various packets in the message will take different routes through the networks, but will all arrive at the

SERVER: a computer that forms the nucleus of a network, and contains the network operating system, as well as case-specific network-based applications.

UNIFORM RESOURCE LOCATOR (URL): the address of a resource on the World Wide Web. The URL contains the name of the required protocol followed by a colon (normally http:), an identification that a web server is the target (such as //www), and a domain name that identifies a specific web server followed by a slash (e.g., gm.com/), and perhaps a specific file name (such as index.html) to make http://www.gm.com/index.html. Increasingly, the letters www are no longer required as web servers are assumed unless otherwise specified. Index pages are often assumed as well.

Figure 3.1   Client-Server Network

A client-server network can be analyzed in terms of clients and servers.

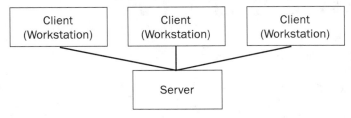

General Motors
www.gm.com

same server at the other end and be reassembled according to the instructions embedded in the packets.

However, what a person sees after logging onto the Internet is typically only a part of the Internet—the World Wide Web. When the Internet was first implemented, it had several components, including Gopher, Veronica, and FTP. These were simply sets of functionality for certain specific purposes. For example, Gopher was used to find and retrieve certain kinds of information, Veronica was used for searching for information, and FTP was used for transporting large files or data sets. None of these functions were user-friendly, and this created serious limitations on the usefulness of the Internet for non-technical people. User interfaces were character-based rather than graphical or icon-based, and required the knowledge of various commands that users had to enter in command lines to make the system work.

WEB BROWSER: software with a user-friendly interface that enables users to connect to and navigate on the Internet.

In 1993, however, a new tool emerged in the form of a user-friendly, graphics-capable interface that would run on the Internet. It was known as Mosaic. This new interface software, which became known as a **web browser**, led directly to the emergence and popularity of the World Wide Web on the Internet. Mosaic evolved to become Netscape Navigator, one of the most significant pieces of software that helped make possible the Internet as we know it. Navigator (or Netscape Communicator, which includes Navigator) is now one of the two most popular web browsers, the other being Microsoft Explorer. The World Wide Web

Figure 3.2   Overview of the World Wide Web Network

This figure specifies some of the major characteristics of the World Wide Web as a client-server network.

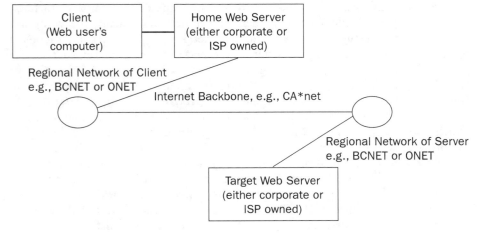

consists of a special set of servers on the Internet, known as web servers, that can communicate with web browsers. The WWW provides a bridge to the other older technologies that remain on the Internet, such as FTP, to facilitate file transfers and other functions by clicking on icons rather than entering the old commands.

Other Technologies

So far we have outlined two of the most important types of technology used on the Internet—the TCP/IP protocol and web browsers. Other technologies are also critical to the Internet, including CGI, HTML, HTTP, and XML.

Common Gateway Interface (CGI) **Common Gateway Interface (CGI)** is a method used by a web server to pass a user's request that has come over the Internet to an application program and receive data that can be sent back to the user. It is a standard Internet-based method and therefore can be recognized by web servers around the world.

HyperText Markup Language (HTML) **HyperText Markup Language (HTML)** is a code that must be inserted in a file in order for it to be displayed on the World Wide Web. It essentially amounts to a specialized type of programming language that tells the web browser how to display the words and images in the file on a web page. Figure 3.3 shows the HTML **source code** for the main entry web page of the website for St. Francis Xavier University. In that source code can be seen the **metatags** that are used to identify the contents of the page. In this case, the metatags are near the top of Figure 3.3, and are inside the word <title>. Metatags are used by search engines to identify web pages. Accordingly, the words included within metatags on a website are very important, since for a business site, the owner of the page wants web users to find the site when they enter a search on a search engine. Other lines in the source code reproduced in Figure 3.3 show the content that appears on the actual page that the web users will see.

HyperText Transfer Protocol (HTTP) **HyperText Transfer Protocol (HTTP)** is a set of rules used in exchanging hypertext files (such as text, graphics, sound, and video) for display on the World Wide Web. It is by far the most common protocol used for reading web pages on the Web.

Secure HyperText Transfer Protocol (HTTPS) Secure Hypertext Transfer Protocol (HTTPS): a secure form of HTTP. It is a web protocol built into Netscape Navigator that encrypts (scrambles) and decrypts (unscrambles) transmissions between the user and the web server. **Secure HyperText Transfer Protocol (HTTPS)** is a secure form of HTTP. It is a web protocol built into Netscape Navigator that encrypts (scrambles) and decrypts (unscrambles) transmissions between the user and the web server, thus creating an environment in which sensitive transactions (such as payments) can be executed on the Web. HTTPS is commonly used by banks for the benefit of customers who do banking transactions on the Web. Without a secure protocol, Internet banking would not be feasible.

Extensible Markup Language (XML) **Extensible Markup Language (XML)** is similar to HTML in that they both contain symbols to describe the contents of a page or file. While HTML describes the content only in terms of how it is to be displayed and interacted with, XML describes the content in terms of what data is being included—for example, "phonenum". This provides more flexibility in execution of the file; for example, the phone number could be stored, displayed, or

COMMON GATEWAY INTERFACE (CGI): a method used by a web server to pass a user's request that has come over the Internet to an application program and receive data that can be sent back to the user.

HYPERTEXT MARKUP LANGUAGE (HTML): code that must be inserted in a file in order for it to be displayed on the World Wide Web.

SOURCE CODE: the format in which a program is written that can be read by humans and that is converted into a different format that the computer can recognize.

METATAGS: identifiers within HTML code that indicate the content of the website.

HYPERTEXT TRANSFER PROTOCOL (HTTP): a set of rules used in exchanging hypertext files (such as text, graphics, sound, and video) for display on the World Wide Web.

SECURE HYPERTEXT TRANSFER PROTOCOL (HTTPS): a secure form of HTTP. It is a web protocol built into Netscape Navigator that encrypts (scrambles) and decrypts (unscrambles) transmissions between the user and the web server.

EXTENSIBLE MARKUP LANGUAGE (XML): markup language similar to HTML in that they both contain symbols to describe the contents of a page or file, but while HTML describes the content only in terms of how it is to be displayed and interacted with, XML describes the content in terms of what data is being included.

Figure 3.3   A Site's Source Code

This shows the source code for the entry website of St. Francis Xavier University.

```
<!DOCTYPE HTML PUBLIC "-//W3C//DTD HTML 3.2 Final//EN">

<HTML>
<HEAD><TITLE>St. Francis Xavier University, Antigonish, Nova Scotia,
Canada</TITLE>
</HEAD>


<body bgcolor=#FFFFFF text=#23238E link=#9A6400 vlink=#0000FF>
<table WIDTH=610 border=0 cellspacing=0 cellpadding=0>
<tr><td><img src="../images/lines.gif" width="154" height="13"></td>
<td><a href="/about/"><img src="../images/about.gif" border=0 width="74"
height="13"></a></td>
<td><a href="/whatsnew/"><img src="../images/news.gif" border=0 width="81"
height="13"></a></td>
<td><a href="/campus/schedules/calendar/"><img src="../images/events.gif"
border=0 width="68" height="13"></a></td>
<td><a href="/search/"><img src="../images/search.gif" border=0 width="57"
height="13"></a></td>
<td><a href="https://webmail.stfx.ca/"><img src="../images/webmail.gif" border=0
alt="St. Francis Xavier University Users Only:" width="82" height="13"></a></td>
<td><a
href="http://www.stfx.ca/campus/admin/advancement/Campaign/expandingfutures/welc
ome.htm"><img src="../images/expfut1.gif" border=0 alt="The Campaign For StFX"
width="94" height="13"></a></td>
</tr>
</table>

<table border=0 cellspacing=0 cellpadding=0>
<tr><td><img src="../images/1.gif" width="103" height="61"></td>
<!--- <tr><td><img src="../gord/1.jpg" width="103" height="61"></td>--->
<td><img src="../images/2.gif" width="157" height="61"></td>
<td><a href="http://www.stfx.ca/tresearch/"><img src="../images/teach.gif"
border=0 alt="Excellence and Commitment!" width="213" height="61"></a></td>
<td><a
href="http://www.stfx.ca/campus/admin/advancement/Campaign/expandingfutures/welc
ome.htm"><img src="../images/expfut2.gif" border=0 alt="The Campaign For StFX"
width="137" height="61"></a></td>
</tr>

<tr><td><img src="../images/3.gif" border=0 width="103" height="61"></td>
<!--- <tr><td><img src="../gord/3.jpg" border=0 width="103" height="61"></td> --
->
<td><img src="../images/4.gif" width="157" height="61"></td>
<td><a href="http://www.stfx.ca/pinstitutes/"><img src="../images/proj.gif"
border=0 alt="Outreach and Best Practice!" width="213" height="61"></a></td>
<td><a
href="http://www.stfx.ca/campus/admin/advancement/Campaign/expandingfutures/welc
ome.htm"><img src="../images/expfut3.gif" border=0 alt="The Campaign For StFX"
width="137" height="61"></a></td>
</tr>
```

dialed. The data described can be in a separate server; thus XML can be used to gather information from across the Internet.

All of these technologies are needed to be able to use the World Wide Web for business purposes. Although the Web worked for some years without XML, nevertheless XML is becoming an essential part of the Web because of its power and flexibility. Another technology that is not a part of the core set of technologies, but that has become important to the display of web pages, is Java. **Java** is a programming language that was originally invented by Sun Microsystems for the purpose of dressing up web pages. It is the program that is used, for example, to create many of the little animated icons one sees moving about on web pages. Various other technologies are used on the Web for similar purposes, such as Flash and Shockwave, but while important for modern web pages, they are not considered core technologies.

JAVA: a programming language that was originally invented for the purpose of enhancing web pages and is used to create animations and moveable, interactive icons. Since its inception, its use has grown markedly beyond web pages to include many business and e-business applications.

Making a Website Visible on the Web

Since the Web is so large and widespread, simply launching a new website does not provide any assurance that people will find it. The idea of metatags is one of the means available to help people find a website using a search engine. However, there are numerous considerations that must be kept in mind to ensure that a site is visible. These include:

- obtaining a good domain name;
- proper website design, including metatags;
- registration with search engines; and
- launching an e-business marketing program.

Obtaining a Good Domain Name Domain names are controlled internationally by InterNIC at www.internic.net. InterNIC is organized under the U.S. Department of Commerce, but it allocates domain name registration for the *.com*, *.org*, and *.edu* domain names. It also licenses various other organizations around the world to provide these domain names. For example, in Canada, domain names can be purchased from A Technology Inc., MrDomReg.com Inc., TUCOWS.com Inc., and ZiD.com. (Figure 3.4 shows the website for ZiD.com.) These organizations also provide the *.ca* domain name for Canadian companies. Domain names take the user to a particular IP address, and are, in fact, just a simple way of naming web server locations, one that is easier to remember than an IP address. For example, the domain name for the *Globe and Mail* newspaper is globeandmail.com, and the IP address for that web server is 199.246.67.250. The

InterNIC
www.internic.net

Mr.DomReg.com
www.mrdomreg.com

Tucows downloads
www.tucows.com

ZID.com
www.zid.com

Figure 3.4   ZiD.com

ZiD.com is one of the primary registrars for Canadian domain names.

website can be accessed by entering http://www.globeandmail.com or by entering http://199.246.67.250. The domain name is much easier to remember.

A domain name is portable from one server to another, so the possession of a domain name adds stability to the name of a site. The IP address, however, changes from time to time. It is generally desirable to have a domain name that is similar to the business name, but this is not always possible because many names have been taken by others. Despite popular misconception, however, there is some control over this practice. If a company owns a copyright to a name, such as Loblaws, it is very difficult for another company to obtain that domain name. Various national and international committees have been set up to control the distribution of domain names. Initially, there was a brisk trade in domain names of various companies in recent years. A famous case took place in 1994, when a young technology writer noticed that the domain name mcdonalds.com hadn't been registered. When McDonald's Restaurants wanted to register it, it was, of course, taken, and so a legal battle ensued. After much expense, the dispute was settled by McDonald's giving a donation to a charity. After this high-profile case, much better control was exerted over domain name distribution, and now, companies who have a trademarked name, such as McDonald's, have priority rights to domain names using that name.

Proper Website Design, Including Metatags Website design is a fundamental feature of a good site that goes beyond the issue of finding the site. However, it is important to take this matter into consideration when designing a site. Search engines look for many different words to find sites of interest, so it is important that the most critical words be strategically located at or near the top of the main pages, or within metatags. For example, one of the metatag lines on the site for the *Globe and Mail* is:

> META NAME="Keywords" CONTENT="canadian news, national newspaper, daily news, breaking news, political news, world news, canadian business news, canadian newspapers online, international news, report on business, national news, canadian sports, travel information, globe and mail, globe & mail"

This metatag line enables search engines to find the site if any of these search terms are used.

Registration with Search Engines To enable a search engine to find a website, it is highly desirable to register the site with the search engines in the markets in which the e-business is intended to operate. For example, registration with the Yahoo.com search engine will make the site show up on searches in the United States and other countries that use that site. If the sole intent is to do business in Canada, then registration with Yahoo.ca is needed. Similar reasoning applies to doing business in Europe and Asia. This topic will be explored further in Chapter 11.

Launching an E-Business Marketing Program Marketing in an e-business context requires development of a specialized Internet-based marketing program. This matter will be discussed in detail in Chapter 11.

Intranets and Extranets

Intranets

An intranet is a network that is internal to an organization and uses Internet technologies. Since these technologies include the use of browsers, the network appears to users to be the same as the Internet. Since it uses the same protocols as the Internet, such as TCP/IP, it can interact seamlessly with the Internet. Intranets have all of the advantages of the Internet, including ease of use, compatibility with other systems, and simplicity.

Intranets play an important role in the e-business strategies of many organizations. Initially, they were used to convey information to employees that once was printed—documents like procedure manuals, personnel manuals, policy statements, and major announcements. Essentially they were used to save printing costs and to speed up the dissemination of information.

In the next step of their evolution, they began to be used for applications that employees could use to input information into corporate applications. For example, they have been used to input time reports on assignments in process and make changes to personnel information such as addresses and telephone numbers. Essentially, applications like this on intranets transfer the input process to the employees, empower the employees to maintain their own records, and support those who are travelling by giving them remote access to the intranets. The latter use is an example of how intranets support and facilitate e-business, as they enable employees to work from outside their offices, or in client's offices, and input timely information for management and others with whom they must collaborate. The E-Strategy box provides an example of how Shell has found intranets useful as a strategy for dealing with a particular specialized need of their business.

Extranets

Extranets are networks that are available to users outside of a company and use web technology. In the case outlined in the E-Strategy box on page 50, if Shell is successful in opening the application up to customers, then the intranet that was available only to employees will become an extranet because it will also be available to customers.

Shell.com
www.shell.com

Extranets have all the advantages of intranets but extend those advantages to outside parties—most often, suppliers and customers. Accordingly, a prime purpose of the use of intranets and extranets is to automate and streamline the supply chain. For suppliers, extranets are used to enable companies to place purchase orders online and for the suppliers to fill those orders. On an extranet, companies can place their catalogues online, and their customers can place orders online. All of the documentation can be in electronic form, and if the applications are sophisticated enough, all of the transactions can be executed online.

An extranet can also be an excellent way to deal with inquiries about availability, delivery times, and other customer concerns and to provide promotional information to the customers. For suppliers, extranets have been extended to implementing joint applications such as vendor managed inventory (VMI) applications, in which the suppliers manage the company's inventory levels by monitoring quantities on hand and automatically replenishing the stock when needed. Applications like this are critical to contemporary e-business. They reduce costs, improve the timing of business transactions, and foster key business relationships. These are the reasons why extranets have proven to be powerful and popular business tools adopted by a growing range of companies. The E-Business in Global Perspective box, which provides the example of Hyundai Motors using an extranet to build parts sales, illustrates how e-business can help the overall business to succeed.

Hyundai Motors
www.hyundai.com

E-STRATEGY

Handling Waste at Shell

When a company like Shell Oil Co. moves hazardous chemicals, the chemicals must be accompanied by a safety sheet. The purpose of safety sheets is to make available information about the health hazards and flammability of a particular substance to anyone who handles the products. For Shell, the preparation of these sheets has always been costly. To address this cost factor, the company rolled out an intranet application for creating and distributing "material safety data sheets" to employees and perhaps customers. With the intranet, the safety sheets can be easily distributed online.

Users and analysts say intranets are gaining popularity in the chemicals industry as an efficient and inexpensive way to manage many safety sheets. Other companies are likely to follow Shell's lead. One consultant said that companies can save as much as 25 percent of the cost by distributing safety sheets on an intranet.

Besides the savings in printing and handling paper, there are savings in computing costs. If Shell had used a mainframe system for this purpose, it would require accounts for each user who needs access, which would have to be paid for whether they were used or not. With the intranet, access can be provided to anyone with a web browser, so departments can be charged based on actual usage rather than the number of accounts. Also they have many different technologies in the company, and web technology can run on many different PC operating systems.

Shell is such a diverse group, with numerous subsidiaries having their own computing standards, that it couldn't even launch a client/server system. If it had used the existing set of technologies for tracking safety sheets, it would have been required to develop multiple versions of the client application and then redistribute them every time the application changed. The intranet application, on the other hand, can be updated once

in a central database and accessed through web browsers, which run on many operating systems.

The U.S. Occupational Safety and Health Administration's (OSHA) Hazard Communication Standard requires widespread access to the distribution of the safety sheets. Shell has obtained legal opinions that electronic access satisfies the requirement as long as PCs are readily available to workers.

At present, uncertainty about the OSHA requirements is preventing Shell from using the intranet to distribute the safety sheets to customers. The company must be able to prove that the appropriate data sheet reached the customer by the time the chemical did, and it is unclear whether web access logs will be sufficient from OSHA's viewpoint to provide this proof.

Shell spent between US$3 million and US$4 million to develop and deploy the intranet application. Eventually, it hopes to recover some of the costs by selling the software to other companies.

Questions

1. How did the use of web technologies make this application possible?
2. What issues would management have had to deal with to make this application viable?

SOURCE: www.computerworld.com.

Virtual Private Networks

Many extranets and intranets actually run on the Internet, in order to save the cost of acquiring broadband network capability, dedicated telephone lines, and the other paraphernalia that is necessary to set up a conventional network. The major distinguishing feature of an intranet or an extranet from a normal website in this circumstance is the existence of a login requiring a user ID and a password to obtain access. Clearly, having a network on the Internet exposes it to the well-known

E-BUSINESS IN GLOBAL PERSPECTIVE

Scrapping Paper at Hyundai

Hyundai Motors America has built an extranet to link car dealers, auto parts distributors, and independent repair shops to boost the sales of parts by, they hope, as much as 10 percent. Parts sales have been declining. The extranet, which runs on the World Wide Web, is also intended to help Hyundai build a database of information on the independent repair shops as well as customers. The extranet was formally launched on April 6, 2001.

Before the launch of the extranet, repair shops seeking information on the 35 000 parts Hyundai sells had to use either paper catalogues and microfiche documents or call the Hyundai office in New Jersey. Because of the time-consuming nature of this process, repair shops often tended to go simply with third-party products that are cheaper but not always of the same quality.

By using the extranet, repair shops and other registered users will be able to order vehicle parts from an online electronic catalogue that will then be fulfilled by participating dealers. Hyundai figures that the extranet will be much faster than catalogues or microfiche and can also be used to provide certain information, such as the status of an order, that is needed for everyday operations.

Dealers and distributors must pay US$50 monthly to participate in the extranet, but the payback is that they can use it to order parts wholesale, check parts inventories, and monitor order and account status information. By launch time, more than 40 percent of Hyundai's 470 dealers in the United States had signed up on the extranet.

The extranet project is part of an overall Hyundai strategy to make its parts more readily available to consumers. Hyundai also initiated a separate supply-chain project in which it is building small warehouses for auto parts at 50 of its largest dealerships to replace three large centres in California, Chicago, and New Jersey. With this approach, the parts will be closer to the customers, and all of the inventories will be available through the extranet.

Questions

1. How will the extranet help to solve the problem of declining parts sales for Hyundai?
2. How does the use of web technology inherent in an extranet help to achieve this objective?

SOURCE: www.computerworld.com.

security shortcomings of the Internet. A good hacker can find the intranet or extranet by surfing the Internet and only has to crack the ID and password to gain access—a comparatively easier job than if the network is set within the bounds of the corporate networks.

A **virtual private network (VPN)** is one answer to these concerns that has been adopted by many companies. A VPN is a secure and encrypted connection between two points across the Internet. VPNs transfer information by encrypting the data in IP packets and sending the packets over the Internet by a process called **tunnelling**. Most VPNs are built and run by Internet service providers and have been used to replace remote access and international proprietary networks.

By using the Internet, VPNs reduce networking costs and staffing requirements, somewhat akin to outsourcing, but with better cost reductions. Companies use VPNs instead of international frame-relay and leased-line connections. Using VPNs for international networks is quicker than waiting until links can be established by the carriers.

VIRTUAL PRIVATE NETWORK (VPN): a secure and encrypted connection between two points across the Internet.

TUNNELLING: process under which data packets are transmitted over the Internet by including an additional header that establishes its route through the Internet. This adds some assurance and security to the transmission process because it is known where the data are and where they are going at all times. The route to be followed by the data is called a tunnel.

FIREWALL: a high-security computer system that acts as the entry point into a network from the Internet. It includes sophisticated security features as well as encryption capabilities to render the data unreadable by unauthorized persons. A firewall also includes security-related policies and procedures that make it effective as a secure entry point.

When a user sends data through a VPN, it goes from that user's PC to a **firewall**, which encrypts the data and sends it over an access line to the company's Internet service provider. The data is then carried through tunnels across the Internet to the recipient's Internet provider. From that point, the data travels over an access line, through another firewall where it is decrypted and sent to the recipient's PC.

How VPNs Facilitate E-Business Transactions

VPNs are driven by a need for wide-ranging networks with the advantages of the Internet in terms of cost and availability, but without the disadvantages of the Internet in terms of security. By providing a secure environment, VPNs address the Internet's limitations and, as a consequence, add considerable flexibility to a company's network options. In other words, they make the Internet more available as a viable business system.

VPNs are used as a framework in which to develop extranets as well as intranets. Extranets range outside a company and, therefore, tend to serve the need for wide area networks. Intranets, on the other hand, are internal to a company. However, in large companies, the network must cover a large geographical area, and may well be global in scope.

KEY TERMS

packet switching

protocol

Transmission Control Protocol (TCP)

Internet Protocol (IP)

asynchronous transfer mode (ATM)

Megabits per second (Mbps)

point-of-presence (POP)

fibre optic

Internet backbone

client

server

Uniform Resource Locator (URL)

web browser

Common Gateway Interface (CGI)

HyperText Markup Language (HTML)

source code

metatags

HyperText Transfer Protocol (HTTP)

Secure HyperText Transfer Protocol (HTTPS)

Extensible Markup Language (XML)

Java

virtual private network (VPN)

tunnelling

firewall

Chapter Summary

The Internet is the world's largest network, connecting millions of computers from more than 100 countries. The size of the network and the number of users are growing rapidly. It began as a military project in 1968 when the U.S. Defense Advanced Research Projects Agency (DARPA) formed a network intended for sharing research and development work among corporate, academic, and government researchers. They formed a new network called ARPANET and a protocol to make it work—TCP/IP.

In Canada, the Internet began in 1990 when CA*net was created. The purpose of CA*net was to provide Internet connectivity between universities and research organizations in Canada. In 1997, CA*net II was formed by linking with international organizations using the Internet Protocol. Then, in 1998, the federal government began working with CANARIE to build a national R&D Internet network, CA*net 3, based on fibre optic technology. CANARIE's mission is to accelerate Canada's advanced Internet development and use.

The Internet Architecture Board (IAB) is the coordinating committee for Internet design, engineering, and management. The IAB established the Internet Engineering Task Force (IETF) to help coordinate the operation, management, and evolution of the Internet. The IETF is a large open community of network designers, operators, vendors, and researchers concerned with the Internet and its protocols. The Internet Research Task Force (IRTF) was formed by the IAB to promote research in networking and the development of new technology.

The World Wide Web (WWW) is a special set of servers on the Internet, known as web servers, that is equipped to communicate with web browsers.

The main technologies used on the Internet are TCP/IP, Common Gateway Interface (CGI), HyperText Markup Language (HTML), HyperText Transfer Protocol (HTTP), and Extensible Markup Language (XML).

An intranet is a network that is internal to an organization and uses Internet technologies. Since these technologies include the use of browsers, the network appears to users to be the same as the Internet. Since it uses the same protocols as the Internet, it can interact seamlessly with the Internet.

Extranets are networks that are available to users outside of a company and use Internet technology. On an extranet, companies can place their catalogues online, and their customers can place orders online. Applications like this are critical to contemporary e-business. They reduce costs, improve the timing of business transactions, and foster key business relationships.

Many extranets and intranets actually run on the Internet, in order to save the cost of acquiring broadband network capability, dedicated telephone lines, and the other paraphernalia that is necessary to set up a conventional network. Clearly, having a network on the Internet exposes it to the security shortcomings of the Internet. A virtual private network (VPN) is one solution that has been adopted by many companies. A VPN is a secure and encrypted connection between two points across the Internet. It can transfer information by encrypting the data in IP packets and sending the packets over the Internet by a process called tunnelling. Most VPNs are built and run by Internet service providers and have been used to replace remote access and international proprietary networks.

Tools for Online Learning

To help you master the material in this chapter and stay up to date with new developments in e-business, visit **www.pearsoned.ca/trites** . Resources include:

> **Review Questions and Exercises**

> **Problems for Discussion**

> **Recommended Readings**

> **Updates to Boxes, Case Studies and textual material**

> **Links to demonstration tools related to course topics including sample Web sites**

> **Streaming CBC Videos with Cases**

CHAPTER 4

Enterprise-Wide and Inter-Enterprise Systems

learning objectives

When you complete this chapter, you should be able to:

1. Describe what is meant by enterprise-wide systems.

2. Describe how enterprise-wide systems fit with e-business strategy.

3. Identify the key features of enterprise systems.

4. Describe how inter-enterprise systems are created.

5. Evaluate the structures for setting up enterprise and inter-enterprise systems.

6. Explain how enterprise and inter-enterprise systems are crucial to e-business.

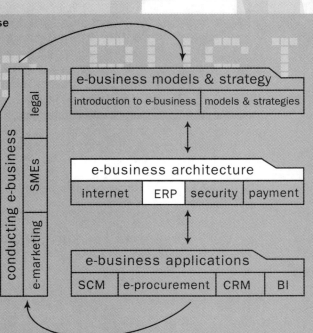

e-business models & strategy	
introduction to e-business	models & strategies

e-business architecture			
internet	ERP	security	payment

e-business applications			
SCM	e-procurement	CRM	BI

conducting e-business — legal | SMEs | e-marketing

Introduction

In a broad sense, **enterprise-wide systems** are any information systems that are deployed throughout an enterprise. They are intended to make information available to all personnel in the enterprise who need it, regardless of where they are located. They are based on the concept that the personnel should have confidence that the information they have is as accurate and up to date as what others in the enterprise are receiving and, therefore, everyone is "on the same page."

Enterprise-wide systems became widely used as business enterprises continued to spread out around the globe and management decisions were pushed down in the organizations so that local managements had more autonomy to make decisions, but still needed to be up to date on activities in the rest of the organization. Such systems take many forms, including enterprise resource planning (ERP), supply chain management (SCM) systems, and customer relationship management (CRM) systems.[1]

Some companies link systems by using **middleware** and Extensible Markup Language (XML), and the linked set of systems can be referred to as an enterprise-wide system. These types of systems are discussed in the following sections. The advent of e-business spurred on the development of enterprise-wide systems since they are needed to enable an enterprise to fully integrate its data and systems for purposes of enabling the parts of the supply chain to respond quickly to customer needs.

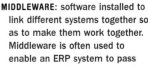

ENTERPRISE-WIDE SYSTEMS: any software systems used throughout an enterprise with the intention of enabling a consistent type of functionality as well as enterprise-wide access to the same data.

MIDDLEWARE: software installed to link different systems together so as to make them work together. Middleware is often used to enable an ERP system to pass data back and forth between it and a legacy system.

ERP Systems

Enterprise resource planning (ERP) systems have all the characteristics of what is described above as enterprise-wide systems. They are specifically designed to enable personnel throughout an organization to view the same set of data. Accordingly, ERP systems are large, have a comprehensive set of functionality, and utilize centralized databases to hold the data of an organization so that all personnel are, in fact, reading the same data.

The five largest vendors of ERP systems are Baan, J.D. Edwards, Oracle, Peoplesoft, and SAP. Because of the importance of systems integration in e-business and the important role that can be played by ERP systems in that integration, all of these vendors are positioning their products as e-business solutions, as can be seen in the example of SAP in Figure 4.1.

A typical ERP system has numerous modules, such as those shown in Figure 4.2. The breadth of the applications is immediately apparent—they cover the entire range of business applications, including areas like financial accounting, sales and distribution, materials management, and human resources.

The financial accounting module includes all the bookkeeping requirements for a company. This module collects all the transactions of the company and assembles them into the financial statements and other reports regarding profitability and financial position. As with all modules of SAP, the financial accounting reports can be used on a "drill down" basis, where the overall financial results can be presented in a report, and then the user can drill down to reports according to divisions, geographic areas, and particular stores by clicking on selected numbers in the report. In this way, detailed information about the company can be made available throughout the organization.

The sales and distribution module captures all the data about individual sales, records it, and then develops the necessary information to see that the product

Figure 4.1   SAP Website

SAP is positioning itself as an e-business solution.

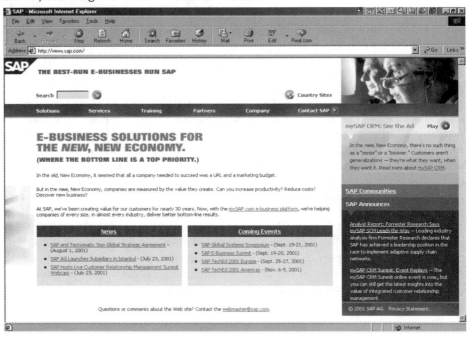

SOURCE: "Home Page." *SAP*. <http://www.sap.com>. November 2001. Reprinted with permission.

Figure 4.2   The SAP ERP System

SAP's ERP system includes various applications modules.

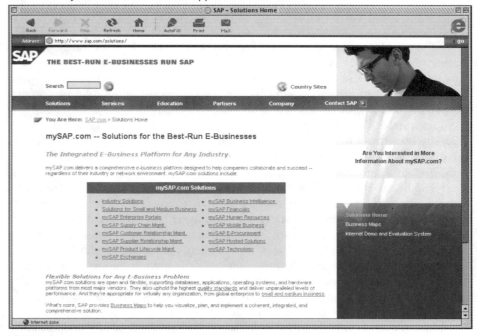

SOURCE: "SAP ERP System." *SAP*. <http://www.sap.com>. November 2001. Reprinted with permission.

sold is passed along to the shipping area of the company. The data on sales and shipments is then passed along to the financial accounting module for inclusion in the "bookkeeping" records and the financial reports.

The materials management module is used to manage all the materials that go into the production of the final product. For example, if automobiles were being built, this module would keep track of the inventories of the individual components, such as engines, seats, fenders, and headlights. Detailed specifications and costs of these components would also be kept in this module. Again, this module would integrate with the financial accounting module.

The human resources module, of course, includes the payroll system as well as all the records the company must maintain about the personnel in the organization. As with all modules, the data in this module can integrate with other modules as needed.

The scope of the modules is one of the defining characteristics of ERP systems. Another defining characteristic is the fact that the system works across an entire organization, whereas companies that do not employ ERP systems often have a variety of different systems in place, some to serve areas covered by the different modules and some to cover the different geographical areas and business units of a company. Finally, the sheer size of the system is a defining characteristic of ERP systems, and one of the characteristics that leads to many of the implementation and management issues usually associated with ERP systems.

Characteristics of ERP Systems

Client-Server Systems A significant characteristic of ERP systems is that they are **client-server systems** built on **relational database systems**. There are various forms of client-server systems, the differences primarily defined by strategic objectives. There are three basic elements to any information system—data, processing (applications), and output (display). The strategic forms of client-server systems are derived from the idea that these three system elements can be distributed between the client and the server in several ways. The processing element, for example, can be distributed to the clients, giving rise to a form of client-server system called a distributed processing system. Systems that simply have servers and clients are referred to as two-tier client-server systems. When the applications are distributed to servers dedicated to applications (i.e., when the processing is done), the system is referred to as a three-tier client-server system. If the data itself is distributed to the clients, the resulting system is known as a distributed data client-server system. Most ERP systems are configured as three-tier client-server systems, which means they have applications servers available in the organization. A system like this makes the applications more manageable, making it possible to place them closer to the user groups who are responsible for using them. This is illustrated in Figure 4.3.

While client-server systems began to gain popularity in the 1980s and '90s, the ERP systems have been found to be a good basic technology to use. However, there has been a strong movement to extend this model beyond that to create what has become known as web-enabled applications. As an example, SAP has invested a great deal in a new system called MySAP.com, which is a highly web-enabled kind of system that extends the capabilities of ERP to the Internet. Its leading competitor, Oracle Corp., also introduced a new version (Oracle Applications IIi) of its basic software that was web-enabled as well, and then introduced an integrated suite called Oracle E-Business Suite (see Figure 4.4). Of

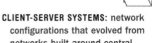

CLIENT-SERVER SYSTEMS: network configurations that evolved from networks built around central computers (servers) to provide computing power to the users on their own desktop computers (clients).

RELATIONAL DATABASE SYSTEMS: logical database model that relates data in different tables within the database by sharing a common data element (or field) between them. The common data element can serve as a reference point in the tables to other data elements in a data record.

Oracle Corporation
www.oracle.com

'Figure 4.3   Three-Tier Client-Server System

This graphic shows the basic structure of a three-tier client-server system, with the clients in the top row, the application servers in the middle row, and the network server in the bottom row.

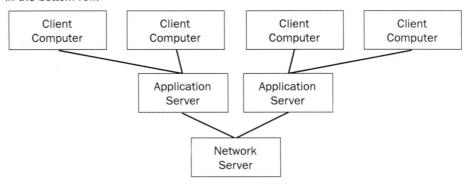

course, web-enablement is crucial to the effective use of ERP systems in e-business since it makes the integration of the ERP systems with the Internet much more effective and seamless.

The integration of the Web into the ERP products is having an impact on the basic architecture of ERP system, to the point that some vendors are touting their products as having moved from a client-server system to a network-computing architecture. Oracle, for example, in announcing version IIi of Oracle

Figure 4.4   Oracle E-Business Suite

Oracle's E-Business Suite website shows the components of the software, which represent a wide range of functionality across the e-business spectrum.

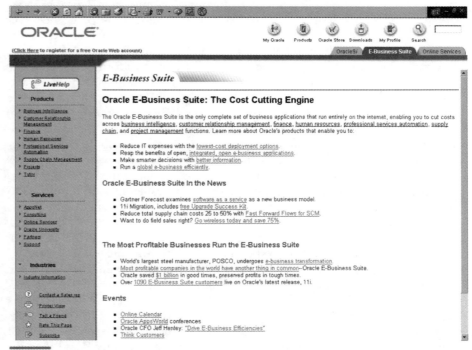

SOURCE: "E-Business Suite." *Oracle Small Business.com.* <http://www.oraclesmallbusiness.com>. December 2001. Reprinted by permission of NetLedger Inc. All rights reserved.

Applications, made that statement, arguing that a client-server model is too rigid. They point out that in a network-computing model such as the Internet, the architecture of the network is fluid, placing the data, processing, and output where it makes sense. In fact, in many ERP systems, the initial configuration of the software can reflect this flexibility. It does become much more difficult, however, to change the system after the initial configuration.

Relational Databases The fact that ERP systems are built on relational database systems is an important feature of ERP systems, since they provide a vehicle through which the data in the organization can be held and managed. All ERP systems use a relational database for this purpose, with some providing more flexibility than others as to exactly which one can be used. A very common database used for these purposes is Oracle, which of course underlies the Oracle Applications ERP system. Oracle also is one of the most common database systems used for SAP. Others are Microsoft's relational database (SQL Server) and IBM's DB2.

Database systems consist of files that contain fields of information. For example, a database containing sales information would have fields for customer number, customer name, address, product number, and product name, among other information. Databases consist of several different files like this, all linked in various ways. Relational databases are linked by identifying a common field between two or more individual files in the database, where the applications can go to look for information related to that field. This field that is common to both files is known as a "relational" field. In the example above, both files might have a field to record a customer number—a common relational field—in which case, this field can be used as the relational field. Complete systems contain many files and many relational fields.

Package Software *Package software*, as a characteristic of ERP systems, means that it is software that is bought off the shelf in a form that is installed and then operated. This is a characteristic distinct from the idea of software that is developed in-house. While the program code for packaged software is not normally changed, the program itself does need to be customized as much as possible to the specific company adopting it. Such customization must be carried out by using the functionality contained within the software as provided. Because of the size and complexity of ERP systems, the customization process is in itself a large and complex project.

Business Process Reengineering Business process reengineering (BPR) is one of the characteristics of ERP systems in the broad sense because all of them require extensive BPR to fit them into the business, or more correctly, to fit the business to the software. By definition, BPR means that the business processes being carried out by the organization must be substantially changed to accommodate the processes that are built into the software. These changes can involve changing the steps carried out during the processes, changing who does them, combining them, or replacing them. The BPR element of ERP implementations is one of the most difficult aspects of such projects.

Implementing ERP

Several notable news stories have emerged in recent years about specific failures with regard to ERP implementation projects. A widely publicized story concerns Hershey Foods and a major implementation in 1999 that ran into trouble.[2]

Hershey Food Corporation
www.hersheys.com

In late 1999, Hershey Foods announced that problems in the final phase of its ERP implementation project had resulted in delays in filling its orders to the extent that it was taking them more than twice as long to fill orders than previously. Their announcement was made during their busiest season, when back-to-school and Halloween orders were flooding in. Retailers scrambled to find other suppliers, and Hershey lost out significantly, particularly with the lucrative Halloween trade. To make matters worse, there were reports that many of those customers stayed with the other suppliers they had found for the Christmas season as well.

The impact of all this on Hershey's financial statements was substantial. Their reports showed that in the third quarter of 1999, sales were down about US$60 million from the same period in 1998, and net income fell by US$20 million. For the fourth quarter, sales were down US$42 million and earnings were down US$11 million from the fourth quarter of 1998.

In a statement released with the third-quarter results, Hershey CEO Kenneth L. Wolfe said, "our third-quarter sales and earnings declined primarily as a result of problems encountered since the July start-up of new business processes in the areas of customer service, warehousing and order fulfillment. These problems resulted in lost sales and significantly increased freight and warehousing costs."

Hershey's implementation plan involved replacing about 80 percent of its legacy systems with a system that included SAP R/3 combined with other software from Manugistics and Siebel Systems. The implementation team was formed in early 1997, with a view to going live by the spring of 1999. It was a tight deadline, with little room for error. As with many ERP implementations at the time, they were driven to complete in time for the **Y2K** deadline. They also had a strong interest in preparing themselves for the emerging world of e-business—the world of the 21st century.

As always with major projects, some things went wrong, and the pressure wrought because of the tight deadlines skyrocketed. The timetable slipped and the last phase of the implementation, which included the critical functions of warehouse management, transportation management, and the order-to-cash process, was moved to the third quarter. This happened to be the company's heaviest shipping season. They couldn't keep up and orders couldn't be filled in time, customers were unhappy, and lower earnings followed.

Hershey, SAP, and the press had lots of possible reasons and excuses for this outcome. Lack of adequate training was frequently cited. Also, some pointed to a lack of distribution capacity, although it's hard to see how this factor could be attributed to the implementation process. One author put forward the view that Hershey's computer network just couldn't handle the new system, and that Hershey didn't check it out well in advance—a classic **systems sizing** issue. They wouldn't have been the first company to run into this oversight. It's not unusual for an enterprise to implement a complicated system only to find the infrastructure can't handle it. This is especially true of an ERP system, which is huge, causes a heavy traffic flow, and requires lots of capacity for data transmission and storage. With a big-budget implementation, it makes sense to do everything possible to eliminate the risks, and one of the first places to look is to check the platform on which the system is intended to run.

There were no reports from Hershey as to whether they checked their network before starting the implementation project, so it's not known whether this was the problem or not. Some reporters thought it might have been, pointing out that with a full probe of the network, modelling it and profiling the applications

Y2K: term referring to the year 2000. Y2K was a common abbreviation to identify the computer glitches that were widely predicted to take place when the calendar turned to the year 2000.

SYSTEMS SIZING: process of assessing the volume and processing requirements that will be placed on a new information system and thereby determining the size of system required, including hardware and software.

that would run on it, Hershey could have checked the impact of the R/3, Manugistics, and Siebel systems on its network. By doing this, they could have seen the loads those applications were going to put on the network, and would have been able to identify problem areas. Put another way, thorough testing of the system, including **stress testing**, might have done the job.

Another issue was training. Some informed people felt that this was the main problem—that Hershey underestimated the amount of training required and so the people running the system couldn't cope. Even with modern high-tech systems, the people running it are critical to the process. An enterprise must make sure the people have the skill sets needed to operate and support the new system, and that proper processes are in place for supporting the users (see the Global Perspective box for an example).

STRESS TESTING: process consisting of high-volume entry, processing, and output of test data designed to determine whether the system has the capacity to handle the volumes that will be required of it.

E-BUSINESS IN GLOBAL PERSPECTIVE

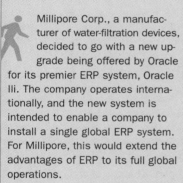

Global ERP at Millipore

Millipore Corp., a manufacturer of water-filtration devices, decided to go with a new upgrade being offered by Oracle for its premier ERP system, Oracle IIi. The company operates internationally, and the new system is intended to enable a company to install a single global ERP system. For Millipore, this would extend the advantages of ERP to its full global operations.

As a preliminary to implementation, the company moved its European ERP system from their own ERP server to one at company headquarters in Bedford, Massachusetts, leaving only its Japanese division on a separate system. Millipore executives said putting everything on the U.S. server should reduce data centre costs, in addition to giving users a unified view of the company's business. The project team knew they needed to be careful, however,

because their users would be very unforgiving if response times suffered, even a little bit.

At the same time as centralizing the servers, the company also began a six-month project to create a common accounting structure for Millipore's business units, as well as an overhaul of the company's network infrastructure.

The new system also required a database upgrade, changes in the order management module, and a change to Oracle's graphical user interface (GUI). The database upgrade needed to be tested heavily to determine how well the centralized system would be able to handle end-user workloads. A whole 12-person team, working with Oracle development personnel, had to be assigned just to test and debug the new order management module.

The switch to Oracle's GUI required strengthening the company

networks by installing new switches to double or even triple its wide-area bandwidth. However, Millipore didn't have a good understanding of the bandwidth requirements of the new GUI—just that it would definitely require a much higher capacity. They needed to initiate performance testing for this aspect of the initiative.

They had a tight deadline, with testing scheduled for the summer and "going live" scheduled for October. They ran into a setback when Oracle announced a delay in the release of the new upgrade. That was when Millipore decided to go ahead more cautiously. They wanted to be very sure the new upgrade would work well in all environments. In some of the less technologically developed areas of the world, they could run into problems, but they didn't have the option of skipping them in the implementation. It was all or nothing.

Questions

1. What issues would Millipore have had to consider when it did the risk benefit analysis for this project?
2. What would be the implications of the delay in the project?
3. Do you think they made the right decision to move ahead cautiously?

SOURCE: Computerworld.com.

Integrating ERP

ERP systems that are implemented across an organization offer the most direct way of integrating systems. (Table 4.1 provides an outline of the steps for ERP in-

Table 4.1   Steps in ERP Implementation

These steps are recommended by Oracle Corporation in its methodology for implementation of an ERP system.

Phase 1: Definition

1. Set up and organize the project team.
2. Conduct project team orientation.
3. Plan the implementation project.
4. Identify and document the overall business and system requirements.
5. Define the future business model of the organization.
6. Describe the application and information technology architectures.
7. Develop a training plan for team members.

Phase 2: Operations Analysis

8. Collect the business process information and requirements.
9. Fit the required business processes to the standard built-in ERP processes.
10. Develop the business requirements scenarios and the gap analysis.
11. Refine the applications and technology architectures.
12. Prototype business processes.
13. Begin consideration of the feasibility of the business process design.

Phase 3: Solution Design

14. Develop detailed documentation of business procedures.
15. Consider and set specific application configuration options for customization.
16. Design any custom extensions, interfaces, and data conversions.
17. Determine process and organizational changes required to enable implementation.

Phase 4: Build

18. Code and test the customization carried out, including all enhancements, conversions, and interfaces (development team).
19. Create and execute performance, integration, and business system tests.

Phase 5: Transition

20. Conduct data conversion.
21. Conduct final training for the users and support staff.
22. Conduct a production readiness check.

Phase 6: Production

23. Cutover to production.
24. Fine-tune the system to make sure it is actually running as it was intended.
25. Begin the process of regular maintenance.
26. Turn over the system to the continuing management of the organization.
27. Begin ongoing support by the continuing IS personnel.

SOURCE: "Using Oracle Applications" (Boss Corporation, Indianapolis, 2000). Reprinted with permission of NetLedger Inc. All rights reserved.

tegration, as outlined by Oracle Corporation.) If, for example, all the modules of SAP are implemented, then the modules will automatically be able to "talk to" each other. The major issue that arises in this situation is that the fit between the enterprise's systems and the overall ERP system is likely to be less, requiring more business process change in order to implement, because with the large systems in particular, the business processes must be changed to fit the software, rather than changing the software to fit the existing processes. Also, the interface with users is standard across the modules, minimizing the training required for personnel who change their jobs within the company.

On the other hand, implementation of a number of systems in an organization by choosing the best fit for particular functionality—a "best-of-breed" approach—enhances the possibility of attaining a good fit between the business processes and the software, requiring less business process change. However, more time must be spent during implementation on the interfaces between the systems, and sometimes these interfaces don't work as well as the users would like. The E-Strategy box outlines a best-of-breed approach that was used at Dell Computer. The essential point is that good integration is absolutely essential for e-business purposes.

E-STRATEGY

Best of Breed at Dell

When Dell Computer Co. decided to implement enterprise-wide systems, it chose the ERP software of Glovia International for inventory control, warehouse management, and materials management as part of its strategy. Dell had also chosen i2 Technologies' Supply Chain Management system and Oracle's Order Management system in implementing what is known as a best-of-breed strategy. The concept of a best-of-breed strategy is to choose specific functionality from a variety of software packages instead of relying on one all-encompassing product. Then the packages need to be knit together by using middleware and other linkages.

The company had tried to implement SAP's R/3 ERP system in 1994 for manufacturing applications, but had felt it to be "too monolithic" to be able to keep up with their changing business needs. After trying to implement over the next two years, they finally cut back the effort in 1996, using SAP only for human resources. They had tried to customize the product to match their business model, but found they couldn't keep up with the very rapid changes in this area.

Dell management pointed out that the Glovia software was scalable on Dell hardware, but also flexible enough to integrate with the other software they had chosen to run. In addition, they felt Glovia had the capability to break into smaller pieces for implementation. This was before SAP modularized its software to offer the same capability.

Dell undertook a global implementation of Glovia in 2000, with approximately 3000 Dell employees in the United States, Ireland, and Malaysia slated to use the software.

Questions

1. Based on what you know of Dell, evaluate their best-of-breed strategy against a single-vendor strategy.
2. What are the risks of a best-of-breed strategy?
3. Which strategy—best-of-breed or single-vendor—is likely to remain valid for the long term?

SOURCE: Informationweek.com. May 11, 1998

Middleware

The term "middleware" is used to designate any software that is used to link applications together. It differs from the idea of importing and exporting information between applications, because middleware involves the creation of a direct linkage through which data can flow uninterrupted. For example, accounting applications, such as Simply Accounting by Computer Associates, have functions in their menus that specifically allow data and reports to be imported from and exported to spreadsheets for further analysis. This process is not middleware because it requires the import and export functions to be executed. The use of middleware between applications like accounting software and spreadsheets is seamless (i.e., it is not seen by the user). The data moves as though it were still in the same application.

Middleware is used in enterprise systems because it is important that data move freely and easily across the enterprise. While the large systems like ERP and CRM systems are large enough to minimize the use of middleware, they do not eliminate that need. The process of using middleware to knit applications together across an enterprise is known as enterprise application integration (EAI).

Examples of middleware include Microsoft Message Queue Server (MSMQ), which is also known as Falcon. This software is designed to enable application programs to communicate with other application programs through a built-in messaging system that asynchronously sends and receives messages. Database systems, such as Sybase, DB2, and Oracle, are also used as middleware by providing a direct linkage to specific data and a repository of data that is in transit. Data often resides on networks, midrange, and mainframe systems, and database systems can provide direct, read/write access to integrate that data into an application. Such linkages are used in e-business to build data warehouses, automate sales forces, and integrate Internet-based applications.

Extensible Markup Language (XML)

In Chapter 1, Extensible Markup Language (XML) was defined as a very powerful tool that is similar to HTML and is compatible with it, but does not rely on single preset tags to identify information. Instead, XML provides a mechanism for any document builder to define new XML tags within any XML document. This means that in addition to being a markup language, XML is a meta-language that can define new tags. Data can be tagged within a system using XML and then found quickly by an XML-enabled browser.

As with HTML, tags can be identified in XML by words that are bracketed by "<" and ">". Tags within such brackets can also be definitional, such as <name="value">. A major difference between HTML and XML, however, is that HTML specifies exactly what each tag means, while XML uses the tags only to identify the data, and leaves it up to the application reading the data to find that data. For example, an XML document might be a report that shows the total sales of a company. The XML tag might read <total sales> for that part of the report where the number is intended to appear. The XML tag will be sent to another application and that application will read the tag and go to the data fields for total sales and insert the number in the document. Of course, in order to do this, the application needs to be "XML enabled," which means it contains the software code that enables it to read and interpret the tags.

XML is used for the integration of systems from the Internet back into the basic information systems of the company, the CRM and ERP systems, the accounting systems, and any other components of the supply chain. The Internet application sends an XML request (tag) back to the source data within the applications, which then sends that specific data back to the Internet. The whole process should be very fast and seamless. In effect, XML is a process for drawing structured data from a variety of sources and placing it into a text file for a user.

XML is not just a single technology, but rather has been referred to as a family of technologies. It is built on specifications that represent agreements within the information systems (IS) community. The core specification is XML 1.0, which defines what "tags" and "attributes" are, but there are several other parts of XML. For example, there is Xlink, which describes a standard way to add hyperlinks to an XML file, as well as XPointer and Xfragments, which are syntaxes for pointing to parts of an XML document. The details of the XML protocol are quite complex, but such detail is not needed to gain an understanding of its applicability for e-business.

Collaborative and Inter-Enterprise Systems

Collaborative systems and inter-enterprise systems are becoming increasingly common as electronic business becomes more sophisticated and companies become more interlinked. Inter-enterprise systems arise because of the growth in collaborative e-business between enterprises and their customers, suppliers, personnel, and competitors.

COLLABORATIVE SYSTEMS: information systems that work between enterprises to enable them to work together on common business initiatives and ventures.

Collaboration with Customers

An early form of collaboration with customers arose out of the customization of products and the involvement of the customers in the customization process. Levi's Jeans was an early innovator in this area. Through their website, they offered customers the option to create their own jeans by inputting their own measurements and then ordering them over the Web. By having the ability to create a pair of jeans that fit their measurements in the way they wanted, customers were essentially collaborating in the design of those jeans. The collaborative system in this case was the Internet. There had to be a way for the input measurements to reach the sales order system within the company, and that would also be part of the collaborative system. This, of course, would require integration of these two parts of the system.

Cisco Systems is one of the world's leading suppliers of technical network equipment like routers, hubs, and switches. They have initiated several applications that use the Web as a vehicle for collaboration with customers. For example, their customers can sign into a website with interactive chat rooms and whiteboard tools that allow customers to interact with Cisco representatives to discuss technical problems. The whiteboard tools are used to exchange drawings to explore possible solutions to the issues. This was a successful initiative and was later expanded to include the capability for customers to simultaneously interact with company representatives using the telephone and the Web. The truly collaborative element comes in when customers click on a "help" button to request an immediate telephone call from a Cisco representative and establish a link between their respective web browsers. As the customer and the representative speak on the telephone, they can navigate the Web together using their linked browsers, sharing electronic documents and completing shared forms on the website.

Cisco Systems
www.cisco.com

Again, this linked browser system is a good example of a collaborative system based on the use of the Internet.

Collaboration with Suppliers

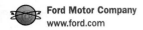
Ford Motor Company
www.ford.com

Several automobile manufacturers are involved in collaboration, to the point that some are saying that the car manufacturers could eventually be out of the car manufacturing business, acting instead as coordinators of the activities carried out by their suppliers. Ford Motor Co. provides a good example of using collaborative techniques for product design. Before the advent of collaboration, Ford would send drawings of new products to their suppliers, who in turn would add in their component and send it back to Ford, who would then pass it along to other suppliers involved in that particular product. Through a process of revision and circulation among suppliers, the ultimate product would evolve. Naturally, this process took a considerable amount of time, even though the drawings were transmitted electronically, because it was a linear process, with each participant revising the drawings in succession.

To improve on this process, Ford adopted a system they called "digital mockup," which operates on a website and enables all of the suppliers to work on the design at the same time. This meant the process changed from a sequential one to an interactive, fully collaborative activity. As with the other examples, the Internet is the prime enabler for this collaborative system. Ford has had had success with this type of system, and uses a very similar system for its "World Car" design, under which collaborators from around the world work together on the system in the design of new cars. Collaborative systems of this type are spreading not only throughout the automobile industry, but other industries as well. The Canadian Snapshot box provides an example of widespread collaboration with many suppliers and others over the Internet.

Collaboration with Personnel

For several years, Lotus Notes has been used in businesses for purposes of collaborative work on projects. The advantage of Lotus Notes is that it is designed for collaboration by enabling personnel on a project to file their papers in a central location and have it fully accessible by other team members, regardless of their location. It was ideal for consulting assignments for large companies, because consultants in Toronto, Halifax, and Vancouver, for example, could work on the company using Lotus Notes, which would maintain their files on a central server, say in Toronto, and enable all of the consultants to view, review, comment on, and even change that documentation. In this way, the working paper files for the entire consulting job can be assembled in a central location on a coordinated basis and thus eliminate duplication and minimize inconsistencies as the job proceeds, rather than just at the review stage. This system can be used between companies as well as within companies.

Collaboration with Competitors

Trading exchanges provide an excellent example of collaboration between competitors, such as the Covisint exchange of the automobile industry described in Chapter 1. Over 2000 exchanges have been formed in the past two years, in virtually all industries. Some have been formed in the chemicals industry, the most recent being one created by 12 major chemical companies, including Dow

CANADIAN SNAPSHOT

Sharing Resources at Venngo

EquityEngine.com is a unique website in which people invest their time and skills, rather than their money, to help build new Internet companies. People with an idea for a new company, but without the skills and capital to make it work, can register on the site. People can also register on the site with their skills, and in exchange for the efforts they make, they receive equity in the startup companies. In addition, people willing to invest money can also register, completing the entrepreneurs' needs.

The dot-com meltdown, however, destroyed this business model because it depended on raising capital through initial public offerings (IPOs) on the stock mar-

ket, and the chances of taking a new venture to the stock market were all but eliminated. The company needed to reinvent its business model.

The company decided to start a new venture, called Venngo Inc., which would offer software—VBN—which would be hosted on the Internet. The VBN software could be installed on clients' internal networks or accessed through the Web. Organizations could purchase licences for the VBN software and use it to post information, conduct transactions, share documents, and manage projects. For example, a small business that needs accounting help could post a notice on the VBN, and another company that possesses the required skills

could provide the help. Venngo is also attracting large companies like Hewlett-Packard Canada Ltd. so that small businesses and entrepreneurs associated with HP will use the network and eventually buy a licence for access to it.

Their idea is to address issues of immediate concern to small business, such as finding funds, employees, and other resources, and landing clients. Also, they know that their appeal will grow with the number of diverse organizations that join them. They recently obtained significant funding, which will be used to develop and market the network, add to the firm's current staff of 14, and outsource maintenance and support of the network.

Questions

1. How did the new business model—Venngo—respond to the new realities indicated by the decline of the dot-com boom?
2. What are the critical success factors for achieving success with Venngo?

SOURCE: Globetechnology.com, May 24, 2001.

Chemical, Du Pont, Bayer, and BP Amoco. Their idea was to form this exchange as an independent company with its own management team. This approach has been followed by other industries, one of the objectives being to go public with the exchange company, thereby raising capital for the trading exchange on the stock market. The purpose of the new exchange is to act as a vehicle for the sale and purchase of goods that are traded on a long-term basis in the industry, which covers a range of goods, from raw materials to the chemicals used in food and drugs. The exchange also offers financing and transportation services.

Since this chemical exchange is set up as a separate company, it has its own information system for carrying out and recording its transactions. The participating companies gain access to the exchange through the Internet, and the access is automated to various degrees, depending on the nature and volume of the business. The core software that is used by the exchange for functions like purchasing, billing, and payment is provided by an outside company on an outsourcing basis, and as a result the technological aspect of the systems are managed on an outsourcing basis. Since the exchange's systems are linked to the systems of the participants through the Internet, the collaborative system consists of the exchange system, the Internet linkages, and those parts of the participants' systems that are linked to the rest of the system.

Managing Inter-Enterprise Systems

Most of the collaborative systems described in the preceding sections are at least partially based on the Internet. Indeed, the Internet has been the prime enabler for virtually all such collaboration in recent years. As collaboration increases in intensity and scope, and as it becomes more complex, the systems will also grow and become more difficult to manage. The management of the systems is being ap-

NEW BUSINESS MODELS

Rationalizing at Rocketdyne

 Bob Carman is a strong believer in the strength of collaboration and the benefits that can come from it. He led a team for Rocketdyne Propulsion and Power that used cutting-edge software and new methods of collaborating on design that reduced the development cost for a U.S. Department of Defense missile system by an incredible factor of 100. That meant that something that cost $1 000 was reduced to $10, what normally took two or more years was cut to ten months, and what took 300 or more people was done by a team of 24. Rocketdyne is a subsidiary of Boeing Co., and has been doing work for the Star Wars initiatives of the United States. Carman's work includes solid rocket boosters that power the space shuttle into orbit, smart nuclear weapons, and high-powered lasers that could shoot down enemy rockets in outer space.

After his initial startling success in making Rocketdyne so much more efficient, he took on the task of remaking the business into smaller, more efficient teams.

Under his new approach, management could be cut to 20 percent of the workforce. To make that possible, Carman designed a new kind of collaborative system drawn from the approach taken in the Manhattan Project and on the old whaling ships of the 19th century.

At first glance, these sources of inspiration seem very unrelated— the Manhattan Project was the team that developed the first atomic bomb, while the old whaling ships, although organized very well for the time, were anything but high-tech. However, they do have one thing in common. Both made extensive use of specialists, but had those specialists work on parts of the project unrelated to their specialty when there was a problem that needed to be solved. The Manhattan Project took this approach throughout their project. In the whaling ships, the analogy was that they needed to have on board a craftsman who knew how to fix masts, even though the chances of breaking a mast were remote. Nevertheless, they needed to be self-sufficient. To keep the

craftsman busy, they had him work on other tasks on the ship.

To add motivation for the personnel, in both cases, their pay was dependent on the success of the project: in the case of the Manhattan Project by virtue of the specific organizational model, and in the case of the whaling ships by virtue of longstanding tradition. This gave the team members a stake in the project, which encouraged them to take part in the resolution of the most critical problems.

Carman's vision builds on this experience. He envisages the development of software that will provide the personnel with a stake in the success of projects and the freedom to do whatever it takes to make the projects succeed. The software would let virtually any member of the team get real-time information on any problems in the production process and allow members to assign themselves to work on the solutions to those problems—a far cry from the old directive approach to project management.

Questions

1. What issues would the collaborative approach envisioned by Carman create for project management?
2. How would the role of the project manager change?

SOURCE: Informationweek.com, January 1, 2001

proached in different ways—by outsourcing, by placing the systems management in the hands of a separate entity (such as an exchange), by establishing a management agreement with one or more of the participants in the collaboration, and by having each of the participants manage the part of the system that simply falls within their own system. The approach depends in part on who is the owner of the system and who is designated as the system manager, which is a matter that can be covered in any governing agreements.

When a collaborative system is adopted, it of course means that specific processes need to be changed, as some are taken over by partners, or by the new entity. As a result, job descriptions change and the need for personnel changes, because of the efficiencies achieved, often in a downward direction. The case of Rocketdyne in the New Business Models box provides one example.

Chapter Summary

Enterprise-wide systems are any information systems that are deployed throughout an enterprise to draw together their data and make it available to anyone who needs it. Such systems may be single systems like enterprise resource planning (ERP) or customer relationship management (CRM) systems, but also can be smaller systems linked together using middleware, Extensible Markup Language (XML), or other tools. E-business spurred on the development of enterprise-wide systems since they are needed to enable an enterprise to fully integrate its supply chain to respond quickly to customer needs.

Enterprise resource systems have all the characteristics of enterprise-wide systems. They have different modules, like financial accounting and sales and distribution, that cover the full range of business activity.

Implementing ERP systems is a major activity, involving considerable risk. Implementations usually require considerable process change and reengineering. With the large systems in particular, the business processes must be changed to fit the software rather than changing the software to fit the existing processes. ERP systems that are implemented across an organization offer the most direct way of integrating systems.

Middleware is used in enterprise systems because it is important that data move freely and easily across the enterprise. While the large systems like ERP and CRM systems are large enough to minimize the use of middleware, they do not eliminate that need. The process of using middleware to knit applications together across an enterprise is known as enterprise application integration (EAI).

XML is used for the integration of systems from the Internet back into the basic information systems of the company, the CRM and ERP systems, the accounting systems, and any other components of the supply chain. The Internet application sends an XML request back to the source data within the applications, which then sends that specific data back to the Internet application.

Different types of collaborative systems exist within companies and between companies that are collaborating. The most common collaborative system is based on using the Internet. A linked Internet browser that is connected to an application system is a good example. Another example is a trading exchange's system that is linked to the systems of the participants through the Internet. In such a case, the collaborative system consists of the exchange system, the Internet linkages, and those parts of the participants' systems that are linked to the rest of the system.

KEY TERMS

enterprise-wide systems
middleware
client-server systems
relational database systems
Y2K
systems sizing
stress testing
collaborative systems

Tools for Online Learning

To help you master the material in this chapter and stay up to date with new developments in e-business, visit www.pearsoned.ca/trites .
Resources include:

> Review Questions and Exercises

> Problems for Discussion

> Recommended Readings

> Updates to Boxes, Case Studies and
  textual material

> Links to demonstration tools related to course topics
  including sample Web sites

> Streaming CBC Videos with Cases

Endnotes

1. Supply chain management (SCM) and customer relationship management (CRM) systems are covered in Chapters 7 and 9 respectively.

2. The Hershey Foods story is reproduced with permission from G. Trites, *Enterprise Resource Planning—The Engine of e-Business.* Toronto: Canadian Institute of Chartered Accountants, 2000.

Security and Controls

learning objectives

When you complete this chapter you should be able to:

1. Identify the security risks of Internet-based business.

2. Describe generally how e-business is made secure.

3. Identify the major components of security systems for e-business.

4. Identify and evaluate the major security strategies.

5. Explain the major issues in implementing good security.

6. Describe the significant types of security tools available.

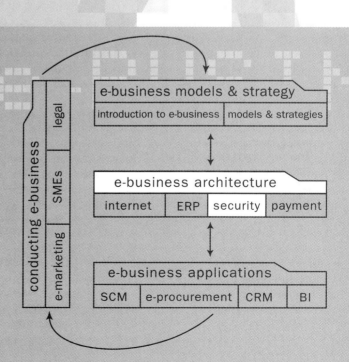

Introduction

Every information system is subject to the **risk** of **error** or **fraud**. The only question that can be dealt with by a company having an information system is the degree of risk that can be tolerated. The risk comes from numerous sources—physical damage to the system through fire, earthquakes, storms, floods, and other natural disasters. Physical damage can also arise from war, accidents, equipment failure, and sabotage. Of course many of the most damaging types of attacks on systems occur at the software level, not the hardware level. At the software level, damage to the system can occur from hacker attacks, viruses, improper use by employees, software glitches, and improper software design and development.

The risk that a business needs to address is that any of these **threats** might result in the erasure or alteration of data, either from fraudulent or careless acts. For every information system, there is always a risk that one or more of these events can happen. Not all can be prevented; for example, nobody can prevent an earthquake from happening if conditions lead it to happen. The only thing that can be done is to take steps to ensure that the data will not be lost if the system is broken or destroyed. In addition, **viruses** will continue to be developed, and sometimes they will succeed. A company can install very tight security and scanning techniques, but some of the viruses will be bound to get through.

Controls

Preventive and corrective measures to deal with the threats to a system, and therefore minimize the risk borne by the system, are known as **controls**. There are two broad categories of controls—physical and logical. Within the logical controls category, there are two types of controls—general and applications. Therefore, there are three types of controls—physical, general, and applications controls. Following is an overview of controls generally, then an examination of those controls that are particularly important to e-business.

All controls are guided by strategy, policy, and implementation procedures. Indeed, the strategy and policy are essential parts of a security system, as they involve institutionalizing the degree of risk that is acceptable and the knowledge and culture among personnel that is necessary to implement security procedures and make them effective.

Physical Controls

Physical controls are those steps and procedures that can be taken by an enterprise to safeguard the physical hardware of the system from damage. These controls include many security features like fences, surveillance equipment, alarms, and security guards. They also include locks on computer consoles, server rooms, and gates. Any measures designed to protect the physical security of the system fall under this category.

General Controls

General controls include several categories:

- security management;
- general access controls;

RISK: the probability of an event occurring that leads to missing, improper, or incorrect information in an information system.

ERROR: an unintentional act or omission that leads to missing, improper, or incorrect information.

FRAUD: an intentional act or omission that leads to missing, improper, or incorrect information.

THREATS: conditions or forces that exist to increase the risk of fraud or error.

VIRUSES: computer programs that are inserted into computer systems on an unauthorized basis, unknown to the system owner or user and with an intent to take some action on that computer that can be mischievous or malicious.

CONTROLS: preventive and corrective measures that are designed to reduce the risk of fraud or error to an acceptable level.

PHYSICAL CONTROLS: measures taken to secure the physical safety of a resource (for example, fences, security guards, and locks on doors).

GENERAL CONTROLS: controls that are not unique to a particular application or applications.

- software development controls;
- operations controls; and
- business continuity.

Security Management The policies and procedures that management adopts and implements in order to guide the security program of the enterprise fall under the security management category. These policies are approved by top management, often as a result of a strategic security plan, and are then monitored by a security committee. Security personnel, such as security officers to manage the access controls, are appointed and policy manuals are distributed to appropriate personnel to ensure that all are aware of the policies and procedures.

General Access Controls There are two kinds of access to a computer system— physical access and logical access. Physical access is controlled by the physical controls described earlier. **Logical access controls** involve the use of user IDs, passwords, and the granting of permissions and rights by the security software. Such controls can be established at various software levels. If they are established at the applications level, then they are considered applications controls. If they are established at the operating system or the database level, they are considered general controls. To look at it another way, if the access controls affect more than one application, they should likely be considered to be general controls. Figure 5.1 illustrates the basic levels of software at which security can be implemented.

LOGICAL ACCESS CONTROLS: controls that are included in software. Accordingly, logical controls are sometimes referred to as "software controls."

Software Development and Change Controls When new applications systems are developed in-house, it is very important that the programs that emerge from the process be those that management approved. This means that through the development process, there must be good control to ensure that errors or omissions are not introduced during the programming, testing, or implementation phases. After that, there must be continuing access controls in place to ensure that the programs are not changed in an unauthorized manner.

Control during the development process is normally accomplished by setting up different directories or sometimes even separate systems in which to carry out the programming, testing, and implementation phases. Figure 5.2 illustrates this process. Programs are written in the development area. They are then tested in the testing area, by the programmer and others. The prime control over these different areas is that access is restricted to those who need it. The development area is accessible only by the programmers, and the testing is accessible only by those doing the testing. Once they are felt to be ready, and the users and management have signed off on them, the new programs are "promoted" to the pro-

Figure 5.1   Security Software Structure

Basic layers at which security is established

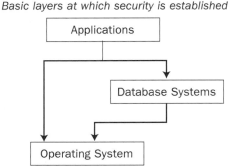

Figure 5.2   Directories for Systems Development

Systems development activities progress through three directories

duction area. This is the area where the programs actually run live and use the data of the enterprise to execute procedures and create reports. The process of following this established approach and obtaining appropriate approvals is crucial to ensuring that the programs that are actually placed into production in the enterprise are the proper ones.

After the programs are developed and implemented, they are sometimes subjected to change because of minor corrections or enhancements. This process, usually referred to as program maintenance, must be subjected to controls similar to development controls, since the same risks and threats exist. However, most enterprises reduce the extent of the controls for practical reasons and because they feel the risks and threats are not as great. This is a matter of judgement in the circumstances.

Operations Controls Control over the operations of a computer system include the operation of the servers, scheduling of jobs, and maintenance of the system. Operations controls are often in the hands of technical support people for networks in the organization. Often, they have particular parts of the operations assigned to them. Operations controls include such activities as review of system logs, monitoring system activity, and review of exception reports on system activity.

Business Continuity Systems must always be available to organizations, and especially when they are involved in e-commerce, downtime can be costly and even disastrous. Therefore, steps must be taken to be able to recover data and programs on a timely basis in the event of system interruptions or disaster. This means the enterprise must have a **business continuity** plan that maps out the steps to be followed in the event of a disaster. The steps must be detailed and the plan must be carefully tested. Normally, the testing is done in as much detail as possible, and all the steps must be documented in detail. Of course, the testing should be repeated periodically and the documentation kept up to date.

An effective **disaster recovery plan** normally addresses at least the following points:

- the nature of potential disasters that might pose a risk (floods, fires, storms, terrorists, etc.);
- roles and responsibilities of information systems personnel and users in an emergency;
- detailed playscripts for all personnel involved in the operation;
- a contact list, including home phone numbers, IS personnel, and external service providers;
- critical processing priorities (to guide the order in which systems will be restored);
- procedures to be followed for testing, review, and update of the plan itself;
- backup hardware to be used, and its location and access requirements;
- location and availability of backup of systems software, application programs, data files, database, and documentation;
- off-site storage location and access requirements of all backups including a copy of the plan itself;

BUSINESS CONTINUITY: the plans that are directed to ensuring that a business can continue in operation after a major disaster or other event occurs that could otherwise disable the computer systems for a lengthy period of time.

DISASTER RECOVERY PLAN: detailed plan of action that enables an information system to be recovered after a major disaster has made it inoperable.

Figure 5.3   The Encryption Process

Sample Method of Encryption

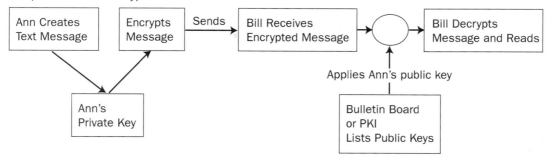

- power requirements and contingency plans if power is down;
- communications requirements and contingency plans if communications are down; and
- detailed procedures for rebuilding the system on the backup computers, including estimated time for completion.

Applications Controls

All applications that a business uses consist of three basic areas—input, processing, and output. Thus, applications controls must be established for each of these areas. In addition, a category that has assumed increased importance is that of communications controls. Input controls include those that validate the input, such as **check digits** and **input masks,** that restricts the number of characters in a section and whether they are numbers or characters. Output controls include controls over the distribution of reports, including access to online reports. If reports are in paper form, then output controls determine the printer that is used, where it is located, and who has access to it. Such controls also include procedures to have the output picked up by authorized personnel for distribution. If the reports are online, access controls are established to determine who can view the reports.

Communications controls are a major aspect of applications controls, are particularly important in e-commerce, and are discussed more fully below. A major communications control is **encryption** (see Figure 5.3), which is discussed further in the sections that follow. Encryption is one of the most important control tools used in e-business.

CHECK DIGITS: redundant digits added to a set of digits that enables the accuracy of other characters in the set to be checked.

INPUT MASKS: established formats for input areas in a screen that allow certain numbers of characters and/or digits to be entered.

ENCRYPTION: the process of scrambling data by applying an encryption algorithm to it. A key to the algorithm is provided to recipients of the data to enable them to unscramble it and read it.

Controls in an E-Commerce Setting

Controls should always be approached in a holistic sense. In other words, all of the controls included in the framework set out above must be included in a control system in order for the system to be secure. This applies as much in an e-business setting as in any other.

The entry of a company into electronic business does raise some unique challenges, and business has adopted various security strategies to deal with them (see New Business Models box). These challenges centre heavily around the use of the Internet as a vehicle of communication with customers and business partners, as well as being an integral part of the IT platform.

NEW BUSINESS MODELS

Outsourcing Security at First American Bank

In recent years, outsourcing has been a strategy in almost every area of business activity, including IT. Many security people feel, however, that security is something that should not be outsourced, especially at the largest and more conservative companies. But in the past few years, the option of outsourcing IT security—through an enterprise known as a managed security service provider (MSSP)—has grown in popularity and respectability. Companies have been handing over key parts of their security structures to MSSPs, including firewalls, anti-virus software, virtual private networks, and intrusion detection.

Some of them, like First American Bank, are relatively small companies that have big security concerns. At that bank, a vice president got a call at 2 a.m. from a technical analyst at the Unisys security command centre. The analyst detected suspicious activity but hadn't been able to isolate and identify the source of the trouble.

He said that if the problem wasn't solved soon, the network would have to be shut down as a security precaution. The VP gave the go-ahead to shut down the network.

A short while later, the security analyst determined that a malicious attack hadn't occurred after all; instead the problem was network interference, caused by local telephone lines. The network was brought up again and the VP went back to sleep. The analyst, or others like him, continued to monitor the bank's network on a 24/7 basis. The VP's attitude was "Better safe than sorry."

Security is extremely important to a bank, as its lack could raise questions about its trustworthiness and lead to a flight of customers. First American had entered into Internet banking and didn't fully understand all the security risks posed by the Internet. For these reasons and also because they did not have sufficient staff resources to mount a sophisticated security system internally, the bank decided

to go with the e-@ction Security Solution offered by Unisys.

When they were asked to provide the service, Unisys did a three-day security assessment, which included an inventory of the bank's IT systems, discussions of their growth plans, and a thorough evaluation of their existing security systems. After the assessment was completed, the bank compared the cost of the Unisys service with that of developing an in-house, round-the-clock network-monitoring operation such as that of the e-@ction Security Solution, and Unisys got the contract.

MSSPs, like most services, don't promise absolutely 100 percent reliability, so companies using their services might also buy hacker insurance. But companies are buying into MSSPs more frequently, for reasons similar to those of First American, and because they can't keep up with all the latest security threats and be in a position to respond to them.

Questions

1. If First American had not gone with the Unisys service, what issues would they have had to address?
2. What are the risks to First American of adopting an MSSP?
3. Discuss the matters First American would have had to consider in making the decision to adopt the Unisys service.

SOURCE: Informationweek.com.

Firewalls

One of the most important elements of control over the security threats posed by the Internet is the use of **firewalls**. In reality, they are not walls at all, but rather computers or routers added to a network system with very high security capability. When the firewall computers are installed, they must be at the only point of entry between the internal network and the Internet. If they are not the only point, then they cannot be effective, because hackers and other intruders will be

FIREWALLS: computers or routers added to a network system with very high security capability.

Figure 5.4   Platform Structure for E-Business Security System

The relationship of a network system to its firewalls

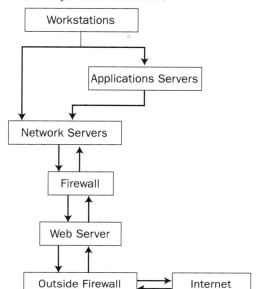

able to enter the system through the least secure point (see Canadian Snapshots box).

Firewalls must be a part of the overall security policy of the company, and must also be accompanied by specific policies that determine how the firewall is configured, who has access to it, and how the firewall actually works.

Normally, a company involved in e-business will make use of two firewalls, as shown in Figure 5.4. The reason for this is that when a network is connected to the Internet, it must have a **web server** that can be accessed by way of the Internet. Of course, this exposure to the Internet can add unnecessary exposure to the network if it is not controlled. Control is achieved by having a firewall placed between the web server and the internet, referred to as the "Outside Firewall" in Figure 5.4, and an inside firewall placed between the web server and the internal network itself.

By using these two firewalls, protection can be gained by configuring the firewalls to play a role appropriate to their placement. The outside firewall is set to accept transactions that only call upon the web server, and it restricts the types of transaction to those that the web server is authorized to handle. The inside firewall is set to process only those requests to the network data that, again, is authorized. For example, the inside server might be set to accept requests to display information on company products, but to reject requests to gain access to payroll information. There are many ways that firewalls can be configured, but all are done with the same objective—to enforce the security and data access policies of the enterprise.

WEB SERVER: a server attached to a network that is dedicated to specific applications that must be run on the World Wide Web, or used by web users, or interface very closely with the Web.

Security Policies

It is clear that an essential element of good security is a set of security policies that establish the acceptable transactions that can be carried out through Internet

CANADIAN SNAPSHOTS

Hackers at Saafnet

Saafnet International Inc. of Burnaby, B.C., has developed products that are based on the observation that high-speed Internet access, through connections such as cable modems and digital subscriber lines (DSL), is always open, making home computer users increasingly vulnerable to hacker attacks.

The company has developed a hardware device called AlphaShield, for production during the summer of 2001, which is placed between a computer and its modem and intermittently disconnects the computer. Users don't notice the disconnections and can surf the Web as usual, but the disconnections do prevent virtual thieves from having enough time to enter and tamper with the system.

The device works by creating a gate that only opens when the user clicks on the mouse button or otherwise activates a command to get information. From the user's viewpoint, it is seamless, but from the hackers' viewpoint, they are locked out of the system because they only have periods of a few seconds while the gate is open—long enough to activate a command—to try to hack into the system.

Saafnet is so convinced that AlphaShield will work flawlessly that the company has announced a planned contest where the prize would be US$1million to anyone who can break through it. The contest would run for five days, with participants invited to go to Saafnet's website and get an Internet protocol address of the computer. Anyone who brought back a piece of code or password that Saafnet preregistered on that computer would be the winner of the grand prize.

Hacking contests have also been held before by other organizations. RSA Corp.'s 56-bit encryption code was broken during a contest held over the Internet in 1996. In September 2000, Secure Digital Music Initiative (SDMI), an industry group, invited hackers to crack into several encryption methods that protect the copying of digital music files. Later that year, Argus Systems Group called on people to try to penetrate software that secures a web server.

Some experts feel that these contests can be misleading and don't prove the product is secure. They say there is no way of knowing whether anyone really tried to break the security of the system or how effective any attempts were. Many people feel there is no such thing as a computer that is 100 percent secure, other than unplugging the computer from any data lines—what is referred to as an "air gap." In a world of wireless computers, even an air gap may not be fully secure.

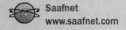
Saafnet
www.saafnet.com

Questions

1. Do you think that hacker contests are a good idea?
2. What other precautions can homeowners with high-speed Internet access take?
3. How serious are the threats against home systems that are exposed to hacker attacks over the Internet?

SOURCE: www.globetechnology.com. April 28, 2001

connections. These policies must be consistent with, or part of, the overall corporate security policies. When the policy is developed, it should be approved by the board of directors for distribution to staff. The major components of a security policy are outlined below.

1. Security Administration

This part of the policy covers the duties of the persons responsible for security administration, including the person in charge of security and the administrators of the various networks, operating systems, databases, and applications. It also establishes to whom the person in charge of security reports. Increasingly, that person is reporting to higher levels of executives, and often has responsibilities for privacy as well as security.

2. Information Management

Many companies include in their security policy an information management policy that describes the importance of the corporate information and identifies the "owner" or custodian of the information. This policy includes details such as all applications and data used in the organization, a description of the level of security required for each application or data set, and identification of appropriate business managers as custodians of the applications and data.

3. Physical Security

Procedures to be followed with regard to safeguarding the physical safety of the hardware, software, and communications infrastructure are normally covered in the security policy. This would include control over servers, the related network/telecommunications equipment, workstations, and access to the premises.

4. Logical Access Control

The policy with regard to logical access control would focus on the user IDs and password system adopted in the company. It would also include the policy guiding the assignment of access rights to specific user IDs, such as which screens, programs, and data a user can access and what actions they can perform on them (such as read, write to, change, or execute). The policy is often broken down into those related to control over personal computers, controls over access to networks, and any other unique components of the system to which personnel might be granted access, such as intranets, database systems, and the Internet.

5. End User Computing Policy

The end user portion of the security policy sets out the responsibilities of users who use corporate computers and systems. This is important for reminding users of their responsibilities for the security of the system and defining those responsibilities. The policy would include items such as reminders that users must comply with corporate security policies and procedures, take care of corporate equipment, and only use the company's computer resources and information for authorized business purposes.

The end user policy also normally sets out responsibilities for backing up data, protecting against viruses, keeping passwords secret, and taking other precautions for protecting the privacy of corporate data. The end user policy also normally identifies the software brands that will be supported by the company.

A major issue with regard to end users is that they often have access to powerful programs and tools that can be used to construct ad-hoc information systems. Sometimes such ad-hoc systems can become unofficially a critical part of the overall information system and, therefore, need to be safeguarded.

To provide proper control over such "unofficial" systems, the security policy needs to define the controls that apply and the levels of system that might require different levels of control.

6. Software Development

It is important in most organizations to take precautions to ensure that any applications are developed using techniques that provide for data integrity and appropriate audit trails.

A security policy on software development would define a procedure for setting up and managing the various directories that are used in the process, such as development, testing, and production. It would include the process for review and approval, who owns the programs, and the required documentation and access rights to various parts of the system that are used in development.

7. Personnel Management

Highly qualified IT personnel are necessary to enable an enterprise to operate and manage the system, but there is a risk to having them in that they have the skills to circumvent established controls. Therefore, a security policy must deal with the area of personnel management, including training and education. This would include matters like distribution of duties, confidentiality agreements, passwords, and control over equipment.

8. Security Monitoring

Monitoring of systems activity is crucial in establishing a secure system, as it helps the security personnel identify inappropriate activities both on the part of staff and on the part of unauthorized intruders. The security policy should establish how monitoring will take place, who will carry it out, and reporting procedures on events that occur, such as usage anomalies and security violations.

A memorandum must be issued to users to advise them that monitoring is being done, the type and frequency of monitoring, and the implications of breaching security.

9. Disaster Recovery and Contingency Planning

The basic existence and general nature of the disaster recovery plan should be outlined in the security policy, which should also stress the importance of the plan, who is responsible for it, and generally how it is administered.

One of the essential elements of disaster recovery and contingency planning is the provision for backup of systems. The security policy should therefore contain detailed guidance as to the backup procedures in force within the company for all systems including communications.

Control over Communications: Encryption, Authentication, and Non-Repudiation

Encryption techniques are fundamental to control over the communications process, a process that is central to e-business. Encryption is the conversion of data into a form, called a cipher, that is very difficult to read without possession of a "key." The encryption conversion is achieved by applying an algorithm, or formula, to the data bits that comprise the data, converting it into the cipher. The

E-STRATEGY

Insurance at Counterpane

Counterpane Internet Security Inc. (see Figure 5.5), a California company involved in the managed security services market, offers to its clients the purchase of up to US$100 million in insurance coverage to protect against loss of revenue and information assets caused by Internet and e-commerce security breaches. The insurance is backed by Lloyd's of London.

Other insurance companies have offered policies that are designed to compensate for security-related losses under loss-of-business or act-of-vandalism clauses, but they usually carry very high premiums and it is difficult to collect the benefits. Their product, which they call "Internet Asset and Income Protection Coverage," specifically provides insurance for losses resulting from a breach of security or technology failure related to damage to information assets such as data, customer lists, credit-card numbers, and other digital information. Claims can also be made for related business interruption losses. Premiums are more comparable to other forms of business insurance.

Lloyd's security insurance covers the cost of repairing and replacing data or software following the destruction or corruption of electronic devices from an attack. It also covers lost revenue following a service interruption or service impairment caused by malicious hackers.

The concept for the insurance coverage is that the insured company must demonstrate that it has met the requirements of the insurable risk model that is prescribed and accepted by Counterpane. Assistance in a security crisis and any subsequent negotiations, even including payment of a ransom demand, is also part of the package.

Until this package was developed, there did not exist an acceptable model of risk control assurance from security companies that insurance companies could use to write policies against. One of the benefits of this service, besides the insurance coverage, is the incentive it provides for companies to maintain acceptable levels of control over their systems.

The insurance plan is only one of the services that Counterpane offers in its managed security business. They provide managed, around-the-clock incident response services that are designed to help companies formulate responses to security-related incidents. They offer security experts for their clients' staff and their board, in an overall approach to security. Their experts undertake continuous monitoring for flaws in security technologies to help companies make the most of their security products. The alternative for most companies would be to hire a security manager to watch the system logs and report on the activities.

Counterpane locates its security experts in two security centres where they monitor customer networks through encrypted tunnels. They collect audit information from clients' existing security products, including servers, firewalls, and intrusion detection products. The service operates on a 24/7 basis.

The security experts use a system called "Socrates" to manage the network information they gather with data on known attacks to prioritize events, pinpoint attacks, and filter out false alarms. Socrates can be configured to monitor specific network systems and maintains its own separate logs to help prevent intruders from erasing logs to mask incursions. If an attack occurs, Counterpane reacts with pre-set procedures to deal with it.

 **Counterpane Internet Security**
www.counterpane.com

Questions

1. Why does the concept of insurance fit with security strategy?
2. To what extent is the use of Counterpane an outsourcing exercise?
3. What would management need to do in including Counterpane in its security strategy? What would be their responsibilities and duties?

SOURCE: Informationweek.com.

key is a set of data that can be applied to the cipher to convert it back to the original data. Application of the key is referred to as the decryption process.

Figure 5.5 Counterpane Internet Security Homepage

Counterpane Internet Security Inc. provides insurance coverage to protect against Internet and e-commerce security breaches.

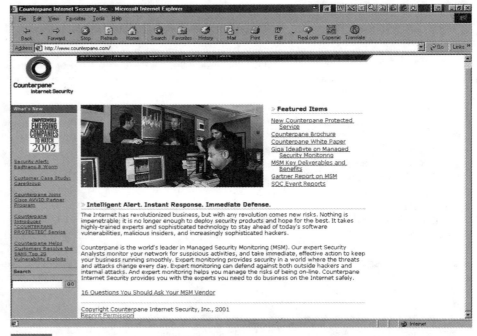

SOURCE: "Home Page." *Counterpane Internet Security Inc.* <www.counterpane.com> December 2001. Reprinted with permission. All rights reserved..

Encryption is used in various aspects of e-business, including e-mail, transmissions to execute banking transactions on the Internet, and other sensitive transmissions. The major web browsers—Netscape Navigator and Microsoft Explorer—include encryption capability, and strong encryption is available for these products as well.

There are various strengths available in encryption, measured by the length of the key. The most common standard is the 56-bit encryption key, which is supplied as a standard feature of the two web browsers. There are over 72 quadrillion (72 057 594 037 927 936) possible keys in the 56-bit DES system. The 56-bit encryption was broken in 1997 by a team led by Rock Verser, a freelance computer consultant. Verser had formed the "team" by sending out messages on the Internet asking people to download some keys and run them against a test program. He had 14 000 members on his team, and they tried about 18 quadrillion keys before finding the right one.

Despite the fact the 56-bit encryption code was cracked, the Verser episode illustrated the magnitude of effort that is required to decrypt a message using even the 56-bit encryption technology. It is still used because most people do not have the capability to go through such a process. However, the fact that it has been done has led to the use of the 128-bit technology for more sensitive transmissions. For the standard browsers, 128-bit encryption can be downloaded from the websites of the browsers' manufacturers and added to the browsers to make them capable of high-encryption transmissions. For Internet banking, the banks in Canada require their customers to install the 128-bit encryption technology for their browser before they can obtain access to

Internet banking. Links are provided on the banks' login web pages to simplify this process.

Encryption works by using a key that is generated by the person who initiates a transaction and then providing a key to the recipient that will enable the transmission to be decrypted. This can be done on a symmetric basis or an asymmetric basis. When it is done on a symmetric basis, the sender of the message simply provides the recipient with the same key used for the encryption.

The asymmetric approach is carried out by using a system of private and public keys, which together are created in pairs. A **private key** is known only to the person who generated it. A **public key** is made known to outsiders, and can be obtained by the recipient of the message. In a typical transmission, Ann might send a message to Bill that she wants to keep secret. She encrypts it with her private key and when Bill receives it, he decrypts it using her public key. Only her public key will decrypt a message encrypted using her private key.

Since the public key works on the message, Bill knows that Ann sent the message, which establishes the property of **authentication** of the user. In addition, since the public key worked in the decryption, Ann cannot deny she sent the message, establishing the property of **non-repudiation**.

On the other hand, if Ann wants to make sure that only Bill can open the message, she will encrypt it with Bill's public key. Only his private key can open the message and, of course, only he has that key. In practice, a combination of symmetric and asymmetric encryption is used, usually by using the **Secure Socket Layer (SSL) Protocol**. Also used, particularly for web pages, is the **Secure HyperText Transfer Protocol (S-HTTP)** that provides security for transmissions involving web pages (see the E-Business in Global Perspective box for an example).

Under the SSL protocol, a system of server authentication is used by making use of server-related **digital certificates** administered by **certificate authorities (CAs)** and **digital signatures.** Using SSL involves a series of negotiations when a browser contacts a web server. First, the browser obtains the server certificate and examines the digital signature on it. The digital signature would have been placed on the certificate by the certificate authority using the CA's own private key. The browser checks that this is a CA that it trusts and then decrypts the signature with the CA's public key, thereby establishing the authenticity of the certificate authority. Access to the public key is accomplished by accessing the CA's online database. The browser and the server then agree on a master key for the session, which is used to encrypt and decrypt all transmissions for that session. The master key is generated by the browser and then sent to the server by encrypting it with the server's public key. Since it can only be opened by the server for which it is intended, the identity of the master key is secure. From that point on, the encryption process for that session is carried out on a symmetric basis.

Public Key Infrastructure (PKI)

The importance of digital signatures for business, and the essential role that public and private keys play in them, means that there is a need for a great many keys. Since the public keys must be accessible by anyone, they need to be stored in a database that is accessible to the public. In addition, there is a need for a reliable system for managing the keys—one that is secure and backed by a reputable organization. This is where a public key infrastructure (PKI) is used.

A **public key infrastructure** is a system that stores and delivers keys and certificates as needed and also provides privacy, security, integrity, authentication, and

PRIVATE KEY: a set of data used to encrypt and decrypt data transmissions that is known to only one person.

PUBLIC KEY: a set of data used to encrypt and decrypt data transmissions that can be shared with anyone.

AUTHENTICATION: the property that confirms that a particular person or server is, in fact, the person or server that is identified in a transaction.

NON-REPUDIATION: a property that confirms that a particular person did indeed send a message and cannot deny that fact.

SECURE SOCKET LAYER (SSL) PROTOCOL: a security protocol associated with TCP/IP that establishes a secure communications channel between web clients and servers.

SECURE HYPERTEXT TRANSFER PROTOCOL (S-HTTP): a security protocol that works with HTTP to wrap transmissions in a secure "envelope" created with encryption technology.

DIGITAL CERTIFICATES: electronic documents that contain the identity of a person or server and the related public key. They are used for purposes of authentication.

CERTIFICATE AUTHORITIES (CAs): organizations that issue digital certificates and sign them with digital signatures to establish the authenticity of the certificates.

DIGITAL SIGNATURES: encrypted appendages to documents and data transmissions that utilize combinations of private and public keys to establish the authenticity of the signature. They fill the same role as manual signatures on paper documents.

PUBLIC KEY INFRASTRUCTURE (PKI): a system that stores and delivers keys and certificates as needed and also provides privacy, security, integrity, authentication, and non-repudiation support for various technological and e-business applications and transactions.

S-HTTP at Terisa

Recently, a coalition consisting of America Online Inc., CompuServe Inc., IBM, and Netscape Communications Corp. took equity investments in Terisa, a California company that had developed a commercial version of S-HTTP. An interesting aspect of this investment was the involvement of Netscape, since they had been promoting their SSL protocol.

Both SSL and S-HTTP are part of the Open Systems Interconnection protocol, albeit at different levels, and are quite complementary to each other, rather than competitive. SSL works at the network level to secure TCP/IP sessions, while S-HTTP works at the message level for HTTP-based web servers and clients.

There had been a good deal of competition between the two protocols, which had been confusing the marketplace and slowing improvements in security, which were widely known to be needed to enable the growth of e-business.

Other security industry participants expressed less than full enthusiasm for this combination. They said they would rather see activity like this coming through the standards bodies rather than private industry. Their concern was that an integrated S-HTTP/SSL would become a proprietary product rather than being an open system,

available to the public, which S-HTTP presently is.

Many people agree that security protocols need to be openly agreed upon so that recognized security specifications can be built into systems in a form that will be recognized by, and therefore usable in, a variety of platforms and systems.

In response to these concerns, Terisa said it had plans to work with the Internet Engineering Task Force and the World Wide Web Consortium standards bodies to create a common security standard.

In the interim, Terisa planned to begin marketing and distributing its new combined products at prices that would be affordable.

Questions

1. What would be the advantage of combining SSL and S-HTTP?
2. Why do security protocols need to be "open"?
3. What role should the standard-setting organizations, such as the Internet Engineering Task Force (IETF), play in security protocols?

SOURCE: Computerworld.com. April 17, 1995

non-repudiation support for various technological and e-business applications and transactions (see Figure 5.6). A PKI system will provide for the management of the generation and distribution of public/private key pairs and publish the public keys accompanied by certificates that confirm the identity of the key owner. All of this is included in open bulletin boards accessible by the public or all people who need to know the information. The latter qualification is needed to recognize that some PKIs are set up by particular companies, and only make the databases available to the corporate personnel and their business partners rather than the general public.

A PKI structures its data—the keys and certificate authorities—in a logical fashion for orderly management and accessibility. A user's public key and identification are placed together in a certificate. The user's certificate authority then digitally signs each certificate to provide the necessary authentication, which can be verified by using the CA's public key to verify the CA's signature on the certificate. With this system, any user can get any other user's public key from a bulletin board to verify its authenticity.

Figure 5.6   Flow Chart for PKI Systems

This chart shows the parties and procedures involved in the use of a PKI system.

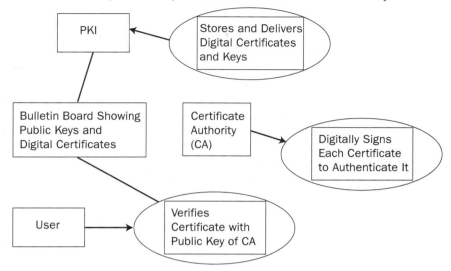

In summary, PKIs integrate digital certificates, public-key cryptography, and certificate authorities into a total, enterprise-wide network security architecture. A typical PKI for an enterprise encompasses the issuance of digital certificates to individual users and servers, end-user software, integration with corporate certificate directories, tools for managing certificates, and related services and support.

VPNs and Security

In Chapter 3 we looked at virtual private networks (VPNs), noting that they include (a) the use of firewalls, (b) tunnelling through the Internet, and (c) the use of encryption.

Firewalls are, of course, a prime tool for adding security to a network. They are usually deployed as part of a VPN system if they are not already in place.

The concept of tunnelling means that messages are directed through predetermined paths on the Internet. This has security implications, since the path through which the messages are directed can be made secure in order to minimize the opportunities of unauthorized persons to intercept those messages through **sniffing** techniques because they can only find the messages on the designated path.

As previously discussed, encryption is one of the key techniques for protecting information residing on, or transmitted through, the Internet. VPNs are set up by installing VPN software, which always includes the ability to encrypt messages being sent and to decrypt them when received. This means that even if messages are intercepted through sniffing, they cannot be read by an unauthorized person.

SNIFFING: the use of electronic devices attached to transmission lines that can detect and capture data transmissions on those lines. Newer models of sniffing devices can work on wireless transmissions as well.

Chapter Summary

Every information system is subject to risk of error or fraud. Preventive and corrective measures to deal with the threats to a system, and therefore minimize

KEY TERMS

risk

error

fraud

threats

viruses

controls

physical controls

general controls

logical access controls

business continuity

disaster recovery plan

check digits

input masks

encryption

firewalls

web server

private key

public key

authentication

non-repudiation

Secure Socket Layer (SSL) Protocol

Secure HyperText Transfer Protocol (S-HTTP)

digital certificates

certificate authorities

digital signatures

public key infrastructure (PKI)

sniffing

the risk borne by the system, are known as controls. All controls are guided by strategy, policy, and implementation procedures, which involve institutionalizing the degree of risk that is acceptable and the knowledge and culture among personnel that is necessary to implement security procedures and make them effective.

There are three kinds of controls—physical, general, and applications controls. General and applications controls fall into the category of logical controls. General controls include security management, general access controls, software development controls, operations controls, and business continuity. Applications controls include input, processing, and output controls.

All controls must be approached in a holistic fashion. This means that the e-business controls must be completely integrated with and consistent with the controls over the enterprise's information systems generally.

The entry of a company into electronic business does raise some unique challenges, and business has adopted various security strategies to deal with them. One of the most important elements of control over the security threats posed by the Internet is the use of firewalls. The other important security tool is encryption. All threats must be covered by good security policies that establish the acceptable transactions that can be carried out through the Internet connections.

Encryption techniques are fundamental to control over the communications process, a process that is central to e-business. The major web browsers—Netscape Navigator and Microsoft Explorer—include encryption capability, and strong encryption is available for these products as well. Most encryption is carried out by using pairs of private/public keys to encrypt and decrypt messages and other data transmissions.

The secure socket layer (SSL) protocol makes use of this key system along with certificate authorities. Under the SSL protocol, a system of server authentication is employed by making use of server certificates administered by certificate authorities and digital signatures. Access to the public key is accomplished by accessing the CA's online database. The master key is generated by the browser and then sent to the server by encrypting it with the server's public key.

A public key infrastructure (PKI) is a system that stores and delivers keys and certificates as needed, and also provides privacy, security, integrity, authentication, and non-repudiation support for various technological and e-business applications and transactions. A PKI system will manage the generation and distribution of public/private key pairs and publish the public keys accompanied by certificates that confirm the identity of the key owner.

Tools for Online Learning

To help you master the material in this chapter and stay up to date with new developments in e-business, visit www.pearsoned.ca/trites . Resources include:

> Review Questions and Exercises

> Problems for Discussion

> Recommended Readings

> Updates to Boxes, Case Studies and textual material

> Links to demonstration tools related to course topics including sample Web sites

> Streaming CBC Videos with Cases

Billing and Payment Systems

learning objectives

When you complete this chapter you should be able to:

1. Describe the techniques for billing and payment over the Internet.

2. Describe how billing and payment techniques relate to corporate strategy.

3. Identify the advantages and disadvantages of these techniques.

4. Evaluate the suitability of billing and payment methods for various e-business scenarios.

5. Explain why many previous techniques have not succeeded.

6. Indicate the trends most likely to prevail in the future.

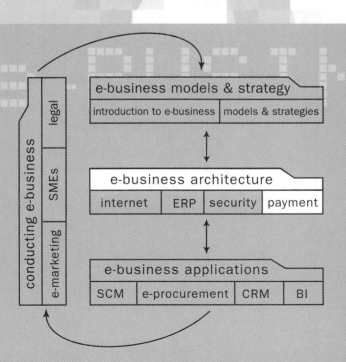

Introduction

Ever since enterprises began to offer goods and services for sale over the Web, there has been a need for some kind of system to pay for them over the Web. One reason is that it is much less expensive to carry out transactions on the Web as compared to other methods. In Figure 1.3 (see page 7), for example, it was shown that the cost of conducting a transaction through a bank branch costs over US$1, while conducting that same transaction over the Internet costs only 1 or 2 cents. This is a remarkable fact that clearly points to the reason why so many businesses are interested in moving transactions to the Internet.

Another reason related to business-to-consumer (B2C) commerce is that if customers can pay online, there is a greater chance that they will buy, as opposed to situations where they must go offline to pay. For business-to-business (B2B) commerce, there is also an incentive to have online billing and payment for economic reasons, as there is a tendency for numerous transactions to be carried out with the same regular customers. The savings in serving these customers can be dramatic; and on the other side of the coin, the savings for the customers in procurement costs can be significant.

There have been attempts to develop systems in the past, but many of them have failed. Some of the more visible of them have included DigiCash, NetCash, NetCheck, First Virtual, Mondex, Intell-A-Check, and NetCard.

The problems have centred on the difficulty of developing a system that is secure, convenient, and accepted by enough people to make it economically viable (see Canadian Snapshots box for an example of one system). The need for security is clear: if there is too great a chance their money will be lost in a transaction, either through fraud or error, consumers will not use the system, and if they do, legal issues will arise for the businesses using those systems. Such a system must also be convenient. People using the Web do not have the time and inclination to enter into significant time commitments just to purchase something online. In face, several companies have noted the unwillingness of consumers to even enter information in a registration screen. Finally, a system must gain acceptance by the customers, the financial institutions, and the vendors in order to be viable. It is far too expensive to initiate a system that is not used.

Characteristics of Traditional Payment Systems

Electronic Data Interchange (EDI)

Electronic Data Interchange (EDI) is a form of conducting transactions, including payment transactions, in electronic form. It is based on the use of widely accepted standards for formatting data in EDI transmissions. Persons using EDI must be signatories to an EDI agreement and must have their information systems configure to be able to recognize and process the transactions.

EDI has been used for many years as a means of settling payments, especially in the B2B world. Traditionally, EDI systems have made use of **value added networks (VANs)** as a platform for operating them. Generally, EDI has been costly and, in its "traditional" form, has been used most often by very large companies. Since the Internet became more widely used for conducting business transactions, EDI has moved from the VANs to the Web. The Web is a much more cost-effective platform for EDI transactions than the VANs, because access to it is much less

VALUE ADDED NETWORKS (VANs): privately owned networks that are rented to users, along with a package of related services, to operate their EDI systems by providing an environment within which they can work and by connecting them to their customers and suppliers.

CANADIAN SNAPSHOTS

Using 900 at Navajo

If a person wants to buy something over the Internet, and doesn't have a credit card or a debit card or doesn't want to use them, there's a problem. What do they use to pay for the purchase? Navajo Networks Inc. has an answer that works for some people—use a 1-900 telephone line.

A 1-900 telephone line is one that is used for a variety of services on a long-distance basis. It's rather like a 1-800 system for toll-free long-distance calls, but in the case of 900 lines, there's a small toll.

The idea that Navajo patented and introduced was one where people buying content off the Web like music and computer games can charge their online purchases to their phone bills without giving credit-card-type information. They say that customers find the system easy to use, it avoids the need to input a lot of personal information, and it is anonymous. The service is called 900 Pay, and it's the first automated 900 pay service in the world that is available to Internet shoppers.

The way the system works is that the customer clicks on a "buy now" button on a vendor's website, and the modem temporarily disconnects from the Internet and dials a 1-900 number. The cost of the call, which is equal to the price of the product, is charged to the customer's telephone bill. The approach of using 1-900 numbers for various charges is, of course, not new. However, the approach of devising a system that allows for automatic online dialling is new.

The service itself is free. Navajo makes its money by making a deal to take a percentage of the fees charged by the telephone carrier, such as Bell Canada or Sprint Canada. Typically, the 900 Pay system earns between 15 and 20 percent of the fees. This commission is built into the cost of the product.

One of the prime markets Navajo sees for this service is the sale of online music that is downloaded from the Internet. The 900 Pay service is built to provide an efficient, easy-to-use payment option for record companies and

other people who want to sell digital music over the Internet. Many figure the service will be popular with young people who buy most of the music and often do not have credit cards.

There are, however, some concerns that customers might not be comfortable with the new system. They might be concerned about how much is going to show up on their phone bills and who is liable for the transaction. A site like Napster, which is moving to a fee-charging service, could present a logical way to use the service. On the other hand, would the customers have their own telephone bill? Or would they end up charging the purchases to someone else's bill?

One of Navajo's first customers was Quikktutor.com, which started using the service on its website to sell virtual tutorials. Quikktutor.com liked the system because it is simple and seamless. Also, it increases their "conversion" rate. That's the number of times their site visitors are turned into customers.

Questions

1. Discuss the pros and cons of using the Navajo system.
2. What issues would a business consider before adopting the system for use by their customers?

SOURCE: Globeandmail.com.

expensive, and the technology is widely recognized and used, making it easier to communicate with various other organizations.

Normally, organizations using web-based EDI set up a web browser interface that links with the corporate systems. For payment purposes, the links would be with the cash systems to enable the payments to be processed through the corporate bank accounts. Such linkages would not be direct, because of security issues.

The use of the Internet for replacing or augmenting existing VANs for EDI transactions is a logical step in streamlining payment systems for B2B commerce.

The conversion of EDI systems from the VANs to the Internet involves many security issues because of the difficulties of securing the Internet and the involvement of cash. In addition, it involves integration of the systems within the company, with the Internet, and with the other parties to the system over the Internet.

Cash

The issue of introducing electronic payments systems for both B2B and B2C purposes leads to the question of what characteristics are required of payment systems in general for them to be effective. It is instructive to consider the characteristics of that most traditional method of payment—cash.

Cash is portable, because it can be carried easily with a person. In addition, it is widely acceptable by stores, other companies, and other people. This means cash can be carried easily from store to store, and customers can be reasonably confident that it will be accepted by the stores for payment of goods. In addition, there is normally no need to identify oneself in order to gain acceptance of the cash. Therefore, cash has the characteristics of portability, acceptance, and anonymity. Finally, the cash provides for an instant transfer of value from the buyer to the vendor.

The acceptability of cash at one time was based on its value relative to gold. There was a commitment of the government that any bank note could be turned over to the government of Canada for gold, equal in value to the denomination of the bank note. During the 1970s, this approach was abandoned and no such commitment of the government has existed since then. The acceptance of the dollar now rests on the strength of the economy, the stability of the currency, and the extent to which it is used. Since Canada generally has a strong economy and a stable government, acceptability has not been a problem in recent years.

The idea of cash providing for the vendor an instant transfer of value is an important one. This is not necessarily the case for other methods of payment. If a credit card is used for payment, for example, the vendor must send the signed voucher to the sponsoring or financial institution for payment in cash. The vouchers themselves cannot be used to purchase something. This takes some time, the actual length of which varies according to the type of card and the method used to process payments. Cash has none of these problems; it can be used immediately by the vendor for purchases.

The anonymity provided by cash is of particular interest in web-based transactions, since there is a widespread concern about the privacy of personal information on the Web. Any system that is set up to protect the privacy of information will be advantageous for this reason.

While traditional cash cannot be transported on the Web, the transportability feature is relatively easy to achieve in the case of electronic cash, as it only requires that the cash be capable of being transported over the electronic media. The means of achieving stability and backing have proven to be much more elusive.

DigiCash

Of the various online payment systems that have been invented and tested so far, one called eCash, developed by DigiCash, is the closest to approximating the attributes of cash. The product did not gain acceptance, and the company itself went bankrupt, but their attempt is interesting and revealing for those interested in the challenges of developing an online cash payment system.

eCash was built on the basis of public key cryptography—involving the use of a private key to sign messages and a public key to verify the signatures. For example, if Laura wants to send a private message to George, she encrypts it with her private key, and when he receives it, he applies her public key to verify that it was sent by her. With this approach, George is able to authenticate Laura as the sender. Because the message was unencrypted with her public key, it means it could only have been encrypted with her private key, because her public key is the only key that will unencrypt a message encrypted with her private key. Her public and private keys are key pairs. No other keys will act with them. Since it can be demonstrated that her private key was used, and that she is the only person with access to that key, she cannot argue she didn't send it, so the eCash system has the feature of non-repudiation. This encryption system can be used for any business documents. Under the eCash approach, Laura would generate a note and sign it with her private key—a digital signature. The bank would verify the signature with its own private key and charge her account. It would send to Laura the signed note and a digitally signed withdrawal receipt for Laura's records.

Laura would then send the signed note to George to pay for some goods. George would receive the note, use the public key of the bank to check the bank's digital signature, and then send the note to the bank, which would credit George's account and return an electronic deposit slip to him. George would then send the merchandise to Laura along with a receipt. With this system, eCash would fulfill most of the characteristics of the old-fashioned cash. Although it would not be portable, it would be easily transferable by electronic means. It would also provide an instant transfer of value, as the cash would be deposited in the vendor's account when the transaction takes place. However, it did not succeed, and other methods have since come forward.

Digital Cheques

Cheques have been used for many decades for settling business transactions and have many of the attributes of cash. They differ from cash largely in that they are not anonymous and carry a greater risk to the vendor accepting them in that they might not be honoured by the bank. For this reason, cheques are most useful for dealing with long-term, regular customers. Several attempts to emulate cheques in the digital environment have been made. One of the digital cheque products was called NetCheck.

NetCheck, like DigiCash, makes use of cryptography to provide the signatures and endorsements that are used in processing paper-based cheques. Except for the fact that NetChecks are electronic, they operate exactly the same as paper-based cheques, can be used with existing chequing accounts, and contain all the same information, although they do provide for the inclusion of additional information. Like DigiCash, however, NetCheck did not gain enough acceptance to enable them to be used widely in daily commercial activity. Electronic cheques are being developed by others, and the idea may still lead to viable products.

One significant electronic project is sponsored by the Financial Services Technology Consortium (FSTC), which has done some important work on electronic cheques in their project that led to the development of eCheck.

eCheck
www.echeck.org

The eCheck website (www.echeck.org) says that these digital cheques:

- contain the same information as paper cheques;
- are based on the same rich legal framework as paper cheques;
- can be linked with unlimited information and exchanged directly between parties;

- can be used in any and all remote transactions where paper cheques are used today;
- enhance the functions and features provided by bank chequing accounts; and
- expand on the usefulness of paper cheques by providing value-added information.

In fact, eChecks work in exactly the same way as paper cheques do, except for the electronic base. An electronic cheque writer creates (writes) an eCheck and electronically sends (gives) the eCheck to the payee. The payee deposits the eCheck by electronically conveying it to the bank, and then receives credit, and the payee's bank clears the eCheck to the paying bank. The paying bank validates the eCheck by checking the digital signature and then charges the cheque writer's bank account for the eCheck. eChecks are based on the Financial Services Markup Language (FSML), a variation of HTML. They include digital signatures, digital certificates, and other encryption-based features.

The Financial Services Technology Consortium (see the New Business Models box) is a U.S. not-for-profit organization comprised of banks, industry partners, financial services providers, technology companies, academic institutions, and government agencies. It carries out research and development of technology-based solutions to meet financial services industry needs, particularly emphasizing payment systems, electronic commerce, and information delivery. At present, FSTC has a project on electronic cheques as well as one called **Paperless Exchange and Settlement (PACES)**. It also has a project on a **Bank Internet Payment System (BIPS)**. The FSTC issues white papers and reports on their projects, which are very influential. Their white papers are available on the Internet.

An electronic cheque under the FSTC approach would be created by a smart card "chequebook" that would include a digital signature for the cheque along with all the information that would be included on a normal cheque. The cheque would then be delivered by means of an electronic transmission and clear through an electronic clearinghouse.

The fact that the cheque originates from a smart card provides a degree of security because the smart card is not connected to the computer system and, in addition, has its own password system. Of course, the digital signature adds considerable security because it is based on public key encryption, enabling any authorized party to the transaction to authenticate the cheque.

Somewhat related to the electronic cheque project is another project underway by the FSTC on cheque imaging. This is a process involving the creation of a digitized image of a cheque by the payee's bank at the time of deposit. The bank then sends the digital image, not the original cheque, through the payment clearing system. The purpose of the project is to speed up the payment process and reduce the opportunity for fraud. From a business perspective, cheque imaging has appeal because it substantially reduces the costs of processing cheques.

One of the big problems with this system is that images are well known for taking a lot of electronic file size. When they are transmitted, therefore, they require a very wide bandwidth, to the point that it would strain existing bandwidth normally available in most parts of the world. Another issue is that the legal system has not recognized imaged cheques, adding some uncertainty to their use for consummating business transactions.

Finally, the FSTC has a project underway called the "electronic commerce" project, which is focused on creating an infrastructure to process web based transactions through the existing bank payment systems. The first phase of the project involves creating communications links from the Internet to automated clearinghouses and money transfer systems. One of the challenges of this project is to find

PAPERLESS EXCHANGE AND SETTLEMENT (PACES): process for settling cheques within the banking system by using electronic images of the cheques captured at the first bank where they are presented

BANK INTERNET PAYMENT SYSTEM (BIPS): facility offered by banks under which their customers can make payments on the Internet by logging onto a special interface set up by the bank

NEW BUSINESS MODELS

Standards at the FSTC

The Financial Services Technology Consortium (FSTC) has 17 bank representatives and about 75 other financial technology players as members. The group is charged with creating the standards that will direct electronic payments in the future. Several projects have advanced to the point where new standards have been proposed, but some of the key electronic commerce initiatives have been either severely downsized or abandoned.

Standards are one of the most important issues facing global e-business. Standards are what make it possible for different groups, and people in different parts of the world, to do business. Standards make it possible for the participants in business transactions to understand what the others are doing—to communicate with them. In order for standards to work, they must gain acceptance by the people doing business—by the market. An organization such as the FSTC can promulgate the standards, but without this acceptance, they will not serve a useful role. However, there is a pressing need for an organization like the FSTC to develop those standards and send them out into the market.

One of the areas concerning the FSTC is the role of banks in the payment system for transactions on the Internet. They want to make sure that the banks play a dominant role because of their established expertise with payment systems and their financial credibility. Because of the growth of business on the Web and the variety of methods available, almost half of all online credit-card payments are processed by non-banking organizations. Several of the founding members of the FSTC are major banks, such as the Bank of America, Citibank, and Chase Manhattan Bank. Through the standards they create, the FSTC hopes to make the position of the banks more competitive.

The FSTC initiates a project by signing up interested members, who then ante up enough money to fund it. Entry into their cheque-imaging project, for example, was US$250 000, which could either be paid in cash or in kind by means of a gift of equipment or the time of a knowledgeable person.

The FSTC feels that use of the electronic cheque is the best way to eliminate its paper equivalent. They have done some testing of the system they propose, and they planned a pilot program among a group of banks and consumers in 2001.

Questions

1. Discuss how the initiatives of the FSTC could benefit e-business.
2. What are the chances that paper cheques will be eliminated eventually? If they are eliminated, what method of payment is most likely to replace them?

ways to attach the payment systems to the Internet without compromising their security.

Mondex

A well-known payment method that has received support from financial institutions is the Mondex electronic cash system. Mondex utilizes a smart card, which is a plastic card that looks like a credit card but contains a microchip that is used like a purse to store information about cash transactions and cash on hand. The card also contains some security features, designed to protect transactions between it and another Mondex card. It also contains security that restricts access to the information on the card. Mondex is easily transportable over digital connections, telephone lines, and the Internet, since it is electronic.

The idea is that the card would be "loaded" by the owner at a bank or at a Mondex-compatible ATM machine and then used at retail and other locations to buy goods, rather like a debit card, except that it is paying out the money stored in its own memory rather than having to log into the buyer's bank account. In this way, Mondex can act as an electronic substitute for cash.

Mondex can be applied in two broad areas, unlike eCash. While eCash can be transported over communications media, it was never designed to be carried by a person like real cash. Mondex, however, can be used in both arenas—the card can be carried around by a person and the signals can be sent over the Internet. This additional flexibility brings it closer to the functionality of real cash. Its acceptability depends on its acceptance by the financial institutions, which in Canada has largely been accomplished, at least in principle. Although they have been slow to implement Mondex, most of the banks still say that it will be launched. There have been field tests in several cities in Canada, including Guelph, Sherbrooke, and Toronto. In addition, Mondex's acceptability for use by people in the streets and in stores depends on the extent to which the stores themselves have adopted the card readers that are necessary to make the system work.

Mondex is already being used in many parts of the world, particularly in France and some other European countries. One of its major difficulties now, however, is that other systems are evolving that might make the Mondex system obsolete before it gains usage. These are discussed below.

Credit Cards

When commerce over the Web began, the payment mechanism often took place offline. Typically, a website would provide a page that people could download, print, and fax to the company. In addition, many people would review websites for research and comparison purposes and then go to the store to buy the goods. While this is still common, it was much more common when web-based commerce began. Slowly, the idea of providing the capability of people to input their credit card information into the website itself and consummate the transaction online became more common. The issue that companies had to deal with, however, was that the security provided on the website needed to be significantly increased.

The need for increased security was related to the needs of both the company and the customer. From the customer's point of view, the security is needed to ensure that their credit card information is not made available to other people who might make illegal use of it. In addition, for reasons of personal privacy, customers normally do not want any information about themselves to be passed along to others without their knowledge and permission. From the company's point of view, there is a need to provide good security in order to safeguard their customers' interests—and to avoid the possibility of litigation being brought against the company if web customers' reasonable expectations of security are not met.

As a consequence, the websites that accept credit cards have normally adopted high-security techniques, such as high encryption and the use of S-HTTP and SSL, as described in Chapter 5. Normally, when a user enters into the secure parts of websites, a warning will appear on the browser screen that indicates that he or she is entering a secure area. In addition, if Netscape Navigator is being used, a small lock on the lower left-hand corner of the screen will move into a locked position. When the user moves out of the secure area, a warning to this effect will also appear. There is an option in the browsers to turn off these warnings, at the discretion of the user.

In addition to these features, sites will use the **Secure Electronic Transaction (SET) protocol**, which was developed by MasterCard and Visa and a consortium

SECURE ELECTRONIC TRANSACTION (SET) PROTOCOL: a method of securing credit card transactions that makes use of encryption and authentication technology.

of other companies, based on public key encryption and authentication technology developed by RSA Data Security. By using public/private key technology, encryption, and digital certificates, SET enables the cardholders to check that online parties are valid merchants qualified to accept their particular credit card and also allows merchants to validate that the prospective customer has a valid card. SET also provides for the confidentiality of order and payment information transmitted and ensures the integrity of the transmitted data through the use of encryption techniques. Since its development, SET has become a standard for credit card payments on the Web. (see E-Strategy box.)

Where credit cards are used for payment, numerous systems offer customers the opportunity to register by entering information about themselves, including their credit card information, in a personal profile that is kept in a secure area by the vendor. Then when the customer enters the site to buy products, that customer needs only to log into the personal profile and does not need to enter all the additional information many times. Of course, the vendor has an interest in

E-STRATEGY

SET at VSB

On July 1, 2000, a trial period began in the Netherlands for a new service offered by VSB International/Visa Card Services B.V., the company that administers Visa cards in that country. The service essentially involves the ability to pay for goods bought over the Internet using the Secure Electronic Transaction (SET) protocol. It is the first time a service has been launched in the Netherlands using SET, the security protocol developed by Visa and MasterCard.

SET has been criticized for being too slow and complicated to be viable in commercial environments, but there is a feeling that it may have a better chance of acceptance in Europe than in other places because e-commerce is not as well advanced there as else-

where, so people have not become used to faster methods, such as the SSL system used in the United States and Canada. A recent study projected that European online purchases of books, music, air travel, and software will reach US$3.3 billion in 2002, compared with US$37.5 billion in the U.S. This vast difference certainly does not reflect the relative size of the populations or wealth.

It is largely because of security concerns that e-commerce has been slow to develop in Europe. The credit-card companies hope that trials such as this one will encourage people to buy over the Web. The new system has been adopted by three major merchants: Shop.nl, a diversified consumer goods company; Dunnet, a vendor of hardware

and software; and the Database Co., which sells golf equipment.

The software being used in the trial includes an electronic wallet, which is a browser plug-in that can be downloaded to the customers' PC to enable users to send encrypted credit-card information. Also included in the system is a certification authority for the generation and control of digital certificates and cryptographic keys. Finally, there are links to financial institutions to process the payments.

SSL and SET essentially operate as rivals in the area of e-commerce security. SSL just encrypts credit-card and personal-identification numbers, whereas SET also uses digital certificates to verify the identities of the customer and the merchant.

Questions

1. Discuss the advantages to customers of using the SET protocol in the European trials.
2. What are the advantages and disadvantages to the merchants of the SET and the SSL protocols?

SOURCE: Computerworld.com, August 3rd, 1998

doing this to make it easier for the customer to buy, and the customer has an interest in doing this to save the time required to input information every time. An additional advantage of this system is that the credit card information is only entered and transmitted once, reducing the risk of detection by unauthorized parties during transmission.

When a vendor accepts a credit card, over the Internet or otherwise, there is always the risk of accepting an invalid card. The risk is probably greater where the Web is used, since the person cannot be seen by the vendor. Services are available to the vendor to fill the need for verification of the card. ICVERIFY is a common service for credit authorization, which includes not only credit card authorization, but also cheque guarantee and **ATM/debit card** authorization.

The ICVERIFY system includes software that enables vendors to deposit most major credit card vouchers into their existing bank accounts, and also captures and stores the transaction data. In addition, the software enables the vendor to export the data into spreadsheets and other programs. Other services similar to ICVERIFY do exist and are used by many organizations around the world.

ATM/DEBIT CARD: bank card used for bank transactions at ATM machines and for purchases from retail outlets where payments are made directly from the user's bank account.

Micropayments

When goods and services are bought over the Internet, often the charges are very small. Sometimes, however, the price that could reasonably be attributed to a certain item is so small that it would not be feasible to incur the cost of processing that payment. In such cases, the vendor loses the opportunity to charge for a product, and must decide whether to offer it at all. On the side of the purchasers, the opportunity is lost to be able to obtain certain items over the Internet, simply because of this shortcoming.

Several companies have been addressing this issue by developing systems that render the processing of micropayments (very small payments) cost-effective (see E-Business in Global Perspective box). One of the early developers was Digital Corporation, which initiated the product MilliCent. It was developed for buying and selling products that can be downloaded and sold for a price ranging from one-tenth of a cent to about $10.00. MilliCent is installed by a vendor on its website and can then be run for a number of products, generating numerous revenue streams. It can be used for selling and buying anything, including articles, newsletters, audio, MP3 music, electronic postage, and many other items.

MilliCent Microcommerce Network
www.millicent.com

To use MilliCent, users need to open an account with the MilliCent network on its website. Users can finance their account with an online credit card, a debit card, by direct billing, or through pre-paid cards purchased in convenience stores. They need to maintain a balance in the account, and the funds are kept in the account for them until a purchase is made. When a purchase is made, MilliCent processes the actual payment, including any currency conversion that might be required.

When vendors decide to implement the MilliCent system, they also need to log into the MilliCent website and register. They must select a licensed payment-hosting provider from the site, which could be an ISP, a commerce-hosting provider (CSP), or MilliCent itself. During the registration process, the vendor opens an account with MilliCent or one of its licensed brokers.

After opening an account, the vendors must assign prices to individual products or groups of products to be sold. Then they must place this pricing on their own website for the benefit of the customers. The set-up process only takes a few hours. The interaction with MilliCent can take place through communications

E-BUSINESS IN GLOBAL PERSPECTIVE

Small Payments at British Telecommunications

People in Britain who buy over the Internet should have an easier time of it when British Telecommunications (BT) launches its new payment service called Array. This is a micropayment system that allows users to purchase inexpensive products and services online without having to enter a credit-card number every time. The service involves a number of merchants who agreed to be part of it. EMAP's *Internet Magazine*, for example, is one subscriber. Array works by requiring the users to register on the BT Array site and enter their credit-card information. This information is transmitted over a SSL connection to BT's Array server and then resides on that server, which is not connected to the Internet, making it very secure from Internet hackers.

After registering, users can buy from any Array-registered vendor simply by entering their password and user name. The system will activate the registration file and charge the purchases to the credit card in that file. Users can view their credit card balance and the Array transactions processed through it.

When a user actually makes a purchase, the transaction is recorded on the vendor's server, which activates a script on that server that brings up the price. The price is then sent to BT's Array payment server from the vendor's server. BT verifies the user name and password, matches up the credit-card information, and authorizes the purchase to the merchant. Then BT processes the sale, charging the credit card with the cost. BT will make money on the scheme by taking a percentage of the transaction value as payment.

The purpose of Array is to facilitate sales of small-value transactions, and BT plans to target online software vendors, publishers, and video game providers. BT says that in the future, they will extend Array to accept payments from debit cards and other credit cards and, eventually, Mondex cards.

Questions

1. What are the advantages of Array to customers who want to buy on the Web? What are the disadvantages?
2. Would Array be an effective means of purchasing on the Web? How would the addition of Mondex help?

SOURCE: Computerworld.com, February 17, 1998

---

links or through an integration process. The two approaches have an impact on the speed of response available to customers. The integration approach gives the vendors more control over the service provided to customers, better integration into their day-to-day operations, and elimination of any fees that would otherwise be charged by MilliCent for hosting services.

IBM Micro Payments is an emerging technology that gives vendors the ability to charge just a few cents for anything from customized news summaries and analyses to specialized searches, translations, reviews, and games. Such transactions can be processed and billed for one cent or even less—and generate a profit. The success of such a system depends on a volume that makes it worthwhile to the business, as well as a critical mass of companies adopting the system. The system needs to be simple and easy to use.

Unlike the digital cash and cheque systems discussed earlier, Micro Payments does not require a vendor to establish a network of approved banks and merchants. Instead, the system simply depends on a network of billing servers that can be established by several types of organizations. A billing server can easily be added to the network—it just requires connecting that server with one of the

ibm.com
www.ibm.com

billing servers already in the network. In this way, the network can grow rapidly, giving it a measure of **scalability** and **interoperability** that is necessary to gain the needed critical mass of buyers and sellers. IBM Micro Payments attempts to address risk issues by enabling the vendors to manage their own risk. They deal with their own billing server and can control the degree of security in place. They can choose their customers and establish the credit limits for different buyers. Generally, they can administer the entire process themselves, and assume whatever degree of risk is acceptable to them.

SCALABILITY: the ability of a system to adapt or be adapted to changing sizing requirements. A system that can easily be expanded to accommodate a growing business is referred to as scalable.

INTEROPERABILITY: the ability of two or more systems to conduct operations processes with each other.

Emerging Billing and Payment Systems

So far, we have discussed payment systems. With the growth of web commerce, there has been a great deal of interest among businesspeople in developing efficient and effective methods of billing and payment systems over the Web—in other words, systems that incorporate online billing as well as payment. The cost-effectiveness of web-based transactions has been a major factor in sustaining this interest, as well as the opportunities to develop an additional channel of business. As a result, the billing and payments systems in place have evolved considerably and continue to evolve. The principal billing and payment systems in current use include those established by (1) epost, (2) the banks, and (3) the vendors.

Canada Post

The billing and payment system referred to as epost was developed by Canada Post Corporation and the Bank of Montreal (see Figure 6.1). The epost system is an electronic mailbox that people can use for several mail functions, including the ability to receive and pay bills through the epost website. An individual must register with the site and select the bills they wish to receive online from those available through epost. Then the bills will be received electronically and can be paid online by using a credit card or electronic funds transfer that will enable a connection to a bank's payment system.

Canada Post's epost
www.epost.ca

    Epost emulates traditional mail to the extent possible in an electronic environment. It makes use of high security and provides an electronic post office box free of charge. All pieces of mail are stamped with an electronic postmark to guarantee they have not been opened or tampered with. The security environment includes firewalls and 128-bit SSL encryption technology.

The Banks

On their websites, the banks have provided systems for billing and payment that are among the most popular of this type of service. For several years, the banks have offered their customers the capability to log into their online banking pages at their websites. Online banking has offered customers the ability to use their debit card number, together with a password, to log in and view their bank account balances and transactions. They also have the capability to transfer funds from one account to another and pay bills. Ultimately, It will likely be possible for people to deposit and withdraw funds from their home computer, but this will depend on the introduction and integration of smart-card technology, such as that of Mondex, by using card readers that plug into the user's computer.

Figure 6.1   Canada Post's epost Site

The login screen for epost.

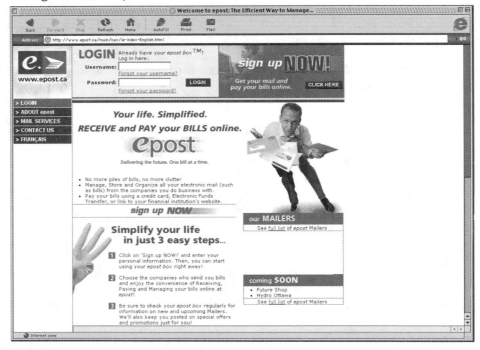

SOURCE: "Home Page." *epost*. <http://www.epost.ca>. January 2002. Reproduced with permission.

In recent months, the banks have expanded their online banking to include electronic billing. While bill payment has been possible for several years, it has been used in relation to bills mailed through the old "snail-mail" system. Customers would receive their bills—say from American Express—and then go to the online banking function on their bank's website and pay it online. To make this payment, they would need to select American Express from the list of participating organizations as one of the organizations they would be paying to, and then make the payment. Once the selection is made, it would remain in their profile and would not have to be selected from the main list again.

With the addition of electronic billing to their online banking functions, the participating organizations can elect to have the bills sent electronically rather than by regular mail. This means that bills can be transmitted faster and more cheaply, and paid online just as the mailed bills would have been paid. This system is gaining support from many organizations and has a great deal of potential for the future.

The Vendors

In some cases, the vendors themselves offer online billing and payment systems on their sites. Most of these systems are similar to those of epost and the banks, offering the ability to transmit and receive bills electronically, view them on the company website, and then pay them online using a variety of payment methods. As with the other systems, the customer can be notified by e-mail that a payment has been received.

Figure 6.2   PalmPilot

This screen capture from Palm shows pictures of various Palm Handheld Computers.

An emerging system is that of personal digital assistants (PDAs), such as the PalmPilot (Figure 6.2) and BlackBerry (Figure 6.3) systems. These small handheld devices are wireless and contain infrared capability that can communicate with

Figure 6.3   BlackBerry

Developed by Research In Motion, the BlackBerry has become an extremely popular PDA.

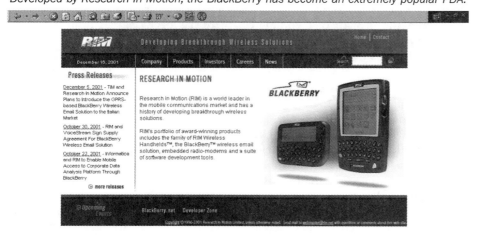

other electronic devices. If electronic cash registers are enabled to use infrared communications, then payments might be made by using such PDAs, either directly from the owner's bank account or from an electronic wallet embedded in the device. PDAs have become extremely popular in recent years, particularly as personal electronic organizers, and more recently for surfing the Internet and sending e-mail. Because of their popularity and their infrared capability, they are more likely to be adopted for payment purposes than Mondex cards.

KEY TERMS

value added networks

non-repudiation

Paperless Exchange and Settlement (PACES)

Bank Internet Payment System (BIPS)

Secure Electronic Transaction (SET) protocol

ATM/debit card

scalability

interoperability

Chapter Summary

Payment systems traditionally have included cash, cheques, and credit cards. Attempts have been made to emulate all of these in digital form for use on the Internet. Early attempts to develop digital cash and cheques have failed to gain acceptance by financial institutions and users.

Credit cards continue to be a prime method of payment, but concerns about their security and safety remain. However, the Financial Services Technology Consortium has been developing a system for electronic cheques and other payment systems that might gain acceptance. Public/private key encryption techniques are a prime way to provide security. The Secure Electronic Transaction (SET) protocol uses public/private key technology, encryption, and digital certificates to enable the cardholders to check that online parties are valid merchants qualified to accept their particular credit card, and also allows merchants to validate that the prospective customer has a valid card. Where credit cards are used for payment, numerous systems offer the customer an opportunity to register by entering information about themselves, including their credit-card information in a personal profile that is kept in a secure area by the vendor. Services are available to the vendor to fill the need for verification of the card. ICVERIFY is a common service for credit authorization, which includes not only credit-card authorization, but also cheque guarantee and ATM/debit card authorization.

Mondex is a well-known payment method that has received some support from financial institutions. Mondex utilizes a smart card, which is a plastic card that looks like a credit card but contains a microchip that is used like a purse to store information about cash transactions and cash on hand. It also contains security data that restricts access to the information on the card.

With the growth of e-commerce, there has been a great deal of interest among businesspeople in developing efficient and effective methods of billing and payment systems over the Web. As a result, the billing and payments systems in place have evolved considerably and continue to evolve. The principal billing and payment systems in current use include those established by Canada Post, the banks, and the vendors themselves.

Canada Post's epost system is an electronic mailbox that people can use for several mail functions, including receiving and paying bills. Banks have also provided systems for billing and payment that are among the most popular of this type of service. For several years, banks have allowed customers to log into their online banking pages in their websites. In some cases, vendors themselves have also offered online billing and payment systems on their sites. Most of these systems are similar to those of epost and the banks, offering the ability to transmit and receive bills electronically, view them on the company website and then pay them online using a variety of payment methods.

Finally, there has been a growth in the number of "micropayment" systems available. These systems enable very small payments to be processed in an economic manner. This in turn enables businesses to charge for items on the Web that would not have been feasible before these systems were available. It also enables businesses to streamline their billing and payment procedures for small items.

Tools for Online Learning

To help you master the material in this chapter and stay up to date with new developments in e-business, visit www.pearsoned.ca/trites . Resources include:

> Review Questions and Exercises

> Problems for Discussion

> Recommended Readings

> Updates to Boxes, Case Studies and textual material

> Links to demonstration tools related to course topics including sample Web sites

> Streaming CBC Videos with Cases

Supply Chain Management

learning objectives

When you complete this chapter you should be able to:

1. Describe the process and components of supply chain management (SCM).

2. Identify and describe the forces affecting SCM.

3. Explain how e-businesses can use technology in SCM.

4. Contrast the traditional supply chain with the Internet-enabled supply chain.

5. Outline how business-process reengineering can be carried out and why it is necessary as part of implementing SCM.

6. Describe partnership strategies and implementation concerns for SCM.

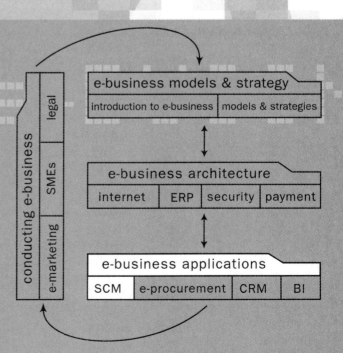

e-business models & strategy	
introduction to e-business	models & strategies

e-business architecture			
internet	ERP	security	payment

e-business applications			
SCM	e-procurement	CRM	BI

conducting e-business

legal

SMEs

e-marketing

SUPPLY CHAIN MANAGEMENT (SCM):
a business technique involving strategic decisions enabled through the application of technologies.

Introduction

Supply chain management (SCM) has become an increasingly important component of corporate strategy in the past several years. Driven by the need for companies to reduce costs and prices while improving customer service and product quality, SCM is also recognized as an essential aspect of e-business implementation. Dell Computer Corporation is an excellent example of a company that has been able to maximize the efficiency of its supply chain to allow for reduction of costs, reduced inventories, increased speed of delivery, and customized (made-to-order) products for its customers over the Web or by direct order. (See the New Business Models box for a discussion of Dell's make-to-order approach.) SCM is a business technique involving strategic decisions enabled through the application of technologies. Throughout this chapter, both the strategic and technological aspects of SCM will be discussed.

NEW BUSINESS MODELS

Innovations in Supply Chain Management at Dell Computer Corporation

Dell Computer is widely recognized as a leader in the sale of customized computers through the Web. Users can log in (www.dell.com), build the computer they want, and order it online. Dell's job is to source the components, assemble, and ship the computer in the very short timeline that online customers have come to expect. A key to Dell's ability to achieve this performance is its use of SCM. Dell is one of the world's leading companies in supply chain management. Its make-to-order approach to e-business was recognized early as an industry-changing concept that involved numerous changes to the supply chain. The initial goal at Dell was to reduce inventories, increase efficiency, reduce obsolescence, and facilitate the delivery of custom products to customers. To achieve this goal, Dell began to "substitute information for inventory." By 1998 Dell had reduced its inventory levels to approximately seven days but

was not satisfied. Compared to many traditional industries and other competitors, seven days was a risky inventory level that could result in stockouts and poor customer service.

Supply-Side Streamlining

Dell decided that it was necessary to increase the level of information sharing with key suppliers to better facilitate planning. Customized web pages for top suppliers were created that allowed access to Dell's forecasts, sales data, customer information, defect rates, and other product-related information. In addition, Dell began to require its suppliers to share the same types of detailed information, to allow for improved planning at their point in the supply chain. Through effective communication, high-technology solutions, and sound planning, Dell has reduced inventories for many items to a level measured in only hours rather than days—

creating a true just-in-time inventory system.

After establishing strong links with suppliers, Dell also extended its communications through a supplier portal called Valuechain.Dell.com, allowing for more complete exchange of information between suppliers and the company. In late 2000, Dell extended the portal with a web-based supply chain initiative (coined DSI2) aimed at improving forecasting further up the supply chain. The goal was to share information with second- and third-tier suppliers and increase the effectiveness of the complete supply chain (see Figure 7.1).

Customer Focus

Dell has also worked to implement SCM on the customer portion of its supply chain. To improve sales and customer service, Dell created "Premier Pages" for many of its business customers (80 percent of its business), which aimed to

(continued)

Figure 7.1   Dell's Supply Chain Configuration

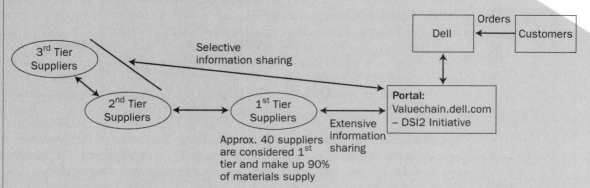

reduce the complexity of ordering. The Premier Pages were established in conjunction with customers such as Ford Motor Co. and held information on pre-approved product configurations and established pricing—effectively taking several steps out of the traditional purchase order process. Ford estimates that this initiative alone saved U.S.$2 million in procurement costs and is very satisfied with its relationship with Dell.

Service Enhancement

After achieving great success in the core of its supply chain, Dell decided to apply similar management concepts to its customer service and support divisions. Again focusing on the customer, Dell set goals to provide high-quality service, on time and at reasonable prices, as a means of bolstering commitment to the brand. To improve its service area, Dell decided to partner with SonicAir for parts inventory management and distribution to ensure its important same-day and next-day services. Through effective partnership and supply chain strategies, Dell has achieved a 95 percent service level for parts availability and on-time delivery. Considering that Dell handles approximately 60 000 calls per day, this is an impressive accomplishment.

Calls are screened first at the high-tech call centre where the staff connect through the Internet to the customer's machine to identify any problems. Each product is embedded with diagnostic equipment so that Dell is able to analyze many functions remotely as well as access product information and configuration to ensure parts availability. Unless the call is handled remotely, the service request is logged and Dell's service processes take effect.

Dell uses EDI and Web technologies to relay service requests immediately to both SonicAir and a technician to facilitate planning on a tight schedule. At that point SonicAir's logistics system ensures that required parts are moved to the appropriate location and confirms the schedule with Dell. Technicians are scheduled to work at either a repair depot or the customer's location, and arrival of the parts and technician is coordinated. Reducing downtime and providing high-quality after-sales service again scores high marks with Dell's customers.

Dell exhibits leading-edge management strategies for the supply chain and e-business in general—combining strategic planning, technological innovation, and strong implementation.

Dell Computer Corporation
www.dell.com

Questions

1. Dell has enjoyed success in its strategy for several years. Why are others having difficulty in copying it?
2. What other industries do you think would benefit from Dell's supply chain model?
3. Should Dell get into bricks-and-mortar retail operations to expand its potential market to those who don't buy online?

SOURCES: Saccomano, Ann, "Dell Computer Builds Service," *Traffic World*, 1999, 259:4, 26–27; "Dell Aims Web-based SCM Program at Forecasts," *Electronic Buyers' News*, August 2000; Stein, Tom, and Jeff Sweat, "Killer Supply Chains," *Informationweek*, November 1998.

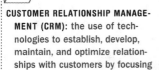

SUPPLY CHAIN: the set of processes that encompasses raw materials or resource purchases through to final delivery of a product/service to the end consumer.

The **supply chain** is the set of processes that encompasses raw materials or resource purchases through to final delivery of a product/service to the end consumer. Therefore, the supply chain includes sourcing, transportation, manufacturing, distributing, wholesaling, retailing, and final delivery of goods. The chain is not necessarily a linear or simple process: some authors have suggested that "supply web" is a more appropriate term to describe the complex interrelationships involved in the supply chain.

Supply chain management is the process of coordination and optimization of all product/service, information, and financial flows among all players of the supply chain, from raw material provider to the end consumer. SCM includes functions such as ordering from suppliers, shipping, warehousing, manufacturing, logistics, sales, and delivery to the end consumer. Therefore, we can say that the supply chain includes upstream, internal, and downstream components, all of which need to be effectively managed.

A number of terms are used in practice that are interchangeable with or closely related to supply chain management, such as *value chain management, integrated logistics, integrated purchasing strategies*, and *supply chain synchronization*. Keep in mind that many business terms are adapted to suit specific industry and company preferences. *Logistics* is the term you may commonly hear used and is now considered to be nearly interchangeable with SCM.

CUSTOMER RELATIONSHIP MANAGEMENT (CRM): the use of technologies to establish, develop, maintain, and optimize relationships with customers by focusing on understanding needs and desires.

In essence, the supply chain integrates a number of very important topics in e-business. For instance, business-to-business (B2B) e-commerce is an essential component of managing the buy-side (and often the sell-side) of the supply chain. Business-to-consumer (B2C) e-commerce is an essential component of managing the sell-side of the supply chain for *organizations* that deal directly with the end consumer. B2B has been affected substantially by SCM, as well as e-procurement and trading exchanges, which are discussed in more detail in Chapter 8. Both B2B and B2C have been shifting to the customer focus of business through **customer relationship management (CRM)**, which is the topic of Chapter 9. In this chapter, SCM is discussed from an inter-organizational perspective to allow the reader to fully understand its importance to success in e-business.

The Traditional Supply Chain

PUSH SYSTEM: supply chain in which suppliers produce goods based upon their efficiencies and push them to customers rather than rely on demand to determine production.

In the traditional supply chain model (see Figure 7.2), suppliers produced goods in the most efficient manner for their business (typically large batches), and sent large orders to customers (either retailers or wholesalers). This system was referred to as the **push system,** where the supply chain is driven by vendors supplying product downstream until the end consumer chooses whether or not to purchase what has been made. The system was most effective in the early days of manufacturing, as a means of driving unit costs down and bringing prices within the reach of most people. The best example of this is the mass production techniques used by Henry Ford. The system worked best for highly standardized products in markets where there was very high demand. The movement of large orders was considered to be a cost-effective method of production that required inventory to be held at various stages of the supply chain. The manufacturer would hold raw materials as well as finished goods, while downstream members of the supply chain would each hold inventories of their own. As buyers became more discriminating, and markets more narrowly defined, the supply chain model of the past became full of inefficiencies that increased production costs, storage costs, cycle times, obsolescence, and consumer wait times.

Figure 7.2   The Traditional Supply Chain

The traditional supply chain was focused on efficiency of production gained through batch manufacturing that often resulted in excess inventories throughout the supply chain.

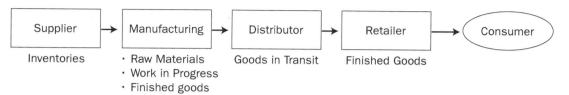

Supplier	Manufacturing	Distributor	Retailer	Consumer
Inventories	• Raw Materials • Work in Progress • Finished goods	Goods in Transit	Finished Goods	

In the past, supply chains have been burdened with excess inventories created by the push-type system. Creating large batches of product was considered efficient for each individual company.

Early attempts to improve the efficiency of the supply chain made use of **electronic data interchange (EDI)** for communication between supply chain firms. Despite the efforts to improve communications, many firms were unable to drastically improve performance due to difficulties in setting standards for the EDI format across many supply chain members. In addition, the data being transferred was often based on data that came from legacy systems (lacking timeliness and often accuracy).

Common attempts at supply chain management have focused on reducing inventories and achieving some levels of efficiency within the value chain. However, simply reducing inventory levels along the chain is not enough in today's business environment.

ELECTRONIC DATA INTERCHANGE (EDI): a form of conducting transactions, including payment transactions, in electronic form. It is based on the use of widely accepted standards for formatting data in EDI transmissions.

Forces Affecting Supply Chain Management

The rapid pace of change in the business world today has affected SCM in a number of ways. Some of the major forces of change include:

- globalization
- mass customization
- price sensitivity
- customer focus and time to market
- just-in-time inventory and inventory reduction
- enterprise resource planning
- outsourcing

Globalization

While companies continue to expand their global presence, challenges to the efficiency of the supply chain become more complex. For example, establishing a reliable transportation and delivery system in a foreign country is complicated by domestic policies, tariffs, and customs regulations. When customers are waiting for delivery, the supply chain needs to perform: slow delivery from a foreign supplier could result in a lost sale, future lost business, and negative publicity. (A further analysis of the impact of globalization on e-businesses is provided in Chapter 13.)

Mass Customization

The advent of e-business has shifted power from companies to consumers (in some respects at least), resulting in consumers asking for products or services that are tailored to their specific needs. The Internet and computer technology have played a major role in allowing businesses to meet the needs of consumers more easily by simplifying the process of customization, data capture, and information sharing with partners in the supply chain. For example, Dell allows customers to customize their computer system for any component from internal RAM to external colours, while providing a very rapid turnaround time. To support this service successfully, Dell must be able to quickly establish production plans, purchase required components, and arrange shipping of its products. This form of customization is very popular with customers and is likely to reach into other products as well in the near future.

Price Sensitivity

The Internet provides individuals with the ability to easily compare prices and gather product information. This shift has resulted in customers becoming increasingly sensitive to price, and when combined with the preference for customized products discussed earlier, this requires businesses to have a very strong grasp of their competition and their supply chain partners. Internet companies like Priceline.com have also changed the nature of pricing—consumers can now name their price and allow a company to accept or reject their offer. Auctioning sites have had a bigger impact on pricing, since auctioning has made its way into B2B through trading exchanges.

Customer Focus and Time to Market

The ability to create and deliver new products has become critically important in many industries. Not only is it necessary to be able to innovate and develop high-quality products, it is crucial to be able to do it quickly and continuously. Competitors Intel and AMD are examples of high-tech chip manufacturers that focus on time to market in order to maintain their coveted market share of the computer industry. A combination of research and development, partnerships, and supply chain management allows these companies to continually create high-quality products at "Internet speed."

Just-in-Time Inventory and Inventory Reduction

Inventory reduction has been attempted for many years; however, the increasing use of the Internet and Internet Protocol (TCP/IP) has reduced the difficulty for firms to share information with other supply chain members. Data sharing and communication have traditionally been major obstacles to reducing inventories, since it is necessary to have all members of the supply chain working in concert in order to reduce inventories while meeting customer demands and maintaining order fill rates.

Enterprise Resource Planning

Enterprise resource-planning (ERP) applications have become the norm in large organizations and, to a great extent, help an organization to facilitate SCM. With legacy systems, firms could spend days or even weeks trying to integrate data from sales, inventory, and purchasing systems in order to effectively plan for future production. This lack of data integration has been largely overcome with ERP systems, which use centralized databases, allowing companies to ensure that everyone is using the same data and to make decisions in real time. Through the use of centralized data, and the linking of the applications that sit on that data, ERP is an effective tool for integrating the supply chain and thus expediting SCM.

Outsourcing

Outsourcing is increasing and requires supply chain managers to make important supplier selection decisions. For example, Nortel Networks signed a seven-year outsourcing contract in the summer of 2000 for its IT function.[1] Although it may seem ironic that an IT company would outsource its internal IT operations, this strategic decision allows Nortel to concentrate on its own customers and products. The decision to outsource is often made in order to focus on core competencies, but the supplier effectively becomes a partner who can dramatically affect the ability of the business to meet its objectives. Coupled with customization and time-to-market forces, outsourcing requires that the supply relationships be strong and well managed. The outsourcing partner must be willing and able to react quickly to required product changes and demand fluctuations. Many of the concepts discussed earlier in this book such as the use of extranets can be helpful in establishing effective outsourcing strategies by allowing the supplier to access crucial information on a timely basis.

Nortel Networks
www.nortel.com

The Internet-Enabled Supply Chain

The Internet economy has resulted in drastic changes to the entire supply chain. The current business environment often results in what has become known as a **pull system** of production. In the Internet-enabled supply chain (see Figure 7.3), the customer drives the entire process by initiating an order (often for a specific/customized product) that results in information flows being passed upstream to suppliers from the firm, which may be a manufacturer, distributor, or wholesaler. In some organizations, no product is made until the customer order is known (e.g., Dell), while in others the customer order results in updates to supplier orders so that appropriate inventory levels can be maintained (e.g., Wal-Mart). The major change from the traditional supply chain is that the predominant information flow is upstream as opposed to downstream.

PULL SYSTEM: supply chain in which the production of suppliers is determined by the needs of customers who request or order goods necessitating production.

Fiigure 7.3   Internet-Enabled Supply Chain Information Flows

In the Internet-enabled supply chain the customer drives the process, and information flows primarily upstream.

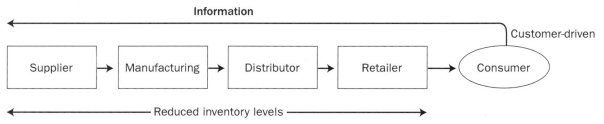

DISINTERMEDIATION: a change in the supply chain where the provider and consumer interact directly with each other, thereby eliminating the need for an intermediary.

The Internet supply chain has also resulted in substantial changes to more than just information flows. Early in the electronic age, some technology analysts felt that major changes to supply chains would result in disintermediation and that many businesses would fail if they did not counteract this phenomenon. **Disintermediation** is a change in the supply chain where the provider and consumer interact directly with each other, thereby eliminating the need for an intermediary. The two major categories of disintermediation are (1) where the supplier of a good or service circumvents another member of the supply chain, such as a distributor, and provides the good or service directly to the end consumer, and (2) where a new intermediary enters the market using a new business model (often lower cost) in order to drive out existing intermediaries.[2] The analysts were correct in some respects; however, in many industries the bricks-and-mortar companies have been able to leverage their brands and maintain a foothold over new entrants.

The travel industry is an example of one that has seen some level of disintermediation take place (see Figure 7.4). In the past, nearly all airline and other travel was booked through travel agents who had access to information and provided it to the customer. The airlines provided information to travel companies who, in turn, rolled out that information to their agents. The agents would then provide information to interested customers, which at times would be inaccurate or out of date by the time the end consumer was reached. Reliance on manual/computerized processes reduced timeliness and accuracy of information.

Figure 7.4   Travel Industry Information Flows

The travel industry supply chain has been drastically changed by e-commerce and the Internet.

Traditional Supply Chain

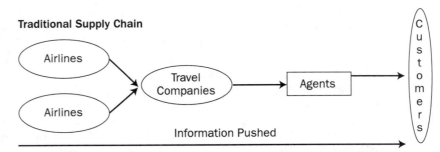

Internet-Enabled Supply Chain

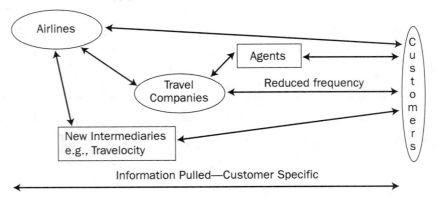

With the advent of Internet communication, the travel/airline-booking industry has been completely transformed. Customers now have access to a great deal of information from a variety of sources, including information directly from the airlines. Thus the travel/flight-booking industry has undergone disintermediation in both major formats. Customers can book flights now in a variety of ways: online directly with the airline, online with new services like Travelocity.com, or through a travel agent. Essentially, the flight-booking/airline industry has shifted from a push system to a pull system, whereby the customer can extract information from a variety of sources and make an informed decision.

While disintermediation has significantly changed the travel industry, these changes simply force the industry to compete in different ways. This leads to a process known as **reintermediation**. Reintermediation is the process by which companies constantly reinvent themselves in order to survive. Many travel agents feel that their services will remain in demand because they are better able to offer travel packages and provide customized solutions and recommendations to travellers than websites. While this may be true at present, this balance of power is rapidly changing. Customers can comparison shop quickly and easily in the comfort of their home at their own pace, forcing the industries involved to ensure they offer a quality, valuable service.

The travel industry is not the only industry to feel the impact of disintermediation. Others that have experienced the phenomenon in various ways include the book industry (Amazon.com, Chapters.Indigo.ca), the investment industry (eTrade.com), and postal services (e-mail). Also, recent attempts have been made to disintermediate the grocery industry (see the E-Strategy box). Not all attempts at disintermediation have been successful. Levi's attempted to offer online, custom jeans direct to consumers but was met by difficulties when retailers/distributors became angry and demand was not what had been estimated (since customers had difficulty trying the jeans online). As business continues to change, we can expect many other industries to be affected by changes in the Internet-enabled supply chain.

REINTERMEDIATION: process by which companies constantly reinvent themselves in order to survive by entering a market as a new intermediary.

Integration of Technology

The supply chain concept has been introduced as a management process so far in this chapter. SCM has been strongly affected by the growth of the Internet but is also enabled through a number of other technologies such as extranets, enterprise resource-planning applications, business intelligence software, and application service providers.

Use of Extranets

The sharing of information between supply chain members has been made significantly more manageable through the use of extranet technologies. In order for supply chain members to reduce costs and increase efficiency, information needs to be shared in a reliable, cost-effective manner. Extranet technologies have reduced the usage of EDI as an information-sharing technology due to the simplified standards of using TCP/IP. The cost of providing information on extranets, however, is much more manageable if an organization is fully integrated in its back office (likely through ERP), which allows provision of current inventory, demand, and other data.

E-STRATEGY

Online Grocery Shopping at Peapod.com

Peapod is a dot-com grocery business that has been operating in eight major U.S. cities since the early 1990s. As an early entry into the online retail world, Peapod has learned the importance of effective supply chain management, since customer satisfaction is achieved through the responsive delivery of goods. In addition to being quick, the process must reduce handling in order to prevent damage to produce and other items. The major problems in managing Peapod's supply chain include demand management, accurate ordering to prevent stock-outs, efficient storage/warehousing for speedy and damage-free picking, and efficient scheduling and routing for deliveries. The direct-to-consumer approach requires Peapod to adjust its delivery quantities to the customers' orders, meaning that bulk shipping as manufacturers do is not applicable. Pallets full of like products cannot be loaded and sent; the company must tailor its product delivery system to the customer order. Peapod must be able to package a loaf of bread, box of cereal, carton of milk, and canned goods in a manner that minimizes damage and space in the delivery vehicle, to ensure customer satisfaction and remain efficient.

Initially, Peapod delivered goods within 24 to 72 hours of an order; however, customers demanded more, and Peapod had to focus on supply chain management and logistics functions to reduce the order-to-delivery time. Its goal is less than one hour within local areas. The rapid delivery is further complicated by the ability of customers to select specific delivery time blocks. Again, the customer is the focus, so Peapod must be able to deliver between 6:00 p.m. and 6:30 p.m. if the customer desires. The delivery cycle requires the use of advanced planning and transportation models similar to those used by major airline reservation systems.

Peapod originally sent its shoppers to grocery stores to buy the items requested but, as growth continued, this fulfillment method became extremely inefficient. Today, Peapod uses its own distribution centres, which allow it to optimize warehousing for its own picking, as opposed to retail displays. This also allows for better control over inventory levels. Providing a convenience service such as grocery delivery requires stock to be available, and Peapod has found that stockouts were initially one of its major customer complaints—not receiving one item for a recipe, for instance, can be a significant inconvenience to customers.

Technology assists substantially in the overall SCM strategy at Peapod. Automated ordering provides data to handheld scanners for picking items. As items are picked, they are scanned, updating inventory records and triggering a reordering process if necessary. The automated order also triggers a routing schedule for delivery that optimizes the route by grouping times, weights, and sizes appropriately. Orders received in advance (up to one week) allow Peapod to place its just-in-time orders to suppliers for perishables and other goods that cannot be stored for lengthy periods.

The major strategic differences that Peapod has encountered in supply chain management are driven by the customer-oriented (pull-type) supply chain they are involved in. Rather than optimizing delivery quantities and routes based solely on costs, Peapod must focus on meeting customer service expectations in the first place, while keeping costs under control. Peapod's e-strategy continues to unfold as its e-tailing business grows and evolves and it considers expanding its product offerings to capitalize on its infrastructure and supply chain.

Peapod
www.peapod.com

Questions

1. Peapod's strategy is to be a leading logistics provider. Why don't they just contract that part of the operation out to UPS Logistics or another major logistics provider?
2. Will major grocery chains like Loblaws and Sobeys soon be entering the online market to compete against pure-play companies like Peapod?
3. Do you think pure-play companies will be more successful than those established in the industry?

SOURCES: Peapod.com; and "SCM at Peapod," *Supply Chain Management Review*, March/April 2000.

Extranets allow for companies to share information in a much more timely manner than was previously available through EDI. The use of EDI required complex standards to be developed, and the request for an order would be sent to a supplier and require a reply. Extranet/Internet technology allows for the demand forecast to be adjusted constantly, giving the supplier advance notice and allowing for production planning changes to take place sooner. This increase in timeliness of information should reduce the production-to-delivery timeframe and also reduce supply chain costs over the long run. Effective information sharing is allowing companies like Dell and Wal-Mart to become highly effective supply chain managers.

Thomson Consumer Electronics Inc. makes extensive use of an extranet to facilitate communication and information sharing in its supply chain. Analysis of Thomson's customers was carried out through a survey, which revealed that its supply chain effectiveness was considered weak in on-time delivery and stockouts. As a result, Thompson implemented an integration project by using an extranet and i2's supply chain management system (see Figure 7.5). Customers such as Best Buy, Circuit City, and Kmart agreed to provide detailed information on sales and forecasts to Thomson. Thomson uses i2 to analyze the information internally and updates its plans and forecasts that are shared with suppliers. In effect, the extranet facilitates communications and allows supply chain members to improve planning. Thomson's supply chain strategy has improved its supplier relationships, increased sales, and reduced rush shipments due to last-minute decision-making.

Thomson Consumer Electronics Inc.
www.thomson-electronics.com

ERP in SCM

Enterprise resource-planning systems have truly become the backbone of any e-business. In order to improve decision-making in the digital economy, it is absolutely essential to have access to up-to-date information. ERP systems allow for effective monitoring of the entire organization and provide essential information to the

Figure 7.5   SCM at Thomson Consumer Electronics

Thomson Consumer Electronics uses an extranet along with sophisticated applications to control its supply chain.

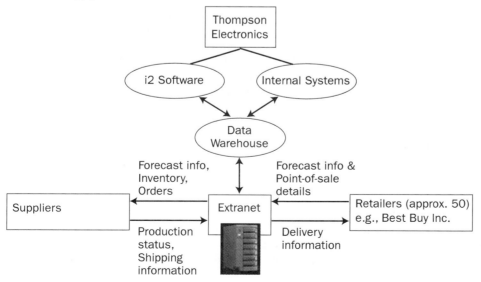

functions of SCM. Imagine trying to place orders to suppliers for a toy manufacturer without an ERP system. The major difficulty in legacy systems was coordinating and synchronizing data sets to ensure that inventory levels, purchasing requirements, and production plans were all based on accurate information in order to meet upcoming orders. In today's business world, a manager is constantly aware of customer demand information and can instantly revise purchasing, staffing, financial, and production information based on an integrated ERP system.

Business Intelligence Software

In an era of information overload, it is essential for companies to have strong data analysis tools in order to identify critical operating information. A number of software tools and techniques have emerged to turn raw data into business information, such as data mining techniques, decision support systems (DSS), and most recently **business intelligence** software. As discussed in the previous section, ERP systems allow organizations to capture data, and many of these systems include analysis tools such as SAP's Business Warehouse (BW) and Executive Information System (EIS) modules. The SAP EIS functions allow for high-level reporting of data and is intended to simplify the analysis of data for information appropriate to decision makers. Most organizations, however, have traditionally determined that custom reports are necessary for their specific organization, which is where the Business Warehouse is targeted. This data warehouse allows for customized queries and reporting to be carried out, based on the SAP data.

Business intelligence and specialized software makers such as SAS and Cognos have emerged to improve the usability, impact, and understanding of critical data. For example, Cognos products allow organizations to integrate any and all data sources (such as ERP, legacy system, and website data) into one business intelligence system. Cognos products can then be customized with preset, company-specific information such as quality level warnings, whereby returns under warranty related to a specific supplier would be automatically flagged. This information can be more carefully examined through a drill-down interface to determine source locations, manufacturing dates, and other critical information that can then be passed back to the supplier. The system also allows the company to establish a web browser-based interface for suppliers to log into and analyze the data in their own way, thus providing a high level of information sharing.

Business intelligence software is being used primarily to facilitate critical issues in supply chain management, such as information analysis and sharing. As the pace of change accelerates, the usefulness of business intelligence increases exponentially.

Application Service Providers

The growth of application service providers (ASPs) is affecting SCM in a number of ways. ASPs are allowing companies to access software through the Internet without hosting and maintaining the systems in-house. This method of providing technology is expected to grow rapidly for several years, since it allows businesses to select core components of ERP applications or other software at lower cost. To date, logistics and supply chain software have experienced difficulty in providing technology through the ASP model because customization is often required for each business. However, as standards develop and ERP providers increasingly

BUSINESS INTELLIGENCE: the environment that supports analysis of data from any source (internal or external) to provide valuable information for making operating, tactical, or strategic decisions.

Cognos
www.cognos.com

move toward ASP models, the provision of SCM technology through the Internet will become much more commonplace.

Strategic SCM

To operate effectively, an organization must employ its technology strategically. The adoption of leading-edge technology will yield little benefit unless it is used to facilitate corporate goals, and the same is true of SCM software/applications. The technology to be chosen for SCM must be carefully planned and coordinated so that benefits may be achieved through integration and information.

Boeing recognized that its supply chain was in crucial need of revision in 1997 when delays forced the closure of its production facilities. Since that time, Boeing has planned extensively to build its new technological infrastructure, which consists of Baan (its ERP backbone), i2 (forecasting software), factory floor software, and Internet communication tools.[3] Each of the applications was implemented with a common goal in mind—to turn Boeing's assembly line and supply chain into a highly efficient operation. Starting with a backbone ERP system, Boeing added applications that would allow it to more specifically target areas crucial to its success. Given that the lead-time to order a plane was approximately three years in the late 1990s, it is essential to be able to forecast several years in advance to achieve supply chain effectiveness. As such, Boeing adopted i2 forecasting software to allow for advanced planning and also changed many manual processes to EDI and Internet transactions. For example, customers can now order parts through the Boeing PART web page (see Figure 7.6). In addition to

Boeing
www.boeing.com

Baan
www.baan.com

i2
www.i2.com

Figure 7.6   Boeing PART Web Page

Illustration of the Boeing PART web page through which customers can efficiently and effectively order spare parts.

adopting technological solutions, Boeing carried out product changes to stream-line internal processes. The core components of the aircraft were redesigned in order to allow for a more "Henry Ford"-like production line, with customization taking place at the end of the process wherever possible.

Boeing provides a good example of a company that made strategic use of technology: it established a strategic vision for its supply chain, adopted techno-logical applications in support of that vision, and made process changes internally and externally in support of its strategy. Strategy must drive the business—not the technology!

Reengineering Processes

Business process reengineering was popularized with Hammer and Champy's *Reengineering the Corporation*, and reflects the requirements of corporations to initiate change to fundamental business processes as a result of the changing busi-ness world. They define a business process as "a collection of activities that takes one or more kinds of input and creates an output that is of value to the cus-tomer."[4] In terms of SCM, business processes include procurement processes, in-ternal operations, sales processes, and numerous other fundamental processes in the business. As discussed in the previous section, the evolution of e-business is requiring that companies change business processes as technological advances are made in order to achieve success. The adoption of ERP, forecasting tools, and e-procurement are all changes that will require an organization to re-evaluate and often revise its business processes.

BUSINESS PROCESS REENGINEERING: fundamental rethinking and radical redesign of existing business processes to add value or prepare for new technologies.

Business process change can occur at three major levels—streamlining, reengineering, or organizational change.[5] Streamlining involves relatively minor changes or "tweaking" of existing business processes in order to facilitate changes occurring in the business. **Business process reengineering** is defined as "funda-mental rethinking and radical redesign"[6] of existing processes and is therefore a large undertaking. Organizational change has been described as the creation of a process organization by modification of organizational structure. In a process or-ganization, new management-level positions are created that focus on maximiza-tion of process efficiency.[7] As discussed in Chapter 4, ERP systems such as SAP require that specific processes be adopted in order to facilitate the technology's "best practices" model. The adopting corporation's current processes often de-termine the extent of change required, because streamlining may be adequate in cases where processes are similar.

Many organizations have achieved tremendous results through reengineer-ing. IBM's senior vice-president of technology and manufacturing stated, "As we set out to reengineer our company, we knew that having world-class information technology simply wasn't enough. Since speed and efficiency were fundamental elements of our strategy, we needed entirely new approaches to our operations management."[8] Through technological innovation and reengineering of opera-tions, IBM saved hundreds of millions of dollars (see the Global Perspective box for more information).

ERP systems are not the only cause of business process change. When or-ganizations begin to more closely integrate with supply chain members, it is often necessary to align processes more closely with other organizations. For example, assume a key supplier of e-Co wishes to be able to quickly monitor demand in order to adjust its production plans. In order to facilitate this information sharing, e-Co may decide to use an extranet to share inventory levels, customer orders, and

E-BUSINESS IN GLOBAL PERSPECTIVE

Refining the Global Supply Chain and Service Call Management at IBM

International Business Machines (IBM) Corporation is one of the world's largest technology companies, operating in over 160 countries worldwide. The range of services and products provided by IBM includes manufacturing, software design/sales, personal computers, servers, and after-sales service. Revenues were over US$80 billion in 2000. Operating on such a large scale requires IBM to have an effective supply chain strategy in place, ensuring that research and development, purchasing, manufacturing, delivery, and sales channels are all properly integrated to deliver products on time, within budget, and of superior quality.

Global Supply Chain Reengineering

In the mid-1990s, IBM decided that inventory levels were too high and that customer service levels could be improved. Operations analysts began reviewing the supply chain and determined that the length of time from purchasing materials until the product was manufactured (called the **cash-to-cash cycle**) was excessive. The results of a long cash-to-cash cycle include increased inventory levels, customer service delays, excessive write-offs of obsolete inventory, and high dealer discounts.

In order to improve the global supply chain, IBM needed to develop a strategic approach to improvement. Management determined that in-house expertise within the IBM Research division would be able to assist in the development of a simulation tool that was named the Asset Management

Tool (AMT). The AMT is a sophisticated optimization tool that examines inventory levels, forecasts, supplier information, and products to develop optimal supply chain plans. In addition, AMT must be able to integrate foreign currency transactions, duties, tariffs, and tax concerns in order to make accurate decisions. Given that IBM deals with such large volumes of product, the AMT needs to carry out many analytical functions. For example, AMT analyzes products manufactured in all countries to identify common parts requirements and carries out detailed analysis of shipping and purchasing costs, combined with activity-based costing methods, to determine whether all parts should be sourced from common locations or sourced from the nearest company. This analysis can now be carried out across the 3000 hardware and 20 000 software products and analyzed in further detail by supplier. Essentially, AMT demonstrates the need for advanced systems in large organizations that can accommodate uncertainty.

The global reengineering initiative has netted IBM in excess of US$750 million and reduced the cash-to-cash cycle by four weeks to six weeks. The goal of reduced cost and improved customer service was met, and IBM continues to improve its world-class SCM practices.

Service Call Management

IBM also recognized that the increasing complexity of its Global Services division was an area where effective planning could improve results. Dealing with approximately 22 000 service calls per

day, more than 7000 service representatives need to be scheduled throughout the world. At first glance, one could assume that this task could be simple—just give each representative three or four service calls per day. However, factoring in the diverse products, parts availability, language, location, call/problem complexity, and service representative expertise, the task becomes overwhelming.

Once again the IBM Research group was called in to help develop a customized solution, after a manager recognized the similarity of the situation's complexity to chess. The IBM Research group had been able to develop algorithms for the chess match between then-world-champion Gary Kasparov and IBM's Deep Blue computer. The programming was designed to handle the multiple iterations of moving chess pieces and was also able to develop an advanced call centre management system for Global Services.

The solution is able to analyze huge volumes of data in order to reduce customer response time and minimize idle time, travel costs, and delays by focusing on the integration of data. Available service reps are first assigned to service calls as they come in (by qualifications), and then the system begins to optimize the assignments through global and local locations by analyzing costs and other factors. The schedule also needs to be recomputed every 10 minutes in order to ensure that new service calls are allocated in an optimal manner—often juggling the calls already within the system. IBM estimates that the time spent

(continued)

at service calls has been reduced by 10 to 35 percent through better assignment, and that idle time has decreased as much as five-fold in some locations. A combination of technological solution and strategic vision has resulted in success at IBM.

IBM
www.ibm.com

CASH-TO-CASH CYCLE: the length of time from purchasing materials until a product is manufactured.

Questions

1. In a large company like IBM, how can management be sure that the supply chain initiatives are improving operations?
2. Can other organizations effectively manage service calls like IBM without the use of high-technology systems?
3. What complications does the global operation of IBM add to the supply chain management process?

SOURCES: ibm.com; Dietrich, Brenda et al., "Big Benefits for Big Blue," *OR/MS Today*, June 2000.

sales forecasts with this supplier. However, e-Co has always been very cautious in releasing information related to sales and also guards its forecasts closely. In addition, e-Co's production manager meets with the purchasing department manager once every two weeks in order to establish appropriate purchase order amounts. In order for the extranet to provide useful information, e-Co will have to modify business processes such as budgeting and ordering. As such, the duties of the production and purchasing managers will also change. This simple example illustrates how information sharing and technology adoption can result in tremendous change within an organization—e-business must be willing to embrace change to achieve success.

Partnerships of the Supply Chain

Throughout this chapter we have discussed the need to form supply chain partnerships in order to achieve success. Forming partnerships, however, is only partially facilitated through the use of technological tools discussed earlier. Sharing of information is a difficult task to achieve in a business world where information has been traditionally safeguarded. In this next section, partnership formation is discussed in further detail from a management of relationships perspective.

Partnership formation and strategic alliances of the supply chain are as crucial to supply chain success as the technology and information systems. Appropriate sharing of critical information will not take place unless both exist. Establishing strong lines of communication is the first step in ensuring that supply partnerships will succeed. Since the technology is only an enabler of the information sharing, decisions need to be made about what information should be shared, when, and who is responsible for it. Clarifying these basic terms early will help in develop trust.

Supply chain success can often be attributed to the development of a relationship based on trust. **Trust** "involves one party having confidence in or relying on another party to fulfill its obligations. The existence of trust in a relationship reduces the perception of risk associated with opportunistic behavior and allows each party to believe that its needs will be fulfilled in the future by actions taken by the other party."[9] As it is in personal relationships, trust is formed over time and begins with honest and open communication among parties. Having appropriate managers involved in the partnership development is key to success.

TRUST: the confidence in another party (business or individual) to meet its end of a bargain that is established through a relationship over time.

The relationship of trust can be created more quickly if discussions centre on:

- realignment
- performance measurement
- dispute resolution
- security

Realignment

The creation of a supply chain partnership does not simply entail setting up an extranet and sharing information. In many cases, success will be best achieved by realigning work responsibilities, selectively outsourcing, and realigning decision-making. For example, many organizations have realigned the decision-making related to purchasing by moving toward vendor-managed inventory. **Vendor-managed inventory (VMI)** is the process by which suppliers take over the monitoring of inventory levels through the use of technology and are responsible for replenishment of stock. Wal-Mart has adopted the use of VMI for many of its products, thus reducing the reliance on internal decision-making and allowing suppliers such as Procter & Gamble to be responsible for their own products. Research has shown that VMI often leads to reduced inventory levels and substantially lower stockout rates,[10] as suppliers are keen to ensure that consumers are always able to purchase their products.

Selective outsourcing may be necessary or economically feasible in some supply chains for functions that are traditionally problematic. If both partners evaluate the outcomes as positive, transportation of rush orders may be outsourced to courier companies in order to reduce costs and improve delivery times. Outsourcing may also mean the movement of work from one organization to another in the supply chain to improve overall supply chain effectiveness. While customization of products in the computer industry was normally carried out by computer resellers, Dell's business model moved the customization function to the manufacturer rather than the reseller. Outsourcing decisions will vary by industry but should always be made on the basis of improving customer value, reducing complexity, and/or controlling costs.

VENDOR-MANAGED INVENTORY (VMI): the process by which suppliers take over the monitoring of inventory levels through the use of technology and are responsible for replenishment of stock.

Performance Measurement

Performance measurement is a complex task in any setting, and e-business changes the dynamics of performance measurement by changing the dynamics of information and rate of change. In order to allow supply chain partners to contribute positively to the partnership and later evaluate the relationship, partners should create joint metrics for performance measurement. Establishing the terms by which success will be measured at the onset allows partners to develop plans to meet those goals.

Performance measurement goals should be established for delivery timelines, decision effectiveness, quality procedures, and any other outcomes that are considered important to the relationship. The partnership can also make use of benchmarking studies to establish realistic goals, which can later be re-evaluated.

Dispute Resolution

Given that we are in an age of lawsuits and expensive legal debates, it is wise, as with other business functions, to take dispute resolution into account in supply chain planning. Supply chain partners need to document and plan ahead for areas of concern such as security, copyright, and asset title when changes to the supply chain process take place. Trademark and copyright concerns need to be dealt with up front so that partners are willing to share critical information without the risk of losing a "trade secret." In addition, simple changes to the process can result in confusing terms of title that should be clarified with contracts and partnership agreements. As in health, prevention (of disputes) is the best medicine.

Security

Sharing information digitally poses additional concerns to security in the supply chain partnership. Security issues such as remote access and data warehouse sharing over extranets or virtual private networks should be clearly documented and monitored to ensure that security breaches do not occur. Partners need to establish policies that each is comfortable with and may monitor the compliance continually (and may be included in internal and external audits as well).

Essentially, trust will be the result of a well-planned and communicated supply chain partnership. Managing the changes in sharing of confidential information and job duty modification will often be a major task. As all of the issues are considered, we see that e-business and SCM are major business issues.

Order Fulfillment/Delivery

Order fulfillment has emerged as a critical component of the supply chain in the e-business era. In the early 2000s and the Christmas of 1999, fulfillment failures and difficulties tarnished the reputations of many e-tailers, including toy sellers and electronics retailers. The inability of many dot-coms to deliver goods on time for Christmas tarnished the growth of e-commerce and disappointed a number of children waiting for Barbie and Hot Wheels models, or computer systems. Since that time, a number of new fulfillment possibilities have emerged, and organizations—both bricks-and-mortar and dot-com—have dedicated substantial management and financial resources to modifying the fulfillment process.

The 1999 EC problems were to a great extent the result of unexpected demand, combined with underdeveloped supply chains and inventory control, and unrealistic delivery promises. In addition, the relatively new supply chains often lacked full integration on the B2B end, which resulted in increased pressure on the e-tailers to take late shipments and turn them into on-time deliveries, often at excessive costs. Admittedly, at the early stages of EC, demand was unknown; however, many of the early e-tailers had committed relatively little to planning and were focused on other important areas such as security and advertising. General business studies have taught us that a business is an integrated enterprise, and emphasis on select functional areas at the expense of others often leads to failure.

Order fulfillment consists of many procedures grouped into the main areas of order processing, warehousing, and shipping and transportation planning (see Figure 7.7). Fulfillment is the front-end and back-end processes necessary to convert an order into a sale by completing the company's responsibility of providing a product or service. Order processing includes activities such as credit checks, inventory availability determination, accounting, billing, and replenishment requests. A great deal of the work in order processing is now automated through ERP and web-based systems.

ORDER FULFILLMENT: process that consists of many procedures, grouped into the main areas of order processing, warehousing, and shipping and transportation planning.

Figure 7.7   The Order Fulfillment Process

Order fulfillment includes many business processes in areas such as order processing, warehousing, and shipping and transportation planning.

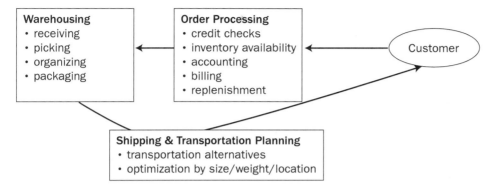

Warehousing includes processes such as receiving orders from suppliers (if not previously in stock), picking, organizing, and packaging goods for delivery. Initial attempts by online sellers to have suppliers package orders for shipment direct to the consumer had to be revised as customers began ordering multiple products and were dissatisfied with having to be available to receive multiple deliveries. Consider, for example, Wine.com (originally Virtual Vineyards), an e-tailer of wines and other gift products. When a customer ordered wines from the California region, Wine.com would relay the orders to individual vineyards for shipment to the consumer. Ordering wine from more than one vineyard would result in an inconvenience to the customer who might receive delivery at various times. As a result, Wine.com needed to centralize its fulfillment centre into a warehouse to provide quality service to customers.

Shipping and transportation planning (STP) is the process of getting finished goods to the consumer quickly and efficiently. STP requires businesses to coordinate all their orders cost-effectively by analyzing sizes, weights, packaging, and transportation alternatives. Like many other e-business functions discussed in this book, STP and order fulfillment require the use of sophisticated technologies to implement.

Fulfillment is similar to the moment of truth in service organizations, whereby delivery of a quality service or product is the only thing that a customer truly sees. The **moment of truth** is the critical moment in a service transaction when the customer's expectations are met, exceeded, or disappointed. The customer is not aware of or concerned with how complex the supply chain is or the number of processes involved—the customer wants to receive what was ordered, when it was promised, and at the cost quoted. To meet these needs, many companies have chosen to outsource the fulfillment function in order to remain focused on core competencies. For example, ToysRUs.com decided to outsource its fulfillment function to Amazon in order to focus on inventory management and procurement, which are complicated processes in the toy industry.[11] Amazon had strong fulfillment capabilities in place and could capitalize on existing infrastructure, allowing Toys "R" Us to control internal functions, manage its upstream supply chain, and concentrate on its new e-strategy.

A growing number of outsourcing companies are coming to light, including some of the well-known courier companies like FedEx and UPS. UPS signed an agreement with Samsung Electro-Mechanics Co. in the fall of 2000 to provide

SHIPPING AND TRANSPORTATION PLANNING (STP): the process of getting the finished goods to the consumer quickly and efficiently.

MOMENT OF TRUTH: the critical moment in a service transaction when the customer's expectations are met, exceeded, or disappointed.

outsourced global supply chain management services. The UPS Logistics Group offers services such as supply chain analysis, transportation, brokerage, and financing to companies wishing to move SCM outside of the organization. Samsung determined that its focus should remain on quality, production, and management, and UPS offered a competitive price, leading technology, and proven expertise.[12] Partnerships and outsourcing with firms such as UPS and FedEx have allowed many organizations to reduce the demands of SCM. While outsourcing is common, it can be an expensive alternative to in-house management and should be carefully evaluated. The size of an organization, product features, industry, and complexity of the supply chain will all affect the costs of carrying out SCM.

Large organizations with established management structures and supply chain expertise can develop top-performing fulfillment systems by capitalizing on technological structures in place. ERP systems hold a great deal of the information required to develop efficient fulfillment, such as inventory information (quantities on hand and on order, delivery information, backorders), customer information (credit limits, shipping addresses), and financial information (sales prices, shipping cost information, etc.). In order to leverage the information in the ERP system it is necessary to ensure that fulfillment is based on ERP data and integrated in order to deliver real-time updates. Order status information needs to be provided back to the ERP system from custom applications (such as shopping cart applications or shipping partner data, so that data need not be entered twice) and allows customer service to provide meaningful feedback to customer service calls.

CANADIAN SNAPSHOTS

The Partnerships that Made Empori.com

Empori.com was formed as a division of Oxford Properties Group, one of Canada's largest property development and management firms. Recognizing the problems of dealing with fulfillment in the B2C marketplace, Empori set out to provide a valuable service to businesses and consumers. Many e-tailers recognized that an impediment to online buying was the availability of the customer for delivery at home. Empori provided an alternative to this fulfillment procedure by offering consumers the option of having goods delivered to drop-off locations throughout Toronto. This business model allowed individuals to order items on the Internet while at work or home and pick items up after work at a convenient time/location rather than attempting to be home when the courier service arrived.

Empori's business model allowed e-tailers to partner with a fulfillment firm that provided convenience and flexibility to consumers. Chapters.ca established a partnership with Empori and allowed shoppers on its site to select Empori locations for delivery of books, toys, and music.

This innovative business model provided customers with convenient alternatives and removed some of the barriers to e-tailing. Despite its innovativeness, Empori went out of business in late 2001. The limited growth in the e-tailing sector combined with a general decline in investment in Internet companies forced Oxford Properties to close the company. The model does, however, have potential if the right drop-off locations can be found.

Questions

1. How do you think the Empori model could have been turned into a success?
2. What types of products are well suited to use this model of fulfillment?
3. Why would a large company like Oxford Properties have given up on its investment after such a short period of time?
4. Can you think of companies that are well suited to compete using the Empori model?

SOURCES: Empori.com, Chapters.indigo.ca.

Warehousing concerns have resulted in major changes within e-business as companies strive to reduce delivery times while controlling costs. The classic example is that of Amazon.com. Amazon's original business model was to operate as an online sales organization with no inventory on hand. Amazon chose to move from a dot-com organization to a "bricks and clicks" business that holds some inventory in strategically located warehouses throughout the United States. Amazon now stocks high-volume books in high-tech warehouses and has the ability to better meet its objectives of shipping overnight for most customer orders. Wine.com has taken a similar approach by using warehouses as storage points for high-volume items and as a receiving point for integrating and packaging orders. The B2C marketplace has transformed through the pure Internet phase to a model where it is often necessary to hold some inventories in order to provide rapid customer service and delivery. A unique and interesting model for dealing with fulfillment in the B2C market is described in the Canadian Snapshots box.

As shipping and transportation companies embrace the technological advances in business, it becomes easier to provide high levels of customer service. UPS and FedEx allow customers to track packages on the Internet by entering an identification number. The ability of these transportation service providers to deliver information at all stages of the delivery channel is made possible through information systems and Internet technology. In addition, wireless devices are allowing businesses to better provide services to customers. For example, Global Forwarding Company Limited of Dartmouth, Nova Scotia, has the capability to monitor the movements of its fleet of transfer trucks through satellite tracking systems, allowing customers the ability to accurately forecast order delivery (see Figure 7.8). In an age where delivery speed is often measured in hours or days,

Global Forwarding Company Limited
www.globaltransport.ca

Figure 7.8   Global Forwarding Company Website

Illustration of website of Global Forwarding, through which equipment can be tracked by the "Truck Locator" button.

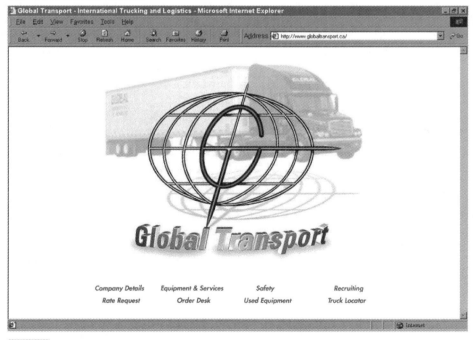

SOURCE: "Home Page." *Global Transport*. <http://www.globaltransport.ca>. November 2001. Reproduced with permission.

this type of information becomes crucial to success. The combination of wireless and Internet technologies is creating excellent opportunities for transportation and other companies to gain substantial benefits throughout the fulfillment process—improving customer service, increasing revenue, and controlling costs all at the same time.

Reverse Logistics

REVERSE LOGISTICS: the process through which customers can return items purchased either for a refund or for warranty/repair.

Internet research has demonstrated that returning products is both a concern for buyers and an important issue for sellers. **Reverse logistics** is the process through which customers can return items purchased, either for a refund or for warranty/repair. Having an effective mechanism for dealing with returns is helpful in making sales but also must be designed to ensure that fraud cannot be perpetrated easily.

Bricks-and-mortar businesses that have been in the catalogue sales business have dealt with the problem of returns for many years. However, pure online stores need to establish policies, drop-off locations, and credit procedures in order to effectively handle returns. For instance, clothing e-tailers found early on that buyers would purchase a medium and a large of the same style and then return the item that did not fit properly. Without proper procedures in place, the return of items can be very costly—incurring shipping costs, banking and transaction costs, and the expense of storing and dealing with excess inventory. Policies that assist with returns include many items that are common to retailing such as time limits on returns, responsibility for shipping costs, and reasonable use limitations for warranty-related concerns. Establishing clear policies and communicating them to customers assists greatly in controlling reverse logistics.

Outsourcing has once again become an important strategy in dealing with reverse logistics. For example, Buy.com determined that having an effective delivery system encouraged customers to purchase products and have confidence in the company. Initially, Buy.com allowed customers to make returns by calling and obtaining an authorization code, and then later a mailing label would be sent to the customer for the product's return. The process was cumbersome and slow, so Buy.com outsourced the function to UPS. Customers now obtain authorization for returns online and can enter their authorization code into the returns section of the website, which allows them to print out their own packaging label from UPS. The package can then be dropped off at a UPS location or picked up by the courier service. Once again, customer service has dominated.

C-Commerce: The Future

COLLABORATIVE COMMERCE: the application of technologies to allow trading partners to synchronize and optimize their partnerships; performed in collaboration.

The Gartner Group coined the term **collaborative commerce** (c-commerce) in late 1999 in a strategic planning note examining the future of e-business.[13] C-commerce is the application of technologies to allow trading partners to synchronize and optimize their partnerships and is performed in collaboration. As SCM and other applications develop, we will watch c-commerce emerge as an extremely important component of the supply chain, facilitating strong relationships, fuelling efficiency, and driving customer-oriented decisions.

Essentially, c-commerce is the advanced stage of many of the topics discussed in this chapter. It involves employing technology to improve partnerships, gain efficiency in processes, make effective decisions, and satisfy the customer.

Trading exchanges and customer relationship management are part of the development of c-commerce and are discussed later in this book.

Chapter Summary

Supply chain management is the process of coordination and management of the product, information, and financial flows among members of the supply chain. As e-business has emerged, SCM has become an important aspect of success by allowing businesses to gain efficiencies and improve customer service in a fast-paced environment. The Internet-enabled supply chain has a customer focus from the beginning, whereby the entire chain is driven by the pull of the customer.

Technology is an important component of SCM. ERP systems provide the backbone for information exchange. The Internet provides the medium through which much communication and "collaboration" take place. Extranets and other technologies allow partners to securely share information in a convenient, cost-effective, and user-friendly manner.

Strategy plays a key role in SCM by setting the direction for partners to work toward. Like many other aspects of business, technology is a critical tool for SCM, but success is achieved by making strategic decisions and effectively managing the people who employ the technologies. Companies like Dell have employed SCM to achieve their goal of providing the customer with customized products, at a competitive price, within a short period of time.

KEY TERMS

supply chain management (SCM)

supply chain

customer relationship management (CRM)

push system

electronic data interchange (EDI)

pull system

disintermediation

reintermediation

business intelligence

business process reengineering

cash-to-cash cycle

trust

vendor-managed inventory

order fulfillment

shipping and transportation planning

moment of truth

reverse logistics

collaborative commerce

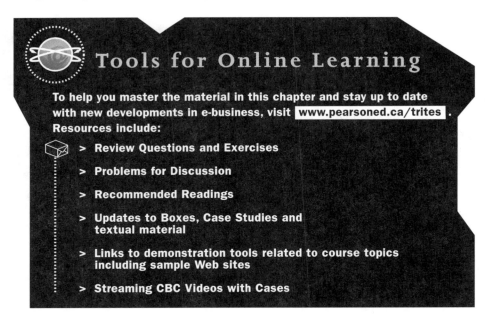

Tools for Online Learning

To help you master the material in this chapter and stay up to date with new developments in e-business, visit www.pearsoned.ca/trites. Resources include:

> **Review Questions and Exercises**

> **Problems for Discussion**

> **Recommended Readings**

> **Updates to Boxes, Case Studies and textual material**

> **Links to demonstration tools related to course topics including sample Web sites**

> **Streaming CBC Videos with Cases**

Endnotes

1. Advertising Supplement, *Canadian Business,* September 2000.
2. Evans, Philip, and Thomas S. Wurster, *Blown to Bits: How the New Economics of Information Transforms Strategy.* Harvard Business School Press, p. 237.

3. Stein, Tom, and Jeff Sweat, "Killer Supply Chains," *Informationweek*, Nov. 9, 1998.

4. Hammer, Michael and James Champy, *Reengineering the Corporation*. New York: HarperCollins Publishers, 1994, p. 35.

5. Trites, Gerald, *Enterprise Resource Planning—The Engine for E-Business*. CICA, 2000.

6. Hammer, Michael, and Steven Stanton, *The Reengineering Revolution*. New York: HarperCollins, 1995.

7. Hammer, Michael, and Steven Stanton, "How Process Enterprises Really Work," *Harvard Business Review*, November-December 1999.

8. Dietrich, Brenda, et al., "Big Benefits for Big Blue," *OR/MS Today*, June 2000.

9. Kevin R. Moore, "Trust and Relationship Commitment in Logistics Alliances: A Buyer Perspective," *International Journal of Purchasing and Materials Management* 34: 24–37.

10. Lee, Hau, "Creating Value through Supply Chain Integration," *Supply Chain Management Review*, September/October 2000.

11. Tedeschi, Bob, "Internet Merchants, Seeing Landscape Shift, Adapt to Survive," *New York Times*, Dec. 18, 2000.

12. UPS.com, Samsung.com.

13. Bond, B., et al., "C-Commerce: The New Arena for Business Applications," Gartner Group, August 1999.

E-Procurement, Trading Exchanges, and Auctions

learning objectives

When you complete this chapter you should be able to:

1. Explain the e-procurement process and why e-procurement is important in today's business world.

2. Outline the major benefits of e-procurement and what types of goods are often procured.

3. Describe trading exchanges and what functions they have.

4. Explain the issues exchange providers are facing.

5. Categorize auctions and explain how the different types could be used.

6. Identify the critical stages of the auctioning process and describe how an auction would be carried out online.

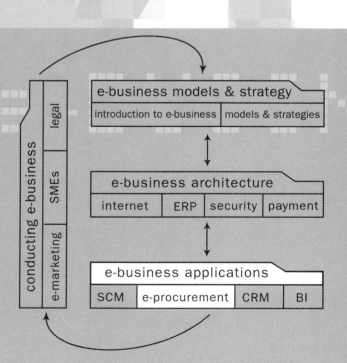

Introduction

Marriott
www.marriott.com

Hyatt
www.hyatt.com

Raytheon
www.raytheon.com

FreeMarkets
www.freemarkets.com

E-PROCUREMENT: the complete business process of acquiring goods through electronic means, from requisition through to fulfillment and payment.

Businesses have become increasingly interested in the area of e-procurement as a means of cutting costs and improving efficiency in the early 2000s. While the dot-com craze of the late 1990s corrected itself and disappointed many, the benefits of B2B transactions, e-procurement, and trading exchanges are just beginning to be realized. A variety of strategies have been adopted in the B2B arena in an attempt to capitalize on the benefits. For example, the Marriott and Hyatt hotel chains moved their procurement staffs outside the organization into a joint venture called Avendra LLC. Raytheon, a large U.S. defence contractor, has used its own in-house e-procurement efforts to "rationalize" its number of suppliers and cut costs, while also using outsourced procurement services from FreeMarkets.[1] While a variety of strategies are used, one thing is clear—e-procurement is a critical area of e-business that will continue to evolve for the next several years as companies strive to achieve completely digital, integrated B2B e-commerce. In this chapter we will examine the e-procurement process, trading exchanges, implementation challenges, and directions for future development.

E-procurement can be defined broadly as the complete business process of acquiring goods through electronic means, from requisition through to fulfillment and payment. The process of e-procurement involves more than just the purchasing of goods, as it deals more broadly with the complete cycle, including selection and payment. The e-procurement process is illustrated in Figure 8.1.

Figure 8.1   The E-Procurement Process

E-procurement encompasses numerous tasks that are increasingly being carried out in integrated, electronic formats.

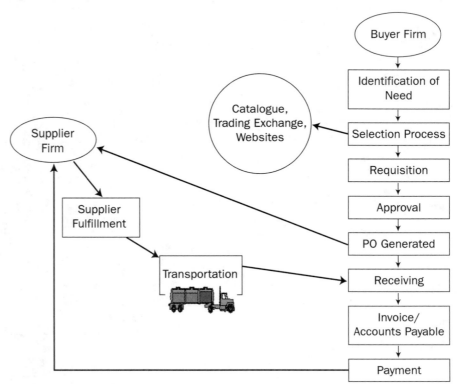

The E-Procurement Process

E-procurement's process can be described by referring to Figure 8.1. The process itself will vary somewhat by organization, but a simplified analysis of the components will allow us to better understand the concept. Once a firm identifies a need for a good or service, an employee would begin the selection process to find a good to fill the need. This process could be carried out through catalogues, either online or through the corporate intranet, through a trading exchange, or by examining websites of potential vendors. Other possibilities such as auctions will be discussed later. Once the employee has identified the specific good to be procured he or she would create a requisition electronically and forward it to the appropriate signing officer if approval is required. Purchases of specific types of goods or within certain dollar limits may be automatically approved by the system.

The approval of the requisition will result in the creation of a purchase order that will be transmitted to the supplier firm. The transmission could take place in any number of formats including EDI, XML, or through a secure Internet transaction in another format. The transmission of the purchase order may occur directly through a trading exchange, through the Internet, or could be through a proprietary VAN, depending on the technologies of the firms involved.

The supplier firm may then carry out all of its fulfillment processes and arrange for transportation to the buyer firm. Once the buyer receives the goods, the payment process will begin. The receiving information should be entered in the buyer's ERP/accounting system to update inventory, and when the invoice is received it is matched to the receiving information and purchase order to confirm receipt of the entire order as well as pricing information. The accounts payable will be paid in the normal sequence by the buyer, and again the format of this would depend on the particular circumstances. Increasingly, the steps described in this process are carried out electronically and integrated into the back office systems.

Surprisingly, by mid-2001 the level of integration achieved in these processes by many large companies was rather limited. Texas Instruments claimed that it wished to emphasize efforts on improving the capability of itself and its suppliers to integrate systems to expand the products acquired through e-procurement. A great deal of information was passed through e-mail and spreadsheets and then later re-keyed into their ERP system, leading to inefficiencies and errors.[2] Many organizations have identified improved integration as a key issue for stimulating B2B transactions through trading exchanges and e-procurement, thus creating a lucrative opportunity for technology firms in this area.

Goods and Services Procured

When e-procurement began, the most common use was for the purchase of office supplies and maintenance, repair, and operating (MRO) items. As businesses began to realize the potential for cost savings, the purchases expanded into computer equipment and corporate travel services, and later into production-related goods such as raw materials.

It is critical that processes for e-procurement are established while considering the types of goods and services being acquired in order to be both efficient and effective. Like paper-based transactions, the dollar value and urgency of the purchase impact how processes function and how quickly they occur. Despite this, it is important to keep the electronic processes in check. Consider the following example from Microsoft, where Bill Gates discovered inefficiency within digital processes:

I thought every company had this kind of explicit review for expense approval. I learned I was wrong when I demonstrated our Intranet to a group of CEOs. Paul O'Neill of Alcoa, which is the world's leading producer of aluminum, came up to me after my talk and asked, "It's great that everything is digital and efficient, but why should you have to review expense reports? You've got better things to do with your time."[3]

This example illustrates exactly what businesses must be careful not to do—simply automate paper processes. In this case there was no need for Bill Gates to authorize the travel expenditures of senior-level VPs, even though it may have only taken a relatively short amount of time. As for many other aspects of e-business, processes often need to be reengineered for procurement when moving to electronic processes.

Businesses will not want to allow automatic approval on many types of goods being acquired but should consider carefully thinking through the approvals process. For example, it may be reasonable to establish budgeted amounts for basic office supplies that are purchased through specified vendors rather than dealing with individual purchase order review and approval. The expenses may be audited later for control purposes, but the time saved should exceed the cost of any potential employee wrongdoing.

Maintenance, Repair, and Operating Expenses Maintenance, repair, and operating (MRO) expenses are other areas where automatic approvals may be delegated to specific individuals. For instance, the production manager may have approval to create a purchase order up to a specific dollar limit in order that machine breakdowns can efficiently be dealt with. If downtime within a manufacturing business is expensive, then allowing the production manager to quickly deal with a problem would benefit the business, whereas a detailed process of approvals could delay the repair and impact the bottom line. This example is not intended to imply that MRO should always be automatically approved, but simply that each business must carefully evaluate its processes when establishing e-procurement policies.

Travel Services Travel services and meals and entertainment costs represent a major expense for many of today's service-based businesses. Therefore, the ability to deal with travel services in an integrated fashion has the potential for major cost savings. Microsoft saw this potential in the late 1990s and established a partnership with American Express so employees could access negotiated rates and discounts through the e-procurement portion of the corporate Intranet, dubbed "MS Market" (see the E-Strategy box). Allowing employees to book their own travel at approved rates resulted in more than just improved rates—it also satisfied employees who wished to manage their own schedules and have the flexibility to make changes if necessary.[4]

Computer Equipment The acquisition of computer equipment represents another major category where businesses have begun to employ e-procurement. Not only can computers be acquired through exchanges and vendors' websites, but increasingly, corporate intranets can be linked to specialized pages of the vendors. For example, Dell has created "Premier Pages" (see Figure 8.2) for many of its customers, which allows a number of benefits, including negotiated pricing, preconfigured systems, and knowledge of corporate infrastructure. Arrangements such as this allow for computer systems within budget limits to be purchased with little involvement of supervisors and technical support staff. The cost savings of consolidating purchases with a few suppliers can also be substantial. For example,

E-STRATEGY

MS Market at Microsoft

Microsoft began its efforts in the e-procurement arena in the mid-1990s with MS Market. MS Market was an intranet project that Microsoft tied in with several of its other intranet-based initiatives, such as Microsoft Archives, MS Reports, and MS Sales. Recognizing early the importance of employee self-service to create increased efficiency, cost reduction, and employee satisfaction, Microsoft built an application for procurement that would address a number of important cost areas for the company, including office supplies and travel.

In *Business @ The Speed of Thought*, Bill Gates describes some of the "growing pains" that MS Market went through as well as how some problems were addressed. For example, then-President Steve Ballmer (who later became CEO) was hesitant to make use of the application and the MS Market product manager confronted him over his concerns. Ballmer was disappointed that he was unable to determine if other managers had already reviewed and/or approved

orders that he was responsible for, as no routing application was in place. In addition, he was unable to review supporting documentation for purchase orders. Within weeks the routing requirement was resolved, and documentation support was available within a few months.

The key reason that the MS Market issues were addressed was that the product manager was fully in control of the project and sought advice from the user group in a manner they understood. Issues were resolved quickly and users began requesting other functionality that both saved them time and saved Microsoft money.

Microsoft's digital capabilities allow it to manage employee time and information from the point of application through the online résumé tool through to dealing with Human Resources information. After an employee has been hired they are able to use self-service for a number of functions including ordering office supplies, business cards and also the ability to deal with human resource issues, like benefits selection and charitable

donations, all through the corporate intranet.

The Microsoft and American Express travel partnership, AXI, is a 24/7 service that allows employees to book corporate-discounted fares on airlines and negotiated rates at preferred hotels. Travel policies are built into AXI so that routine travel is automatically approved, while non-routine requests are routed to the appropriate manager for review. Gates estimated that employee time to book routine domestic flights would be reduced "from seventeen minutes and six phone calls or e-mails to approximately five minutes."

MS Market was used to conduct over US$1 billion of transactions in its first year and was estimated to reduce administrative procurement costs by US$35 million—an e-procurement success. E-procurement implementation strategies, like all other implementations, need to be carried out with swiftness and flexibility in order to succeed.

Microsoft
www.microsoft.com

Questions

1. Does the fact that Microsoft was working on e-procurement before many other large businesses indicate that they should have made a lot of money by selling their expertise in this area?

2. Gates made several presentations to share information regarding MS Market with fellow CEOs. What would be the motivation behind this? What can Microsoft gain from these "show and tell" sessions?

SOURCES: Gates, Bill, *Business @ the Speed of Thought*, New York, 1999; MS Market Technical Deployment White Paper, August 1999; and www.microsoft.com.

Bristol-Myers Squibb claims to have saved US$20 million per year by consolidating its purchases from both Dell and IBM with e-procurement.[5]

Production Items The cost savings and benefits obtained through e-procurement for non-production items have led many businesses to look to e-procurement for

Figure 8.2   The Higher Education Homepage of Dell.ca

Dell's Premier Pages allow corporate and other large customers to access tailored web pages and pre-configured systems, which provide excellent service and ease of use.

SOURCES: "Higher Education." *Dell Canada*. <http://www.dell.ca/en/hied/defalut.htm>. November 2001. Reprinted with permission of Dell Canada. All rights reserved.

production items (also referred to as direct spending), such as raw materials and components. There are, however, some significant differences between production and non-production goods, which are making this transition more difficult. For example, non-production goods can be acquired more easily through poorly integrated systems since their arrival date and update are less critical. Production items need to be acquired within specific time frames in order to keep manufacturing schedules and inventory levels in order both for internal planning purposes and for customer notification. Therefore, production items need to occur through an integrated e-procurement system or they will require re-keying of information.

In addition to currency of information, production items tend to have other important concerns that need to be addressed, such as product quality, payment terms, delivery arrangements, and supplier capabilities for collaborative product design. Essentially, the concern for using e-procurement, trading exchanges, or auction models to procure production goods is that price is only one part of the buying decision.

Benefits of e-Procurement

The benefits of e-procurement to businesses are still being discovered, but early indications are that the practice has a tremendous payoff. Some of the benefits include cost and efficiency, strategic procurement, and authorized buying.

Cost and Efficiency   The benefits of e-procurement are many, including price reductions and process efficiencies. Recent studies have found that companies reported benefits such as faster order times, convenience, time savings, easier price comparisons, and cost savings.[6] While the initial jump to adopt e-procurement was to create more competitive markets and reduce prices, a number of businesses claim that the "primary benefit lies in streamlining internal processes."[7]

It is interesting to consider how costs have been reduced from approximately US$120 to process a purchase order to the US$5 to $25 range. Paper-based procurement is laced with inefficiencies such as approvals of all purchase orders, despite the dollar amount or importance. In addition, the length of time to process a purchase order has been reduced by many businesses by nearly 75 percent due to the removal of "the paper chase." Microsoft claimed to have reduced its paper forms related to procurement from 114 to 1, significantly reducing the paper chasing in that company.[8] The reduction in cost and increase in efficiency also results in a reduced administrative workload for procurement staff.

Strategic Procurement With the implementation of e-procurement in a business, the staff from the procurement area will be able to focus efforts on more important areas, such as strategic sourcing and supplier relations. As discussed in Chapter 7, efficient supply chains depend on reliable suppliers, and the ability of staff to spend more time in developing relationships is very beneficial. In addition, procurement staff may become involved in managing procurement processes that now occur through electronic means.

Authorized Buying Another area where benefits of e-procurement have been obtained is in consolidated buying from approved vendors. By controlling which suppliers employees may order from, the business should be able to demand improved pricing by increasing volume. The impact, for example, on a large business with tens of thousands of employees, each of whom purchases their own office supplies at the local supplier rather than consolidating purchases, could be tremendous. Limiting employees to the suppliers in the e-procurement system can reduce this **maverick buying**. In addition to potentially reducing costs, these limitations reduce the volume of payments required and the headaches that may arise.

MAVERICK BUYING: the unauthorized purchasing of goods by employees through non-routine and poorly controlled means, such as acquiring office supplies with petty cash.

The benefits of e-procurement are broad in scope and will vary by organization. However, one thing is clear—e-procurement is a strategy that all e-businesses are working on now, or will be working on in the near future. See the Canadian Snapshots box to see how the Canadian government is moving into e-procurement.

Trading Exchanges

Business-to-business trading exchanges are Internet-based sites in which businesses can sell or purchase products and services or share information to advertise products and services. Trading exchanges lead to reduced reliance on other forms of communication in the procurement/selling process, as illustrated in Figure 8.3. During the year 2000, the popularity of trading exchanges resulted in the formation of more than a thousand online exchanges; however, the limited growth in trading through these exchanges was unable to support this number, and by mid-2001 many of the startups had shut down. For example, Chemdex, which had been touted as one of the trading exchanges with great potential, discontinued operations in April 2001. Forrester Research predicts an exchange shakeout will leave fewer than 200 significant B2B companies in operation.[9] Despite this fact, a number of trading exchanges, both public and private, are operating successfully today and offer extended benefits to e-procurement activities on the buy-side and selling opportunities on the sell-side.

CANADIAN SNAPSHOTS

E-Procurement at Merx.ca

The Canadian federal and provincial governments are moving in the direction of e-procurement with their electronic tendering service known as Merx.ca. Merx is powered by Cebra Inc., a Bank of Montreal company, and provides contractors and businesses both large and small with the opportunity to bid on tenders from purchasers in the federal, provincial, and MASH (municipal, academic, school, and hospital) sectors.

Essentially, Merx is an electronic tendering service, meaning that an Ottawa-based contractor can easily search for any contracts in the Ottawa area with the federal government, the City of Ottawa, local municipalities in the region, or government agencies (a complete list of purchasers through Merx can be found on their website). If tenders of interest are posted on the site, the contractor simply requests the tender documents and pays the shipping fees. As of early 2001 bids were still conducted through paper-based means, but Merx was looking at the creation of electronic bid submission capabilities.

In early 2001, Cebra and the Canadian Chamber of Commerce signed a deal, which would see nearly 170 000 Canadian businesses able to take advantage of the billions of dollars of government tendering opportunities. This agreement is expected to triple the number of suppliers able to access the site, taking into account that many of the Chamber members were already paying users of the site. The details of the new payment scheme in place are unclear; however, the 2001 cost to join Merx was a mere $7 per month.

New Developments

A new auction service was announced by Cebra to be introduced in late 2001 and offered initially to Merx users. The service would create a secure buyer and seller auction site and allows business-to-business transactions to be conducted through the Internet. Renah Persofsky, CEO and President of Cebra Inc., said, "Most of the auction sites available in Canada today are business-to-consumer or consumer-to-consumer focused. Through this auction solution we will be offering a service which is designed specifically for the B2B market."

Merx
www.merx.ca

Cebra Inc.
www.cebra.com

Questions

1. Would it make sense to allow Chamber members to access the Merx site at no charge? Would Cebra Inc. wish to pursue this model?
2. What benefits would this result in for the buyers from government?
3. What extensions to the existing e-tendering strategy should Merx be working on in order to improve the overall procurement process?
4. Should the government be getting involved in any fashion with the auction site? Why or why not?

SOURCES: merx.ca and cebra.com.

VERTICAL TRADING EXCHANGES: trading exchanges that have an industry or specific market focus, such as healthcare or energy products and services.

HORIZONTAL TRADING EXCHANGES: trading exchanges that have a product or service focus, such as computers or office equipment, and do not target any specific industry.

Trading exchanges may also be referred to by a number of different names in practice. Terms such as *hubs*, *e-hubs*, *marketplaces*, *consortiums*, and combinations of these (sometimes with B2B added) are used in trade literature and magazine publications. In this book, we will refer primarily to trading exchanges, that being the most comprehensive term.

Trading exchanges can be grouped into two major categories in terms of products and services exchanged: vertical and horizontal. **Vertical trading exchanges** are those that have an industry or specific market focus, such as healthcare or energy products and services. **Horizontal trading exchanges** are those that have a product or service focus, such as computers or office equipment, and do not target any specific industry. Figure 8.4 illustrates the concept of vertical and horizontal exchanges.

Figure 8.3   Trading Exchange Facilitating Role

Trading exchanges can consolidate numerous forms of communication into one medium.

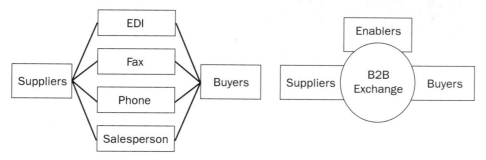

Trading exchanges are also categorized as either public or private, depending on the controls in place and any access limitations. For example, when General Electric first began its Global eXchange Services (GXS), it was limited to a few specific buyers who were soliciting goods and services from sellers who had been given access to enter the exchange, an example of a **private exchange**. GXS has evolved over time and continues to provide exchange services such as network infrastructure, software, hardware, and consulting services to major clients like JC Penney and Procter & Gamble.[10] (See the New Business Models box for more information on GXS). Private exchanges continue to evolve and range in the methods by which they allow sellers and buyers to join.

Public exchanges are those in which buyers and sellers register to join, and there are few limitations to joining. For example, VerticalNet describes itself as the "leading business-to-business e-commerce enabler"[11] and hosted nearly 60 vertical exchanges by mid-2001 (see Figure 8.5). VerticalNet allows buyers and sellers to register and use its exchange services, providing little control over the transactions since it is primarily an "enabler."

PRIVATE EXCHANGE: trading exchange that limits participation to specific buyers and sellers—normally related to the exchange provider's supply chain.

PUBLIC EXCHANGES: trading exchanges in which buyers and sellers register to join, and there are few limitations to joining.

 **VerticalNet**
www.verticalnet.com

Figure 8.4   Vertical and Horizontal Trading Exchanges

Trading exchanges are often categorized as either vertical or horizontal based upon the way they operate.

Vertical Exchanges: Chemical, Communications, Energy, Environment, Financial Services, Healthcare, High-Tech, Manufacturing, Telecommunications

Horizontal Exchanges: Computer Equipment, Office Supplies, Cleaning Supplies

NEW BUSINESS MODELS

The GXS Trading Exchange at GE

General Electric (GE), at first glance, may not strike individuals as a particularly exciting company; however, their strengths in the world of e-business may just be unknown. GE's history is full of innovation, adaptation, and change, which are characteristics that should serve it well in the world of e-business. GE has a history of over 120 years and in that time has been involved with product innovation in the areas of lighting, aircraft engines, mainframe computers, and now B2B trading exchanges. GE is a very diversified company with business units dedicated to supplies, medical products, plastics, trucking, appliances, insurance, and other products.

In the late 1990s, GE began working on its own e-procurement processes by automating purchases through the Internet. As the pure-play dot-com businesses expanded into trading exchanges, GE realized that its work on its own Global eXchange Service (GXS) could be a very valuable asset. The company's CEO, Jack Welsh, recommended major innovation and devotion to the project and in early 2000 spent several hundred million dollars in the GXS project.

What makes GXS different from many of the other dot-com trading exchange enablers is their core strength in working with EDI. While many other enablers struggle with integration, GXS uses the experience of GE with EDI to allow integration to take place over the Internet. By early 2001, approximately 5 percent of trading exchanges had the processes integrated with ERP systems of users. To expand the possibilities of GXS, partnerships were formed with leading companies in the area, including Commercial One and Tibco Software.

The GXS private exchange successfully built exchanges for large bricks-and-mortar businesses such as JC Penney and DaimlerChrysler, and realized that it had the ability to provide excellent service in the area. To capitalize on this experience, GXS, in partnership with others, helped launch a public exchange known as Express Marketplace.

Despite its involvement in trading exchanges, both use and design, GE has opted not to become involved in public exchanges with its own products. GXS sees that a great opportunity in the exchange area will be to create means of integration between separate exchanges that will create better experiences and processes for users. The old bricks-and-mortar organization known as GE has shown clearly that the world of e-business is not just for startups.

Commerce One
www.commerceone.com

Tibco Software
www.tibco.com

Questions

1. Why would GE choose not to engage in selling its own products through public exchanges?
2. Should GE abandon its "traditional" product lines of appliances and lighting products to focus on its technological capabilities? Why?
3. At a time when outsourcing has become extremely common, does it make sense for GE to focus its attention on the development of trading exchanges?

SOURCES: Burke, Jon, "The Last Internet Company," *Red Herring*, December 19, 2000; www.ge.com; www.geis.com.

Trading Exchange Functions

Trading exchanges operate with a variety of service levels and allow for varying degrees of integration. The functions of a trading exchange can range from simplistic, in which members share company information and then conduct transac-

Figure 8.5   **Progression Stages for Trading Exchanges and Marketplaces**

B2B trading exchanges range from basic brochureware sites to complex collaborative environments.

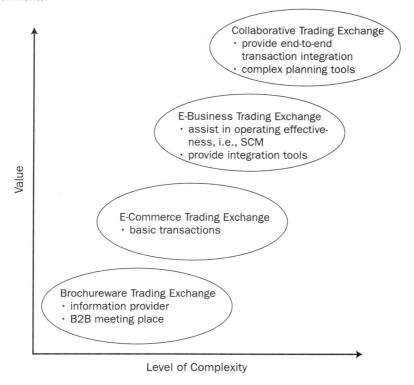

tions offline (similar to the brochureware phase of the Internet), to catalogue sites, to fully integrated collaborative environments (see Figure 8.6). In the collaborative environments, contract terms and payment can be carried out completely online and integrated with the buyer and seller back-end systems, and products and services may even be designed online.

In this section we will look at trading exchanges from the perspectives of buyers, sellers, and exchange enablers. To illustrate the points being discussed, the automotive trading exchange, Covisint, will be highlighted. Covisint was formed in the spring of 2000 by General Motors Corp., DaimlerChrysler AG, and Ford Motor Company. The exchange had previously been known as the Automotive Network Exchange (ANX). This industry consortium aims to create a business community of buyers, sellers, designers, engineers, and third parties within the global automotive industry.[12]

Covisint
www.covisint.com

Covisint developed plans for expansion during the year 2000 and early 2001 in order to begin facilitating its role by mid-2001. Renault SA and Nissan Motor Company later joined the Covisint exchange as automotive partners and both Oracle and Commerce One joined as technology partners. By May 2001, Covisint said it had more than 250 customers on the exchange carrying out some functions of auctions, quote management, and collaborative design. Products and services, however, at this point in time are focused primarily on procurement and the supply chain.[13]

Covisint has a development plan that aims to move far beyond the use of the exchange for procurement. The categories of the Covisint development plan are procurement efficiencies, supply chain optimization, and product development. See Figure 8.6 for an illustration. Each of these stages relates back to Figure 8.5 as well, where the progression is from a transaction automation basis to a collaborative exchange in the future.

For Buyers Trading exchanges offer buyers the ability to search, select, and acquire goods and services in an efficient manner from numerous suppliers. Suppliers can register with an exchange in order to list their products in catalogue form on the exchange so that buyers may seek their products.

In addition to hosting catalogues, exchanges can facilitate trade by providing additional services that the buyer may consider valuable. For example, the exchange may provide services related to the review of potential suppliers in terms of quality and past customer satisfaction. Trading exchanges may also work closely with buyers to deal with issues of integration, technology requirements, and training, as well as numerous other offerings. See Figure 8.7 for a listing of a number of services potentially offered by trading exchanges.

Covisint, an industry-led exchange, offers a number of services to its buyers (such as Ford and GM), who are also the founding members of the exchange. Members of the exchange can carry out procurement activities through catalogue

Figure 8.6   Covisint Trading Exchange

The Covisint trading exchange aims to move toward the collaborative environment by providing services for supply chain management, collaborative product development, and e-procurement capabilities.

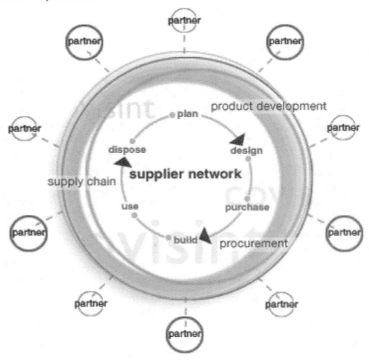

Figure 8.7   Potential Trading Exchange Functions

Trading exchanges have the potential to provide numerous value-added services to members on both the buy-side and sell-side of transactions as they increase in complexity.

• Supplier certification, reputation	• Contract administration
• Transportation management	• Tariffs and duties assessment
• Product life cycle management	• Planning, scheduling, forecasting
• Warehousing and inspection	• Promotions/campaign management
• Risk mitigation services	• Profiling and personalization
• Catalogue display/maintenance	• Authentication/security
• Financing	• Complex pricing
• Product configuration	• Private markets, negotiated terms
• Derivative instruments	• Post-sale support, warranty programs
• Community news, employment, etc.	• Receivables management
• Returns processing, repair claims	• Scrap management/reverse logistics
• Payment processing/order management	• Inventory availability
• Order explosion/routing	• Partner/team selling and promotions
• Workflow and business rules	• Backorder management

methods or use auction or reverse auction methods (these will be discussed later in the chapter). Other services at Covisint include supply chain optimization, integration of supply chain technologies, and hosting of applications to allow for collaborative design and development of new products in a virtual workspace. This industry-led consortium essentially allows buyers to deal more efficiently with suppliers, to reduce costs, and to make gains in effectiveness by using collaborative tools designed specifically for the industry.

For Suppliers Suppliers to trading exchanges are attempting to attract additional business through a medium that allows for efficient sales to take place. By listing products and services on a public trading exchange, a supplier may be aiming to reach new customers across a range of industries. On the other hand, a supplier may join a private trading exchange in order to more efficiently and effectively deal with customers it has sold to previously. See the E-Business in Global Perspective box to further examine the potential benefits of exchanges to buyers and sellers.

Covisint offers suppliers access to a huge market as well as an exchange backed by leading players in the automotive industry. Suppliers can look forward to accessing customers on a more cost-effective basis as well as begin using collaborative functions over the next few years to become more closely involved in the design process. Covisint also allows suppliers who deal with several of the major automakers the ability to use one major interface to conduct business, thus simplifying the process for employees. These functions should develop strong bonds between trading partners who successfully participate and demonstrate their ability to provide input and meet commitments (which may be tracked and disclosed by the exchange).

Issues for Exchange Providers

Business-to-business exchange providers have a huge challenge ahead of them to deliver on the demands of both buyers and suppliers over the coming years. In

E-BUSINESS IN GLOBAL PERSPECTIVE

Industry Exchange at TransLease Pro

Fleet management for leasing companies and other fleet operators in Britain has become much more efficient since the introduction of TransLease Pro. TransLease Pro is a product/service of Cap Gemini Ernst & Young, which has been launched in Britain and is growing steadily.

The general manager of fleet operations for TransLease Pro's largest customer, Motability Fleet Limited, stated, "The reduction in paperwork and administrative time resulting from TransLease Pro will deliver substantial annual cost savings in excess of £9 million by 2002 compared with what we would have spent using a traditional fleet management process." Benefits to the e-procurement/ exchange service are numerous and the product has become well accepted by fleet managers as well as repair and maintenance providers.

Assume for a moment that you lease a vehicle in London and are travelling to a nearby city when your vehicle breaks down. Since repairs on many of the leases are included in the cost, you must call the leasing company and get an approval for repair work at the nearest garage. Then the repair garage can either charge you for the work (and you can be reimbursed by the leasing company later) or the leasing company can pay the garage directly if the repair garage is comfortable with the account receivable. Basically, this sounds like one extra headache that is not needed when dealing with vehicle maintenance, doesn't it?

TransLease Pro was developed to streamline the process described above as well as provide additional valuable services to the leasing companies. A customer with a problem now can call a central location and be directed to an approved repair garage nearby. The garage can use its internal system to authorize the transaction and then receives payment very rapidly. Vehicle owners, garage operators, and fleet managers are all happy with the improvements in the process created by streamlining the procurement of repairs. By mid-2000, TransLease Pro had nearly 600 000 vehicles in the database (growing by 10 000 per month) and 2400 registered maintenance and repair garages.

TransLease Pro also provides an extensive array of services such as:

- approving garages to carry out work based on experience and basic business requirements;
- analyzing trends and costs for vehicles across multiple companies to allow improved analysis of model/repair information; and
- handling the payment process to dealers, thus reducing the work involved for its customers (the leasing companies).

It seems that TransLease Pro has created a new intermediary in the fleet management and leasing industry, which provides services that satisfy a number of members of the supply chain.

Cap Gemini Ernst & Young
www.businessinnovation.ey.com

Questions

1. Why couldn't the leasing companies use a standard B2B trading exchange to facilitate the processes described here?
2. Are there any concerns for the leasing companies with respect to privacy of data held by TransLease Pro?

SOURCE: www.businessinnovation.ey.com

addition, those exchanges that have gone through the IPO process have high expectations from shareholders. The challenges ahead for B2B exchange providers include integration, profitability, governance, and legal issues.

Integration: Making It Work Early participants in B2B exchanges provided only basic services, such as corporate information on products and contact details.

Exchanges, however, have moved quickly beyond that point and participants now demand the ability to conduct transactions in real time and integrate the data into their own back-end systems. By early 2001 only about 5 percent of companies involved in trading exchanges had achieved full integration of processes with back-end ERP systems.[14] The difficulty is that exchanges may facilitate transactions between companies that use dozens of different back-end systems.

One initiative aiming to make the process of integration a little easier is the **Universal Description, Discovery and Integration (UDDI) initiative**. UDDI is a collaborative effort among three founding companies—Microsoft, IBM, and Ariba—which aims to improve the ability of businesses to carry out electronic transactions with each other. Essentially, UDDI will create a listing of businesses involved in B2B e-commerce and describe in a standardized manner how each business handles electronic transactions. As active participants in the B2B arena, trading exchange providers must get involved in this initiative to provide value-added services to users.

Advances in technology and improvements to existing standards will assist in the process of integration; however, like most areas of technology, complexity also continues to rise. The promise of extensible markup language (XML) to assist in integration was initially hailed as very strong, but unfortunately many of the ERP systems were unable to adequately deal with the language. Other attempts to standardize formats such as EDI have been largely unsuccessful. Exchange enablers like Ariba and Commerce One have established partnerships with leading ERP vendors such as SAP and Oracle in order to address these very issues. Collaboration in the technology area must continue to be developed in order to facilitate B2B integration.

UNIVERSAL DESCRIPTION, DISCOVERY AND INTEGRATION (UDDI) INITIATIVE: a collaborative effort that aims to improve the ability of businesses to carry out electronic transactions with each other.

UDDI
www.uddi.org

Profitability B2B exchange enablers are struggling with issues similar to many of the failed dot-coms—notably, how to charge for services. It is essential that exchange enablers adopt pricing schemes that will allow them to become profitable enough that they can continue to grow and invest in new technologies. An oft-quoted example of an exchange enabler that failed to find an appropriate revenue model is the New York Stock Exchange, which facilitates over US$7 trillion in trades but has revenues of just US$100 million.[15] Similarly, online exchange providers struggle with similar issues—whether fees should be based on per-transaction amounts, dollar amounts traded, or a membership signup fee.

Covisint, for example, began by charging no fees in order to encourage participation, but later changed to a fee per transaction to cover the costs of operating the exchange. Other exchanges tie fees more closely to services offered and utilized by the particular customer. Establishing a pricing model for an exchange is not dissimilar to pricing in any other business—determine what drives costs, estimate costs, evaluate the market, and establish a profitable pricing system.

Governance Trading exchanges run into additional complexity when they attempt to establish policies and procedures to govern their operation. Some of the concerns which may arise include: Who can join the exchange on both buyer and supplier sides? Is data owned by the exchange or individual members? Do members have the ability to demand access to data? Are members restricted in their rights to participate/own other exchanges?

Addressing issues such as those outlined above will vary depending on the format of the exchange. Private exchanges and public exchanges will address these concerns in different manners but each has the same objective—to provide the most value possible to all members of the trading community.

Restricting membership in an exchange may be necessary in either public or private exchanges. As mentioned previously, the exchange may provide a service of supplier accreditation, which effectively limits membership to those suppliers who pass the codes of accreditation established. In other circumstances, however, exchanges will experience pressures from members not to allow competitors to join, in an effort to keep a competitive advantage. Exchanges must clearly document methods by which membership is restricted and enforce policies to achieve consistency and provide a valuable service to members.

Data privacy will be a key concern to all members. Consider the repercussions if DaimlerChrysler were to find out through Covisint that Supplier X had been giving General Motors a better price and higher service levels. In this age of litigation, this situation would likely lead to several costly lawsuits. Privacy of data and details of its ownership must be clearly laid out in the exchange's policies to prevent situations such as those described here.

The rights of members are another area of concern for exchange governance. The Covisint exchange members, for example, are not restricted from using other exchanges but the question of their commitment arises when you consider that several of the founding members also operate their own private exchanges. Private exchanges will need to address the issue of member rights in order to stimulate a community of collaboration where members are not competing directly with the exchange and/or borrowing valuable resources from the exchange itself.

Legal Issues The growth in the size of trading exchanges and the establishment of Covisint has brought attention to legal issues surrounding B2B trading. The sheer magnitude of Covisint sparked the U.S. Department of Justice and Federal Trade Commission to examine the impact of such exchanges on competition and antitrust laws. Covisint was given approval to go ahead based on its policies, which did not strictly limit competition, despite some concerns by suppliers that they would be heavily pressured to reduce prices. Legal issues that could arise are far-reaching and should be carefully considered in advance by exchanges, both public and private.

Auctions

Internet-based auctions have been popularized by the success of eBay.com in developing a model for trading goods between disparate individuals. The development of Internet-based auctions, however, has not been limited to consumer-to-consumer transactions, as businesses have begun to embrace the concept for purchasing and procuring all types of goods. Auctions have been built into trading exchanges as one major method of carrying out transactions and have also been employed by government organizations to conduct commerce online, as discussed in the Merx.ca example earlier in this chapter.

History of Auctions

The Internet has brought attention recently to auctions but they by no means have a short history. Some historical researchers claim that auctions actually date back to 500 B.C., when marriage and slave auctions were carried out. Other auctions are also tied to Ancient Rome around 100 A.D., where auctions took place in the *atrium auctionarium*. Documentation of auctions was limited, and approximately a thousand years passed before information regarding auctions was again written. By the mid-1500s auctions again were documented in France, the Netherlands, and China for slaves, estate auctions, and fine art.[16]

Modern auction giants such as Sotheby's and Christie's were formed in the late 1700s in Britain to sell books, art, and other valuable collectibles. Globalization began to take place in the auction industry in the post-World War II era, as Sotheby's and Christie's expanded internationally with their high-quality and prestigious auctions.

Auctions made their way to the Internet in 1995 when Aucnet, a Japanese company, began selling automobiles at auction. eBay followed closely in September 1995, with its storybook beginnings as a technology to assist the fiancée of Pierre Omidyar (eBay's founder) to sell Pez dispensers over the Internet. During 1999, eBay purchased Butterfield & Butterfield to transform itself into a bricks-and-clicks organization, and Sotheby's formed a joint venture with Amazon.com.[17] By 2001 hundreds of auction sites had begun to replicate and expand upon the model of eBay, including Internet giants like Yahoo! and Amazon.com.

Sotheby's
www.sothebys.com
Christie's
www.christies.com

eBay
www.ebay.com

Types of Auctions

Auctions, both physical and virtual, can take a variety of formats in terms of how the process is conducted and how the winner is determined. The auction format is generally tied to the type of product being sold and the audience where the auction is taking place in an effort to achieve the maximum revenue upon sale of an asset or the lowest price if auctioning for the purchase of products.

A number of different names have been assigned to auction formats, but six types are readily apparent:[18]

1. **English auction.** In the English auction the bidding occurs through an ascending price process when buyers gather in a common location (physical or digital) during specified periods of time. This is the form of auction most would be familiar with as both estate auctions and online auctions.

2. **Yankee auction.** The Yankee auction is similar to an English auction except that multiple items are sold by price, quantity, and earliest bid time. This form of auction can be used by businesses that are buying products where price is not the only factor to consider and quantity available is a key consideration, such as purchasing supplies where a small quantity would be insufficient and would necessitate buying from multiple suppliers.

3. **Dutch auction.** Dutch auctions use a descending price format whereby the auctioneer begins with a high price and buyers can bid on specific quantities of inventory as the price falls. This type of auction can be used for perishable goods or any other type of commodity in which the process is predicted to have good results. The buyers must purchase the goods they wish to obtain before the price falls to a level such that demand rises enough to deplete the inventory.

ENGLISH AUCTION: auction in which the bidding occurs through an ascending price process when buyers gather in a common location (physical or digital) during specified periods of time.

YANKEE AUCTION: auction format similar to an English auction except that multiple items are sold by price, quantity, and earliest bid time. This form of auction can be used by businesses that are buying products where price is not the only factor to consider and quantity available is a key consideration.

DUTCH AUCTION: auction that uses a descending price format, whereby the auctioneer begins with a high price and buyers can bid on specific quantities of inventory as the price falls.

4. **Reverse auction.** Reverse auctions again use a descending price format but in this case the buyer creates the auction to receive bids from potential suppliers. Suppliers must bid lower than the most recent bid in order to gain the sale in this auction-type format, which has been used quite frequently on the Internet through trading exchanges and other formats.

5. **Sealed-bid auction.** The sealed-bid auction is often used for products/services where price is only one consideration to the decision. For example, construction contracts often go through a sealed-bid process, as the buyer will consider capabilities, product quality, timelines, and past experience of the contractor before awarding the contract. Many of the auctions conducted on Merx.ca, which was discussed earlier, use the sealed-bid format.

6. **Vickrey auction.** The Vickrey auction format is an ascending price format in which the highest bidder wins the auction but must pay the price submitted by the second place bidder. The objective of this auction type is to encourage the price upwards by allowing the buyer to pay the next highest price.

A number of variations on these auction types exist where conditions of anonymity, "opting out," and restrictions are used to control the process. A number of studies have been conducted that indicated that the outcomes of many of the auction formats are very similar in nature, with a few minor exceptions.[19]

The most common formats of auctions used on the Internet to date have been English auctions for consumer-to-consumer (C2C) transactions (such as those on eBay) and reverse auctions for B2B transactions (such as those often used at FreeMarkets.com). The English auction format appears to work well in the C2C arena and could also be used in the B2B arena for selected products and services. In addition, governments are being strongly recommended to adopt auction models to become more efficient and effective in carrying out their mandates.[20]

The reverse auction model, as noted above, suits itself particularly well to addressing the needs of buyers looking to procure products and services in a cost-effective manner. FreeMarkets, for instance, assists numerous customers through the reverse auction process and claims to reduce costs—often by as much as 50 percent.[21]

EDS Canada used a reverse auction to acquire contract technical staffing services after first issuing a **request for proposal (RFP)**. The RFP process was used in order to short-list qualified suppliers in terms of qualitative aspects such as service capabilities, experience, and guarantees. Initial requests for pricing information were included in the RFP, but it was made clear to suppliers that pricing details would be dealt with later. In association with eBreviate, the auction provider, EDS provided the six short-listed candidates with information on the auctioning process. In discussing the time involved to carry out the reverse auction, Patricia Moser, Director of Global Purchasing, commented that turnaround time was quite impressive since, "We knew that the bids we were receiving reflected the going market rate for our size and type of organization. Instead of having to go through a research house for this information, we were able to get this information during the auction."[22] EDS Canada was able to successfully carry out the auction and within two months had hired a labour contractor for a two-year

EDS Canada
www.eds.com/canada/

period, using a new purchasing strategy. Previously, this process would have taken up to six months, and would have involved a lot more administrative work.

E-Auction Requirements

In order to successfully carry out online auctions either to sell or acquire products/services, it is necessary to properly plan and administer a process that uses the appropriate technologies. For auctions to be fair to participants, the process requires full disclosure and security procedures, which prevent the "rules of the game" from being broken. In addition, e-auctions must provide the capability to integrate data, notify users of recent information, and process/facilitate payments.

Full Disclosure To function efficiently, auctions must provide participants with all relevant information related to the prospective purchase or sale. In addition to basic descriptions of product/service types and quantity information, it is necessary to provide details of quality levels, warranty programs, transportation agreements, payment terms, and after-sale support mechanisms. In essence, an auction will only work properly when participants are aware of what they are getting involved in. Similar to the "viewing period" in traditional auctions, where buyers are given time to view the items for sale and determine their own preferences, the disclosure of information in an electronic auction will yield better results and create more active participation. Where possible, emerging technologies such as streaming video and collaborative discussions should be used to provide visual support to the disclosure of information.

Integration The use of auctions creates some unique considerations for integration of the auctioning system with the back-end ERP system. For sellers, it is important that the ERP system can be integrated with the auction's front end or auction provider's system to capture details of pricing and shipping information so that the transportation-planning process can be carried out effectively. Buyers also can benefit from integration as details of incoming shipments can be captured, as well as cost information for acquired assets or upcoming expenses.

Notification Mechanisms Auction providers, whether external (such as FreeMarkets) or internal, must develop notification mechanisms that are effective at ensuring that all participants in an auction are up to date at all times. Early auction sites used e-mail extensively for communication, but developments in the area have led to the use of push technologies, which allow the auction server to frequently update clients directly through the Internet browser. Information relating to the current status of the auction can be critical in gaining new business for sellers or cutting costs for buyers, so it is essential that mechanisms are in place to provide details. EDS Canada's first e-auction made use of timed bidding whereby if any bid was placed during the last 10 minutes of the auction time block, a 15-minute extension would be added to ensure that other suppliers had an adequate opportunity to resubmit.

Auction Security Auction security is crucial to ensure that the process is executed appropriately and that hackers are unable to sabotage an auction. In addition, it is necessary to ensure that information that is meant to be confidential is in no way breached or the use of auctions in the future could be compromised. For example, if a product's design and manufacturing details are released to a potential buyer but the auction mechanism inappropriately released the information to a competitor in the auction, the reputation of the auction provider and buyer could be damaged. To prevent mishaps such as this, the auction process will need to use cryptographic techniques similar to other electronic transactions. In addition, the system will need to adequately create audit trails so participants can rely on the technology to conduct the auction according to the rules and award business to the appropriate supplier.

Payment Capabilities The requirement for payment capabilities differs depending on the nature of the auction, the products/services, and the participants (whether B2B or C2C). However, the ability for auction providers to facilitate payments will become increasingly important. Early in the life of eBay, the potential for the business was limited due to the lack of convenient payment mechanisms. The growth of numerous payment schemes for online commerce however (such as PayPal) has allowed eBay to successfully grow and for consumers to sell to one another by paying for goods through online mechanisms. Similarly, B2B transactions with unknown suppliers have been limited by payment mechanisms. Technology advances are helping in this area as well (see Chapter 6), while other services like escrow payments and funds transfer are also helping to make these transactions possible.

The Auctioning Process

Auctions are used extensively in B2B trading exchanges, as discussed earlier, to procure all types of goods and services. The process of conducting an auction online varies depending on the type of auction and the rules adopted, but a basic process is as demonstrated in Figure 8.8.

Auction Configuration The auction initiator (who may be either the buyer or seller) and auction enabler must establish the preliminary requirements for the auction at the beginning of the process. The auction type (English, reverse, etc.) must be decided upon, as well as the details of the products/services involved

Figure 8.8   **The Auctioning Process**

The auctioning process must be carefully executed to be efficient and effective.

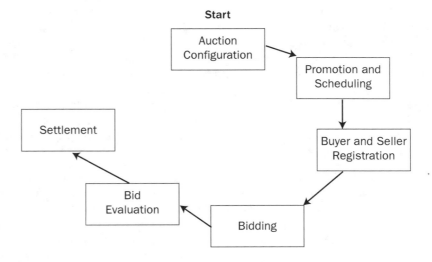

(quantity, quality, etc.). In addition, the configuration will control the timing details of the auction, minimum bid amounts, minimum bid increments, auction closing rules, and other details.

Promotion and Scheduling In coordination with the auction enabler, the initiator will carry out promotion and advertising consistent with the strategy for the auction. This may involve simply notifying a number of potential participants that the initiator is familiar with or an advertising campaign to a broad or targeted audience. This stage of the process may also involve soliciting participants from other exchange or auction providers to expand the number of participants in order to improve the outcome of the auction.

Buyer and Seller Registration In this step of the process, both the buyer(s) and seller(s) must register with the auction provider and deal with such concerns as sharing of cryptographic keys, contact information, and other basic details. At this stage, the process can be either "open" or "by invitation only" depending on the preferences of the initiator of the auction. Participants may be investigated or evaluated at this phase as well to ensure that they meet standards they have claimed (e.g., ISO certification) and to verify credit if necessary.

Bidding The bidding phase of the auction may last for minutes, days, or weeks depending on the parameters outlined at the configuration stage. While this stage is primarily concerned with carrying out the auction and executing the process, it may also include a training element. For example, new participants may be able to use a demonstration to evaluate the bidding process and train members of their firm. There may also be a number of standby mechanisms such as the ability to use fax or voice in the event of bidding process problems. Once the bidding has begun, this stage essentially carries out the details of the configuration by controlling minimum bid increments and notifying participants of changes in auction/bid status.

Bid Evaluation The evaluation of bids may be automatic or may involve human intervention depending on the format of the auction chosen. For example, a reverse auction may automatically notify the "winner" at the end of the bidding time period, whereas a sealed-bid auction would simply notify participants that their information had been received and they would be contacted later. If factors other than price are involved at this stage, the process is complicated; however, alternative methods can be utilized such as pre-screening participants for qualitative factors (as EDS Canada did).

Settlement The final stage of the process involves settlement of contractual terms, payment, and transfer of goods. The ordering and method of carrying out this stage may differ based on a number of factors, but the key is to execute payment and enter a valid contract. This stage may be entirely electronic (besides delivery of tangible goods) or may involve an in-person meeting, again depending on the preferences of the parties involved.

The auction process as described here could take only a few hours in total or could occur over a period of months. The importance of the process outlined is that each of the stages needs to be thoroughly planned and executed, taking into account the auction requirements discussed earlier in order for the process to be successful.

Figure 8.9   An Automotive Metamarket

The consolidation of auctions and B2B exchanges may lead to the creation of metamarkets such as this automotive market.

Fully integrated, informational and transactional marketplace

Automobile Metamarket
- Auto manufacturers
- New car dealers
- Used car dealers
- Newspaper classifieds
- Auto magazine
- Peer and expert opinions
- Financing companies
- Insurance companies
- Mechanics
- Service shops
- Spare parts dealers

The Future of Auctions

DYNAMIC PRICING: the use of market-based, negotiated prices for transactions.

The use of auctions in the procurement and sale of goods is projected to increase dramatically over the next few years. Some pundits go so far as to predict the demise of fixed prices in business, with a move to **dynamic pricing**.[23] Dynamic pricing is the use of market-based, negotiated prices for transactions, which some analysts argue can be easily accomplished through Internet-based auction technologies. While the demise of fixed pricing may be unlikely, the increasing use of auction models for conducting business will continue to occur.

In order to facilitate the improved use of auction models to carry out commerce, the idea of metamarkets and meta-auctions has been discussed. Essentially, a metamarket would result in the linking of all related auctions and markets together to form a large base of participants with common interests. Figure 8.9 provides an example of a metamarket for the automotive industry. The difference between this concept and the concept of industry exchanges is that the metamarket would allow for various exchanges and auctions to integrate all of their participants to achieve a critical mass, which would lead to a more efficient market of "frictionless commerce."[24]

E-procurement, trading exchanges, and auctions will continue to converge and be more easily integrated with back-office technologies over the coming months and years. The creation of metamarkets is an ideal that may be in the distant future, but it gives competitors in this area something to strive for.

Chapter Summary

E-procurement has become one of the major initiatives of e-business in the last few years. Recognizing the potential for reduced administration costs, increased turnaround time, and improved pricing, businesses have begun to embark upon e-procurement initiatives to automate paper processes. The major success factors for e-procurement are the ability of organizations to integrate digital procurement data into the ERP system and the flexibility of the organization to modify existing business processes.

Trading exchanges form an important part of an overall e-procurement strategy. Exchanges provide a medium through which buyers and suppliers can transact business in an efficient manner. Horizontal exchanges are those that target business across numerous industries, such as an office supplies exchange. Vertical exchanges are those that target business within a specific industry throughout the supply chain, such as a healthcare industry exchange. As trading exchanges evolve, they progress towards a medium through which e-procurement, supply chain management, and customer relationship management are conducted.

The growth of the online auction industry sparked by consumer-to-consumer giant eBay has resulted in increased awareness of auctioning applications. The business-to-business community has commenced the use of auctioning techniques in the e-procurement process as an efficient means of executing transactions for many types of goods and services. B2B transactions have commonly been carried out through the use of reverse auctions, and as the industry and technologies develop many of the trading exchanges are facilitating auctioning processes.

The auctioning process employs numerous technologies in order to operate efficiently and effectively. In order that all auction participants are treated fairly, it is essential that auction policies are provided and that bidders are kept up to date throughout the auction period. Auctions in the future are predicted to increase the use of dynamic pricing in business, possibly in both B2B and B2C transactions.

KEY TERMS

e-procurement

maverick buying

vertical trading exchanges

horizontal trading exchanges

private exchange

public exchanges

Universal Description, Discovery and Integration (UDDI) initiative

English auction

Yankee auction

Dutch auction

reverse auction

sealed-bid auction

Vickrey auction

request for proposal (RFP)

dynamic pricing

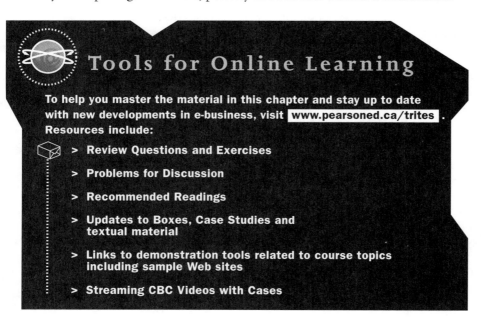

Tools for Online Learning

To help you master the material in this chapter and stay up to date with new developments in e-business, visit www.pearsoned.ca/trites. Resources include:

> Review Questions and Exercises

> Problems for Discussion

> Recommended Readings

> Updates to Boxes, Case Studies and textual material

> Links to demonstration tools related to course topics including sample Web sites

> Streaming CBC Videos with Cases

Endnotes

1. Wilson, Tim, "e-Procurement Revisited—More than Cheap Supplies," *Internetweek*, Manhasset, April 23, 2001.
2. Atkinson, William, "Web ordering, auctions will play limited role," *Purchasing*, April 5, 2001.
3. Gates, Bill, *Business @ the Speed of Thought*, New York, 1999.
4. Ibid.

5. Geriant, John, "Drug company triples cost savings via e-procurement," *Supply Management,* London, March 15, 2001.

6. "e-Procurement savings," *The Controller's Report,* New York, April 2001; *"e-Procurement Saves,"* *Internetweek,* April 2, 2001.

7. Ibid.

8. Gates, Bill, p. 49.

9. "eMarketplaces Boost B2B Trade," Forrester Research, February 2000.

10. Burke, Jon, "The Last Internet Company," *Red Herring,* San Francisco, No. 88, p. 55.

11. www.verticalnet.com/aboutus/.

12. www.covisint.com/home/.

13. Bennett, Jeff, "Covisint becomes corporation: Online parts exchange defies doubters in Europe," *Detroit Free Press,* December 12, 2000.

14. Burke, Jon.

15. Ibid.

16. www.auctionwatch.com/awdaily/features/history/index.html.

17. www.auctionwatch.com/awdaily/features/history/index.html.

18. Wyld, David, "The Auction Model: How the Public Sector Can Leverage the Power of E-Commerce Through Dynamic Pricing," Grant Report, October 2000.

19. Kumar, M., and S. Feldman, "Internet Auctions," IBM Research Division.

20. Wyld, David.

21. Wyld, David.

22. Atkinson, William, "IT firm uses reverse auction for big contract labor buy," *Purchasing,* December 22, 2000.

23. Wyld, David.

24. Sawhney, Mohanbir, "Making New Markets: Sellers Need to Better Understand Buyers to Achieve the Promise of the Net Economy," *Business 2.0,* May 1999.

Customer Relationship Management

learning objectives

When you complete this chapter you should be able to:

1. Describe the concept of customer relationship management and explain its relevance to e-business.

2. Identify the sources of data for CRM and how that data can be turned into information.

3. Outline the goals of CRM and how those goals are accomplished with the use of technology.

4. Name and describe the core Internet-enabled CRM technologies.

5. Describe the process of implementation of CRM.

6. Identify potential problems that may arise during implementation and how those problems can be addressed.

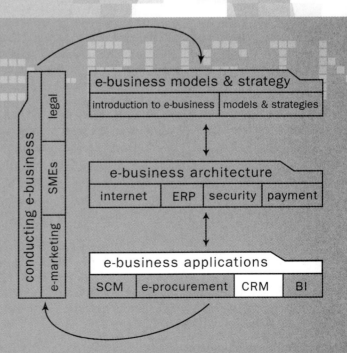

Introduction

Today's business world has begun to adopt the customer-centric approach to strategy that has been recommended by analysts for the past several years. Having gone through a period of cost-reductions and downsizing, businesses must now look to the customer to increase profitability and stock prices. The key to developing these customer relationships is the application of available technologies to better understand, communicate, and develop relationships.

Customer relationship management (CRM) is the use of technologies to establish, develop, maintain, and optimize relationships with customers by focusing on the understanding of needs and desires.[1] By integrating technology, business processes, human resources, and strategies, businesses can focus on CRM to deliver powerful results such as increased sales and decreased costs. With the creation of a single access point, e-businesses can allow customer information to be commonly used throughout the organization to improve the relationship with customers (either businesses or end consumers) at every point of contact.

Canadian Tire Corporation
www.canadiantire.ca

Blue Martini Software
www.bluemartini.com

Customer relationship management has been adopted recently by organizations large and small, online and offline. For example, Canadian Tire Corporation adopted some of Blue Martini Software's (a CRM provider) applications to better serve and interact with customers both online and through its call centre. Online customers are able to benefit from Canadian Tire's loyalty program and Canadian Tire Money, and the company gets to better track and understand its customers' online shopping habits with Blue Martini. In addition, the online store is enabled to customize prices based on the shopper's postal code since prices at each store vary, being established by each store's independent franchise owner. This results in customers seeing prices that correspond with the prices at their local stores. Offline customers who phone the Canadian Tire call centre are better served because customer service representatives (CSRs) are automatically provided with account histories and information on the customer.[2] The application of CRM technologies is helping Canadian Tire retain its leadership in the retail market for automotive, sports, and home products.

CRM may seem to be a relatively simple concept, and in many ways it is; however, successfully carrying out a CRM implementation and developing the appropriate attitudes with employees can be very challenging. Similar to other major technology implementations (such as ERP systems and e-procurement systems), the focus of the implementation needs to be on the business processes. Ensuring that goals remain focused on achieving established strategic objectives rather than on the specifics of the project is essential for a successful implementation. While the concept of focusing on the customer has likely existed since business began, CRM offers a revolutionary means of fully understanding, predicting, and responding to customers and potential customer actions, as we will see in this chapter. See the E-Strategy box for an example of CRM by an online retailer.

The CRM Process

CRM must cut across the organization in order to create a framework that will allow employees of the organization to better fulfill customer needs. The key areas for CRM include marketing, sales, and service. Marketing can use CRM to establish new relationships as well as develop and optimize existing relationships by better understanding questions such as:

E-STRATEGY

eBags Focuses on the Customer

eBags is an online retailer of bags, luggage, and travel accessories based in Denver, Colorado. eBags' management feels that the key to maximizing profitability is understanding the customer and designing advertising campaigns and websites based around their customers' needs.

eBags decided that a customer loyalty program was required to retain existing customers and chose Broadbase e-Marketing for its program. As well as focusing on the loyalty program, eBags is integrating its front-end website and back-end (J.D. Edwards ERP and Oracle database) with Broadbase applications. Other information sources such as e-mail, chat interactions, and telephone conversations are also being captured to allow eBags to better understand customer behaviour.

The president and CEO of eBags, Jon Nordmark, describes the importance of the CRM initiative as follows:

Conversion rates are the best measure of customer satisfaction. Improving those rates means making continuous improvements on click-throughs on emails, getting more browsers to put items in their shopping carts,

and getting more shopping carts all the way to the order desk.

The CRM application allows eBags to more quickly analyze its customers, up to five times as fast as previous analytical tools, which can save the company numerous lost prospective customers.

Once the website redesign and customer analysis techniques were in place, eBags began to employ e-mail marketing and campaign management using its CRM application. By capturing all data related to the campaigns, including response rates, buy rates, and customer analysis, eBags aims to gain 10 to 30 percent on its conversion rates while improving customer service levels—potentially increasing return visits.

eBags has learned a number of important facts about its customers through the use of technology, such as how its e-mail campaigns work. The analysis of data has led eBags to the conclusion that customers are much more likely to buy items placed at the beginning or end of an e-mail ad. This information allows eBags to design more profitable campaigns by placing high-margin items at the beginning and end of e-mail campaign lists.

eBags didn't stand still after successfully employing its CRM application; in fact Nordmark stated that he wanted the company to link its databases and share information extensively with those of its suppliers and partners. Since the eBags system is already automated, Nordmark argues that collaboration is simply the next logical step.

Looking to expand its online presence and brand image, eBags has partnered with notable companies such as Bluetags A/S and United Airlines. The United Airlines partnership provides customers with the opportunity to earn United Mileage Plus bonus miles when shopping through the site, and customers at the United Airlines site can purchase travel necessities through the eBags site. The Bluetags partnership allows eBags the exclusive rights to sell wireless-enabled bags designed by the Danish company throughout North America. The wireless applications, including Bluetooth, allow travellers in equipped airports to track their bag throughout airports by their cell phone or PDA, and the bags can be programmed for routing through baggage, thus reducing lost items.

eBags
www.ebags.com

Questions

1. What possible advantage could eBags see in sharing its CRM data with suppliers and partners?
2. Do partnerships such as the United Airlines one complicate the CRM process and data capture? How?
3. What information might eBags like to be able to track with regards to the Bluetags travel products with wireless technology?

SOURCES: www.ebags.com; www.broadbase.com/casestudy_ebags.html.

- Who are our customers?
- What do these customers really want from us?
- What advertising methods are most effective?
- Which channels are likely to be most successful in gaining repeat business?

UP-SELL: the process of encouraging customers to purchase higher-priced products or services.

CROSS-SELL: the process of encouraging customers to purchase complementary or additional products or services from the firm.

In addition, marketing can better develop and manage campaigns by using centralized customer data, rather than the piecemeal information that was often used in the past. The concept of e-marketing is explored more fully in Chapter 11.

The sales area will benefit from CRM by better providing sales representatives with information that they can use to **up-sell** or **cross-sell** products and services. If a business customer phones a salesperson and the CRM application can automatically provide the customer's purchase history, credit details, and other information, the salesperson may be able to generate more sales dollars than would be possible without the information. If the salesperson can up-sell a customer from a mid-level product to a higher-quality product, sales will increase and the customer ends up with a better product offering—an example of up-selling. The salesperson may also be able to provide customers with information regarding optional equipment that is available or details of how industry participants combine other products to enhance their capabilities—an example of cross-selling. In advanced systems, these selling opportunities may even be scripted (see Figure 9.1 for an example) and provide additional details the customer may wish to know, such as how the product compares to the competition.

The customer service area of many businesses also offers the opportunity to become involved in selling while providing valuable customer service. For example, when a bank customer phones looking for information on current interest rates, a CSR can see that the customer has outstanding credit card debts for the past few months but has a strong credit rating. A scripted discussion may appear on the CSR's screen that guides them through the process of "selling" the customer debt services by consolidating high-interest credit cards into a personal loan. This situation essentially can turn a service-based interaction into a selling opportunity and increasingly organizations will be using techniques similar to this to improve the customer relationship and the bottom line.

Figure 9.1   Siebel Call Center

This illustration of Siebel Call Center application shows selling prompts and other details.

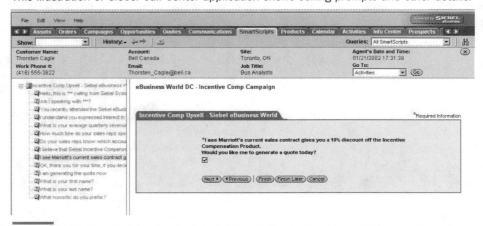

SOURCES: "Call Center Campaign. Products-Solutions." *Siebel*. <http://www.siebel.com>. November 2001. Reproduced with permission.

To better understand the processes and technologies involved in CRM, an illustration of the CRM process will be discussed. Figure 9.2 illustrates the core components of CRM, which include the integration of internal departments, gathering data from all touch points, and utilizing advanced technologies for data capture. Integration of internal processes across the organization must include all potential areas that may impact the customer, directly or indirectly. For example, sales would be an obvious area to include in CRM, but research and development (R&D) is another important integration point. Information on customer feedback needs to be linked to the design process, while information about R&D relating to new products and product improvements needs to be communicated to sales and marketing internally, and selectively to customers—establishing two-way communication through a central medium.

The process of CRM can be described as the capture of data, data analysis, strategic decision making, and implementation (see Figure 9.3).

Data Capture

The first stage, capture of data, occurs from each of the touch points in Figure 9.2 including online sources (web forms and e-mail), offline sources (warranty registration cards), and back-office data integration. Data is stored in a **data warehouse** and will generally be formatted and modified to suit the particular requirements of the organization by removing unnecessary data elements and adding any necessary data descriptions. In some organizations, data from each touch point may be stored in a **data mart** prior to being transferred to the data warehouse.

DATA WAREHOUSE: a central data repository utilized to organize, store, analyze, and report upon data for decision-making purposes.

DATA MART: data repository that is dedicated to specific user groups and is often integrated into the data warehouse.

Figure 9.2   CRM Integration

CRM requires integration of data and access to the application to occur seamlessly across multiple systems.

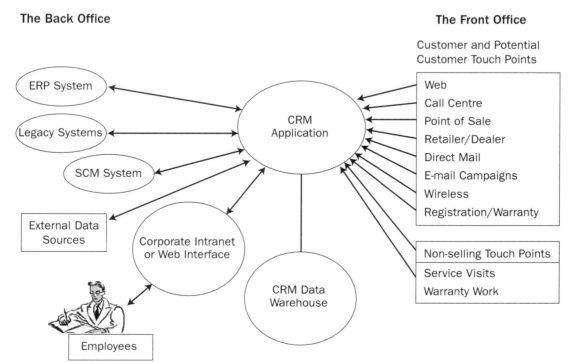

Figure 9.3   The CRM Process

The CRM process is a cycle that begins and ends with the customer touch points.

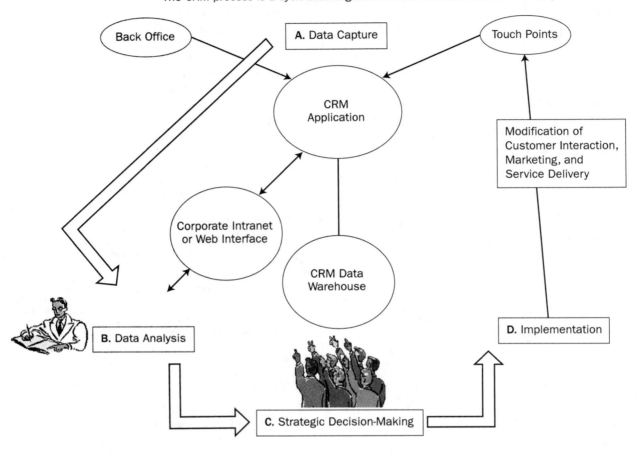

Data Analysis

CRM applications offer a number of tools to analyze and understand customer data. The second step of the CRM process, data analysis, is the use of CRM applications to explore the data to identify relevant customer information. Some organizations refer to this component of CRM as **customer intelligence**. While some predefined settings will assist in identifying trends or alerting management to areas needing attention, the data analysis stage requires customization and the involvement of individuals who have a strong understanding of the business strategy and the industry. Essentially, data will not be turned into relevant information without the application of logic to identify key areas of concern. This analysis may be carried out by any of sales, marketing, service, or other personnel. Collaboration across departments will often lead to discovery of important factors that may not be learned without a team approach.

Strategic Decision-Making

The information identified through the data analysis stage of the CRM process may provide numerous areas where attention and change are needed or possible. These initiatives may all be relevant, but it is critical that the management team take time to review the information and relate planned initiatives to corporate and departmental strategy. Marketing analysis may identify the potential opportunity to sell a new upscale product; however, management's strategic objective may be to focus on cost-effectiveness. Therefore, the opportunity may be dismissed in favour of others such as the delivery of product and service information through electronic media as a cost-reduction measure. In essence, the point of this stage in the process is to narrow the initiatives identified by data analysis to those that most directly relate to current strategic objectives.

Implementation

Once strategic objectives have been clarified, the implementation of change can begin. This may involve change to the method by which information is delivered to customers, modification of marketing campaigns, revisions to the online store, or numerous other possibilities. Implementation, however, is a critical stage in the process where objectives must be clearly understood and outcomes should be predicted. The prediction of outcomes on a measurable basis is optimal so that ongoing evaluation of any process changes can be measured. Cross-departmental teams may be required in some circumstances to effectively implement change, while in other cases implementation may come down to a single group or individual within the organization.

CRM vs. Business Intelligence

While CRM makes use of data warehousing technology and data analysis techniques it is not the same as business intelligence (BI). CRM data may be used within a BI application but would only form one component of the system. As illustrated in Figure 9.4, business intelligence is broader in scope and carries a different focus than CRM. As technologies continue to converge, CRM applications are becoming offerings within BI applications. Business intelligence is examined fully in Chapter 10.

Figure 9.4   CRM and Business Intelligence

CRM overlaps with BI but has a different focus and scope.

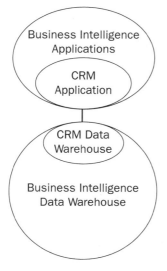

Goals of CRM

The goals of CRM are many and can be organized into a number of key areas, such as marketing, sales, and service. The overall goal of any CRM implementation should be to improve upon customer relationships by providing better service, improved sales efforts, and reduced marketing costs.

Marketing Goals

The goals for CRM in the marketing area are many and in many cases overlap with other areas. Some of the marketing goals include improved marketing planning, sales forecasting, competitor intelligence, trend analysis, and performance analysis. While many of these goals are related specifically to marketing, others are cross-functional due to the integrative nature of CRM.

Sales Goals

In the sales area, CRM strategies aim to improve the sales process by increasing efficiency, improving customer interaction and service, and simplifying the process for salespeople. In addition, the sales goals include the redirection of sales to the most efficient and effective selling channels (e.g., telesales, Internet sales, trading exchanges, etc.).

CRM efforts have developed naturally from some firms' efforts in the area of sales force automation. **Sales force automation (SFA)** is the process of simplifying sales in the field and the integration of sales activity into the corporate information structure.[3] CRM is a much more encompassing strategy than SFA, but the two share some common goals. SFA efforts began with simplistic tools such as contact managers, and later emerged into sophisticated technologies to track leads, integrate databases, and share information with back-end systems. Some of the leading CRM application providers have evolved from being SFA providers in the past.

SALES FORCE AUTOMATION (SFA): the process of simplifying sales in the field and the integration of sales activity into the corporate information structure.

Service Goals

The service areas of businesses pursuing CRM strategies aim to strengthen and develop the customer relationship from the date of original sale. Service departments and CSRs also have the capability through the use of technology to become effective sales contacts by developing an understanding of customer needs. Similar to other areas within the organization, customer service needs to examine its role as a customer touch point and learn which service methods are effective for customer groups. (See the Canadian Snapshot box for a look at customer service goals at Hydro-Québec.)

CRM Metrics

CRM initiatives will aim to gather large volumes of data that may be analyzed to better understand the customer. The large volumes of data, however, will run into storage capacity problems and result in slow analysis if unnecessary data is not purged from the system.

Some of the CRM metrics that should commonly be used for many businesses can be centred on the areas of marketing, sales, and service. Each of these areas can be used to structure the types of outcomes and information that the CRM sys-

CANADIAN SNAPSHOT

Hydro-Québec Improves Customer Service

Hydro-Québec is one of Canada's largest providers of energy, with more than 3.5 million customers throughout North America. With the ensuing deregulation of the energy markets, Hydro-Québec has decided to adopt a proactive strategy in dealing with customer service and relationship management.

Hydro-Québec's vision statement includes the following statement, "Customers are the reason we are in business and we must show them that, at Hydro-Québec, the customer comes first. Whether in Québec or on international markets, we want to satisfy our customers by supplying energy products and services of a quality that meets their needs at competitive prices." While numerous companies may have statements similar to this, Hydro-Québec has taken action by adopting Siebel applications to assist in CRM.

Hydro-Québec adopted Siebel Sales to improve relationships with corporate customers and improve information sharing among sales and service staff. Realizing that

deregulation may bring substantial competition, the company began implementing its CRM strategy with corporate customers who make up a large portion of sales and offer a stronger opportunity for relationship development than residential customers.

Siebel Sales allows company representatives to consolidate and share customer information in a manner that was never before possible. Previous attempts to automate the system based on periodic updates resulted in little success due to missing information and lack of timeliness. The adoption of CRM has allowed employees to work more successfully as a team, and management claims that customer service has been improved with more accurate and up-to-date information available.

Sales contact in the past had been primarily in person, and Hydro-Québec realized that customers were beginning to demand more personalized and timely service. The company plans to improve upon its CRM strategy by adopting additional products from

Siebel, including Siebel eChannel and Siebel Handheld. Siebel eChannel will allow customers to communicate with the company by Internet, e-mail, and cellular channels while continuing to capture data and provide seamless customer service. Siebel Handheld is an application that lends support to sales staff so they may interact with the CRM application anytime, anywhere.

Hydro-Québec's implementation of Siebel applications is being integrated with both the back-end ERP system (Oracle) and the front-end applications, allowing efficient transfer of information. One of the key selling points of the Siebel applications to Hydro-Québec was the integration of French-language support that was well designed and reduced requirements for translation from some other applications.

The benefits of CRM at Hydro-Québec include improved customer service, enhanced information sharing and team selling, faster sales cycles, and an increase in customer retention rates.

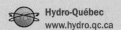
Hydro-Québec
www.hydro.qc.ca

Questions

1. Should deregulation have been the motivator for Hydro-Québec to get involved in CRM?
2. What types of communication are likely to take place through Siebel eChannel with corporate customers? How is this more efficient?
3. Will CRM assist Hydro-Québec in any way to develop relationships with residential customers? How?

SOURCES: www.hydro.qc.ca; www.siebel.com.

tem should be able to provide. An example of some of the specific measurements that may be derived from the data warehouse is demonstrated in Figure 9.5.

The basic metrics for CRM may be programmed as standard reports within the application. While these metrics provide useful information, the most valuable information will often be garnered from custom queries and analysis tied to the company's specific industry and strategic goals.

Figure 9.5   CRM Metrics

Numerous metrics can be useful in measuring the performance of a business in the area of CRM.

Marketing and Sales Metrics
• Customer Segmentation
• Profitability by Customer/ Product/Channel
• Demand Forecasting
• Campaign Analysis
• Channel Effectiveness
• Sales Analysis
• Cost-to-serve
• Revenue Optimization
• Customer Value
• Up-sell and Cross-sell Success
• Customer Churn Analysis

Service Metrics
• Customer Satisfaction
• Customer Complaints
• Product Quality Analysis
• Warranty Cost Analysis
• Service Quality

Internet-Enabled CRM

CRM has become much more powerful with the increasing use of the Internet. Internet technology allows e-businesses to efficiently gather and distribute customer data as well as provide a new medium for communication with customers. Websites were originally used as simplistic marketing tools, but the increasing use of multimedia and other components allows businesses to transmit large volumes of data, provide customer support online, and reach potential customers through a flexible interface.

The data capture process described earlier is simplified by technology that can easily gather data from customers and prospects. Information typed into on-line forms or through e-mail can be automatically moved to the data warehouse through automated tools. While a bricks-and-mortar retail business may never realize that a potential customer was in the store but couldn't find the product they were looking for, online stores can gather valuable data from prospects through click-stream analysis, log-file analysis, and efficient feedback systems (discussed below).

Online Contact Management

Internet-based contacts can be a valuable resource as long as they are not allowed to easily get away without a reasonable sales attempt. A number of methods exist to establish contacts, but gathering information is important in both B2B and B2C e-commerce. While researching this book, one of the authors was contacted by several salespeople after registering online for free demos and product white papers. The CRM systems at these businesses were designed to capture information on prospective buyers based on registration details so that a salesperson could later follow up with the individual, attempting to make the sale. Some studies have indicated that personal follow-up to contacts resulted in a 20 to 37 percent increase in sales. The Internet can be a tremendous means of gathering prospects, but it is necessary to use that information in an effective way—either through e-mail or telephone follow-up.

Online Data Analysis

The completion of business transactions online provides companies with a tremendous opportunity to collect data. Online data analysis is the analysis of data collected through e-commerce transactions and other online technologies. Several forms of online data analysis can be carried out in order to discover important information related to CRM.

Click-Stream Analysis **Click-stream analysis** is a method by which a user's path through a website can be tracked and analyzed. The key here is to analyze the data to identify important trends such as difficulty in finding specific sites or information, searches that yielded no results, or constant "back" movement through the site. By analyzing click-stream data, an e-business can identify website design errors, which can be corrected before other customers run into them. In other circumstances click-stream analysis may be correlated with other factors about the customer, such as demographics or business industry, that may lead to the discovery of trends related to specific target markets. For example, the correlation of user registration data, such as industry type, or other offline information with click-stream analysis may lead an organization to the conclusion that its website is not organized in a manner well suited to particular industries. The site could then be reworked to better suit specific industries or a specialized design could be developed to address this problem. The use of data to identify problem areas and make improvements is another example of CRM in action.

CLICK-STREAM ANALYSIS: a method by which a user's path through a website can be tracked and analyzed.

Cookies Click-stream data is enabled by a number of technologies. **Cookies** are small text files stored by a website on individual computers that allow the site to track the movements of a visitor.[4] Cookies are often added to an individual's computer the first time that a site is visited and can track a great deal of information, such as time spent on a site, passwords, shopping-cart information, preferences, and the most recent site visited. Privacy concerns have often been raised about cookies; however, many people are satisfied that they are not harmful and do not invade privacy. The primary concern over cookies is the fact that they are stored on the user's computer and can potentially provide information regarding other sites visited, preferences, and shopping habits. The use of cookies as an online technology has become standard practice but will continue to evolve as privacy concerns are worked out. The personalization of a website can be accomplished through the use of cookies, which remember your profile and organize the presentation of websites you view. The privacy concerns tend to relate to the use of cookies to analyze your shopping habits and create targeted marketing for you. For example, after searching for several books related to golfing on Chapters.ca, you may notice that the banner ads on the site are for several golf-related products and that featured books the next time you visit the site are golf-related. The personalization of websites by this means can be beneficial to the user but to some is too intrusive to be acceptable. Privacy concerns are considered more fully in Chapter 13.

COOKIES: small text files stored by a website on individual computers that allow the site to track the movements of a visitor.

Log File Analysis **Log files** are another data source that can be used to capture and analyze information online. Log files essentially provide details of site traffic by focusing on the user's IP address and the movements throughout the site. **Log file analysis** can be carried out by a number of means including basic database techniques or advanced Internet-based products such as those offered by WebTrends. See Figure 9.6 for an illustration of a sample WebTrends report.

LOG FILES: data source that can be used to capture and analyze information online.

LOG FILE ANALYSIS: the process of analyzing information with regards to the movements of users throughout a site based upon data captured in server log files.

WEB BUGS (CLEAR GIFS): image files embedded into a web page that can track user movements without the user knowing.

Web Bugs **Web bugs** (also known as **clear GIFs**) are image files embedded into a web page that can track user movements without the user knowing. Essentially, web bugs are clear images or images that blend in with the background of a page you are viewing. The web bug sends information to a server (belonging to the company itself or an advertising firm) each time you request a new page and thus tracks your movements. This allows the analyzing firm to understand your movements throughout the site and is one method of capturing click-stream data.

Any and all of the methods described here (and others) can be used in the data capture stage of the CRM process (discussed earlier) to pull information related to the Internet operation into the CRM application. The analysis of click-stream data within the CRM application will allow for additional variables to be considered, such as the impact of advertising programs on website hits and usage, potential cannibalization of delivery channels, and other factors related to the increasing use of the Internet. As this data can demand very large storage requirements, it is necessary to determine what factors are critical to be stored and to evaluate storage limits carefully when implementing a CRM solution.

Online Marketing Campaigns

CRM analyses should lead to the ability to create targeted online marketing campaigns by better understanding who online customers are, how their needs may differ, and what predictors of buying are relevant. As businesses move to an online sales channel, historic information regarding customer segments and buying patterns may need to be completely re-evaluated. Customers making use of

Figure 9.6   WebTrends Report

This illustration of a WebTrends report analyzes shopping cart activity.

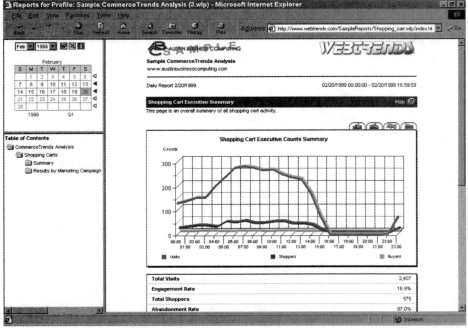

SOURCES: "Shopping Cart Executive Counts Summary." *WebTrends.* <http://www.webtrends.com/ SampleReports/Shopping_cart.wlp/index.html>. November 2001. Reproduced with permission.

Internet technologies for purchasing may have different demographics and new prospects may be found who would not have been identified through traditional campaigns.

E-mail Campaigns The use of e-mail for sales is a controversial but important area for e-businesses to consider. Sending a large volume of general-interest e-mails will likely result in negative attitudes by customers; however, targeted e-mail may be very beneficial. Past customers are known to be those who are most likely to buy again, so e-mail offers to existing customers, if done appropriately, can result in additional sales. Some organizations choose to send e-mails only to those who have agreed to receive information on new offers, known as **permission marketing**. Other businesses send e-mail offers to contacts based on their demographic or CRM analysis and allow customers to opt out of future mailings.

PERMISSION MARKETING: the process of marketing only to potential customers who have agreed to receive information on products, new offers, and sales.

CRM applications such as Siebel Systems include advanced tools for creating, managing, and analyzing e-mail campaigns as described here. To improve upon past experience, it is essential that e-mail campaigns be carefully monitored. Details of sales arising from e-mail campaigns should be integrated with both online and offline sales to evaluate campaign success, and any past analysis techniques should be re-evaluated based on the outcomes.

Real-Time Chat The Internet brings a number of technologies to the table in order to create relationships with customers or potential customers, an important one being the use of chat technologies. A number of service providers are available that can integrate live chat into a website so that a user can ask to chat immediately with a human being. For example, HumanClick.com provides chat applications that sites can use to provide improved customer service (see Figure 9.7).

Chat technologies have been known as a way to waste time online with groups of people with common interests; however, the business applications of this technology are impressive. A potential customer can get information immediately from a sales representative, for instance, rather than having to dial a 1-800 number (potentially having to go offline to do so). Many "browsers" would not go the extra step to phone with a question, but the live chat session makes the inquiry convenient and hassle-free, potentially leading to new business. Existing customers can also utilize real-time chat to be assisted with finding specific product information or to learn about special offers for existing customers.

Advanced technologies also allow chat sessions to be interactive, with the support person actually guiding the user through the Web. A support person can see on their screen what the user is looking at and is able to give detailed advice on where they should be moving. In some applications the support person can actually move the user interactively through the site—effectively taking them to the site they are looking for. These capabilities are allowing businesses to establish stronger relationships by providing customers and prospects with service when they need it.

Voice Over Internet Protocol Similar to the usefulness of real-time chat sessions, Voice over Internet Protocol (VoIP) is an application that can enhance service to customers and prospects. **Voice over Internet Protocol** is the use of an Internet telephony protocol that relays voice signals across the Internet, whether in a computer-to-phone call or a computer-to-computer call. VoIP allows users to phone a customer service representative through the Internet, again by clicking on a "Phone us now" or similar link on a website. As broadband technologies improve, the application of VoIP is likely to increase, allowing users a convenient, low-cost method of connecting with businesses to receive service.

VOICE OVER INTERNET PROTOCOL (VOIP): the use of an Internet telephony protocol that relays voice signals across the Internet, whether in a computer-to-phone call or a computer-to-computer call.

Figure 9.7   Real-Time Chat

Example of a live chat session with HumanClick.com.

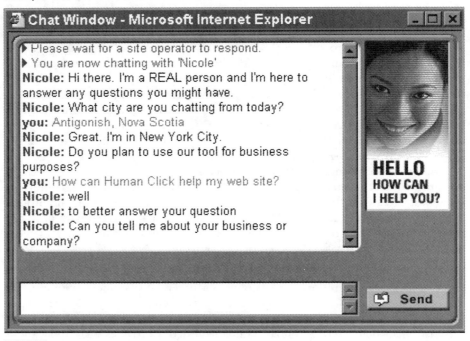

INTELLIGENT AGENT: a program designed to assist users on the Web to carry out tasks such as searching for information or automate tasks.

Intelligent Agents   An **intelligent agent** is a program designed to assist users on the Web to carry out tasks such as searching for information or automate tasks.[5] Intelligent agents are also known as "web bots" or "bots" (from robots). Intelligent agents allow companies to implement tools that can assist users to find products or information throughout their site and may result in automated up-selling and cross-selling of products. If a business customer was examining a supplier's site and had difficulty identifying the specific part required, an intelligent agent could pull information about the customer's existing equipment, past buying patterns, and other details to select web content that may be useful to provide. The intelligent agent may come back with a few options that would work for the customer, including higher-quality products or supplemental items that can be purchased (perhaps at a discount as well). While intelligent agents are still in their infancy, integration with CRM systems and application to many industries is a promising prospect.

E-mail Management   The volume of e-mail requests sent to many organizations with a successful web presence quickly outpaces the capability of individuals to respond. A CRM strategy would imply that e-mail requests be handled in a reasonable period of time, which users and customers are shortening every day. E-mail management technologies are available which can assist in dealing with the mass of e-mails that are sure to come with growth.

E-mail represents one of the many customer/prospect touch points discussed earlier and as such is a form of data that needs to be captured. Leading CRM providers' applications integrate e-mail data into the CRM applications so that call centre staff who later receive contact from a customer can review former correspondence, thus remaining up to date with all business–customer information.

Incoming e-mail can be sorted and redirected to appropriate individuals by applications that seek out keywords in the e-mail and identify those within the organization who can address the concern or question. In addition, many applications can put together draft responses to questions based on pre-defined templates (or FAQs), which employees need only review quickly prior to responding to the customer or prospect. Other features such as auto-acknowledgement of requests, statistical analysis, and standard e-mail system integration are also available.

Customer Self-Service

Another important aspect of Internet-enabled CRM is the ability of customers to "serve themselves," thus reducing costs and simplifying service. Customer self-service may take many forms but is essentially the application of technologies that allow customers to easily identify problems, seek out service information, and in some cases solve their own problems (e.g., software downloads). Technology-based products are particularly well-suited to customer self-service since customers often have employee expertise related to the product and may be happy to identify and solve difficulties on their own. Allowing those customers who are content to service their own concerns to do so also allows the business to focus its time on those customers who wish to have personal (person-to-person) service.

Internet-enabled CRM is an important area of CRM that includes numerous tools and applications to better serve the customer. (See the New Business Models box to see how Eddie Bauer is coping with the vast changes in the CRM area). Ranging from simple tools like e-mail applications to complex integrated systems, Internet-enabled CRM is growing in importance and will continue to develop over the next several years.

Technologies and Integration

Many of the technologies discussed in this book are used to allow CRM applications to operate in an integrated fashion. Businesses are investing heavily in the development of integrated systems and CRM efforts require a number of integration points to be considered. To develop customer relationships, it is necessary to capture, process, and share information across the enterprise, which may originate in the ERP system, the SCM application, within legacy systems, or in external data sources.

The ERP system is the cornerstone source for data within the internal side of the business. For example, all current information related to the customer (such as orders placed, in production, or being shipped) should be up to date within the ERP system. This data needs to be available to the CRM system in order that salespeople or customer service representatives can discuss issues in a current fashion at the various touch points they deal with. The integration of the CRM application and ERP system is critical and its implementation will vary depending on the particular systems employed.

The integration of data from the supply chain will also be important in successful CRM applications. In order that customers can gain access to information regarding expected delivery dates or other factors, the CRM application must be interfaced with the SCM system. Much of the data within the CRM system will

NEW BUSINESS MODELS

CRM at EddieBauer.com

Eddie Bauer is a retailer of casual lifestyle clothing, accessories, and home furnishings, and has over an 80-year history as an excellent service provider. The company had stores around the world and extensive sales through catalogues as the e-business era approached. To maintain its foothold in the retail industry, the company launched eddiebauer.com in 1995 to begin selling many of its products over the Internet.

The traffic on the website increased rapidly and Eddie Bauer began to experience concern over the level of customer service being provided. Customer service representatives began to be overwhelmed by the volume of e-mail questions, and telephone queries related to the website were on the rise—dramatically increasing costs while customer service was getting slower. To combat this problem Eddie Bauer began seeking new technology in hopes of capturing some of the lucrative 1999 holiday season.

Eddie Bauer chose Broadbase Services technology as its provider of CRM applications that could assist in improving online customer service. The initial concern by Eddie Bauer staff was over the e-mail volume that was being handled on a first-come-first-served basis by the CSRs—so an e-mail application was added that sorted the queries based on CSR expertise and forwarded them to the appropriate in-box.

Intelligent agent technology was added to the site as well, and is known as "Ask Eddie for Help" (see Figure 9.8). Ask Eddie is an intelligent agent that can respond immediately to customers seeking self-service by compiling standard responses from FAQs and employee e-mail responses. By 2001, up to 80 percent of the users of Ask Eddie had no further questions, indicating "Eddie" had adequately answered their requests. This resulted in reduced demand on CSRs to respond to routine requests and allowed the e-mail requests to be answered within two hours rather than days.

EddieBauer.com also employs live chat technologies to improve customer service. Chat is available both in the service and sales areas of the site. In service, chat allows the customer to immediately query a knowledgeable CSR without the use of the telephone and while still on the site—potentially increasing the likelihood of purchasing on the site or strengthening the relationship with the customer. In the sales sections of the site, chat is available throughout the purchase process so that nervous buyers can discuss the checkout process with a CSR.

Utilizing Internet-based technologies and CRM applications, Eddie Bauer has now transformed itself from a bricks-and-mortar retailer to a leading bricks-and-clicks retailer. Eddie Bauer has embraced the changes brought forth in the era of e-business and utilized technology to become a leading player in the field.

Eddie Bauer
www.eddiebauer.com

Broadbase
www.broadbase.com

Questions

1. Do you feel the application of technology such as intelligent agents can actually improve the business–customer relationship?
2. Would the company require as many CSRs as in the past? What other roles could those employees take on?
3. Eddie Bauer is an upscale retailer. Does online selling impact that image?

SOURCES: www.broadbase.com; www.eddiebauer.com.

also be useful for SCM processes such as forecasting and demand analysis. In order that the entire value chain operates effectively, it is essential that integration of internal and external data be carried out.

The use of external data sources is one that complicates the process of data integration. As companies aim to integrate across enterprises, the intricacies of each ERP system and other application in the process can create major roadblocks to data sharing. Some of the tools used to overcome these difficulties are discussed in the next section.

Figure 9.8   Ask Eddie for Help

Eddie Bauer's "Ask Eddie" application provides users with customized self-service, thus reducing e-mail and telephone enquiries.

SOURCES: "Customer Service. Ask Eddie for Help." *eddiebauer.com*. <http://www.eddiebauer.com/eb/custserv/ae_splash.asp>. December 2001. Reprinted with permission. All rights reserved. Copyright 1999 eddie Bauer, Inc.

The integration of data must be carried out as a critical component of developing a CRM strategy. Identification of relevant data sources must be followed by developing an understanding of the technologies to be employed and creating data structures that will allow the data to be easily analyzed. The complexity of the data must not be allowed to encroach on the usefulness of the information that can be garnered through analysis.

Implementing CRM

Implementation of CRM is a project that requires planning similar to other major technology projects but also requires managers to deal with a number of implementation concerns. The implementation process may take several months or more than a year to complete and will progress through a number of stages as the "learning curve" is worked through.

Implementation Concerns

A number of implementation concerns related to CRM projects (similar in many ways to ERP projects) can result in failed implementations. It is important when undertaking such an implementation to consider the political, cultural, and technological concerns that are likely to arise as the project progresses. Like ERP implementations, technology is important, but it is critical that business strategies and processes drive the implementation.

Political and Cultural Political and cultural concerns can throw any technology project into trouble as employees struggle with changes in responsibility and processes. Team-based approaches with strong buy-in from management tend to reduce the concerns in this area, but they will still invariably arise. For example, CRM implementation will require various departments such as sales, service, and marketing to review their data requirements, processes, and customer touchpoints in order to plan for the implementation. As these and other topics are considered, the "ownership" of customer touch points is likely to become an issue, necessitating management to deal with the changes that are inherent in developing a true customer-centric approach.

CRM implementation will also require a number of employees to adjust their responsibilities when dealing with customers. For example, customer service representatives may now become responsible for selling products or services, as described earlier in the chapter. This change alone may require the development of new compensation arrangements within the firm, whereby the traditional "salesperson" is no longer the only employee receiving commissions or performance bonuses based on sales. These types of cultural changes are likely to cause a number of difficulties as the CRM strategy is adopted, but can also be valuable learning tools for adept managers who identify means by which customer relationships can be improved throughout the enterprise.

Technological Technological concerns for a CRM implementation project focus on integration with existing technologies and planning for new technologies. As discussed earlier in this chapter, the CRM system needs to be integrated with ERP, SCM, and other applications in order to be an effective tool, and this can create difficulties for information systems departments dealing with numerous other applications. CRM applications vary a great deal in structure as well, ranging from typical client-server approaches to web-based designs.

Many of the linkages required to integrate CRM will be based on enterprise application integration (EAI) tools such as middleware. Middleware is software that allows communication between different systems by reformatting data into a form that can be interpreted by the other system. In addition to middleware, XML has been touted as a language that will simplify the integration of technologies by permitting applications to read and understand the self-described format. Despite the capabilities of middleware, EAI, and XML to allow organizations to integrate systems, some analysts claim that possibly only 10 percent of organizations have achieved integration at a sophisticated level.[6]

Other technology concerns will focus on the integration of the numerous touch points and processes involved in CRM. Customer contacts that occur, for example, at a wholesale outlet or via a website should attempt to gather similar data from the customer and store it within the data warehouse. In addition, call centres need access to integrated customer data that may require the business to adopt computer telephony integration.

Computer telephony integration (CTI) is a technology that allows telephone systems to integrate with computer systems to aid in customer service and data capture. An example of CTI in action would be a customer service request coming in by phone. As the phone system recognizes the caller (through caller identification), the call is redirected to an appropriate CSR within seconds, and information is pulled from the CRM system related to the customer and output to the CSR's computer screen. Without any demands being placed on the CSR, the customer is now ready to be serviced by a knowledgeable employee who has a great deal of information related to the customer. This information can be used

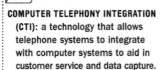

COMPUTER TELEPHONY INTEGRATION (CTI): a technology that allows telephone systems to integrate with computer systems to aid in customer service and data capture.

to provide service and potentially to sell products or services that the customer is likely to buy based on the system's analysis.

Technological concerns will vary in complexity and cost but must be considered in relation to the implementation project's objectives. The critical stages of implementation for technologies include the CRM application selection stage and integration stage. CRM application selection will dictate how the project proceeds and the capabilities of the system for integration. Once again, the use of cross-functional teams at the planning stage is critical to allow the best application to be chosen for the organization.

Implementation Stages

The implementation of CRM will evolve through a number of stages over the term of the project. Some implementations will end up with only basic functionality, while others will evolve into advanced systems that are used extensively throughout the organization. Various methodologies exist but most CRM implementations will progress through the following stages: planning, process redesign, integration, education, analysis, and change implementation. See the E-Business in Global Perspective box for a discussion of the implementation process at National Australia Bank.

Planning The planning phase of CRM adoption and implementation is an important foundation to the entire project. Setting the stage for the remainder of the implementation, planning will address such areas as needs analysis, software selection, project responsibilities, and project timelines. The planning phase may consider some preliminary requirements for process change and will evaluate and have input into the CRM strategy.

The planning process should be carried out by a cross-functional team of employees (and consultants) to establish input from the entire enterprise. As discussed earlier, the team approach will allow concerns of various departments to be raised early in the process and establish a communication process for the implementation. It is important to have consultants involved at the planning process as well so that the project goals and timeline are reviewed for reasonableness. Consultants will also be able to offer important advice as to how departments can plan for the implementation and what process revisions are likely to be required.

Process Redesign Business processes are likely to change as the CRM implementation project moves forward, accommodating technological requirements and revised employee/departmental responsibilities. Process redesign and business process reengineering (BPR) will occur throughout the implementation of CRM and often afterwards as well, but should be planned for early in the implementation process.

Early planning for BPR will allow employees and their departments time to consider the changes and provide feedback on the proposed changes. Some process changes may be dictated by the CRM application that is chosen, but others will be necessitated to achieve the strategic goals of the CRM implementation. Feedback and discussion of the process redesign will allow employees to feel they have input into the process and will often result in suggested improvements that better the overall implementation.

Integration The implementation project's technological aspects will focus on integration of data once the CRM application has been installed. Relating back to

COMPUTER TELEPHONY INTEGRATION (CTI): a technology that allows telephone systems to integrate with computer systems to aid in customer service and data capture.

E-BUSINESS IN GLOBAL PERSPECTIVE

Implementing CRM at National Australia Bank

National Australia Bank Limited (NAB), formed in 1858, is a leader in the employment of CRM. NAB has holdings in Australia, New Zealand, Ireland, United Kingdom, and the United States and has developed a CRM strategy over the past several years that allows it to manage customers globally by segments.

As a large financial institution, NAB may not have been a likely candidate to lead the CRM charge, but it began working on its CRM initiatives in 1988. At that early date, NAB began developing its strategy for CRM and a management and profitability system that would integrate customer-related information. Over the next seven years, NAB continued to develop its CRM systems, expanding to additional product lines and customer categories. By 1999 NAB implemented a complete CRM data warehouse, which linked customer data from Australia, New Zealand, and the U.S., and had begun to identify important information to capitalize on opportunities across a number of countries in its holdings.

During 2000 NAB began a global implementation of a CRM solution to allow it to focus on its "franchise strategy." NAB, unlike many other banks, had organized its holdings to operate primarily as franchises rather than completely independent companies. Each franchise, such as the National Irish Bank, would look after its own regional and country-specific initiatives, but the management of customer segments was done on a global basis using all CRM data.

The franchise strategy approach allowed NAB to enable participation in strategic initiatives by all of the banks it controlled but recognized that customer segments tended to perform in a similar manner globally.

In progressing to the stage where NAB is a progressive manager of CRM data, the company has gone through a series of developments and revisions. The early initiatives focused on learning who customers were and what types of services the customer segments tended to use. Later the company explored the profitability of customer segments and how customer contact and follow-up impacted the likelihood to buy. A number of technologies have been used during the years that CRM strategies were implemented, including NCR's Teradata data warehouse, NCR's Relationship Optimizer, and Siebel's eBusiness Applications.

NAB attempts to approach CRM as both a proactive and a reactive process. The company proactively uses information from its data warehouse to conduct custom campaigns and implement targeted selling strategies. Reactively, NAB looks for customer trends to reduce risk, increase customer loyalty, and attempt to respond to customer concerns in a reasonable manner. For example, a reactive approach may take place after the CRM system notifies an investment advisor that a major customer has accumulated a large deposit balance in the past week, resulting in a sales call that can benefit both NAB and the customer.

While NAB doesn't claim to know all there is to know about CRM, the company has developed an advanced system and a strategic operational approach to focusing on the customer.

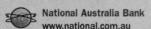

National Australia Bank
www.national.com.au

Questions

1. What customer segments might NAB analyze that are similar in all of its markets?
2. What role should the subsidiary banks (e.g., National Irish Bank) have in the CRM strategy?
3. What other complications do you see in operating a CRM strategy on a global basis?

SOURCES: www.national.com.au; Khirallah, K., "Case Study: Optimizing Relationships at National Australia Bank, Ltd.," Tower Group, January 2001.

---

the goals established at the planning process, the implementation team will work towards integrating any systems required for project success. This integration stage will often continue to evolve as further stages of the implementation take place. Future investments in integration will occur once management and employees buy into the CRM approach and continue to demand further capabilities from the system.

Education The implementation of any new technology will involve a learning curve and an educational process. For CRM implementations, the educational process will involve both technology training and CRM-focused learning. The training required of most employees can be minimized by adopting systems that are web-enabled, allowing basic point-and-click interaction. However, despite ease of use, training for advanced queries and capabilities will be required for those users who will be responsible for aspects of the CRM application beyond basic reporting.

CRM-focused learning sessions should be provided to all employees who will interact with customers in order to implement a common strategy of customer contact. The CRM strategy's goals can only be achieved if employees are aware of the requirements and understand the customer-centric approach being adopted. The learning sessions also serve to inform and educate staff on the process revisions adopted so that customer touch points have common service levels.

Analysis The analysis stage of CRM implementation comes once the implementation has reached a stage where data is collected and the CRM application can begin to provide some information. An interesting analysis of the stages of growth for CRM was written by Ronald Swift, who outlines the stages as reporting, analyzing, and predicting (see Figure 9.9).[7]

The reporting stage of analysis is characterized by the use of pre-configured reports and queries on the data. In this initial phase of implementation, users become familiar with the system by developing an understanding of who the customer is, what products and services sell well in specific areas, and other basic analysis. The reporting phase is primarily historical in focus with the limited use of ad-hoc querying.

The analyzing stage of analysis is a step up from reporting, whereby managers and users begin to ask questions such as why things are occurring. This stage of implementation begins to truly develop a CRM mentality, whereby users question what the causes of specific events and trends have been. Analyzing data may look more specifically at understanding why specific product lines did not meet targets,

Figure 9.9   CRM Application Use Growth

The usage of CRM applications tends to move through the stages of reporting, analyzing, and predicting.

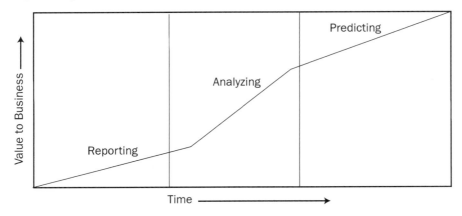

why a marketing campaign was so successful, or other information-discovering questions.

The final stage of the analysis phase of a CRM implementation is the predicting phase in which the business begins to truly capitalize on the CRM initiative by utilizing the data for strategic purposes. In the predicting phase, businesses begin to set marketing strategy, service goals, and modify touch points based on analysis from the CRM system. For example, the marketing and sales departments may perform analysis to identify which customers are most at risk of going to alternative suppliers and carry out proactive relationship measures to retain them. In this phase of CRM implementation, users are very familiar with the system and have developed an appreciation for the value of CRM.

The analysis stage of implementation is one that will progress hand-in-hand with other activities such as education and process redesign. The time that individual businesses will spend at each stage will vary and, despite large investments, those who don't spend adequately on education and change management efforts will never progress to the predicting stage of analysis.

Change Implementation The change implementation stage of CRM implementations is the point at which businesses begin to capitalize on their investments. This will normally occur after the business has been able to reach either the analyzing or predicting phases, described above, and truly understands customers.

At this stage, businesses will focus on efforts such as redesigning processes after successful or unsuccessful efforts have been evaluated. For example, a firm may run an Internet-based advertising campaign based on CRM analysis, which has identified a target group likely to buy through this channel. If this campaign is successful, the firm may continue with this strategy by modifying processes that strengthen and support the use of this channel by specific groups, such as creating specialized websites for their use. This implementation of change should further develop customer relationships by making it easier for them to deal with the company through the channel of their choice.

KEY TERMS

up-sell

cross-sell

data warehouse

data mart

customer intelligence

sales force automation (SFA)

click-stream analysis

cookies

log files

log file analysis

web bugs

clear GIFs

permission marketing

Voice over Internet Protocol

intelligent agent

computer telephony integration (CTI)

Chapter Summary

Customer relationship management (CRM) is the use of technologies to establish, develop, maintain, and optimize relationships with customers by focusing on the understanding of customers' needs and desires.

The key areas for CRM include marketing, sales, and service. The customer service area of many businesses also offers the opportunity to become involved in selling, while providing valuable customer service. The process of CRM can be described as the capture of data, data analysis, strategic decision-making, and implementation.

CRM applications offer a number of tools to analyze and understand customer data. Data analysis is the use of CRM applications to explore the data to identify relevant customer information. Some organizations refer to this component of CRM as customer intelligence.

While CRM makes use of data warehousing technology and data analysis techniques, it is not the same as business intelligence (BI). As technologies continue to converge, CRM applications are becoming offerings within BI applications. The overall goal of any CRM implementation should be to improve upon customer relationships by providing better service, improved sales efforts, and reduced marketing costs.

In the sales area, CRM strategies aim to improve the sales process by increasing efficiency, improving the customer interaction and service, and simplifying the process for salespeople. The service areas of businesses pursuing CRM strategies aim to strengthen and develop the customer relationship from the date of original sale.

Internet technology allows e-businesses to efficiently gather and distribute customer data, as well as provide a new medium for communication with customers. The data capture process described earlier is simplified by technology that can easily gather data from customers and prospects.

Leading CRM providers' applications integrate e-mail data into the CRM applications so that call centre staff who later receive a contact from a customer can review former correspondence and thus remain up to date with all business–customer information. This ability to integrate data to aid in customer service is a major development for companies in both the B2B and B2C arenas.

The critical stages of implementation for technologies include the CRM application selection stage and integration stage. The implementation project's technological aspects will focus on integration of data once the CRM application has been installed. For CRM implementations, the educational process will involve both technology training and CRM-focused learning. In order to implement a common strategy of customer contact, CRM-focused learning sessions should be provided to all employees who will interact with customers.

 Tools for Online Learning

To help you master the material in this chapter and stay up to date with new developments in e-business, visit www.pearsoned.ca/trites. Resources include:

> **Review Questions and Exercises**

> **Problems for Discussion**

> **Recommended Readings**

> **Updates to Boxes, Case Studies and textual material**

> **Links to demonstration tools related to course topics including sample Web sites**

> **Streaming CBC Videos with Cases**

Endnotes

1. Fox, T., and S. Stead, "Customer Relationship Management: Delivering the Benefits," White Paper, *CRM* (UK), 2001.

2. Customer Successes on www.bluemartini.com/.

3. Kalakota, R., and A. Whinston, *Electronic Commerce: A Manager's Guide*. Toronto: Addison Wesley, 1996.

4. Deitel, *e-Commerce and e-Business for Managers*. Toronto: Prentice Hall, 2001.

5. Ibid.

6. Kalakota, R., and M. Robinson, *e-Business 2.0: Roadmap for Success*. Toronto: Addison Wesley, 2001.

7. Swift, R., "The Stages of Growth for CRM and Data Warehousing," *DM Review*, September 2000.

Business Intelligence

learning objectives

When you complete this chapter you should be able to:

1. Explain the importance of business intelligence to business strategy.

2. Compare and contrast how business intelligence and ERP systems handle data.

3. Name and describe the major functions of business intelligence systems.

4. Explain the types of technologies used in business intelligence systems.

5. Discuss the implementation of business intelligence systems and what stages need to be followed.

6. Describe how businesses may use data warehouses and data marts within the business intelligence infrastructure.

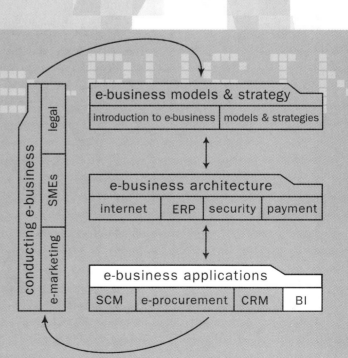

Introduction

Corporations globally are struggling to keep pace in the "information economy," and the rapid growth of the Internet and related technologies is strengthening the demand for data management strategies. Business intelligence (BI) has emerged as a powerful tool that allows businesses to capture, analyze, interpret, and report on data—thus creating valuable information for the enterprise. Massive investments in ERP systems over the past decade have resulted in huge data storage mechanisms. In addition, the deployment of electronic commerce strategies on the Internet results in large volumes of data, such as click-stream information. Business intelligence is the environment that supports analysis of data from any source (internal or external) to provide valuable information for making operating, tactical, or strategic decisions.

The concepts of business intelligence are not entirely new and have emerged from data-mining techniques, decision support systems, data warehousing, knowledge management, and other business tools that have been used for many years. Business intelligence differs from these other tools in that it is a completely integrated approach to data management and has been made possible by advances in technology such as the Internet, ERP, and database systems.

CLEARNET
COMMUNICATIONS INC.
www.clearnet.com

COGNOS INCORPORATED
www.cognos.com

Clearnet Communications Inc., based in Scarborough, Ontario, has adopted BI technology as a means to improve its decision-making in the competitive wireless communication industry in Canada. After examining the offerings of solution providers of business intelligence technology, Clearnet chose Cognos Inc., which is based in Ottawa. Cognos has numerous offerings in the business intelligence market and has developed a global reputation of excellence in the industry. Clearnet's intelligence strategy was to develop a data warehouse that would allow for user-friendly data analysis and reporting while also being powerful enough to allow ad-hoc queries and analysis to be carried out. Clearnet adopted the Cognos Impromptu and PowerPlay products, which met the company's needs and were flexible in their deployment. Using Cognos business intelligence tools, Clearnet can more quickly analyze its business and leverage data.[1]

Business intelligence applications can be closely related to CRM strategies, as discussed in the previous chapter (see Figure 9.4 on page 161), and in many instances the two go hand in hand. For example, Clearnet may use Cognos tools to identify customer segments that are highly profitable and develop strategies to ensure that it retains those customers (a CRM activity). In a similar light, however, a business analyst may use business intelligence applications to identify wireless infrastructure that is most likely to become problematic based on historical data in the system and deploy additional service and upkeep in that area (an operating activity). Essentially, business intelligence can be used any time that an organization wishes to better understand its data to improve decision-making. See the Canadian Snapshots box for a discussion of decision-making capabilities and relationship building with business intelligence technology at the Bank of Montreal.

Business Intelligence Functions

Business intelligence has evolved from previous data management systems such as data warehousing. As businesses struggle to gain a competitive advantage, BI offers the potential to improve decision-making and improve profitability. However, many organizations have recently undergone massive investments in ERP systems, which promised an integrated data environment—leaving many wondering why BI is even necessary.

BI at the Bank of Montreal

The Bank of Montreal (BMO) is one of the largest banks in North America, with over $200 billion in assets and 30 000 employees. During the late 1990s, BMO recognized that its huge IBM DB2 database had excellent potential to provide management with the information they needed to compete in the increasingly competitive financial services industry.

BMO was worried about common bank concerns such as customer attrition, profitability, and risk and wished to utilize business intelligence technology to provide a user-friendly method to better manage key areas. BMO formed an implementation team and selected the MicroStrategy platform to provide the BI functionality from its IBM data warehouse.

BMO's successful implementation resulted in numerous improvements in business analysis, customer service, and risk management. Each day the BI platform performs over 500 queries against the database and provides detailed reports to the appropriate employees. The capabilities in reporting are much greater than previous reporting systems and easily allow users the ability to drill down for further details.

Customer service has been improved in a number of ways. BMO has a separate CRM strategy but utilizes BI information to understand which customers are at risk of leaving the firm, which are most profitable, and similar important analysis. The information gleaned from the BI system allows BMO to proactively work with customers to identify their needs and attempt to reduce attrition. BMO has developed point-of-sale interfaces for its employees that provide them with key customer metrics from the BI application when they are meeting with clients. This custom interface provides the employee with details that previously would have taken hours to research, and allows for easier negotiation of interest rates and terms of service.

Risk analysis is a key factor in the financial services industry but is also a very complex and data-rich area. BMO's BI application has been custom designed to allow executives and high-level users to quickly spot business segments that are approaching or exceeding predefined risk levels by the use of colour-coded symbols. A yellow or red indicator would let the executive know, for example, that a decision made to extend a loan in a Calgary branch has increased the overall credit risk in the Alberta segment to an unacceptable limit. While the executive would not likely override the approval of a specific loan arrangement, the analytical information would allow BMO to actively reduce credit risk in other areas of Alberta to compensate for the overall increase in risk.

The BI application at BMO has provided the opportunity to make improved decisions in multiple areas of the business. In competitive industries such as banking, this information may be the only thing that can help sustain profitability and growth.

Questions

1. Does the BI initiative at BMO give it a competitive advantage?
2. How does Bank of Montreal's BI strategy differ from CRM?
3. What other major types of analysis would BMO likely carry out within the BI application?

SOURCES: MicroStrategy.com; BMO.com.

ERP vs. BI

Enterprise resource planning (ERP) systems promised businesses a single data environment to capture transaction data and integrate all parts of the business. ERP implementations have ranged widely in their successes but in the reporting and analysis area have lacked the ability to satisfy users. A number of important reasons exist as to why ERP systems are not suitable for data analysis, reporting, and decision support—the most important being that ERP was designed as a transaction-based processing system. See the E-Strategy box for an example of how an ERP company is utilizing BI technologies to manage its own company.

E-STRATEGY

Intelligence at J.D. Edwards

J.D. Edwards is one of the world's largest ERP vendors and has developed a strong focus on business intelligence for both its own internal use and for deployment within its enterprise software. After completing its IPO in late 1997, J.D. Edwards began to recognize that the huge volume of data it had accumulated was not being used to its full potential for decision-making. The company reviewed the options available in the intelligence area and chose MicroStrategy's Intelligent E-Business Platform as its internal BI application.

The MicroStrategy product allows J.D. Edwards employees around the globe to analyze data using a simple web interface. David Wilmore, Director of Worldwide Decision Support Services at J.D. Edwards, describes the BI initiative as an online reporting solution for mission-critical information around the globe. Analysts can easily review information such as forecasts and identify areas of concern that may impact budgeting, production, and other plans within the company. Executives are also able to easily review high-level information on investment decisions, profitability, and regional analysis, and then drill-down into that data if they wish to see further details. The ease of use of the solution allowed implementation to be carried out rapidly.

J.D. Edwards's implementation of the initial phase of BI was up and running within two months after the vendor selection had been carried out. The training requirements were limited due to the use of browser-based movement within the system and users' ability to relate the technology to surfing the Internet. The company expected the investment to have a payback period of approximately six months, based on initial estimates, and early indications from its users were that the technology would "save the company millions of dollars by increasing productivity, improving the quality of forecasting, and generating time savings."

The second phase of implementation of BI at J.D. Edwards was to adopt MicroStrategy Broadcaster. Broadcaster will allow users to have important information transmitted to them without request by cellular phone, pager, PDA, e-mail, or fax. The application of BI to information transmittal is expected to further improve management decision-making at J.D. Edwards.

In the summer of 2001, J.D. Edwards announced the launch of J.D. Edwards Business Intelligence, a comprehensive monitoring and analytical reporting system to be used by its customers. The company prides itself on being a leader in the development of software that enables collaborative commerce. The J.D. Edwards BI product, however, is not designed by the company itself—it is actually a MicroStrategy application that has been tied into the ERP application. J.D. Edwards was so satisfied with the products they had been using for a few years that they formed a partnership to provide the functionality within their software for their own customers.

J.D. Edwards has begun the quest of bringing ERP and BI closer together by forming an alliance with one of the leading BI providers. Time will tell how this trend will end, but it is likely to continue for some time.

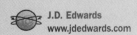

J.D. Edwards
www.jdedwards.com

Questions

1. Does it damage J.D. Edwards's reputation to use another firm's technology for BI when it aims to be a leader in enterprise-wide systems?
2. Why would MicroStrategy wish to allow J.D. Edwards to brand its product and distribute it under a different name? Is this a wise strategy?
3. Do you think J.D. Edwards is likely to gain a large market share in the BI sector? Why or why not?

SOURCES: jdedwards.com; MicroStrategy.com.

ERP transaction systems capture data from the operation of a business into a complex structure of thousands of tables and fields. The structure of ERP is in part dictated by the need to service multiple industries from a single system. The disparate structure of the data results in difficulty attempting to create reports specific to the company, since the data fields need to be selected from numerous tables. In addition, the ERP data structure cannot be "cleaned" to a structure more compatible with reporting, since the transaction system would be impacted.[2] While ERP systems have succeeded in integrating the transactional systems of business, they have been unable to satisfy all of the information needs—leaving a place for business intelligence strategies.

In addition to the complexity of the ERP data structures, the demands on the transaction system also severely limit the reporting capabilities. If you consider a large organization that operates globally, there could be virtually no time during the day when transactions are not being processed. By adding numerous complex queries into the database, analysts could easily hinder the performance of the transaction system. Slow processing time within the transaction system could result in lost sales, data errors, employee frustration, or other difficulties.

Other ERP insufficiencies in the intelligence area include the difficulty in incorporating additional data. Reporting and analysis requirements today reach far beyond the basic debits and credits in the accounting system demanding information on competitors, e-commerce statistics, and supply chain data, which is often not found within the ERP system. It is conceivable that ERP systems could be modified to include other data needs, but due to the reasons already cited, an external data warehouse is a superior solution. Although business changes at a rapid pace, it can be important to carry out analysis over numerous years to identify important trends. Maintaining several years of data within any environment can be difficult, and within ERP, it creates huge storage capabilities that can be reduced by adopting BI. With BI systems the data can be "cleaned" and stored in more efficient formats than possible with ERP.

ERP vendors have recognized the weaknesses of their systems in this regard, and many have begun to address the needs of their customers with new products. For example, SAP has addressed the limitations of its R/3 application in the reporting area with its own data warehousing/business intelligence application, known as SAP Business Warehouse (BW). SAP BW is designed to integrate with R/3 so customers who have not modified the standard ERP system can implement an advanced BI solution relatively easily. SAP has also incorporated SAP BW into its product offering known as Strategic Enterprise Management (SEM), which allows users to integrate ERP data with BW data in a process-oriented and strategic manner for analysis.[3] SEM is intended to replace former Executive Information System reporting, which was limited in capability by the ERP system. In addition to offerings from ERP vendors, numerous business intelligence application providers have created customized interfaces to simplify the data extraction process from ERP systems. For example, Cognos Incorporated has an extraction application designed to simplify the process of gathering data from an SAP R/3 system (see the New Business Models box for an example). Other leading business intelligence providers, such as MicroStrategy, Business Objects, and Brio, have similar applications for various ERP systems as well.

Functions

A number of functions have emerged as business intelligence solutions continue to evolve and business needs for reporting and analysis change. Business intelligence tools should be considered an extension of the power of the ERP system and focus on data integration and organization, data analysis, performance analysis, information dissemination, and collaboration (see Figure 10.1).[4]

NEW BUSINESS MODELS

BI and ERP at NB Power

New Brunswick (NB) Power is the primary supplier of electricity to over 35 0000 customers in the province of New Brunswick. The company is a Crown corporation that generates its power at 15 generating stations using nuclear, thermal, and hydro-electric generation. As the energy industry prepared for deregulation and increased competition in the 1990s, NB Power adopted a proactive technology strategy that would assist the company in remaining competitive.

Similar to other businesses that had long histories, NB Power faced increasing complexity within its IT infrastructure as it continued to grow. The numerous legacy mainframe and mid-range computer systems were difficult to administer and use—thus resulting in a severe backlog in reports. The information systems department was running reports that end-users were unable to do on their own if they couldn't program, and the delay meant waiting from a few days to up to a month to get the information requested.

Realizing that this scenario was unacceptable, NB Power set out to modernize its business and develop a technology platform that could carry it into the new millennium. The company set out to modernize its financial systems and its analysis/reporting capabilities by adopting both an ERP system (SAP R/3) and a data warehousing/BI technology (Cognos Impromptu and PowerPlay).

The data warehousing initiative began prior to the ERP implementation, as the company recognized that much of the legacy data would be required in the system. The software selections did, however, provide the opportunity to simplify future integration since the Cognos applications (Cognos SAP HeadStarts) had the ability to quickly migrate much of the SAP data into the data warehouse.

In addition to internal integration, NB Power's BI initiative has pulled external information deemed important into the system. For example, the data warehouse loads data from the local telephone company in the region to simplify employee work and improve customer service at the company's call centre. Integration of the external data with internal records has improved the efficiency at the call centre dramatically.

The ERP and BI initiatives have placed NB Power among the leading companies in the world. The implementation has improved decision-making, customer service, and even operational planning. The analysis of data has allowed the company to identify areas where power outage risk is higher, based on numerous factors, thus allowing for targeted preventive maintenance to be carried out. This type of information reduces repair costs and improves customer service at the same time.

NB Power has adopted an e-business strategy to lead it from a typical monopoly to an efficient, market-leading organization. When the competition arrives, NB Power plans to be ready.

Questions

1. What benefits would the business intelligence implementation provide to NB Power that would not have been available in the ERP system itself?
2. Why would a Crown corporation with a monopoly over energy in a province be so progressive? Is there a real threat of competition in this industry?
3. How could NB Power expand its e-business strategy to utilize the power of the Internet?

SOURCES: Cognos.com; NBPower.ca.

Data Integration and Organization The business intelligence application performs a key function of integrating and organizing all data considered relevant for managing the enterprise. The sources of data for business intelligence can be numerous, including both internal and external data sources. Internal data sources can include ERP systems, CRM systems, e-procurement systems, legacy systems, and call centres. External data sources may include supply chain partners, industry

Figure 10.1   Business Intelligence Functions

The tools of business intelligence can be categorized into data integration and organization, data analysis, performance analysis, information dissemination, and collaboration.

information regarding competitors, or other external information such as economic indicators (see Figure 10.2). The business intelligence application serves to integrate all of these data sources in a manner optimized for reporting and analysis.

A data warehouse is a central data repository utilized to organize, store, analyze, and report upon data for decision-making purposes. Essentially, a data warehouse is a system that exists outside the **online transaction processing (OLTP)** system or ERP and is dedicated to the analytical aspects of the organization. In some organizations, data warehouses are also divided into smaller, dedicated databases known as data marts. BI solution providers structure their warehousing solutions in a variety of ways, with some focusing on data marts while others focus more specifically on the larger data warehouse.

ONLINE TRANSACTION PROCESSING (OLTP): a program that facilitates and manages transaction-oriented applications, typically for data entry and retrieval transactions across a network.

Figure 10.2   Data Sources for Business Intelligence

Numerous data sources contribute to the BI data warehouse, including internal and external sources.

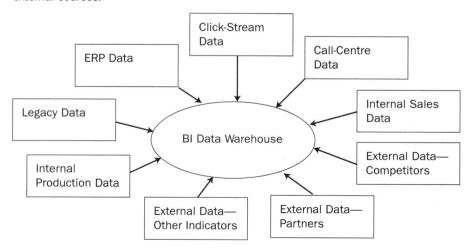

METADATA: a structured definition of data; it is data about data.

EXTRACTION, TRANSFORMATION, AND LOADING (ETL): the process of gathering data from a system, such as an ERP system, which can be simplified and stored within the data warehouse.

DATA CUBES: multidimensional database structures that allow quick drill-down and reformatting of data.

Whether the business intelligence system is based upon a data mart or data warehouse is of little significance when considering the importance of BI. In either case, the data in the system will be structured around metadata. **Metadata** is a structured definition of data—it is data about data. For example, a number of data tables within an ERP system may be consolidated with e-commerce data into a single table when the data is extracted. The extraction process would involve the movement of the data and may also remove unnecessary fields and combine other fields. The changes and combinations of the data may then be described by metadata so that an end-user or data warehouse administrator can better understand where the data has originated and how it has been formed.[5]

The integration of data occurs through a number of methods, as the data warehouse consolidates data from numerous sources. **Extraction, transformation, and loading (ETL)** is the process of gathering data from a system, such as an ERP system, which can be simplified and stored within the data warehouse. Many sources of data will require ETL in order that data from systems such as ERP and legacy can be combined into a common database. The frequency with which ETL will occur within a given organization will depend upon the industry and the type of reporting environment desired. If management wishes to have very up-to-date information ETL could occur daily, while if the reporting is for several past periods, weekly or monthly, extraction may be acceptable. Most e-businesses would require frequent updates of data in order to stay on top of crucial trends and performance indicators necessary to manage the business.

Data Analysis The many users of BI applications in organizations have a great variety of needs in terms of data analysis capabilities. The levels of data analysis may range from basic reporting upon pre-configured data cubes to ad-hoc queries or data mining. Since the demands for data analysis range drastically, it is important that BI applications are flexible and user-friendly. See the E-Business in Global Perspective box for an example of data analysis in a global environment.

Many BI applications make use of **data cubes**, which are multidimensional database structures that allow quick drill-down and reformatting of data. Essentially, a data cube packages data into a cube-like format that has data elements as blocks and data fields within each block (see Figure 10.3). If a user performs an analysis on sales in the Atlantic Canada region, the user would be quickly able to drill down and receive information regarding each province within the region or by sales channel as well. While data cubes are a common format for data warehouses, some critics feel that they lack flexibility and reduce the ability of users to create custom reports. Other more advanced design formats for data warehouses include star and snowflake schemas.

BI allows users to have access to reports and information that previously resided only in the information systems group. By moving the data access directly to users, businesses allow for reduced demands on information systems for routine reporting needs and allow users to more quickly analyze data in the fashion they wish. Information systems staffs can focus their attention on the appropriate hardware, software, and integration issues for which their expertise is required. The types of data analysis and reporting required range from standardized reports through to data mining (see Figure 10.4).[6]

Standard Reports Users will commonly wish to access standard reports such as income statements and inventory lists that may be available within the ERP system as well as the BI system. The data warehouse should provide numerous standard reports for users in order to reduce the need for ad-hoc queries and ERP-based reporting. Many standard reports are provided with purchased busi-

E-BUSINESS IN GLOBAL PERSPECTIVE

Business Intelligence at Monsanto

Monsanto Company is an international company with over 30 000 employees in more than 100 countries. Monsanto operates in the agricultural, pharmaceutical, and food ingredients businesses as a leading biotechnology firm. The diversity of operations and abundance of data led Monsanto to look at business intelligence technologies.

The procurement area at Monsanto operated with disparate systems, and procurement personnel had difficulty consolidating data from each of the operating areas and countries the company operated in. The difficulty of determining, for instance, the volume of purchases from a specific vendor made it difficult to negotiate prices and improve procurement efficiencies. Monsanto decided to begin its BI initiative by adopting

MicroStrategy technology and focusing on improvements in its procurement area.

The Monsanto BI initiative began by building a procurement data warehouse to consolidate and organize the multiple sources of data. The data warehouse was built using Oracle, and MicroStrategy applications were added as the user interface and BI technology to query the Oracle data warehouse.

In addition to reporting functionality, Monsanto was looking for improved decision-making and control with its BI project. The technology succeeded in these areas by allowing procurement professionals to both monitor information for decision-making and control purposes. For example, Monsanto can now identify consolidated purchase volumes from vendors worldwide in order to improve price negotiations

and partnership agreements.

The data also allows procurement professionals to control the processes used by procurement employees to acquire goods in more detail than before. Acquisitions can be summarized and queried by type to identify instances where inappropriate processes have been used, such as purchase order usage for small purchases when a credit card transaction would be more cost-effective.

The BI initiative carried out at Monsanto has been successful to date with the company claiming savings in the millions of dollars. These savings were derived with a focus purely on the procurement area, which indicates that significant additional savings from BI should be possible as the tool is rolled out to other areas within the business.

Questions

1. Was the application of BI to just one area of Monsanto a wise decision? Why?
2. What difficulties might Monsanto encounter as it rolls the BI initiative out to other areas of the business?
3. What specific concerns might arise due to Monsanto's global presence?

SOURCES: MicroStrategy.com; Monsanto.com.

ness intelligence applications. Custom-designed systems will require programmers to create the standard report lists. Standard reports can be considered low value to decision-making, since they tend to lack detail and often necessitate further analysis.

Ad-Hoc Query Ad-hoc query is the ability for users to generate any type of query or report they wish within the system. To carry out ad-hoc queries, users will require sufficient understanding of the data structure and may require additional training with the BI system. The purpose of ad-hoc query is to allow users who have limited understanding of programming languages to create custom reports using the querying capabilities of the BI system.

OLAP Analysis **Online analytical processing (OLAP)** provides the ability for users to perform detailed, summary, or trend analysis on data and allows for drill-

AD-HOC QUERY: the ability for users to generate any type of query or report they wish within the system.

ONLINE ANALYTICAL PROCESSING (OLAP): process that provides the ability for users to perform detailed, summary, or trend analysis on data and allows for drill-down into that data.

Figure 10.3   Illustration of a Data Cube

This illustrates how a data cube may structure data for an Atlantic Canadian company selling via different channels to allow drill-down and data analysis in a structured format.

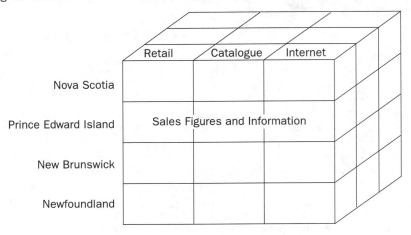

down into that data. Most users will be familiar with drill-down, as it works in a similar manner to the hypertext format of the Internet (in fact, some of the BI providers use HTML as the interface). Figure 10.5 illustrates a drill-down from the overall sales analysis by product category into a more detailed analysis of the electronics product line as an example of OLAP.

Data Mining   Data analysis techniques such as data mining are those that can have drastic impacts on transactional system performance and are, therefore, best suited to BI. **Data mining** is the analysis of data for relationships that may not have previously been known. For example, data mining of sales data at a sports retailer may reveal that customers who buy particular golfing equipment are likely to buy a specific type of hockey equipment in the fall or winter. Discovery of information from data mining can be useful within many areas of the business, from customer analysis to production planning and cost control.

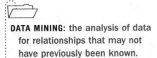

DATA MINING: the analysis of data for relationships that may not have previously been known.

Figure 10.4   Data Analysis and Reporting Methods

The value of BI increases as the complexity of the level of analysis increases beyond standardized reporting.

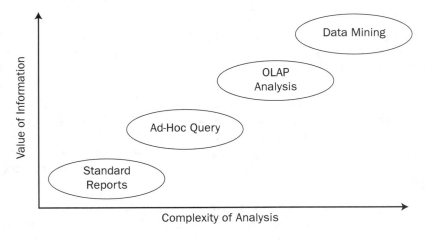

Figure 10.5   Illustration of OLAP

MicroStrategy utilizes HTML reporting and OLAP to enable users to easily drill down through data to identify additional details. Clicking on Electronics brings additional details of the subcomponents of the electronics category.

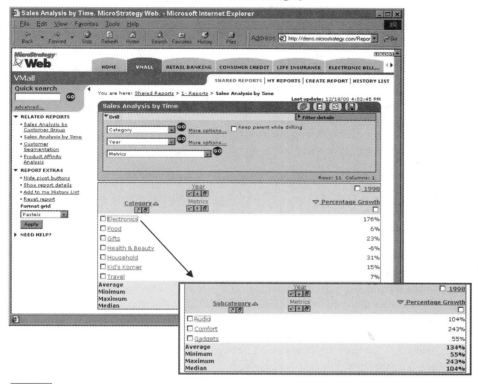

The level of analysis utilized by users will vary with their skill levels both technologically and analytically. While the technology will allow nearly unlimited analysis of data, users need to understand the relevance of reports and output if it is to have any impact on decision-making. For this reason, business analysts within various departments are becoming valuable individuals who can identify important information for management decision-making.

Performance Analysis Performance analysis and monitoring have become important in measuring success as well as evaluating prior decisions in order to improve future decision-making. **Key performance indicators (KPIs)** are important measures that a company measures its performance against in relation to goals, competitors, and the industry. KPIs will vary substantially by industry and firm, depending upon the products or services offered and the corporate strategy. Some common examples of KPIs include market share percentages, revenue growth, and quality deviations. In many cases, the KPIs are linked to a **balanced scorecard**, which is a multidimensional measurement tool aimed to capture performance measures related to accounting/finance, human resources, internal processes, and customers. Robert Kaplan and David Norton developed the balanced scorecard as a means to reduce the limitations of the traditional financial-based performance measures used in business.[7]

KEY PERFORMANCE INDICATORS: important measures that a company measures its performance against in relation to goals, competitors, and the industry.

BALANCED SCORECARD: a multidimensional measurement tool aimed to capture performance measures related to accounting/finance, human resources, internal processes, and customers.

The use of KPIs and/or balanced scorecards for performance measurement and analysis require the capture of large volumes of data. BI and data warehousing technologies aim to capture data for decision-making and performance analysis and, therefore, are well suited to be combined into KPI monitoring or balanced scorecard creation. BI applications can be configured to automatically notify individuals of specific changes in KPIs or other indicators deemed important by management.

Several of the BI and data warehousing vendors have configured their applications to easily support the use of both KPIs and balanced scorecard analysis. SAP's Strategic Enterprise Management suite and Cognos's Visualizer products both use colour-coded information (green, yellow, red) to allow users to quickly identify indicators that are operating within or outside predefined or historical limits. As technology improves, users continue to have additional information at their fingertips for decision-making, and BI provides the perfect environment for performance analysis.

One company that has achieved success in employing BI technology for performance analysis is Grand & Toy. Grand & Toy is the largest office supplies company in Canada and is based in Toronto. Recognizing the need for improved information management at the company, management set out to establish a data warehousing system as they moved away from the use of mainframe technology and standardized reports. Speaking of historical decision-making, the director of marketing commented, "Profitability analysis was based on a combination of dated information, educated guesses, and opinion." The weak reporting system and data was unable to even distinguish retail from commercial sales or easily identify increases in sales attributable to promotions or discount prices.

Grand & Toy
www.grandandtoy.com

Grand & Toy selected Cognos PowerPlay and Cognos Impromptu to build its business intelligence applications. The system was built upon a new data warehouse, and numerous reporting capabilities from standard reports to OLAP analysis are available. The implementation team created customized reports for product profitability analysis and customer analysis that can be monitored easily by the merchandising and sales departments. Analysts can report on products by dimensions such as location, promotion type, stock-keeping unit (SKU), and weekly sales. Customer analysis is similarly powerful.[8] Grand & Toy has recognized gains in both its gross margin on products and overall profitability, which it attributes to improved decision-making based on business intelligence technology.

Information Dissemination Communicating information to users and partners on a timely basis is critical in order to facilitate decision-making at key points in the process. Information dissemination tools are developing which integrate closely with BI applications to carry out this function. For example, MicroStrategy's Narrowcast Server is an application dedicated to delivering the right information to the right user in a personalized format and on a timely basis.[9] The growth in technological tools means that this dissemination of information is now necessary in numerous formats, from e-mail to cellular phones, PDAs, and pagers. Narrowcast Server aims to do just that.

MicroStrategy
www.microstrategy.com

The dissemination of information can be configured to a number of different criteria. For example, a production manager may wish to receive notification of changes in demand above a specified limit over wireless technology so that set-up or other necessary modifications on the shop floor can be planned or commence immediately. Partners of the supply chain may wish to be notified immediately of any changes in production or delivery schedules in order that customers can be updated or orders can be revised to reflect the change in circumstances. The application of intelligence technologies to ongoing operations has limitless potential, as managers increasingly require up-to-date information to make important decisions.

Collaboration   The management of organizations has progressed to the point where focusing on only one enterprise limits the ability to reduce costs and increase sales. Supply chain management, e-procurement, and customer relationship management all require that data and information be shared among members of the entire supply chain. While some of the information to be shared can be facilitated by ERP systems, much information is valuable primarily only for analysis and decision-making by businesses. Business intelligence and data warehousing applications provide businesses with the opportunity to share and collaborate on information useful for decision-making.

During 2001, Home Depot began sharing detailed data with some of its suppliers in an attempt to increase sales and efficiency within the supply chain. Home Depot is marrying information regarding employees, inventory, and sales to allow its major suppliers, such as Georgia-Pacific Corp., to better understand the operations at the shop floor level.[10] This form of collaboration in the analysis and interpretation of data has continued to grow as new technologies simplify the process, and will continue to blossom as the successful outcomes increase profitability.

Collaboration can occur in any aspect of inter-enterprise management and should result in value to all enterprises involved. Retailers and dealers can share detailed information with manufacturers and wholesalers (and vice versa) so that analysis of correlation among variables, such as production costs and rush orders or retail sales trends and manufacturing overtime costs, can be carried out. As businesses learn to embrace collaboration, numerous benefits should be achieved, leading to improved customer satisfaction and supply chain efficiency.

Technologies of BI

To fully appreciate the value of business intelligence applications, it is necessary to give some consideration to the technologies that underlie the user interface. While many vendors have accomplished the goal of simplifying the ease of use of their technologies, it is important to understand the core and enabling technologies employed for the full potential of BI to be obtained. The major technological elements in BI can be described as core technologies, enabling technologies, and solutions.[11] Figure 10.6 illustrates the technological components of a BI architecture.

Core Technologies

Core technologies are those that provide the basic infrastructure for business intelligence. Included in this category are basic networking technologies that facilitate the entire system as well as database management systems (DBMS) and the data warehousing technology. Core technologies create the operating environment within which BI operates and their design and structure will have a significant impact on the success or failure of BI initiatives. In most companies the existing networking infrastructure will be utilized for BI since local area networks (LANs), intranets, or other networking technologies will already be in place.

The use of Internet technologies and protocols such as TCP/IP has significantly reduced the complexity of linking numerous systems. BI implementations

CORE TECHNOLOGIES: those technologies that provide the basic infrastructure for business intelligence.

Figure 10.6   Business Intelligence Architecture

The business intelligence architecture includes core technologies, enabling technologies, and solutions that allow the transformation of data into valuable information for management.

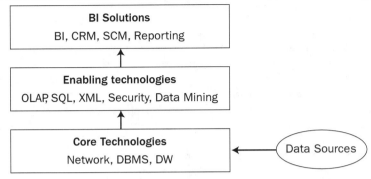

where the application chosen uses an HTML interface (such as the MicroStrategy example provided earlier) can capitalize on Internet technology when dealing with integration issues.

The networking design of a company has substantial impacts on performance in the BI environment as well as the transactional or ERP applications. The number of network servers, their ability to distribute workloads, and overall size of a network are all factors that will impact network performance. Numerous networking technologies such as routers, firewalls, and even operating systems will also need to be evaluated as the deployment of BI and any other corporate applications increase network traffic. The concept of network design and management is a large area and is examined in numerous other texts. The key here is to understand that as a core technology for BI, networking can have dramatic impacts on performance, flexibility, and integration.

The type of core technology chosen for DBMS can vary as well and will be based on numerous factors. The most common form of database is the relational database. A **relational database** is one that uses numerous tables and can relate fields or tables within the database to one another and can easily be reorganized or extended. An example of how a relational database can reduce data duplication can be explained by thinking of a typical sales transaction. A customer order transaction for specific quantity of inventory items could be typed out by an order entry clerk with all fields necessary including date, customer, customer information (address, contact, etc.), purchase order number, inventory items ordered (item number, description, location, etc.), quantities, and numerous other details necessary for an organization to record and track sales. If this same customer were to call again the following day, however, several of the data fields above, such as customer address and inventory descriptions, would be duplicated several times, thus resulting in additional data to store, back up, and manage.

The relational database would reduce this duplication of data by storing different types of data within separate tables and then relating each table to the other in order to identify additional data elements (see Figure 10.7). The order would be entered with a unique order number and date, but the customer information required to be entered is the customer number. The orders table would then relate the customer number to the customer table if additional information is necessary for invoicing, analysis, or reporting. Similarly, an inventory number is entered into the orders table that relates to the inventory table for details of de-

RELATIONAL DATABASE: database that uses numerous tables and can relate fields or tables within the database to one another and can easily be reorganized or extended.

Figure 10.7 Relational Databases

The use of relational databases reduces data redundancy and errors by minimizing duplication and the amount of information that needs to be entered into a system. The database can link to other fields in the customer and inventory tables to get other information necessary, such as price or shipping addresses.

Customer Table

Customer #	Name	Address	Phone	Contact Name
1000	Acme Co	Toronto, ON	416-555-5555	John Summers

Supplier Table

Inventory Code	Description	Manufacturer	Weight	Price
986756	Disk Drive	Seagate	1kg	99.99

Transaction Record

Customer #	Item	Quantity	Date
1000	986756	5	01/01/02

scription, size, weight, and so on. The efficient design and management of a database strategy for BI is crucial to achieving success.

Microsoft Access represents an example of a common relational database you may have seen before. The use of database technologies such as a relational database management system (RDBMS) provides a data warehouse with the flexibility to add additional data sources in the future and redefine the structure of the data if necessary. The data warehouse structure will also be designed so as to reduce the amount of replication of data within the database.

Other forms of databases include distributed databases and objected-oriented programming database systems.

Enabling Technologies

Enabling technologies are those that provide the ability of the BI applications to interact and perform tasks within the core technologies, such as the data warehouse. Some of the key enabling technologies for data warehousing and BI are OLAP, structured query language (SQL), XML, security, messaging/workflow systems, and data mining technologies. The enablers for BI essentially allow either a BI user or a specific BI solution to carry out tasks of reporting, analysis, or modelling within the system.

OLAP (online analytical processing) enables a user to easily and selectively extract and view data from numerous angles and provides the ability for drill-down or drill-up through data. An example of the drill-down capability within OLAP was reviewed earlier in this chapter. The OLAP enabling technology is designed to create ease of use, flexibility, and improved performance in the system by simplifying data structures and organizing standard data elements into data cubes. OLAP applications can require the use of multidimensional as opposed to relational database technology to organize data for analysis. OLAP is carried out in numerous ways by different BI solutions including client-side OLAP, relational OLAP (ROLAP), multidimensional OLAP (MOLAP), and other hybrid forms of the technology.[12]

ENABLING TECHNOLOGIES: technologies that provide the ability of the BI applications to interact and perform tasks within the core technologies, such as the data warehouse.

CLIENT-SIDE OLAP: processing where the data warehouse passes the data from the server to the client machine, where the majority of the processing occurs.

RELATIONAL OLAP (ROLAP): applications that allow multi-dimensional analysis within a relational database. The data processing may take place either at the server, intermediary, or client level.

MULTIDIMENSIONAL OLAP (MOLAP): applications that make use of data cubes to perform analysis on multidimensional databases.

HYBRID OLAP: forms that combine various other formats, such as ROLAP and MOLAP.

Client-side OLAP, also known as "desktop OLAP," is where the data warehouse passes the data from the server to the client machine, where the majority of the processing occurs. Client-side OLAP is useful for laptop users who can effectively move selected information offline for analysis or use and also can reduce server demands for repeated analysis of the same data, such as through drill-down and report reorganization. Both Brio and Business Objects are examples of BI vendors who make use of client-side OLAP.

Relational OLAP (ROLAP) applications allow multidimensional analysis within a relational database. The data processing may take place either at the server, intermediary, or client level. Depending on the networking infrastructure in place, ROLAP can be configured differently, thus allowing for strong flexibility. ROLAP can require larger storage capacity and additional query times due to its use of relational data, but it does have a large capacity. ROLAP is often used in situations where the data changes rapidly or within larger data warehousing environments for analysis purposes, as the ROLAP application can more quickly perform iterative queries than numerous clients could.[13] MicroStrategy's products make use of ROLAP technologies to provide scalable capabilities in the BI marketplace.

Multidimensional OLAP (MOLAP) applications make use of data cubes to perform analysis on multidimensional databases. MOLAP queries can be faster than ROLAP, due to the pre-configured data cubes, if the data is well defined; however, MOLAP runs into scalability difficulties in larger implementations due to its structure. Definition of data cubes and the multidimensional database format are critical stages of creating an efficient MOLAP application. Arbor Essbase and SAS business intelligence applications make use of MOLAP technology.

Hybrid OLAP forms are those that combine various other formats, such as ROLAP and MOLAP. Since ROLAP has strong scalability features and MOLAP has improved performance, it is natural that some vendors have attempted to consolidate the use of the two technologies to get increased benefits. Hybrid applications are more complex in format and development but offer excellent flexibility, scalability, and performance. Microsoft SQL Server 7.0 OLAP Services and IBM DB2 OLAP server are both hybrid applications that provide the benefits described here.

BI Solutions

BI solutions are those technologies that provide the reporting and analysis of data at the client or user end of the process. The focus in this chapter has been on business intelligence applications but, as discussed earlier, the reporting and analysis may take place within other specialized applications as well. Customer relationship and supply chain management technologies may be integrated into or operated separately from the BI application and as such may also share data warehouses or data marts.

The BI solution chosen certainly does not have to be vendor specific. Several companies have adopted products from more than one vendor to suit their particular needs most effectively. Once again, Internet and networking technologies, application programming interfaces, and other technologies can allow numerous systems to be tied together to best accomplish corporate goals.

Implementation

Implementation of a BI initiative requires many common IT project management tools to be employed, as well as numerous BI-specific concepts. The focus of the implementation of BI, similar to ERP, is on business issues and understanding which technological applications can best support the business needs. The basic structure of an implementation will follow a planning phase, architecture design, and execution.

Planning Phase

The planning phase of BI implementation must first focus on establishing reasonable goals for the project and aligning BI goals with corporate goals and strategy. It is essential that this phase clearly identify what areas of concern the BI implementation is attempting to address so that the system is designed appropriately and so that the success of the project can later be determined.

The goals established will assist the project team in defining the scope of the project. As described earlier in this chapter, BI initiatives rely upon data warehouses and data marts. The scope of the project and all implementation phases will be impacted dramatically by the choice of departmentalized data marts versus deployment of a corporate-wide data warehouse. The selection of a major data warehouse does not prohibit the utilization of data marts by departments at a later date, but calls for specific database design and integration tools to be employed. Similarly, the development of a BI initiative that attempts to allow departments to implement data marts that will later be integrated does not prevent the company from developing a corporate-wide BI strategy. This method, however, does require that the individual data mart projects be carried out in unison with strong communication ties so that roadblocks don't develop later (e.g., by using different metadata definitions within each data mart for similar data elements).

The planning phase of BI implementation must also consider specific success factors required for BI. The analysis of industry practices and technological requirements for success will help to prevent the investment of time and money into a project that later needs to be abandoned.

Critical Success Factors for BI In order to be successful, business intelligence applications, similar to other technological tools, must meet a number of requirements. As technologies such as ERP systems, databases, and the Internet continue to evolve, BI will need to keep pace in order to continue providing value to the firm. The critical success factors for BI include ease of use, scalability, flexibility, performance, and security.

Ease of Use The growth in use of the Internet came with the rise of the World Wide Web's graphical interface; similarly, BI technologies will grow in value as they become easier to use. Much of the same data being used in BI applications today has been available for decades, but it was locked within legacy systems. In the mainframe environment, querying data for ad-hoc reports involved a detailed understanding of the data structure within the system, as well as an ability to program in a query language. For these reasons reporting was an expensive task and often took extended periods of time.

Several advances have been made already in improving ease of use of BI tools. The adoption of HTML or web interfaces by many vendors has improved the ability of most users to navigate and find reports. In addition, the use of BI applications drastically reduces the need for programming employees to develop queries into the data. Ad-hoc queries can be carried out by most users with little input from information systems staff, thus reducing costs and time to carry out reporting.

Fannie Mae, the largest financial institution in the world, has adopted data warehousing and BI technologies to allow its employees to more easily create re-

Fannie Mae
www.fanniemae.com

ports. Historical data in the financial industry is critical for long-term analysis, and Fannie Mae maintains large volumes of data back to 1979. In addition to its own data, Fannie Mae stores data from over 70 external sources. In the past, a report requiring access to historical data could take weeks and require several programmers. The mainframe backup system was used to restore data from tapes where programmers would then need to consolidate and query the data to produce the requested reports. Today, Fannie Mae employees can access historical reports directly through their SAS Institute system (a BI provider) within minutes, thus reducing the time for analysis and increasing customer satisfaction.[14]

SAS Institute Inc.
www.sas.com

Ease of use will continue to develop as users request additional functionality and the volume of data increases. The conversion of data from complex ERP systems into data warehouse information supplemented by metadata descriptions will assist users to better understand the reports and data they analyze as systems begin to provide additional help functions. High-level analysis and data mining, however, have limited abilities to become easier. While performing data mining can be simplified by technology, the interpretation and understanding of the results is left to the user.

BI applications have simplified reporting and data analysis through web interfaces and must continue to improve value through ease of use. For example, standard reports must be easy to create and share with other users, tools such as wizards can assist users to build custom reports, and advanced users should be able to share interpretations of data with the user community in a simplistic manner.

Scalability Companies must ensure that the system they implement is extremely scalable. This capability is partially determined by the approaches followed in the implementation phase as well as the configuration of the system, but needs to remain a priority. The volume of data that an organization captures can grow rapidly as the value of BI is realized throughout the enterprise. Scalability and performance are similar and interrelated but not the same. Scalability is the ability of the system to maintain a set rate of performance as the number of users or volume of usage increases.

Many data warehousing/BI projects began to integrate data from ERP and legacy systems. This scenario can result in a relatively predictable volume of data that can be used for reporting and analysis. Once the value of BI is discovered, however, many users will begin to request that additional data from e-commerce transactions, click-stream data, and external sources be captured as well, in order to increase the usefulness of BI for decision-making throughout the firm.

Hardware and software implications must be considered when evaluating the scalability of the BI solution. An obvious hardware issue is hard disk capacity, which can easily reach into the terabytes as data capture grows. In addition, the scalability of hardware performance should be considered as the potential increase in the number of users could bring the speed of the server to a standstill. The hardware selection will likely not be driven by distant future demands on the system, but it is important to be thinking at least a couple of years ahead to avoid wasted capital investments.

Software issues range from operating system selection to BI application selection. As the BI application is chosen, it is important that the entire environment be considered so as to simplify integration and improve compatibility. Other software concerns will include database selection and the use of customized ETL tools. Throughout software evaluation, it is crucial that planned and future demands be considered carefully.

Flexibility The flexibility of the BI system may be put to the test as the adoption of the technology throughout the firm grows. Varying data sources will often place demands on BI applications, and software/hardware selection must consider the needs for flexibility. The number of known data sources at the beginning of implementation will often necessitate specific technology choices, but businesses must plan ahead for potential external sources of data such as web-based data or partner data.

The BI system should also be flexible in allowing multiple data models within large enterprises. Advanced users and data warehousing specialists often disagree on the "best" models to be used for the database design, and flexibility in this regard can be very important. Some data warehouses are constructed so that data is standardized within the warehouse and then data marts are utilized to test alternative models.[15]

Performance Fast and accurate access to information will increase the value and use of BI applications. Hand in hand with scalability design and system selection, performance must be evaluated on an ongoing basis to ensure user satisfaction. Performance can be seriously hindered within a data warehouse by numerous data mining or large-scale analyses. If data mining is to be a common occurrence, policies should be established to control the impact on performance, and alternative system designs should be evaluated.

Performance may also be impacted by the chosen update frequency for the data warehouse. Frequent updates can hinder system performance; however, they result in more up-to-date information. A balance needs to be established in this circumstance.

Data warehouses can be broken down into data marts, as was discussed earlier in the chapter, to provide specific data to divisions or areas within the company. To improve performance of the system as the number of users increase, information systems departments may look to moving highly queried, specialized data into data marts. The performance of the BI system needs to be monitored carefully and is more easily improved if the system is scalable and flexible, as discussed earlier.

Security A data warehouse is designed to allow users to gain information and knowledge from data. However, the presence of confidential data in the system necessitates some level of security to be in place. The security level can range from all users having full access to read, write, and change data records (not reasonable)—to only one "superuser" having complete access to the system (not practical). Within this range, each business will need to evaluate the objectives of its data warehousing/BI strategy and consider the implications of security on the rest of the implementation.

In examining BI objectives, the business must keep in mind that the higher the availability of information should increase the decision-making potential of users. Despite the ease of giving all users access to the data, it is not reasonable to allow a payables clerk to examine the payroll records for the entire company or to "borrow" corporate knowledge for personal gain. As such, the data warehouse needs to be designed with some reasonable security controls over data access to prevent misuse of data.

Consultants in the field of data warehousing have seen significant impacts on performance caused by inappropriately designed security measures. One consultant has observed a 20 to 500 percent increase in query run times.[16] This indicates that although general database design is important, security system design is also important for both authorization and performance purposes.

One of the key decisions in establishing the security framework is deciding whether the security should be built into the business intelligence application or directly into the database (see Figure 10-8). The security design will be impacted by several factors, including the number of users, the number of applications with data access, the operating environment, and others. If ODBC (online database connectivity) is available from the data warehouse, it will be necessary for the security to be built at the database level in order to ensure protection of data access from other connected databases.

Designing security for a data warehouse can be difficult since user access in this environment is much different from the objectives of security in the transactional (ERP) environment. Within the financial environment, the user's role is clearly defined and the requirement for access outside of the functional area is rarely necessary. In the data warehouse environment some users will be limited to the functional area, while others will need the ability to analyze and report upon company-wide data. Numerous security types can be established, but the increase in types leads to increased complexity and upkeep.

In addition to the design of security for employees, it will be necessary to determine what type of access is required for outside users. Some business intelligence proponents argue that sharing specific information with customers, suppliers, and partners has tremendous value from a complete supply chain and relationship perspective. Opponents argue that other methods of overcoming the lack of digital communication can be more successful and less costly. Each organization must decide which approach to information sharing it prefers to take. If outside users will access information, additional security concerns need to be addressed. In most circumstances, outside users will be able to access only information regarding their own relationship with the business. Basic or summarized information regarding supply and demand may also be shared in some organizations. The feeling of many in this regard is that more information leads to better knowledge, which then leads to improved decision-making.

The complexity of security and its potential impact on data warehouse performance suggest that it is not an issue to take lightly. To facilitate implementation in an efficient manner, the security should be designed along with the data warehouse. Building both the security framework and the data warehouse format concurrently may allow for both to occur more efficiently, since database design impacts on security and security impacts database design. Despite the importance of concurrent design of the security and data warehouse, consultants point out that rarely are security issues addressed until later stages of implementation, thus leading to increased complexity, time, and costs.[17]

Figure 10.8   Two Major Approaches to Security in Data Warehousing

Data warehouse security can be established at the application or database level, with the appropriate design depending on many other factors within the organization.

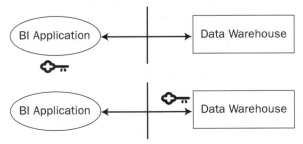

Architecture Design

The design of the system for intelligence applications will be considered at the initial planning phase of the implementation but will need to be revised into achievable project requirements at this stage. Two critical issues to be determined include database design and system architecture.[18]

Database design will be tied in part to the outcomes and analysis methods to be employed. However, the database design will also be closely tied to the vendor applications chosen, meaning that the architecture design stage will be carried out in concert with software selection and consultant recommendations. As discussed previously, the database type and structure can be impacted by the vendor's OLAP type and may also vary if the implementation uses a data warehouse or data mart approach. The design of the database at this phase of implementation also needs to take into account the concerns over security design described earlier.

System architecture is a second critical issue to consider, since the system will impact several of the functions and abilities (flexibility, performance, scalability, etc.). The architecture decisions will also be linked to such factors as software application choice, number of users, hardware selection, and existing corporate infrastructure. One of the considerations to be made at this stage will be whether to use a two-tier or three-tier access design for the data warehouse/data mart (see Figure 10.9). Two-tiered structures are simpler and often less costly, but if the number of users is high, performance can easily be degraded. A three-tier structure allows the servers within the system to balance the load of user requests and is also required for some specific vendor products.

Execution

The execution phase of the intelligence implementation is where numerous common project approaches come into play. Top management commitment needs to exist throughout the project to ensure adequate resources are dedicated and to gain employee buy-in. In addition, a team approach to the entire project is necessary to allow departmental input and evaluation of the project planning and implementation.

Project management techniques should be embraced throughout the implementation so that costs, human resources, and consultants are controlled in a reasonable fashion. Use of project management techniques will assist the project to maintain reasonable timelines and also allow for evaluation of success at critical stages of the implementation.

The implementation of any new technology will also require management to carry out change management. The implementation of BI can create tensions among departments over data ownership issues and user frustration with new applications. Management must ensure that issues of data ownership are addressed to allow the project to be implemented successfully. In addition, the later stages of the implementation should involve strong commitments to training since users will be employing new technologies in their work.

Training will allow users to develop an appreciation for the BI applications and also may provide training in analytical approaches to top-level users. The importance of training is to allow users to truly take the onus of reporting and analysis from the information systems department. Appropriate training will also allow high-level users to understand the impact of data mining and other complex queries on system performance.

During the execution phase of implementation, the business should ensure that it has given consideration to the goals and outcomes defined at the planning

Figure 10.9   Two-Tier and Three-Tier Data Warehouse Structure

Two-tier and three-tier structures for data warehouse design can impact system performance dramatically. The three-tier structure is more easily scaled as the number of users grows.

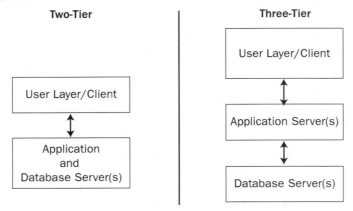

stage. Return on investment (ROI) is a common tool used to evaluate business investments, and many companies have employed ROI as a basis to measure BI implementation success. A study by International Data Corporation found that the overall ROI on data warehousing/BI initiatives among 62 large organizations was 41 percent, with payback periods ranging from two to three years.[19] While ROI is a difficult measure to quantify, it can be used as an overall assessment of the project. Other metrics should also be employed, such as query response time, number of users actively using the system, and analyses of important information discovered to help assess the project's outcomes. Each organization will need to assess the metrics according to their objectives to determine the appropriate mix of financial and operating measures to evaluate.

One organization that has successfully implemented a BI solution and measured its success with primarily non-financial measures is the Vancouver Hospital and Health Services Centre. The Vancouver Hospital is the second largest in Canada and manages over 37 000 acute-care and 81 000 emergency visits per year, in addition to a growing number of surgeries and other medical services. Like other hospitals in Canada, Vancouver Hospital has increasingly found difficulty in keeping up with demand for many of its services, leading to long patient wait times and difficult employee scheduling. Having collected numerous data sources for several years, the Vancouver Hospital began searching for a solution that would allow it to improve its decision-making and patient service. After evaluating their options, the hospital chose Cognos BI as their solution provider to utilize browser-based decision-making and analysis tools.

The implementation utilized a team approach of executives, key users, and consultants to ensure all needs were clearly identified and communicated. The decision was made to utilize data marts rather than a fully integrated data warehouse, since the specific objectives identified did not require full integration within the short term. The solution was built around the parameters outlined at the planning stage, and Vancouver Hospital wished to use metrics such as improved utilization of patient-beds and reductions in wait times for surgery to determine success. In monitoring the overall hospital services, the BI solution employs the balanced scorecard approach to performance measurement. The Vancouver Hospital implementation team has been successful at the initial stages of BI implementation by following logical, business-oriented strategies and working in a team environment.

Chapter Summary

The growth in the knowledge economy has led to the need for a much more sophisticated understanding of business processes, statistics, financial information, and other "information based on data." Business intelligence is the environment that supports analysis of data from any source (internal or external) to provide valuable information for making operating, tactical, or strategic decisions.

The primary enabling technologies of business intelligence systems include both data warehouses and data marts. Data warehouses are repositories of data that have been designed and optimized for analysis and enquiry rather than transaction processing. Data marts are similar to data warehouses but are designed to satisfy the needs of a specific user group within the organization. Implementations of BI applications may make use of both data warehouses and data marts and can take several different forms.

The analysis of data can be carried out in numerous ways with BI systems. Data mining is a common technique used in BI, where the analyst attempts to discover important trends or information within the data. In addition to advanced analysis forms such as data mining, BI can be used to monitor key metrics for the organization—often called key performance indicators. Many organizations also employ BI to gather information to create balanced scorecards, tools that monitor numerous financial and non-financial KPIs important to the industry.

The implementation of a BI system is a complex task requiring sophisticated project management. The design of the system will be driven by the desired outcomes, software applications chosen, data warehouse/mart design, and several other factors. Similar to other technology projects, it is crucial to have management buy-in, team support, and a strong focus on the business processes involved.

The critical success factors for BI include ease of use, scalability, flexibility, performance, and security. In order that the application is useful and meets the objectives established, it is critical that the implementation and software selection carefully consider these factors. The cost and time required for successful BI implementations can be substantial, so it is necessary to put substantial time into the planning process.

KEY TERMS

online transaction processing (OLTP)

metadata

extraction, transformation, and loading

data cubes

ad-hoc query

online analytical processing

data mining

key performance indicators

balanced scorecard

core technologies

relational database

enabling technologies

client-side OLAP

relational OLAP

multidimensional OLAP

hybrid OLAP

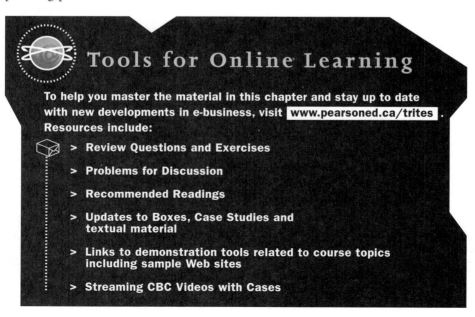

Tools for Online Learning

To help you master the material in this chapter and stay up to date with new developments in e-business, visit www.pearsoned.ca/trites .
Resources include:

> Review Questions and Exercises

> Problems for Discussion

> Recommended Readings

> Updates to Boxes, Case Studies and textual material

> Links to demonstration tools related to course topics including sample Web sites

> Streaming CBC Videos with Cases

Endnotes

1. www.clearnet.com; www.cognos.com.
2. Wyderka, K., "Unlocking Your ERP Data: Business Intelligence for ERP Systems, Part 1," *DM Review,* July 14, 2000.
3. www.sap.com.
4. Kalakota, R. and Robinson, M., *e-Business 2.0: Roadmap for Success.* Toronto: Addison Wesley.
5. Wu, J., "What Is This Data? End User Presentation of Meta Data," *DM Review,* October 2000.
6. Wu, J., "User Requirements for Enterprise Query and Reporting," *DM Review,* April 2000.
7. Oliveira, J., "The balanced scorecard: An integrative approach to performance evaluation," *Healthcare Financial Management,* May 2001.
8. www.cognos.com/company/success/grand&toy.html.
9. www.microstrategy.com.
10. MacDougall, P., "Companies that dare to share information are cashing in on new opportunities," *Information Week,* May 2001.
11. Kalakota, R., and Robinson, M., *e-Business 2.0: Roadmap for Success,* Toronto: Addison Wesley.
12. Ibid.
13. www.whatis.com.
14. Ryan, J., "Cost-Effective Performance, Smarter Decision Support—Alpha Brings it Home to Fannie Mae," Techguide.com.
15. Kelley, C., "Stars and snowflakes: Do you see a snow storm or constellation coming your way?" *Data Warehousing,* February 2001.
16. Silbernagel, C., "Data Security: Protecting the Warehouse from Within," *DM Review,* June 1999.
17. Cunningham, J., "Data Warehousing: A Security Perspective," *DM Review,* November 2000.
18. Love, B. and M. Burwen, "Business Intelligence and Data Warehousing: Crossing the Millennium," Palo Alto Management Group, February 1999.
19. Ryan, J., "A Practical Guide to Getting Started With Data Warehousing," Techguide.com.

E-Marketing and Advertising

learning objectives

When you complete this chapter you should be able to:

1. Understand how e-marketing and online advertising tools fit into the strategy of a business.

2. Explain how the e-marketing process takes place and what components it entails.

3. Describe the types of online research tools that an e-business may use and how they should be used effectively.

4. Discuss the implementation process for an e-marketing strategy.

5. List and describe the major online marketing tools available to e-businesses.

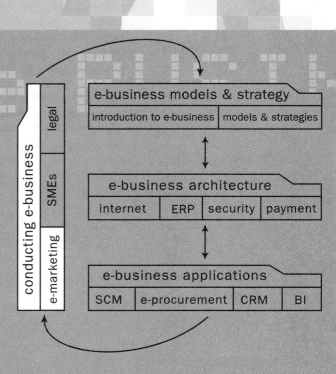

conducting e-business		e-business models & strategy	
legal		introduction to e-business	models & strategies

	e-business architecture			
SMEs	internet	ERP	security	payment

	e-business applications			
e-marketing	SCM	e-procurement	CRM	BI

Introduction

The concept of e-marketing has gone through a rapid cycle of development, from introduction to craze, decline, and stabilization over the past few years. Initially, the promise of global markets, unlimited customers, and improved communication medium led many to the conclusion that Internet marketing and online tools would be the holy grail to businesses pursuing growth. The potential of e-marketing was perhaps misunderstood in these initial stages, and in the recent past the development of the Internet's use for marketing purposes has settled into a more reasonable approach—the Internet represents one important component of an overall marketing strategy.

Ask any individual what five companies they think of when they think of the Internet and you are likely to hear Amazon.com as one of the responses. Why is that? Amazon has developed a successful marketing strategy that incorporates on-line, print, and other advertising methods that have successfully built its brand name as the leading online provider of books, CDs, and many other products. Internet startups like Amazon focused initially on the e-marketing components of their marketing strategy, while competitors like Barnes and Noble stuck to their more traditional markets of bricks and mortar. As the brand recognition of Amazon rose, Barnes and Noble moved towards an online presence with an e-marketing strategy, and Amazon branched out into more traditional media to continue to capitalize on its brand recognition. This example of the development of the online book industry illustrates an important point—whether a company originates as a bricks-and mortar-firm or an Internet startup, e-marketing must form one important component of the business strategy.

E-MARKETING: the utilization of Internet and electronic technologies to assist in the creation, implementation, and evaluation of marketing strategy.

E-marketing is the utilization of Internet and electronic technologies to assist in the creation, implementation, and evaluation of marketing strategy. This chapter will review e-marketing concepts such as online research, Internet advertising technologies, and online consumer behaviour, with reference to the e-marketing strategy process outlined in Figure 11.1. The e-marketing process progresses through a cycle similar to other business initiatives, but may cycle through the process rapidly and numerous times prior to settling on any major strategy. The flexibility of the Internet medium allows for the strategy to be fluid in nature, but numerous changes may be costly and result in poorer than expected performance of future tactics.

Figure 11.1   The E-Marketing Strategy Process

The e-marketing strategy process includes strategy creation, implementation, and evaluation—all within the larger context of overall business strategy.

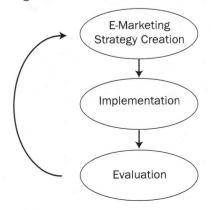

Figure 11.2   The Relationship Between CRM and E-Marketing

The relationship between e-marketing and CRM can be closely related in firms pursuing both strategies, but each is a unique aspect of e-business.

The concept of e-marketing is closely related to customer relationship management (CRM) but is a broader concept that businesses need to consider (see Figure 11.2). CRM and business intelligence (BI) are tools that may be used throughout the e-marketing process. The CRM/BI data may assist in the strategy-creation stage to define a target market, CRM tools may be applied in the implementation stage to provide specific service to customers, and the CRM application may be the tool used to evaluate the success of specific marketing campaigns. CRM and BI applications were discussed in detail in Chapters 9 and 10, and throughout this chapter, areas where the applications hold particular value will be discussed.

Strategy Creation

The creation of an e-marketing strategy will require the use of both traditional and online tools. Similar to any other strategic plan, the development of an e-marketing plan will require the analysis of competition and other environmental factors. One of the major areas of concern at the strategy creation stage will be to evaluate the environment in terms of the legal, ethical, and taxation issues related to the strategy to be devised. These topics are explored in more detail in Chapter 13. In addition, the firm may carry out a market opportunity analysis such as SWOT analysis (strengths, weaknesses, opportunities, threats) in order to identify potential areas of focus. The formulation of the e-marketing strategy must also examine the relationship between the e-marketing strategy and the overall organizational strategy in an attempt to achieve synergies that benefit the business. See the Canadian Snapshots box for an example of an Internet strategy that includes marketing concepts as part of the business model.

The Internet opens up a strong channel for the development of strategy and is a crucial component of successful e-marketing plans. Since the Internet is a developing medium, it is important that firms carefully evaluate their strategies in the context of both traditional customers and online customers. The processes that may be carried out at the strategy creation stage include online research, user behaviour analysis, and advertising planning.

Online Research

The Internet offers a tremendous opportunity to carry out research of use to marketing strategies. An abundance of information is available dealing with demographic

CANADIAN SNAPSHOTS

Discount Brokerage at eNorthern.com

In early 2000 the CEO of Digital Gem Corp. became so frustrated with his online brokerage provider that he decided to start his own. It was this frustration that led to the creation of eNorthern.com, a Canadian provider of online discount brokerage services. The new entrant into the highly competitive market needed to do what many other Internet startups had failed at—attract and retain new customers.

eNorthern describes itself as an online brokerage and financial solutions website that aims to provide a quality service to investors at reasonable rates. The company offers Canadian investors a platform for trading Canadian and U.S. securities, including stocks, options, and mutual funds, in order to satisfy a range of investors from beginner to experienced. While these traits make eNorthern a competitor in the market, they by no means separate them from competitors like eTrade, Datek, TD Waterhouse, and many other online discount brokerages.

The uniqueness of eNorthern's business model is in its approach to reducing the costs of trading—to sell advertising space similar to Amazon and many other online startups. In order to reduce the necessary fees to charge, eNorthern sells advertising space to other e-businesses in a targeted manner based on an understanding of individual preferences, lifestyle, and other information available through the site. This strategy allows the company to provide targeted marketing to users and reduce the fee that users pay to execute trades.

eNorthern has also used some other interesting marketing approaches in an effort to gain customers and build customer loyalty. For example, the company aimed to negotiate a deal with PSInet, a large ISP, to provide free Internet access services to eNorthern users. eNorthern also aimed to create partnerships with financial-planning software makers such as Microsoft's Money. These efforts all led eNorthern to broaden the scope of its offerings while keeping costs under control.

Competitors in the industry, however, are doing many of the same things as eNorthern, and some claim that the number of free giveaways and products won't really help. For example, BayStreetDirect.com's director claims that Canadians seem content to put up with poor service and unfair prices and are, therefore, very difficult to lure away from their traditional service providers. Despite this negativity, eNorthern has gained a small share of the market, and in a *Canadian Business* review of Canada's discount brokers, it scored ahead of many of its competitors in categories such as cost and response time but scored poorly in the telephone service category.

As the financial services industry evolves, eNorthern is also attempting to shed its parent company's history. Digital Gem began as a mining company and attempted to move into the financial services and e-commerce industry through efforts of the CEO, Nadir Desai. In 1999, Digital Gem attempted to sell sapphires over the Internet and then in 2000 it moved into financial services with the creation of eNorthern. The future of this non-traditional financial services company will continue to evolve, but Nadir Desai is happy to be trading through his own company now.

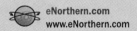

eNorthern.com
www.eNorthern.com

Questions

1. What unique marketing challenges does eNorthern face?
2. How should eNorthern focus its e-marketing efforts? Other marketing?
3. Should the marketing efforts attempt to stay distinct from the Digital Gem past?

SOURCES: Gray, J., "Some Strings are Attached," *Canadian Business*, March 6, 2000; "Trades and Grades: The Best and Worst Discount Brokers Rated by Criteria," *Canadian Business*, October 16, 2000; eNorthern.com.

trends, social and cultural climates, competition, industry statistics, technological innovation, economics, legal data, and political environments.[1] The sources for these types of data are many, and much information can be obtained for free while other information will be fee-based. These data sources are forms of secondary data that are useful in carrying out the environment and market opportunity analyses in the strategy creation stage.

Secondary data is data that has not been developed specifically for the task at hand but may be useful for decision-making. The abundance of secondary data on the Internet provides marketers with information that can be used in crafting a strategy but needs to be used cautiously. For example, the Canadian government's major data centre, Strategis, provides a great deal of information that is from reliable sources such as Statistics Canada. Many of the research firms, such as Forrester Research and Gartner Group, also provide access to some of their research online. However, many other databases and surveys exist online that have been created using unknown and often questionable practices that should not be relied upon without careful review. The key to the use of secondary data is to examine the reliability of the source and ensure that the use of the data within a specific context doesn't reduce its reliability.

The strategy creation stage in most organizations will also lead marketers to gather primary data. **Primary data** is information that is gathered in an effort to better make a specific decision. Typically, primary data will be of a more specific nature than secondary data, and since it is proprietary it will often be more expensive to gather. Many businesses gather primary data on an ongoing basis to assist in evaluation and future planning for their e-marketing strategies. For example, some online retailers ask customers to complete a satisfaction survey after each experience they have with the company. Some of the common methods of gathering primary data online include surveys, experiments, focus groups, and observation.[2] Before examining these data-collection methods, we will look at user behaviour analysis, which is one common analysis type that primary data collection is used for.

User Behaviour Analysis

The understanding of online user behaviour is of extremely high value to organizations whether they sell products and services online or not. The value of understanding user behaviour is the ability to create marketing and advertising strategies that users will find are of value. To better understand user behaviour, companies may be able to rely on secondary data. For example, much research is being carried out regarding the success rates of banner ads in capturing the attention of web users. This type of data may not specifically be designed for a particular company's products but can often be generalized to many different industries. The findings from secondary data analysis may also assist companies in developing the appropriate primary data research tools.

Online user behaviour includes search methods, types of Internet usage, shopping patterns, e-mail usage, and other characteristics. The objective in understanding user behaviours is to be able to improve targeted marketing strategies. If a particular user is very unlikely to buy a product online but commonly seeks information through the Internet, a strategy may be to offer specific discounts for the first online purchase. The key to understanding if this is a valid strategy is to better understand users' behaviour. The use of the techniques described below can assist in developing a user behaviour analysis as well as for other primary data collection.

Surveys Surveys can be conducted online either through the use of e-mail or web-based methods. Early users of online surveys used e-mail extensively; however, the use of e-mail technologies requires the surveyors to develop means of

SECONDARY DATA: data that has not been developed specifically for the task at hand but may be useful for decision-making.

Strategis
www.strategis.gc.ca

PRIMARY DATA: information that is gathered in an effort to better make a specific decision.

capturing the data in a database for analysis, which can be more difficult than with Internet technologies such as forms. Researchers still use e-mail to reach users for their research, but often the e-mail now directs users to a website in order to complete the survey.

The process of collecting data through the Internet is relatively simple with the use of modern technologies. Users simply enter the responses into a survey form, and upon clicking "Submit" the responses can be loaded into a database in the format pre-configured by the data collector. Surveys can be designed and hosted on the Internet using readily available software applications, which significantly reduces the cost of research when compared to postal-based research. In addition, many researchers are finding that the response rates to e-mail and Internet research are very similar to paper surveys.

The use of online surveys allows for significant reductions in time for data collection and analysis. If the data input is automated, the need for data entry and error checking are reduced. Users tend to also respond to e-mail and web-based surveys either very quickly or not at all. The flexibility of design for online surveys also simplifies the completion process for users. Question formats can be customized to responses given in previous questions, and the use of drop-down boxes, radio buttons, and other online tools can make surveys very user-friendly.

Experiments Online experiments are those research methods that attempt to determine a cause-and-effect relationship by exposing participants to different stimuli.[3] The researcher may, for example, ask participants to conduct a search on a particular website and subsequently ask for information regarding the advertising that was on the site. This could lead the researcher to better understand the success of various advertising formats in building brand awareness online. Numerous other types of experiments could be carried out to test website designs, advertising media success, and other characteristics of importance.

Focus Groups The use of online focus groups has emerged with the coming of the Internet as a successful application of the technology. The ability to reach disparate areas at a low cost is one of the major advantages of the Internet for conducting focus groups. Advances in web technologies such as chat, collaboration tools, and browsers allow a focus group leader to carry out effective research at a reasonable cost. Participants in online focus groups can provide feedback based on their analysis of an online presence and are less likely to be influenced by the comments of others.

Critics of online focus groups claim that technology gets in the way of important face-to-face discussion. For many who have conducted focus groups in person, much of the value obtained is the interpretation of actions and facial expressions that often accompany participant feedback. Some critics are also concerned with the ability to confirm the identity of participants; however, advances in technology can overcome this problem relatively easily.

Observation The use of observation in understanding user behaviour online is very valuable. The Internet provides an excellent medium for monitoring user behaviour through such technologies as click-stream analysis. Click-stream analysis, which was discussed in Chapter 9, forms an important component of CRM strategy, as well as website design and e-marketing strategy. The primary importance of observation online is to understand how users navigate websites and then utilize that information to improve the likelihood that users will change their behaviour in a favourable manner, such as staying on the site longer or increasing the likelihood of a purchase.

Market Segmentation   The research process should provide management with the information necessary to segment the market. A **market segment** is a group of customers who share common needs and/or characteristics the selling firm may be able to satisfy. The primary means of segmentation for marketing purposes include demographics, geography, psychographics, and behaviour.[4] Developing an understanding of the market segments that exist will assist the business to identify its target markets and move forward into marketing strategy implementation.

MARKET SEGMENT: a group of customers who share common needs and/or characteristics the selling firm may be able to satisfy.

Many services have been developed to assist businesses in many industries to analyze market segments. The automotive industry is one that relies heavily on demographics, and numerous companies are aiming to lead the demographics analysis segment. DemographicsNow.com has created a large division within its website that provides detailed demographic information as well as geographic breakdowns across vehicle categories.[5] The creation of services such as this provides a wealth of information with which marketers can analyze and predict future sales across numerous markets.

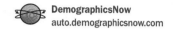

DemographicsNow
auto.demographicsnow.com

Other categories that are used to create market segments are psychographics and behaviour. Increasingly, surveys and research methods aim to gather details about the psychographics of users—such as personality, values, and activities. The understanding of psychographics and online user behaviour, combined with demographic information and geographic analysis, provides the ability to create numerous market segments, which in the past would have taken much more extensive research to gather.

Advertising Planning

One of the major planning components that will take place once the target markets have been identified is advertising and communication planning. Numerous advertising possibilities exist through the Internet, traditional media, and wireless applications, and the business will have to tie the planning to each of the specific target markets identified at this stage. The target markets chosen will impact whether the advertising strategy is mass marketing, niche, or multi-segment—impacting the types of advertising methods to be chosen. Advertising options and technologies are discussed in more detail later in the chapter.

The strategy creation stage should conclude with a comprehensive e-marketing plan. The analysis should have identified proposed budgets and outcome measurements so that the campaign can be analyzed. If the business is involved in CRM, the planning phase will incorporate the marketing strategy and CRM application into the overall plan of action as well. Often the strategy creation stage will necessitate outsourcing to be organized and may also require changes to internal processes as e-marketing and CRM applications are integrated within the enterprise. The e-marketing strategy must be coordinated with all other marketing efforts and evaluated with regard to overall corporate strategy prior to implementation.

Implementation

Implementation of the e-marketing strategy is a stage of both execution and preparation for evaluation. The strategy must be put into place but at the same time e-marketing allows the collection of data to occur during and after the strategy is implemented. Since the e-marketing process can occur rapidly and is flexible in nature, it may be possible for changes to be made during a campaign as well,

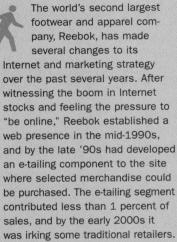

E-BUSINESS IN GLOBAL PERSPECTIVE

Change in the Air at Reebok.com

The world's second largest footwear and apparel company, Reebok, has made several changes to its Internet and marketing strategy over the past several years. After witnessing the boom in Internet stocks and feeling the pressure to "be online," Reebok established a web presence in the mid-1990s, and by the late '90s had developed an e-tailing component to the site where selected merchandise could be purchased. The e-tailing segment contributed less than 1 percent of sales, and by the early 2000s it was irking some traditional retailers.

Recognizing that the potential to the company for online sales was limited and that Reebok's core business was not retail but wholesale, the company set out to revitalize its website along with its new marketing campaign. The new marketing campaign, known as "Defy Convention," was launched in late 2000/early 2001 and traditional media ads included the website URL reebok.com to encourage viewers to visit the site. Following advertising during the Super Bowl and on *Survivor II*, the site saw a one-third increase in visits.

Reebok, however, didn't just use traditional media to drive traffic to the site; it also built the new web presence with the intention to increase loyalty and improve customer service. For example, the website was revised to include not only the ability to search for Reebok retailers within an area but also to find retailers that sell a particular product type. This allows a potential customer to go directly to a store that sells the sneaker line that they are looking for—potentially reducing lost sales. By the end of 2000, Reebok reported an improved market share and increased profitability, and attributes some of the success to the use of an e-marketing strategy within their overall campaign.

Reebok
www.Reebok.com

Questions

1. Why would e-tailing be difficult for Reebok?
2. What other applications could the website hold for Reebok besides providing end consumers with product information and marketing materials?
3. Visit the Reebok site and determine if they have modified their strategy from the one outlined in this scenario.

SOURCES: Lewis, D., "Reebok Defies Convention, and It Pays Off," *Internetweek*, Manhasset, Feb. 19, 2001; www.reebok.com.

based upon preliminary analysis. See the E-Business in Global Perspective box for an example of the flexibility of the Internet in marketing.

The Internet's flexibility allows businesses to move from implementation back to strategy creation relatively quickly. For example, Chapters.ca may decide to reorganize its website, focusing first on the e-business books category, to improve the ease of use and improve its branding effects. After preliminary evaluation however, the company may find that the changes made had reduced the time spent on the site while not improving the purchases-to-visitors ratio. In this case, Chapters may decide to re-evaluate its site revisions and branding strategy prior to moving the new design into other areas of its site. Similarly, organizations conducting promotions through banner ads may decide to abandon banner changes if the click-through rates fall during the campaign.

The implementation of the marketing strategy will focus on a number of interrelated components within each target market. The strategy developed will include plans of action for website design, online advertising, affiliate programs, promotions, partnerships, public relations, and pricing. To examine the complex task of e-marketing implementation, we will examine each of these components below. Keep in mind, however, that the implementation of each of these interrelated components will impact the overall success.

Website Design

The concept of website design has developed very rapidly during the tremendous growth of the Internet from the mid-1990s through to the early 2000s. The basic phases of site design that have occurred to date include the brochureware, interactive, and personalization phases.[6] Early site design was essentially the digitization of existing marketing materials—a phase known as the **brochureware phase** of the Internet. The brochureware phase was the most logical step at the time since it was cost-effective and the true nature of the Internet for commercial purposes was in early development. This phase of site design lasted only briefly for the online innovators who quickly learned that the interactive medium of the Internet offered much more opportunity than simply broadcasting information.

Website innovators began to create sites that were more interactive than early sites and offered two-way communication. Many of the sites in this **interactive phase** began collecting information through online forms and established the ability to conduct e-commerce transactions. The interactive phase of the Internet site design has progressed from simple form-based e-commerce transactions over insecure connections to sophisticated shopping cart transactions over secure networks. Many businesses continue to work within the interactive phase.

The improvement in web programming and site design software, along with a desire to move to "one-to-one" marketing strategies, has led many businesses to the **personalization phase** of the Internet. The personalization of websites allows marketers to tailor the site to the specific wants of the user in an attempt to both improve the chances of making a sale and to improve the relationship with the customer. For example, American Express offers its users the ability to create a My American Express customized page where the user can specify account information, travel preferences, and shopping information (see Figure 11.3). The personalization of websites allows users to see advertising and information closer to their preferences, which increases the likelihood they will stay on a site—known as **site stickiness**. In addition, the personalization allows the business to create more appropriate, targeted ads for the user based on historic transactions combined with preferences.

Personalization has resulted in mixed feedback from users over its adoption by businesses. The key concern over personalization is whether the user can truly control what they see. In many instances the user would prefer to block most advertising and simply focus on information relevant to their Internet usage. However, sites such as My American Express are designed to allow for improved marketing efforts and to increase site stickiness.

Online retailers such as Chapters and Amazon have carried out other personalization efforts. The booksellers have attempted to personalize websites by the use of cookies and user registrations to allow for customized web pages based on users' transaction histories. The difficulty in employing automated tools for personalization is in understanding what preferences truly are. A user who enjoyed reading about golfing and hiking would be happy to see suggestions for reading in this area upon returning to a bookseller's site. However, users complained that booksellers' websites would often tailor the pages with advertising for extended periods of time for items purchased on a one-time event. If, for example, a father

BROCHUREWARE PHASE: an early stage of the Internet's development where commercial enterprises primarily put existing marketing brochures in digital format.

INTERACTIVE PHASE: stage of the Internet's development when websites began to allow two-way communication through e-mail and web forms.

PERSONALIZATION PHASE: stage in the Internet's development when sites began to develop one-to-one marketing techniques through the use of cookies and other tracking tools.

SITE STICKINESS: term to describe the amount of time and likelihood that users will stay on a particular website.

Figure 11.3   My American Express Page

My American Express allows users to personalize a site in order to improve marketing success.

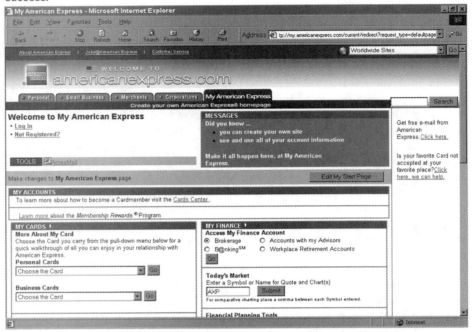

purchased a child's friend a Pokémon book for a birthday gift and was inundated with ads for related products for months afterwards, neither the retailer nor consumer would benefit.[7] Personalization offers the potential to improve marketing efforts but must be used carefully.

Domain Names

The Internet offers the opportunity for businesses to adopt and use domain names in numerous formats. The growth in e-commerce and Internet startups, however, has led to the registration of many domain names. The primary domain name extensions of *.com*, *.net*, and *.org* had limited availability and additional extensions (e.g., *.shop*) have been proposed to increase the ability of organizations to select names related to their business.

The selection of a domain name may not seem to be the most critical area of e-marketing but, as with product naming decisions, can be very important to branding. The first domain names to be taken tended to be those with a short descriptor and the *.com* extension (e.g., Buy.com) to aid in ease of recall. Numerous domain names have been acquired by businesses after the value of their "brand" was recognized for substantial sums. For example, the Business.com domain was purchased for US$7 million to capitalize on the easy-to-remember name. Many factors must be considered when looking into domain name usage, such as competing names, spelling errors, and anti-company sites.

The use of a domain name that is also held by other businesses or Internet users with different extensions can be a risky endeavour. For example, a politician in Nova Scotia registered a domain of his own name with the *.net* extension prior to an election. He was soon embarrassed to discover that the *.com* extension with the same domain name where many constituents ended up in error was a self-promoting porn star—not exactly the kind of publicity he was looking for. Several businesses have run into difficulties with similar scenarios, and for this reason it is often important to register more than one name and attempt to control other similar names.

The ease of registering domain names results in the ability of individuals to capture potentially valuable sites—a practice known as **cybersquatting**. This concept has become problematic and its legality is addressed in Chapter 13. Despite the potential legal means of getting domain names back, many businesses have planned ahead for misspellings and anti-business sites. Encylopaedia Britannica, for example, owns britannica.com (properly spelled) but also owns britanica.com and brittannica.com (spelling errors), along with several other variations. The registration of multiple domain names should always be considered when misspellings are likely. In addition to misspellings, some businesses have taken proactive measures to register various "___sucks.com" domains and other anti-business sites that may damage the brand image on the Web.

Many aspects of website design are based on demographic, cultural, and technological considerations. The nuances of multimedia design, fonts, colour schemes, templates, and other website design issues all need to be considered in order to portray an image of professionalism and encourage users to stay at the site for lengthy periods of time. In order to more fully address these concerns, the complementary website to this book provides additional information on website design.

> **CYBERSQUATTING:** registering of domain names with the intention to use the name for financial gain without legal rights to its use.

Search Engines

One of the major means of driving traffic to a website is through search engine registration. The usage of search engines to identify sites of interest is one of the primary means that users find sites that they are not already familiar with; therefore, being registered with the engines is critical if a website is to be found. In addition to being listed, it is important that sites also show up high on the list of search results—a fact that requires different tactics with many of the different search engines.

Online Advertising

The evolution of website design and online technologies has led to tremendous improvements in the capabilities for online advertising. The understanding that online media is unique and, therefore, requires innovative approaches has led to the development of creative new means to capture attention, create brand strength, and modify payment methods in the advertising area. In this section the common forms of online advertising including banners, interstitials, Superstitials, interactive tools, e-mail, and multimedia are discussed.

Banners Banner advertising has been in existence on the Internet for several years and has grown and changed over time. The first banner ad on the Web appeared on the HotWired site in 1994. Banner ads are graphical images, which may include interactive applications that appear on websites to attract users to click-through to other websites or sections of the present website. Buttons are very similar to banners and are used on the Internet in a similar fashion. Businesses can

Figure 11.4 Illustration of Banner Advertising

The Canada.com website includes examples of both banner ads and buttons in its advertising.

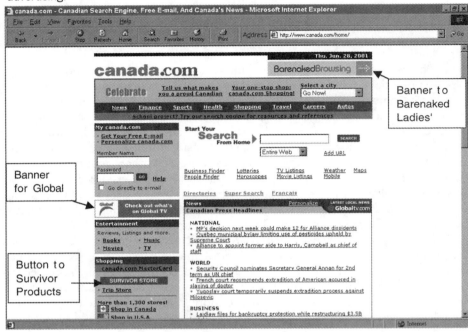

SOURCE: "Home Page." *canada.com.* <http://www.canada.com/home/halifax>. November 2001. Reprinted with permission.

charge other sites through various arrangements to host banners and buttons on their pages that can link users to other organizations. For example, the Canada.com website includes several banners and buttons on its homepage that can take users to other parts of the Internet (see Figure 11.4).

The rising use of banner ads has led to the development of standard sizes and formats for banners. The Coalition for Advertising Supported Information and Entertainment (CASIE) organization in conjunction with the Internet Advertising Bureau developed standard dimensions that more easily allow website designers to integrate banners and allow users to readily identify them.[8] As the technologies used in banner advertising have advanced, new standard formats have been developed which are better suited to interactivity, animation, and multimedia tools within the banners as well.

Banners are easily created using software applications. Many banners are designed and stored as animated GIFs. **Animated Graphic Interchange Format (GIF)** is a file that consists of a series of frames that are shown in a particular sequence. The animation attempts to both capture the user's eye and deliver a more complete message than can be delivered within a single banner's image size. For example, Orbitz.com, the airline portal developed by several airlines to offer rate searches and other services, includes its animated banners on several other sites such as Excite.

Other banners include the ability to select specific sections of a target site by drop-down boxes and other interactive applications (see Figure 11.5). Higher-quality banners can be created in HTML formats or using Flash technology. Some

CASIE
www.casie.net

Internet Advertising Bureau
www.iab.net

ANIMATED GRAPHIC INTERCHANGE FORMAT (GIF): a file that consists of a series of frames that are shown in a particular sequence.

Figure 11.5   Example of Banner with Drop-Down Box

The Globe and Mail's *site includes a banner ad with a drop-down box to allow users to choose where they would like to enter the advertisement's source.*

SOURCE: "Home Page Banner." *Globe and Mail.* <http://www.globeandmail.com>. November 2001. Reprinted with permission from The Globe and Mail..

industry observers have recorded major improvements in click-through rates based on the usage of these forms of rich media in banners.[9]

Banner advertising is the most dominant form of online advertising despite its criticism as a relatively ineffective selling tool. Critics of banner advertising cite low click-through rates of less than 1 or 2 percent as proof of the ineffectiveness of banners. However, some researchers have claimed that exposure to banner ads online has significantly improved brand image and brand perception.[10] The low click-through rates, therefore, may be justified by brand building and explain why companies continue to engage in banner advertising. Banner success measurement (besides click-through rates) is not unlike much media advertising whereby the effectiveness is difficult to measure. DoubleClick, however, has built its business model around measurement of banner ads and other advertising tools (see the New Business Models box).

The cost of banner advertising varies dramatically depending on the location of the advertisement, the host company, and any barter deals that are in place. Costs of advertising are often measured in **cost per thousand (CPM)** impressions. The range in costs can be from US$10 to US$100 CPM, and on premium, targeted sites may even exceed these amounts.[11] The CPM for online advertising is often compared to traditional media costs but marketers must be careful to ensure that the rates are compared based on media-specific terms. For example, the ability to use targeted marketing online is much higher than through broadcast media such as television. Running an advertisement during a prime-time television show is expensive and only results in limited targeting due to the wide demographic bases on television. On the other hand, the use of banner ads would allow the ad to appear on websites specifically targeted to audiences and often related to products that users are searching for.

Banner ads are often run on websites through bartering arrangements. The trading between sites of banners often allows for sites to cooperatively increase traffic and reduces the cash cost of e-marketing. The barter of banners and other advertising has resulted in difficulties in measuring the size of the online advertising market and also has caused complexities in accounting for the costs and revenues associated with online advertising.

One of the major strengths of banner advertising is the ability to measure the effectiveness of advertising in various locations. Banner ads can be created with unique identifiers so that the click-through rates can easily demonstrate which ads have been most effective, what hosting sites have provided the referrals, and comparisons among numerous criteria. These capabilities offer marketers a substantial improvement over the methods of measuring direct marketing initiatives in the past.

COST PER THOUSAND (CPM): standard measure of impressions. Charges are set for each thousand users who visit the site or see an advertisement.

NEW BUSINESS MODELS

Hot Water at DoubleClick.com

DoubleClick was founded in 1995 and aims to assist companies to improve their marketing online. DoubleClick founded the DoubleClick Network, the first and leading advertising network that allowed marketers to conduct advertising through a growing network of companies. In 1999 DoubleClick merged with Abacus Direct, an offline direct mail service, and as speculation grew that the databases could be merged between online, anonymous data and offline data with names, the company came under the fire by privacy advocates.

DoubleClick describes its major capabilities in the e-marketing area as the ability to:

- deliver a more complete understanding of the customer;
- effectively reach and influence customers; and
- measure the results of marketing efforts with a new level of accuracy.

The company offers a broad range of technology, media, direct marketing, e-mail, and research solutions. Most likely, if you have clicked on a banner ad on the Internet, you have become a DoubleClick statistic. The company uses banner ads, cookies, and proprietary technology to understand user behaviour online.

One of the company's major products is DoubleClick AdServer software, which allows sites to maximize their revenue while controlling the ad-serving process internally. The process of managing banner ads and other online advertising is a major task for those organizations that wish to capture relevant data as well as effectively control the income received through hosting advertising.

The DoubleClick Network provides not only access to advertising on leading Internet sites but also uses advanced technology to target markets effectively. DoubleClick's DART (Dynamic, Advertising, Reporting and Targeting) technology provides the capability for a company to specify target audiences and effectively focus advertising campaigns and, therefore, control costs. The advanced tracking of advertising through the Network also allows DoubleClick to gather massive amounts of data regarding online user behaviour and has led it to develop its own research division. The research garnered by DoubleClick allows it to improve its customers' advertising effectiveness and therefore improve its own brand image.

Having first focused on banners and other online advertising, DoubleClick recognized the importance of offering a full suite of services and in early 2001 acquired Flonetwork Inc., a Toronto-based e-mail marketing provider. The acquisition gives DoubleClick an advanced move into the e-mail marketing area, where it had not traditionally focused. During the first quarter of 2001, DoubleClick and FloNetwork delivered a combined 1.7 billion e-mails on behalf of over 240 clients. DoubleClick intends to utilize its DART technology in combination with e-mail to improve targeting and research capabilities across the e-mail frontier as well.

In early 2001, the U.S. Federal Trade Commission (FTC) closed its investigation into DoubleClick's privacy concerns, leaving the way for the company to merge online and offline data— carefully. Health and financial information must not be used, and users must be informed of the uses of the data and have the opportunity to opt out.

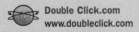

Double Click.com
www.doubleclick.com

Questions

1. How will the information DoubleClick has gained from its online component transfer to the e-mail division?
2. What advantages does the DoubleClick Network provide to marketers? Why?
3. Do you agree with the privacy concerns raised? The FTC's conclusion?

SOURCES: DoubleClick.com; Sperling, N., "DoubleClick Tries to Regain Credibility," RedHerring.com, Dec. 28, 2000; Welte, J., "DoubleClick Grabs Email Firm," *Business 2.0*, Feb. 23, 2001.

Interstitials The use of interstitials is another common form of online advertising that has been used by many businesses. **Interstitials** are web-based windows that pop up as a user enters an Internet site aiming to catch the user's attention. These pop-up boxes, known as **daughter windows**, commonly promote a specific product of a site or aim to gather survey data (see Figure 11.6). The requirement for users to pay attention to an interstitial in order to use it or close it is one factor that proponents of interstitials claim as part of their effectiveness. This same factor is what annoys many Internet users—the requirement to click and close boxes to which they do not wish to pay attention. Clearly planned use of interstitials allows advertisers to gather attention—the key is to find a balance between use and overuse.

Superstitials The rise of Internet advertising led one innovative company, Unicast, to create an advertising format tailored to the Web—Superstitials. **Superstitials®** are Internet advertisement spots that load into a user's browser while the Internet connection is idle and then launch as a daughter window showing a short, TV-like advertisement. A study by Harris Interactive in the summer of 2001 concluded that Superstitials demonstrated equivalent performance to television ads in terms of recall, communication, and persuasion.[12]

Unicast created the Superstitial format to provide advertisers with an improved medium over banner ads and interstitials. The benefit from a user perspective is that the ads do not use up bandwidth while you are attempting to use your Internet connection (see Figure 11.7). Advertisers will be pleased with the

INTERSTITIALS: web-based windows created that pop up as a user enters an Internet site, aiming to catch the user's attention.

DAUGHTER WINDOWS: another name for interstitials or pop-up windows on the Internet.

 Unicast
www.unicast.co

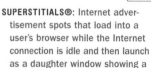

SUPERSTITIALS®: Internet advertisement spots that load into a user's browser while the Internet connection is idle and then launch as a daughter window showing a short, TV-like advertisement.

Figure 11.6   Illustration of an Interstitial Ad

AOL commonly uses interstitials to promote new versions of its products over the Internet. The daughter window appears above the main page that had been selected by the user.

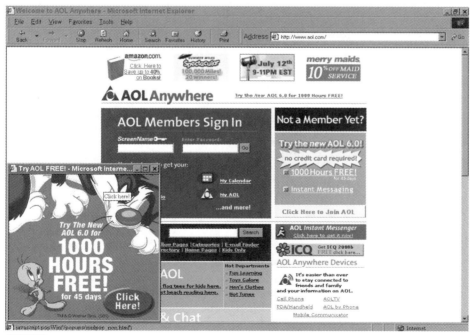

SOURCE: "Home Page. AOL Anywhere." *America Online.* <http://www.aol.com>. December 2001.
Reprinted with permission. All rights reserved.

Figure 11.7   The Superstitial Process

Unicast's Superstitial format is an efficient process designed to minimize user disruption and maximize advertiser effectiveness.

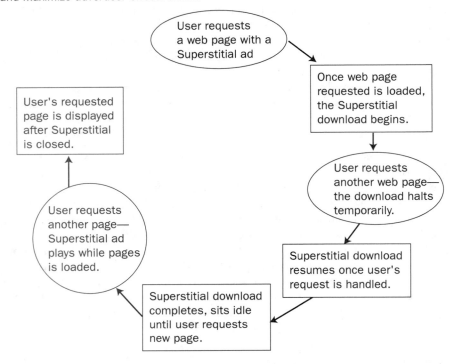

findings in the Harris Interactive report demonstrating the capabilities of online advertising—thus leading to increased use of Unicast's product and the development of similar technologies in the near future. Major companies including Coke, NBC, and Kia, along with hundreds of others, have already adopted the use of Superstitials in their online advertising initiatives. The format not only offers a broadcasting capability but also allows interactivity and direct links to purchasing products—an ability promised but not widely delivered by WebTV for the past several years.

Samples of Superstitials can be viewed at Unicast.com or linked through the website accompanying this text.

Interactive Tools The creation of interactive tools is leading Internet innovators to develop multiple new formats for advertising online. One notable creator of interactive ads is Ad4ever.com, the creator of Toplayer® technology. This technology provides advertisers with numerous capabilities such as branding, interactive selling, and other advertising techniques by using technology that seemingly floats ads over the existing web browser. An excellent example of the use of Ad4ever's technology is the launching of an interactive Chevrolet Corvette when a user searches for specific information at Edmunds.com (see Figure 11.8). In this example, the user can request additional information through a simple request, connect to the General Motors site, or change the colour of their dream vehicle.

Interactive advertisements allow marketers to carry out targeted marketing and branding techniques in numerous formats. Another example of the use of Ad4ever's technology is tying brand awareness into search engines. As a user searches for information at a search engine site or enters the toys section of

Figure 11.8   Example of Interactive Advertising

Ad4Ever's interactive advertisements seemingly hover over the web page and allow users to request information, link to another site, or interact with the advertisement.

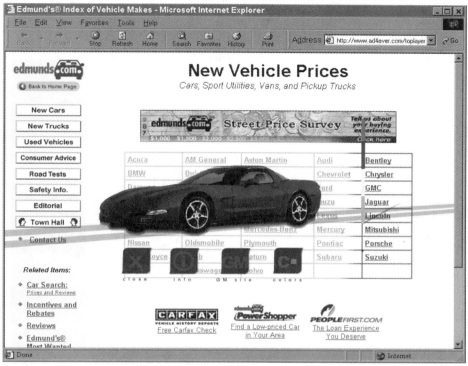

SOURCE: "New Vehicle Prices." *Ad4ever.com*. <www.ad4ever.com/toplayer/demos/corvette/index.html>. November 2001. Reprinted with permission.

Walmart.com, the Energizer bunny ventures across the screen and then rests in a location where the user can follow up. These types of targeted strategies and innovative uses of technology will be major components of online advertising as companies continue to allocate budgets to e-marketing strategies.

E-mail The use of e-mail for corporate advertising and marketing campaigns is an important area but also needs to be used very carefully. The overuse of the ability to send unsolicited e-mail has led to consumer revolt in several instances and can also result in legal problems in some locations. This phenomenon is known as spamming. **Spam** is the name given to the unsolicited sending of e-mail to individuals in an attempt to gain commercial advantage. The rising problem with spam was created by the relative ease of gathering large volumes of e-mail addresses over the Internet through newsgroups, chat sites, and other websites. Many ISPs and online e-mail services (e.g., Hotmail) now provide some protection against spam by picking up largely distributed e-mails and attempting to shield users from the disruptions caused by spam. Despite these efforts, users are still often in receipt of spam offering numerous products and services (see Figure 11.9).

In order to utilize e-mail advertising, marketers need to be careful not to be mistaken for spam. The use of e-mail advertising has become commonly carried out through permission marketing. Permission marketing occurs when users are able to opt-in to receive e-mail offers and advertising such as when registering on

SPAM: the name given to the unsolicited sending of e-mail to individuals in an attempt to gain commercial advantage.

Figure 11.9   Example of Spam "Business Opportunity"

Spam offers continue to spread through e-mail, disrupting users and weakening the effectiveness of e-mail marketing.

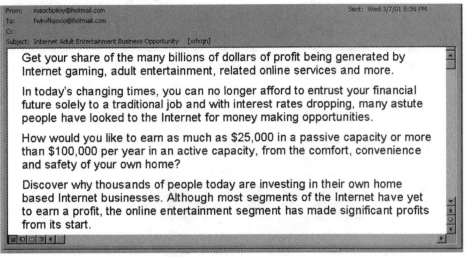

a site for the first time and agreeing to receive offers related to computer products. The use of permission marketing can be witnessed on many sites and allows users to select the types of advertising that they are willing to receive. This assists marketers in targeting potential customers, but because users must opt-in first it results in much less reach.

The use of e-mail marketing has been heralded by some advertisers as a powerful tool. In order to take advantage of e-mail without getting confused with spam, N. Wreden identified several points that should be kept in mind.[13]

1. *The customers should have opted in* to receiving the e-mail and have the ability to opt-out at any time. The spam example in Figure 11.9 contained an unsubscribe option; however, repeated attempts to be removed from the list failed and attempts to contact the "spammer" were unsuccessful.

2. *E-mail is not the same medium as direct-mail advertising and should not be treated the same.* The design of e-mail campaigns needs to be carried out differently from mail ads, which are often long with various typefaces and "free" offers. The growth of promotions on the Web has led many of these "free" campaigns and is reducing their success rate as users become frustrated with the volume. Another difficulty with the design of e-mail campaigns is the incompatibility of various e-mail applications. The formatting of an e-mail due to word-wrap and other functions can be altered by each recipient's software, resulting in an unprofessional appearance if design is not carefully planned.

3. *Giving information away can be a powerful form of e-mail marketing.* Many businesses offer electronic newsletters or information services that provide a great opportunity to build brand image and also sell products and services. For example, Air Canada offers e-mail notification of discount fares on selected destinations to users who have opted to receive the information. The provision of this service allows Air Canada to tout its brand and sell off discount flights to customers.

4. *E-mail marketing is a learning process.* It is important that organizations use the information they have gleaned from other sources such as previous campaigns, CRM, and/or BI initiatives to improve their marketing campaigns. For example, the identification of target markets and preferences of opt-in customers may allow marketers to develop specific campaigns and use trial-and-error methods. It is important that the trial-and-error attempts do not tarnish the brand or lead to categorization as a spammer but are used to determine what campaigns have been most effective for click-through or sales increases.

5. *Ensure adequate resources for e-campaigns.* In order to carry out e-campaigns, human resources, technology, and financial resources will be required. Organizations must balance the commitment of resources toward e-mail campaigns and may wish to look at outsourcing as an option to reduce the human and technology resources required in-house.

6. *E-mail isn't free.* Despite the ease with which we are able to click "send," e-mail campaigns can truly become costly. The use of e-mail for advertising will require extensive upkeep of lists and integration with other applications and may also demand investments in design. As discussed earlier, the use of various e-mail applications by users will require that design is carefully carried out—a job often completed by outsourcing. Whether in-house or outsourced, the successful use of e-mail for marketing and advertising will have a cost.

7. *Always look ahead.* The rapid changes in technology and the Internet will continue to demand a forward-looking firm. The use of wireless technologies, PDA, and voice e-mail access will require that advertisers carefully design campaigns to be effective across numerous mediums now and in the future. Shifts in demand and demographics will continue to impact advertisers for the foreseeable future—necessitating forward-looking plans.

Multimedia The Internet provides a dynamic medium through which advertising can take on a multimedia approach relatively easily. Several technologies such as Shockwave, Java, and Flash provide the capability to integrate animation, sound, and interactivity into web page design. For example, Disney's Internet presence makes use of Flash to build sound and pop-up boxes into its site in numerous places (see Figure 11.10).

The use of multimedia and advanced software on websites has led to some criticism in the past. Multimedia results in increased transfer of data between the web server and the user's computer and also requires the user to have specific plug-ins installed on their system. The increased transfer of data requires advertisers to consider their strategy carefully, as dial-up Internet users may easily become frustrated with slow-loading graphics. The use of multimedia, therefore, requires the consideration of segmenting dial-up versus broadband Internet users and may require alternate website design. This is commonly seen on corporate sites where users may select, for example, Flash-enabled or non-Flash sites.

Multimedia tools are also useful in providing service and information related to the company. For example, RSA Security offers numerous Flash demonstrations that explain security applications and concurrently promote the RSA brand. The use of demonstrations and other information online takes advantage of the unique aspects of the Internet by allowing users to interactively move from a demonstration to additional product details or to purchase the product.

RSA Security
www.rsasecurity.com

Figure 11.10   Illustration of a Multimedia Web Page

Disney's homepage provides a good example of a multimedia-designed site.

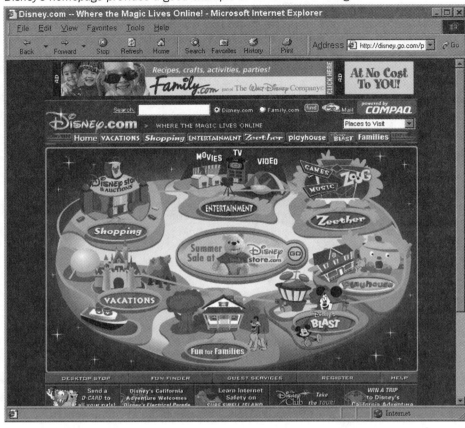

SOURCE: "Home Page." *Disney.com.* <http://www.disney.go.com/park/homepage>. November 2001.
Reprinted with permission of DISNEY Publishing Worldwide. All rights reserved. ©Disney Enterprises, Inc.

Affiliate Programs

AFFILIATE PROGRAMS: agreements between website operators whereby delivery of customers or prospective customers to another company's site results in compensation becoming due.

The use of affiliate programs as part of a strategy to increase website traffic and sales has become a common component of e-marketing strategy. Popularized first by CDnow, **affiliate programs** are agreements between website operators whereby delivery of customers or prospective customers to another company's site results in compensation becoming due. CDnow owners became interested in the concept of affiliate programs when the cost of banner ads seemed risky and was at an expensive stage of its life cycle. CDnow's affiliate program has grown to over 250 000 members and provides a major source of customer acquisition (see the E-Strategy box).[14]

Many companies have created affiliate programs in an attempt to increase traffic to and sales on their websites. The concept is similar for many of these programs but payment amounts can differ. For example, chapters.indigo.ca (see Figure 11.11) offers an affiliate program that nearly any site can join and earn commissions of 5 to 20 percent for click-throughs that lead to sales. The ease of joining and potential for commissions makes affiliate programs attractive. Chapters.indigo.ca provides numerous helpful tools such as pre-designed banner

E-STRATEGY

Affiliate Marketing at CDnow

CDnow is an online music retailer that started out of the basement of a home in Pennsylvania in 1994. Aiming to assist other music lovers to find specialty and hard-to-find music, 19-year-old twins Jason and Matthew Olim started CDnow. CDnow had sales of US$387 in its first month of business, when the only major form of promotion available was to be listed as a website on NCSA Mosaic's "What's New" page. By September 2000, CDnow had grown to be one of the largest e-commerce sites on the Internet and was acquired by Bertelsmann AG, the third largest media company in the world.

Early in the company's development, the Olims recognized that the substantial customer acquisition costs of up to US$500 being paid by some firms were unsustainable, so CDnow began to focus on developing new acquisition tactics. In an era where repeat purchases are not guaranteed and selling products of low-dollar value is increasingly common, CDnow aimed to reduce customer acquisition and marketing costs to a very low amount per customer. Banner ads were still a relatively expensive form of advertising and CDnow was uncomfortable paying for advertising costs that didn't guarantee paying customers. The Olims attempted to get sites to guarantee click-throughs on the banner ads but achieved only limited success.

In late 1994, CDnow and Geffen Records formed a partnership in which Geffen put links to CDnow's site to enable customers to purchase the music of Geffen's artists. The entire concept made sense and CDnow created the BuyWeb program, an early affiliate marketing program. The early edition of the program paid referring sites a commission of 3 percent of sales (now 7 to 15 percent, based upon volume), which provided CDnow with its desired outcomes—pay an "advertising" cost only when the customer actually buys. Now known as the Cosmic Credit and C2 programs, CDnow has an extensive affiliate program with over 250 000 members.

CDnow's overall strategy is described on its website as follows:

> Behind the company's success is a well-articulated, multi-point strategy: offer the most comprehensive selection of music in the world at great prices and with the best service and delivery; build communities of music fans; and strive to always stay at the cutting edge of music distribution technologies. (CDnow.com)

Within this strategy it is clear that CDnow needs to focus on very specific aspects of its e-business including SCM, CRM, and e-marketing. The affiliate programs it has established have become a core component of the e-marketing strategy: with a cost of only 2 percent of its marketing budget, affiliate programs are estimated to bring in over 15 percent of the new customers. CDnow's other marketing dollars are spread among other forms of media as well as online strategic partnerships (24 percent) and online advertising (24 percent). Partnerships and exclusive alliances with sites like America Online contribute another 20 percent of customers, while the online advertising contributes only 5 percent of customers.

CDnow has established itself as a leading online music community and made two young men from Pennsylvania rich in the process. Looking forward and taking advantage of the unique characteristics of the Web, the Olim boys have grown a true e-business in CDnow.

CDnow
www.CDnow.com

Questions

1. Why do you think two young men in their parents' basement were the first to develop an affiliate program?
2. Why would CDnow continue to dedicate 24 percent of its marketing budget to online advertising when it only contributes 5 percent of the customers?
3. What factors would lead Bertelsmann to acquire CDnow? Bertelsmann is the operator of the BMG music club as well, so why didn't BMG have its own online presence?

SOURCES: Hoffman, D. and T. Novak, "How to Acquire Customers on the Web," *Harvard Business Review*, May–June 2000; www.CDnow.com.

Figure 11.11 **Example of an Affiliate Program**

The Chapters-Indigo affiliate program allows other businesses and websites to earn money by bringing customers to their site—referring sites receive a commission on books sold.

SOURCE: "Info Desk. Affiliate Opportunities." *chapters.indigo.ca.* <http://www.chapters.indigo.ca>. December 2001. Reprinted with permission. All rights reserved.

ads and custom HTML codes that allow even novice web designers to integrate the affiliate program.

The affiliate program becomes operational as an Internet user clicks on a banner ad or button at an affiliate site and is redirected to another site (such as chapters.indigo.ca). As the user arrives, the affiliate's referring address is tracked so that if the user purchases a product, the affiliate will be eligible to receive the commission they are due. For the affiliate program providers, one of the major benefits of these programs is that the cost of acquiring customers is only paid if the user actually purchases something. In addition, the affiliate program gains a new customer who may come back to the site directly on the second visit (either through brand recall or e-mail advertising), which results in only paying the affiliate commission once.

Partnerships

The Internet offers unique capabilities for companies to enter into partnerships that can fit into the e-marketing strategy. Online partnerships can be used to create increased traffic or to target specific products and services to a market segment. For example, Lycos and Sympatico formed a partnership in Canada that allowed Lycos (a search engine and web portal) to improve its brand by increasing its use on the popular Sympatico service. Other prominent partnerships have been formed that allow businesses to work together and capitalize on each other's strengths. For example, Amazon and Toys "R" Us formed a partnership that saw Amazon use its existing technologies and e-commerce capabilities to facilitate online transactions with Toys "R" Us.[15] Partnerships can allow businesses to benefit in a number of ways in the online world.

Promotions

The use of promotions is an important aspect of e-marketing and advertising. Promotional tools such as coupons, discounts, contests, points programs, and demos/free trials are all easily employed over the Internet. Several online companies provide tools to create these types of promotions or provide the services for a fee. In addition to using web pages to provide these promotional tools, it is possible to integrate promotions into e-mail campaigns. For example, Figure 11.12 illustrates an e-mail discount offer for an existing customer of International Vision Direct—a targeted and timely advertisement reminding the customer that it is time to replace their disposable contact lenses, and offering a discount at the same time. The e-mail ad also attempts to establish new business by providing compensation for referring a friend to the company.

Figure 11.12 Sample E-mail Discount Promotion

Vision Direct uses e-mail advertising to remind disposable contact lens wearers that it is approaching the time to replace their lenses, and offers discounts for referring other customers.

SOURCE: "Contact Lenses Offer from VisionDirect.com." *Vision Direct.* <http://www.visiondirect.com>. August 2001. Reprinted with permission of VisionDirect.com.

Beenz
www.beenz.com

A large number of companies offer points programs and customer loyalty programs online. These programs range from the more traditional airline miles/points to online cash such as the currency of Beenz.com. Beenz currency is earned by web users for shopping at selected sites, registering for services, and completing surveys. The Beenz can then be spent at specified sites for products and services available. Bricks-and-mortar companies that have loyalty programs have also begun to move their programs online in order to both increase usage and develop online strategies.

The Internet is loaded with locations where users can access free trials and demos. Perhaps most common are software demos that can be downloaded at sites like Download.com. The provision of software demos provides many software businesses with a powerful avenue to display their product and allow users to ensure that they are satisfied with the product prior to purchase.

New applications of trials are aiming to sell products other than software. For example, Johnson & Johnson uses teen chat communities as an avenue to provide trials of its Clean & Clear skin-care products. The company provides teenage girls with the opportunity to send their friends electronic postcards that offer samples of Clean & Clear.[16] While tangible products require either physical shipment or customer pick-up, the Internet provides the opportunity to target and profile these products at a reasonable cost.

Public Relations

Public relations is the activity of creating goodwill or positive company image. Typically, public relations aims to please a wider audience than advertising alone—targeting shareholders, employees, communities, the media, and the public. As an efficient and effective communication tool, the Internet offers numerous methods for satisfying a company's public relations strategy. A review of most corporate websites will reveal a news or press release section whereby current information can be disseminated easily and cost-effectively. In addition, online delivery of information such as annual reports and shareholder information allows for the integration of multimedia and Internet enhancements, along with additional details that cannot be as easily delivered in print.

The proliferation of Internet sites, online magazines, news services, and industry organizations offers tremendous potential for public relations online. Many companies encourage employees to become involved in writing articles for publication on the Internet (and in print) in order to portray an image of excellence and industry leadership. In addition, publication on the Internet is often accompanied by a link to the writer's or employer's website. The combination of published material and interactivity may lead to improved brand image, increased website traffic, and potentially increases in sales.

Pricing

Establishing prices that maximize profitability is a difficult task for businesses. The Internet offers a new medium within which businesses must establish pricing policies that capture potential sales and maximize profits. The traditional practices of establishing prices that remained in effect for extended periods, however, are no longer necessary. The Internet offers the capability of changing prices relatively rapidly and offering varying prices to customer segments. As discussed in Chapter 8, the use of auctions has led many transactions to occur with flexible pricing arrangements.

One concern of many companies to date has been how to deal with pricing between online versus offline sales channels. The online channels originally were thought to become extremely competitive based on price, but the low prices charged by many pure-play competitors forced them out of business. The establishment of multichannel pricing requires a focus on customer segments and also can create additional complexity within an organization. Prices online have not fallen as drastically as some pundits had predicted and, in fact, some online companies claim to use higher prices in their online channel due to convenience, additional services, and appropriate segmentation. In contrast to claims regarding the importance of low prices on the Internet, a McKinsey study found that most online buyers actually do very little shopping around and many tend to return to sites used in the past—suggesting that brand may be as important as pricing.[17]

Low prices may not be the most important factor online, but a solid pricing strategy can lead to substantially improved profitability and market share. For example, some B2B sellers have indicated that they segment customers by the extent with which the customer conducts business with them. Those customers who carry out the majority of their purchases with the seller receive improved pricing, while those who use the seller only as an alternate means of supply may pay a premium price. This form of segmentation led an electronic components company to charge a premium of up to 20 percent to some customers, with little impact on volumes sold.[18]

The Internet provides an opportunity for e-businesses to conduct test pricing and price-related research in an effort to optimize prices. The difficult aspect of altering prices, however, is to do it in a fair manner. As part of a price test, Amazon offered potential customers discounts that ranged from 30 to 40 percent, but was criticized when consumers became aware of the actions. The bad publicity associated with such research requires that companies carefully consider any test pricing strategies they plan to carry out. E-businesses may also optimize prices by making adjustments related to supply and demand on an ongoing basis. The adjustment of prices online can be much simpler than in the traditional sales channels, where price lists, signage, and multiple sales channel firms may all need to be updated with regard to changes.

Evaluation

The ability to modify or refine marketing campaigns is simplified online and can occur several times per week or even per day. Staples.com measures its marketing campaigns by the hour according to a number of key metrics. If those metrics indicate that a particular strategy is not working, the marketing campaign is quickly revised. In addition, Staples adjusts the allocations of its marketing budget on a weekly basis in order to focus on the most crucial elements within a set dollar budget.[19] The development and understanding of key metrics can help businesses adjust e-marketing strategies in Internet time.

The metrics to be used will vary drastically by industry and the particular strategy being pursued. Some metrics that may be considered are banner click-through rates, website view-to-buy ratios, pricing effectiveness measures, market share, revenue growth, and numerous other factors. In developing the e-marketing strategy, the business should determine which metrics are relevant and ensure that an appropriate measurement process exists to evaluate the success of strategy implementation.

Convergence of Technologies

Throughout this book the concept of convergence of technologies has been mentioned several times. For marketing and advertising, convergence may play an increasingly important role in strategy. As technologies like PCs, wireless phones, PDAs, and WebTV can all be used to access e-mail and the Internet, advertising campaigns must carefully evaluate their potential success across numerous mediums. In addition, marketers will need to continually evaluate their demographic and other segmentation measures as each of the converging technologies often has specific consumer segments throughout the technology life cycle.

KEY TERMS

e-marketing

secondary data

primary data

market segment

brochureware phase

interactive phase

personalization phase

site stickiness

cybersquatting

animated GIF

cost per thousand (CPM)

interstitials

daughter windows

Superstitials

spam

affiliate programs

Chapter Summary

E-marketing is an important component of the overall marketing and business strategy of e-businesses. While many dot-com businesses have failed and the spending on online advertising has dropped from its peak, the importance of having an e-marketing and advertising strategy is still widely acknowledged. The e-marketing process includes strategy creation, implementation, and evaluation.

The e-marketing strategy is developed at the strategy creation phase whereby research is carried out, target markets are identified, and a strategy is devised. Secondary research information may be gathered through the Internet as well as other methods, while e-businesses may also engage in primary research. Primary research may be carried out through surveys, experiments, focus groups, and observation.

As in any business, e-businesses must aim to use the data they have gathered to segment the market and identify target markets. The unique aspect of e-marketing is that targeted marketing is often more easily conducted than through offline businesses.

The e-marketing and advertising strategy should be implemented in a fluid manner to capitalize on the capabilities of the Internet. If implemented and carefully monitored, the strategy can be revised mid-stream to better meet the needs of customers. Implementation will include website design, advertising, affiliate programs, promotional techniques, partnerships, public relations, and pricing.

Advertising online has changed dramatically as software and hardware improvements have been made. While simple banner ads are still commonly used, the Internet now allows advertisements to take on television-like appearances with multimedia and interactivity added in. Many advertising tools such as e-mail require careful monitoring, design, and execution in order to be effective—often requiring trial-and-error or outsourcing.

The e-marketing and advertising strategy must be evaluated on an ongoing basis to ensure that the desired outcomes are being met. In addition, the fit of the e-marketing strategy within the general marketing strategy and overall business strategy must be kept in mind as online and offline operations continue to converge.

Tools for Online Learning

To help you master the material in this chapter and stay up to date with new developments in e-business, visit www.pearsoned.ca/trites . Resources include:

> Review Questions and Exercises

> Problems for Discussion

> Recommended Readings

> Updates to Boxes, Case Studies and textual material

> Links to demonstration tools related to course topics including sample Web sites

> Streaming CBC Videos with Cases

Endnotes

1. Strauss, J., and R. Frost, *Prentice Hall's e-Marketing Guide*. Prentice Hall, 2001.
2. Strauss, J., and R. Frost, *Marketing on the Internet: Principles of Online Marketing*. Prentice Hall, 1999.
3. Strauss, J. and R. Frost, 1999.
4. Ibid.
5. "Auto.DemographicsNow.com provides marketing data for auto industry," *Direct Marketing,* Garden City, April 2001.
6. Adapted from Hanson, W., *Principles of Internet Marketing, South-Western College Publishing, 2000.*
7. Hicks, M., "Getting Personal: E-biz Firms Search for Better Ways to Customize Content," *eWEEK, October 2, 2000.*
8. www.iab.net/iab_banner_standards/bannersource.html.
9. Hughes, L., "Rich Media Spicing Up Online Buying Choices," *Advertising Age,* Chicago, February 2001.
10. Briggs, R. and N. Hollis, "Advertising on the Web: Is There Response Before Clickthrough?" *Journal of Advertising Research,* March/April 1997.
11. www.engage.com.
12. www.unicast.com.
13. Wreden, N., "Mapping the Frontiers of E-mail Marketing," *Harvard Management Communication Letter,* September 1999.
14. Hoffman, D., and T. Novak, "How to Acquire Customers on the Web," *Harvard Business Review,* May/June 2000.
15. www.amazon.com.
16. Kenny, D., and J. Marshall, "Contextual Marketing: The Real Business of the Internet," *Harvard Business Review,* November–December 2000.
17. Baker, W. et al., "Price Smarter on the Net," *Harvard Business Review,* February 2001.
18. Ibid.
19. Aufreiter, N. et al., "Marketing Rules: What Sets Winners Apart? More than Anything Else, It's Lightning Fast Marketing," *Harvard Business Review,* February 2001.

E-Commerce and Small Business

learning objectives

When you complete this chapter you should be able to:

1. Understand how e-commerce can be a benefit to small businesses.

2. Discuss the development of strategy for small business e-commerce.

3. Describe the barriers to e-commerce for small businesses and how they can be overcome.

4. Identify and describe some of the useful services and sources of information on the Internet for small businesses.

5. Explain how a small business can establish an e-commerce presence.

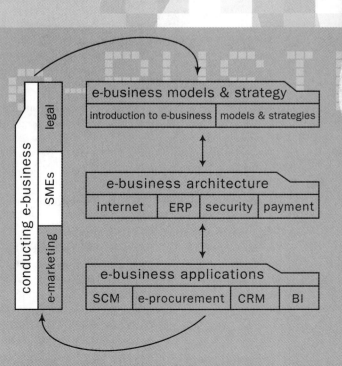

conducting e-business	legal	e-business models & strategy	
		introduction to e-business	models & strategies
	SMEs	e-business architecture	
		internet | ERP | security | payment	
	e-marketing	e-business applications	
		SCM | e-procurement | CRM | BI	

Introduction

E-commerce has brought a great deal of growth and opportunity to the small business sector. The potential to reach new markets, reduce costs of operations, and compete against larger competitors brought the potential of e-commerce to the forefront of news during the late 1990s and early 2000s. The successes of dot-com startups like Amazon and eBay has helped to bring awareness of the importance of the Internet to the headlines of the media. However, the dot-com failures of 2000 and 2001 have produced numerous skeptics and perhaps slowed the interests of the small business sector in becoming involved in e-commerce. In this chapter we will consider the importance of e-commerce to small businesses and consider different ways in which these companies can capitalize on the Internet to suit their own industry.

Small businesses are not unlike large businesses in some ways but tend to vary in the way in which they implement strategy. Despite this fact, it is important for small businesses to develop a strategy for e-commerce, implement that strategy effectively, and constantly evaluate and revise the strategy. One good example of a small business that has successfully developed an e-commerce strategy is Trail Blazer Products of Halifax, Nova Scotia. Trail Blazer is a family-owned business with eight employees that was started in 1987. The company manufactures camping, hunting, and gardening equipment products but is best known for one product. The Take-Down Buck Saw has become the signature product for Trail Blazer—the product is a woodsman's saw that packs in a compact aluminum tube that can be easily stored and carried. The success of this product is evidenced by the prominent list of retailers through which it is sold—Canadian Tire, LL Bean, Home Hardware, Lee Valley, Mountain Equipment Co-op, and others. Trail Blazer had already developed some familiarity with e-commerce prior to establishing an Internet presence through the use of B2B e-commerce with some of its distributors. For example, Canadian Tire required all suppliers to use its extranet to communicate with the company and transfer all shipping and billing documents. As Trail Blazer decided to establish a web presence they had some difficult decisions to make: What should the website's goal be? Will products be sold online? Who will the users of the site be? Who will build and maintain the site?

By evaluating their own objectives and considering the types of products they sold, Trail Blazer established a strategy to use the website to build brand awareness of its products and provide customer service. The company felt that there was a strong potential to sell its products online but was worried about creating conflict with its distributors and retailers—so they chose a different route. The site now includes marketing and other product information and when a user is interested in buying, trailblazerproducts.com directs the user to either the website of one of the retailers or the address of the nearest retailer in the area (see Figure 12.1). Trail Blazer is very satisfied with the investment they have made in the area of e-commerce and feels that the efforts have paid off. A survey conducted of consumers in 1999 found that 68 percent of customers had heard of the product through the Internet, despite the heavy advertising of Trail Blazer in magazines and at trade shows—an impressive statistic indeed![1]

The importance of the small business sector to the economy of Canada and, in fact, to the economies of many countries throughout the world cannot be understated. In Canada, 98 percent of all businesses have fewer than 100 employees and much of the job growth in the country can be attributed to these small enterprises.[2] The number of small businesses combined with their importance to the

Figure 12.1 **Trail Blazer's Website**

Trail Blazer uses its website to service both consumers and other businesses in both a promotional and an educational manner.

economy has led many parties to become interested in developing the use of e-commerce in the small business sector. For example, the Government of Canada has developed an e-commerce strategy and information website through Industry Canada, which includes specific information for small companies, and many regional and provincial government agencies have developed seminars and other incentives. In addition, many technology service providers and online services have developed products and services that are designed specifically for the small business sector.

The doom and gloom brought to online retailing by the death of some major vendors like eToys.com and Pets.com may in fact be an opportunity for small businesses. Larger organizations and many high-growth firms have shifted their focus from the B2C market to B2B and left a massive opportunity for the right individuals. Some pundits predict that small businesses will be able to capture a large portion of the B2C market by focusing on what they do best—providing excellent customer service to niche markets across large geographic areas.[3] See the E-Business in Global Perspective box for an example of a successful niche strategy. How promising B2C will be to small businesses remains to be determined, but the continually increasing number of Internet users represents a market too large to ignore.

Online Retail at Cavendish Figurines Ltd.

Cavendish Figurines Ltd. is a PEI-based manufacturer and retailer of "fine earthenware Anne of Green Gables figurines." This specialty product line has been sold by the company since its formation in 1989 and represents its primary products. In addition to Anne of Green Gables items, the company now produces other PEI-related products including souvenirs based on the Confederation Bridge. The company expanded its operation when the Confederation Bridge opened and now operates a manufacturing and retail facility at the Borden, PEI, end of the bridge.

Cavendish Figurines was approached numerous times by website designers and e-commerce promoters to develop an online strategy, but the owners were reluctant. By 1999, changing circumstances including an internal employee with strong computer skills combined with an attractive offer from an e-commerce consulting partnership prompted the own-

ers to pursue e-commerce. A local ISP has partnered with the Royal Bank and N-gage to develop a catalogue e-commerce solution to be marketed to small businesses, and Cavendish Figurines would be the pilot project.

The online presence seemed to make sense for Cavendish |since many of the customers of the business were tourists and the company's mail-order channel was quite successful. In addition, the popularity of Anne of Green Gables in foreign countries like Japan made the products very suitable to niche marketing online. The key would be to develop a website that could market the high-end figurines to new markets and support existing customers—perhaps transferring some customers from the more costly mail-order channel to the online site.

Following a few glitches in the development stage (one partner in the pilot program went bankrupt), the company's website was launched a few months behind schedule. However, the site re-

ceived only limited traffic and was contributing little in the way of sales. To address this issue, the site was to be optimized for search engines and continuously improved. With modifications and off-line marketing efforts, the site's traffic grew and the owners are now satisfied with their success in the B2C e-commerce area.

Looking to continue growth, Cavendish Figurines would like to expand its abilities in the B2B area. The website, however, is designed primarily for B2C transactions and follows relatively closely to the mail-order catalogues in style. The company is concerned with the impact B2B e-commerce will have on the pricing and payment options used as well.

The key to growth for Cavendish may be establishing core accounts in foreign countries, such as Japan, at both the retail and wholesale levels. The company continues to develop new products and operate a manufacturing plant, retail outlets, and online retailing.

Cavendish Figurines
www.cavendishfigures.com

Questions

1. **What would some of the key issues be with regard to reaching important global markets? Visit the site and decide if you feel it is dealing with these issues.**

2. **What changes will be necessary for cavendishfigurines.com to establish a B2B strategy online?**

3. **What types of complications would the bankruptcy of one of the developing partners have caused for Cavendish Figurines' implementation of e-commerce?**

Source: InnovaQuest, "The State of Electronic Commerce in Atlantic Canada," Atlantic Canada Opportunities Agency, March 2000.

Developing a Small "E" Strategy

The decision to establish an online presence needs to be followed by a consideration of the strategy to be adopted for the website. Trail Blazer, the example discussed earlier, decided to use its website to market the product and provide customers with a service to find retailers rather than attempt to increase sales itself and disintermediate the dealers like Canadian Tire. Within each business, considerations such as these will need to be thought through so as to avoid unintended consequences. One of the difficulties that is often found when dealing with small business owners, however, is that they tend not to use traditional planning and strategy-setting techniques. Therefore, it is important that consultants, government agencies, and other advice givers attempt to have owners think about some of the important issues with regards to going online.

Opportunities for Small Business

The use of electronic commerce by small businesses in Canada has been criticized for severely lagging behind that in the United States. In order to stimulate small business e-commerce in Canada, it is important that small business owners are made aware of the many opportunities and benefits it can offer. The small business owners must also look to how other small businesses have overcome some of the challenges of matching technology and e-commerce use to the small business setting.

The opportunities for e-commerce use in small business are many and have been realized across numerous industries and geographic regions of the world. The benefits can include access to new markets, improved customer responsiveness, increased flexibility, improved profits (through cost reductions and revenue increases), increased innovation, and better-managed resources.[4] The number and amount of benefits received in any of these categories will depend of course on factors such as the industry, products/services sold, and e-strategy chosen.

The use of the Internet can be of benefit to small businesses across many functional areas. To illustrate the types of benefits that can be obtained, we will look at e-commerce and Internet usage across a number of areas and provide examples where appropriate. The use of the Internet can be valuable in the key areas of marketing, customer support, market intelligence, operations, sales transactions, and public relations.[5]

Marketing The capability to market products and services to a wide audience at a reasonable cost was one of the first drivers of businesses onto the Internet. While some may question the value of online marketing, many examples exist of the successful use of online marketing and advertising tools. In addition to attracting new customers, small businesses have found that online advertising has provided valuable, targeted marketing campaigns that have resulted in increased business.[6] One small business operator in the tourism industry is Outside Expeditions of Charlottetown, Prince Edward Island. The owner, Bryon Howard, stated, "Yes, we have landed lots of new business as a result of our website. People have booked tours as a result ... Others have phoned for information, and rather than wait up to 10 days for a brochure to get to the U.S.—I can give them my website address ... and voilà, a reservation is the result, the very same day."[7] Many businesses have had similar findings—the value of an online presence for marketing can at times outweigh other marketing efforts. From finding new customers to building a customer database, the Internet offers businesses a cost-effective means of marketing in a new way. See Table 12.1 for some of the uses of the Internet for small business marketing efforts.

Customer Support One of the key reasons that the Internet is valuable to small businesses for customer support is the availability of the website 24/7. While

Table 12.1   Marketing Aspects of the Internet

- Provide product or service information.
- Find new customers.
- Develop new export markets.
- Educate customers.
- Reduce marketing costs.
- Enhance your image.
- Build a customer/potential customer database.
- Encourage requests for information.
- Support traditional media campaigns.
- Distribute frequently changing information.
- Build brand image.

many small businesses pride themselves on personal support, several enquiries can be easily handled without human contact and the customer is often just as happy to be served in a timely fashion. If, for example, a customer from Los Angeles is looking for product details at 9 a.m. their time, it is unlikely that a business in eastern Canada would be open. Rather than have to wait until the afternoon, the customer can find the information on their own if the supplier has a website. This form of self-service often leads to satisfaction, since it is timely and can reduce the cost of calling long-distance to another business. The customer is now informed of all important product features (assuming a well-designed, useful website exists) and may call or place an order online.

One of the main tools that will reduce routine questions over the phone is a Frequently Asked Questions (FAQ) page on the Web. The FAQ page should pose questions in a manner consistent with how customers normally ask them by phone or in person. Responses can be in basic text format or can integrate text and multimedia to give visual aids to users. The use of FAQs to reduce phone queries can benefit both the customer and the business by reducing the time and cost of dealing with these concerns individually.

Market Intelligence   The Internet offers numerous tools whereby small businesses can more easily gather market intelligence. The monitoring of industry information and competitors can be a time-consuming and costly task, but many Internet sites allow this task to be carried out quickly and at a low cost. For example, online services such as eWatch.com allow users to search for news by company name and even subscribe to receive e-mail notification when press releases or news items occur for selected companies (see Figure 12.2). These types of services range in cost but can be invaluable to businesses in industries where timeliness and competitor monitoring are of crucial importance.

The Internet also holds great potential for small businesses to gather data relevant to their online and offline marketing efforts. For example, the Strategis site is host to a huge volume of data from Statistics Canada and other reliable sources regarding industry statistics, demographics, business listings, and a great deal of other information. Many others, such as the sites for *The Globe and Mail* and National Post, offer the ability to search some archives for free and more distant archives for a cost. The wealth of information online (discussed in more detail later in this chapter) provides useful access to data that may assist business

Strategis
www.strategis.gc.ca

Figure 12.2   Sample of Online Newswire Services

eWatch.com can assist businesses in monitoring the Internet for news on their industry and competitors to ensure that information is used to stay competitive.

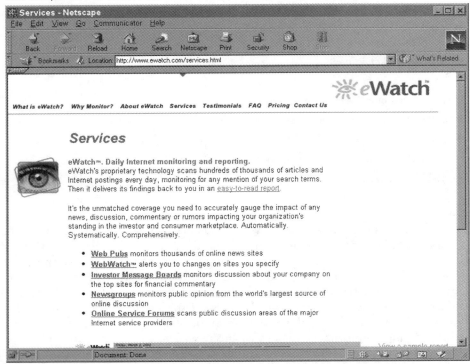

SOURCE: "Services." *eWatch.* <http://www.ewatch.com/services.html>. September 2001. Reprinted with permission of eWatch™ , a service of PR Newswire.

owners in decision-making for everyday issues and in establishing growth strategies during times of change.

Operations The Internet and e-commerce offer small businesses the opportunity to achieve efficiencies for operations in numerous ways. Some of the cost savings that can easily be achieved are through reduced long-distance telephone call (due to e-mail), reduced postage (due to e-mail, websites, and downloads), and the time savings related to these everyday business tasks.

The use of the Internet for sharing business information with business partners can lead to greater efficiencies and improved lines of communication. For example, Trail Blazer (as discussed earlier) communicates almost entirely through the Canadian Tire extranet, thus saving time, phone costs, and frustrating automated message machines in the process. Canadian Tire prefers this means of communication and in many cases demands that suppliers (large and small) utilize the technology. All communication through this means is timely and in many cases more accurate than other communication mediums.

Sales Transactions The Internet offers small businesses the means by which they may generate potential sales leads and/or conduct online sales transactions. The growth of the B2C market has been slower than anticipated but still some small businesses have been successful in building a profitable online sales store. For example, Rogers' Chocolates of Victoria, BC, decided in 1996 to make their "brochureware" site transactional in order to reduce the administrative time required to complete sales and create a stronger online presence. In addition to strong growth in their B2C market, Rogers found that the B2B (wholesale) market increased substantially with their new web presence (see the E-Strategy box).

E-STRATEGY

From Bricks to Clicks at Rogers' Chocolates

Rogers' Chocolates Ltd. opened originally as a grocery store in Victoria, BC, in 1885.

After a short time in operation, the entrepreneur decided that the most popular product, chocolates, should become the focus of the entire business, but the existing supplier was unable to consistently provide the product at a reasonable cost. Then Rogers soon developed their own brand of chocolates and quickly shifted the focus of the business to selling only chocolates to a local market as well as a growing number of tourists visiting the area.

Rogers realized around the turn of the last century that the tourists who had visited the store and been very impressed by the quality products represented an important market. In attempting to continue the company's growth, a mail-order marketing effort began to get the tourists who visited the shop to consider buying more products after they returned home. This represented an early form of "permission marketing," since visitors to the store were asked if they would be willing to receive catalogues and advertisements at home. Growing steadily, the mail-order business came to represent an important market to Rogers' and continues to be a strong component of today's company.

Nearly 110 years after the business had been established, Rogerschocolates.com was developed in 1995 as a marketing site with basic company information and advertising. The company decided in 1996 to become transactional, and today is a full e-commerce site with secure ordering capabilities, Flash-based promotional materials, visual tours, and more. Rogers' Chocolates was an early small business to progress through the major stages of website development.

The website has resulted in e-commerce sales growing rapidly from 1 percent of mail orders in 1996 to 30 percent of mail orders by 1999. Along with the growth in sales, Rogers has developed a high rate of repeat customers in the business-to-consumer marketplace—a significant factor in becoming profitable.

The Internet's growth and the success of the B2C strategy at Rogers led the company to begin development of a B2B strategy as well. The same website is now used to allow potential retailers to contact the company. The wholesale side of Rogers's business grew from just 5 percent of sales in 1989 to 40 percent of sales by 2000. In addition to utilizing the Internet, Rogers uses EDI links with major suppliers and has embraced the capabilities of technology to enhance and improve its business.

The success at Rogers has led to excellent growth in both B2B and B2C markets, increased profile, a global expansion, and development of an important volume of repeat customers. From a mom-and-pop grocery store in 1885 to a successful e-commerce business today, Rogers' Chocolates has shown how a reasonably staged approach can lead even small businesses to capitalize on the Internet. In the future the company aims to establish a secure Internet as well as expand the functionality and services available through the existing website.

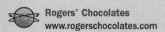
Rogers' Chocolates
www.rogerschocolates.com

Questions

1. Why was the transition to e-commerce a smooth one for Rogers' Chocolates?
2. What uses will an extranet have for rogerschocolates.com?
3. What additional services/features could be added to the website?

SOURCES: Andrews, J., "The More Things Change...," *CA Magazine*, March 2000; www.rogerschocolates.com.

The potential for online sales transactions will depend upon the industry within which the small business operates, as well as the reputation that the company is able to build. Companies that have operated previously in catalogue-sales operations, such as Rogers' Chocolates, will have an easier transition to online sales than those who have no history in the area. Customers will be familiar with the business and the company will have established distribution mechanisms in place.

Those businesses that provide services rather than products may or may not be able to provide those services with only online communication. For many products and services, the value of e-commerce is the generation of sales leads generated online. One example of generation of sales leads is Oven Head Salmon Smokers of St. George, NB, who found that its web presence actually led to enquiries from potential customers who were seeking orders beyond their existing capacity.[8] This type of lead generation is invaluable to any business seeking growth and future profitability.

The conduct of online sales transactions and generation of sales leads combined with the value of online marketing makes e-commerce a very significant tool for most small businesses. Whether the sale actually takes place over the Internet is less significant than whether sales occur that would not have otherwise taken place—and much evidence exists to suggest that this does occur.

Public Relations The Internet offers small businesses the opportunity to more easily broadcast their message to media and other users in an effort to create positive PR. Many newspapers offer e-mail addresses where businesses can send press releases and other information that may be published. By preparing press releases and notifying the media, small businesses may gain exposure in local or even national newspapers that can lead to increased business or traffic to a website. The website can also include PR items that are considered of importance to the local community such as fundraising initiatives that the company is involved in, corporate donations, and community events. The potential for the Internet to generate positive PR is limitless if the business is innovative in its use and may potentially lead to improved brand image and/or increased sales.

Barriers to E-Commerce for Small Business

The small business sector in Canada has been relatively slow to adopt e-commerce and the use of the Internet despite the growth of online commerce. Small businesses are often characterized by the ability to adapt to change quickly and to be innovative, which has created some confusion over their limited adoption of e-commerce. Many studies have concluded that the development of e-commerce in Canadian small businesses has been slower than that in other countries, particularly the United States, and is therefore a concern for the entire economy. The slow development of e-commerce in the small business sector can be attributed to several barriers, notably technological, financial, organizational, and operational barriers.

Technological Barriers The technological barriers to e-commerce for small business continue to evolve as technology and the Internet evolve. Initially, poor Internet access combined with other factors was one of the major barriers to e-commerce. However, Internet access and technology in general have declined in cost and are now more widespread than ever.

The common barrier to technology within small businesses is often cited as a lack of knowledge of computers, the Internet, and technology internally. Small business owners are often very pressed for time just to deal with the core aspects of the business and therefore cannot dedicate time to learning about technologies not considered of crucial importance to the business. The growth of e-commerce has, however, brought attention to the importance of the Internet and sparked the interest of many small businesses.

The complexity of becoming involved in e-commerce is often overstated and misunderstood. Many small business owners interviewed in research studies have indicated that the task of becoming involved in e-commerce seemed too technical and they lacked internal expertise.[9] However, as described in this chapter and throughout this book, it is possible to become involved in e-commerce with only limited technology skills, and many skills can be learned quickly through practice. As businesses increase in size, there is more likelihood that an internal individual may have the capability to implement and manage an e-commerce strategy. Therefore, those small businesses at the upper end of the scale (with 75 to 100 employees) and medium-sized enterprises (those with 100 to 500 employees) are more likely than the smaller enterprises to be involved in e-commerce.

Financial Barriers Small businesses and many large businesses must balance their financial investments across numerous activities, and e-commerce investments to date have often been considered a non-essential investment. As owners are learning the importance of developing an e-commerce strategy and an Internet presence, the costs associated with the investment need to be considered.

The costs that will be borne by small businesses wishing to enter into e-commerce activities will vary widely. The potential costs can include hardware, software, web design, training, and Internet access. The costs that will arise depend upon the strategy chosen, the current technology employed by the business, and the decisions made related to outsourcing.

Organizational Barriers The introduction of change into a small organization is likely to cause as much anxiety, confusion, and resistance as in large organizations. The major difference for small organizations is that if the owner is promoting the change it is much more likely to be accepted than if a manager is promoting change in a large business. If the owner is not the leader of change, however, small businesses may run into many of the difficulties experienced by large ones in implementing new technologies and making business process changes.

The keys to overcoming the organizational barrier of implementation of e-commerce are leadership and communication. The owner/manager is in a strong position to effect change if that person is aware of the importance of the change and is able to clearly communicate the plan to employees. Employees must understand what implications e-commerce will have on the organization as well as their own job responsibilities. The industry, organization's size, and many other factors will also influence the changes necessary to become a small "e" business.

Operational Barriers The small business sector can often experience difficulty in dealing with the operational aspects of becoming an e-business. The impacts that establishing an e-commerce strategy can have on everyday operations can include global issues, fulfillment and logistics needs, hours of operation issues, and several other required changes. These issues should all be thought through at the time when the decision to pursue e-commerce is being made.

The impact on everyday business operations can be tied into the organizational issues if employees are not prepared for the changes that are likely to occur. For example, the introduction of a web presence by a manufacturing firm to attempt to sell direct to consumers will require a complete change in the fulfillment and shipping area of the firm. This may lead to employee dissatisfaction and result in poor performance in the traditional market, the new market, or both. In establishing the e-strategy, small businesses must attempt to plan for all impacts of the implementation on operations.

Other issues that may arise will include language and cultural barriers if operations are expanding globally, and foreign exchange issues. The types of issues that are faced will depend upon the operations of the firm prior to e-commerce. For example, businesses with an established catalogue or 1-800 sales channel will often find the move to e-commerce simpler, since the delivery channel is established, customer service representatives are trained and knowledgeable, and comfort exists with selling to customers who are not present at the retail outlet. The type of industry and product or service will substantially impact the operational issues that the organization will face.

Getting Connected

The first step in becoming involved in e-commerce for those small businesses that are not already connected is to establish an Internet connection. It is not absolutely necessary for a business to have a connection if all aspects of e-commerce are outsourced, but it would be unlikely that a business could understand e-commerce and take advantage of all of its potential without e-mail and web use within the firm. Numerous alternatives exist for businesses as well as consumers to connect to the Internet through an Internet service provider (ISP) such as dial-up, cable, ADSL (asymmetrical digital subscriber line), satellite, and other advanced connection forms. In choosing one of the alternatives from an ISP, a small business needs to consider its needs and then balance a number of tradeoffs.

The range of Internet connections from ISPs will vary substantially in terms of performance, availability, and cost. The evaluation of ISPs should begin with a review of the performance and availability factors of the local service providers, including services offered, speed of access, historical reliability, security system performance, and other areas of concern. For some businesses it will be important to select a provider that can supply access outside of the local area without significant complexity or additional cost. For example, a business owner who travels frequently from Calgary to other locations across Canada may wish to select an ISP that has free dial-up connections that can be used with her laptop across the country. Similar to investigating other business expenses, familiarization with the options available and a review of the various providers will often lead to identification of the best overall service for the firm.

The type of Internet connection chosen should match with the current needs of the business as well as the planned strategy to be followed for e-commerce. For example, if a business wishes to provide only basic marketing information online, a dial-up connection will suffice to allow the company to check e-mail periodically and use the Internet for other business needs on a sporadic basis. However, if a business is going to attempt to build a fully functional Internet site with e-commerce capability and wishes to provide superior service, a more permanent connection may be desired. A permanent connection can allow the company to receive e-mails continuously, monitor online performance, and perform customizations/maintenance on the website on an ongoing basis. The cost of having a permanent connection has fallen drastically in the past several years to the point where it is no longer a prohibitive cost for even the smallest company.

Permanent connections for small businesses are most often in the form of cable or ADSL. A cable or ADSL connection can range from $40 per month and up, depending on the types of services selected. While the cost of a dial-up connection can be lower than this, businesses need to consider whether the dial-up use of a phone line will be a disruption to other customers and, therefore, necessitate an extra phone line. If this is the case, the permanent connection is the preferable method of connection to the Internet.

The selection of the ISP should also be considered in association with other aspects of the e-strategy being developed. Many ISPs exist and the range of services can vary widely. If the business intends to outsource web-hosting and/or e-commerce transaction systems, it may be preferable and less costly to bundle services with one service provider. The telecommunications companies within Canada are often able to bundle their ISP and phone packages as well, which can provide a discount for services. An overall review of the needs of the business as the strategy is implemented will be worthwhile. The selection of a service provider is by no means on a long-term basis and therefore a change in circumstances can easily be changed with a limited cost for most ISPs, such as a one-month required notice/payout.

Information/Services Online

The Internet offers a wealth of information that can be useful to small business owners in a number of ways. In addition, much of the information available online is free or low cost and, therefore, is very valuable to small business. Information available online can be used to evaluate the competition, better understand the industry, research tax and other issues, and monitor governmental programs and services.

As with the use of any external sources, it is important that online information is evaluated as to the validity of the source, its timeliness, and reasonableness. The wealth of information can be overwhelming and therefore can be time-consuming. For this reason it is important that web users become familiar with search techniques and develop an understanding of which sources are most relevant to the business. The sources of information vary widely online and can include government, professional firms, media, industry organizations, and many others. See the New Business Models box for an example of a business model built around information and services for small business.

The various governments and governmental organizations in Canada provide a number of useful websites for small businesses. The Strategis site mentioned earlier and in Chapter 11 is the federal government resource that includes a wealth of information on numerous topics, including a section called "ebiz.enable" that is targeted to e-business B2B users (see Figure 12.3). The ebiz.enable portal provides users with case studies, statistics, and the ability to ask an expert about issues related to e-business. Several other sections of the Strategis site provide information relevant to e-commerce and small business and include useful guides, information, and data related to such topics as retailing on the Internet, e-commerce in service industries, and e-marketing.

Another very powerful part of the Strategis site is the "Business Information by Sector" section. This section can provide useful links and information about very specific categories. For example, a crafts business can select the "Giftware" and "Crafts" sections of the Strategis site and be able to find useful contacts by province or region that may assist the company (see Figure 12.4). By simply clicking on the

NEW BUSINESS MODELS

Catering to Small Business at bCentral.com

The bCentral site is a Microsoft initiative that aims to provide information to small businesses and ultimately sell products and services. The site provides articles and columns with a great deal of information for small businesses, such as how to get online, how to market on the Web, and how to improve customer service. In many of these articles, Microsoft products and services are profiled.

In addition to providing information, the bCentral product offers an online marketplace where small businesses can purchase goods or list their products for sale on Microsoft affiliate sites such as MSN. The positive aspect for small businesses about bCentral is that the site is dedicated to showing small businesses how they can use Microsoft and Internet technology to level the playing field to compete against larger competitors.

The bCentral site represents a component of Microsoft's new .Net strategy and promotes the use of "rented" services/software application as the company attempts to gain a share of the important application service provider (ASP) market. bCentral offers solutions that assist with website management, e-commerce, accounting, and CRM activities to small businesses through secure Internet connections. The informational aspect of bCentral aims to inform and educate small business owners and employees while also promoting the Microsoft products and services.

Topics of information in the portal include information on preparing business plans, financing business investments, human resources, insurance, travel, and many other topics. Many of these resources are not specific to Microsoft products and represent useful advice to small business owners.

The bCentral site allows other organizations to advertise products and services through banner advertising. This represents a means of making the site a revenue generator since the small business market is an important aspect of many B2B strategies.

With Microsoft's acquisition of Great Plains, a leading accounting application, the bCentral site is a logical location for the company to develop further online integration of software and services. The bCentral portal offered some accounting and finance functionality by mid-2001 but made no mention of Great Plains in the accounting topics. Other accounting-related services are likely to be expanded as well, as bCentral competes with Netledger and other leading competitors.

bCentral.com
www.bCentral.com

Questions

1. Is a site like bCentral truly a valuable service to small businesses or just a marketing effort in disguise? Why?
2. What major benefits do ASPs like bCentral have for small businesses?
3. What types of integration will be important if bCentral aims to build functionality from Great Plains into the mix of other products/services offered?

SOURCE: www.bCentral.com.

Statistics link on that page, the user can then find a wealth of data on a specific category of giftware such as the Jewellery and Precious Metals industry information (see Figure 12.5). The information contained on Strategis is reliable and detailed and therefore can be beneficial for numerous businesses.

A common theme on the Internet is the provision of free information, and many professional service firms have excellent websites for small business owners. For example, Grant Thornton LLP (a chartered accounting firm) has a website that includes a complete section dedicated to owner-managers, with news and advice on a broad range of issues. Some of the "Management issues papers" (see

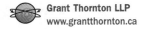

Grant Thornton LLP
www.grantthornton.ca

Figure 12.3   Sample ebiz Page from Strategis

The Strategis site includes information on developing an e-business as well as links to a wealth of useful information.

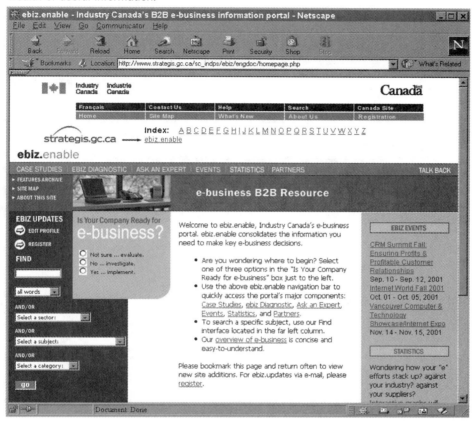

SOURCE: "Ebiz.enable." *Strategis Canada. Industry Canada.* <http://strategis.gc.ca/sc_indps/ebiz/homepage.php>. August 2001. Reprinted with permission.

Figure 12.6) they provide at no cost address concerns such as "Are you a fisherman thinking about incorporation?"; "Doing business outside Canada"; and "Making the most of your audit." Other major accounting and law firms also provide a large amount of information at no cost that can be of significant value to small businesses.

The media is another major source of information on the Internet—including the online components of television and print media as well as online-only media. Online components of print media (such as *The Globe and Mail*) provide free access to Canadian news content, and television media (such as CNNfn) allow users to access a large volume of news at no cost. Other online media, often known as e-zines or online portals (such as CNET and ZdNews), are also huge sources of information regarding technology and e-business, which often include information relevant to small and large organizations.

Building the E-Commerce Presence

The implementation of an e-strategy will require the small business to consider numerous issues. Since small businesses are less likely than larger corporations to

Figure 12.4   Sample of Strategis Industry Information

Details on industries can be obtained within Strategis that are specific and can assist small businesses in gathering useful data.

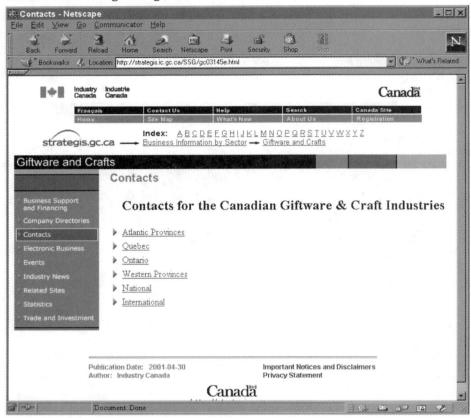

SOURCE: "Business Information by Sector. *Strategis Canada*. Industry Canada. <http://strategis.ic.gc.ca/SSG/ gc03145e.html>. August 2001. Reprinted with permission.

have their own information technology departments with excess time, they will have a high likelihood of outsourcing a great deal of the work involved in building an e-commerce presence. In addition, small businesses must often continue to service and capitalize on existing markets while attempting to utilize e-commerce opportunities without additional staffing. The result of the unique aspects of small businesses entering into e-commerce is that a staged approach (see Figure 12.7) is often adopted whereby firms develop a basic website and then later enhance the site with additional features and capabilities. This growth mimics the stages of website evolution discussed in Chapter 11.

Getting Hosted

The move online will involve establishing both a website location and a website design. These activities can be performed either internally or may be outsourced depending on the capabilities and goals of the firm. The hosting of an Internet site internally requires technologies that many small businesses do not have or wish to invest in; however, many small technology firms do host their own sites due to their expertise in the area. To host a website, the company would require

Figure 12.5   Illustration of Industry Statistics Available from Strategis

The statistics contained on Strategis are reliable and detailed, and therefore can be beneficial for small businesses in numerous industries.

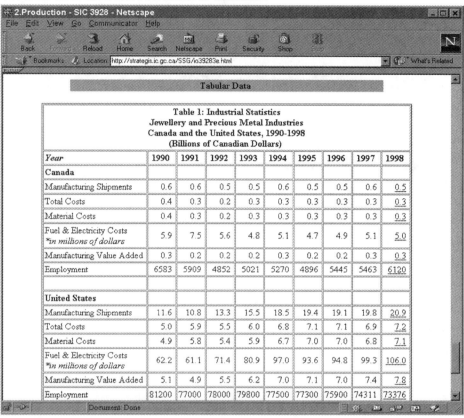

Table 1: Industrial Statistics
Jewellery and Precious Metal Industries
Canada and the United States, 1990-1998
(Billions of Canadian Dollars)

Year	1990	1991	1992	1993	1994	1995	1996	1997	1998
Canada									
Manufacturing Shipments	0.6	0.6	0.5	0.5	0.6	0.5	0.5	0.6	0.5
Total Costs	0.4	0.3	0.2	0.3	0.3	0.3	0.3	0.3	0.3
Material Costs	0.4	0.3	0.2	0.3	0.3	0.3	0.3	0.3	0.3
Fuel & Electricity Costs *in millions of dollars	5.9	7.5	5.6	4.8	5.1	4.7	4.9	5.1	5.0
Manufacturing Value Added	0.3	0.2	0.2	0.2	0.3	0.2	0.2	0.3	0.3
Employment	6583	5909	4852	5021	5270	4896	5445	5463	6120
United States									
Manufacturing Shipments	11.6	10.8	13.3	15.5	18.5	19.4	19.1	19.8	20.9
Total Costs	5.0	5.9	5.5	6.0	6.8	7.1	7.1	6.9	7.2
Material Costs	4.9	5.8	5.4	5.9	6.7	7.0	7.0	6.8	7.1
Fuel & Electricity Costs *in millions of dollars	62.2	61.1	71.4	80.9	97.0	93.6	94.8	99.3	106.0
Manufacturing Value Added	5.1	4.9	5.5	6.2	7.0	7.1	7.0	7.4	7.8
Employment	81200	77000	78000	79800	77500	77300	75900	74311	73376

SOURCE: "Tabular Data." *Strategis Canada. Industry Canada.* <http://strategis.ic.gc.ca/SSG/io39283e.html>. August 2001. Reprinted with permission.

a fast, stable, and permanent Internet connection in order that users can visit the site at all times. The company would also require high-performance hardware, specific software applications (e.g., web server software), and other technologies such as firewalls. This requirement brings with it a number of concerns such as security risks, system performance, and internal expertise, all of which can be costly issues to deal with.

Outsourcing

The complexity of hosting a website prompts many small businesses to outsource. Outsourcing reduces the technological demands within the firm but brings up other issues that the business must consider. The choice of a web host will be based partly upon the service needs of the business. If the website will allow online sales transactions to occur, the host must have the ability to process transactions, whereas a basic marketing site can be hosted by nearly any service provider. A site that allows transactions will also require that the small business is selective in choosing a service provider that has a solid security system in place and is able to provide evidence of its security capabilities.

Figure 12.6   Sample of Free Resources from Grant Thornton

Many professional services firms, such as Grant Thornton LLP, include a great deal of useful information for small and large businesses.

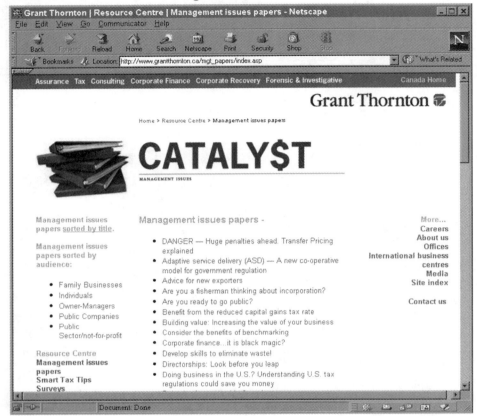

SOURCE: "Cataly$t Management Issues." *Grant Thornton*. <http://www.grantthornton.ca/mgt_papers/index.asp>. Reprinted with permission.

The basic needs for services will assist the business in identifying an outsourcing firm, but just as important will be to find a firm capable of working in manner consistent with the goals of the small business. The development of an

Figure 12.7   Building the E-Commerce Presence

The process of developing an e-commerce presence can be broken down into a continuous process of design and improvements.

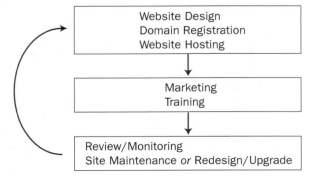

Internet presence will require close communication between the small business and service provider and, similar to other services, quality can vary significantly. Atlantic Canada Home (ACH), a diversified provider of products and services worldwide, is a small business based in Charlottetown, PEI. The company was founded in 1997 and began to establish a website through outsourcing shortly after being formed. Unfortunately, ACH was completely dissatisfied with the progress and outcome of the website under development and decided to shift the entire contract to another service provider. The site was completed successfully by the new service provider, and ACH has maintained its relationship with the firm, which continues to host and maintain the site.[10] This example is one that can commonly occur and results in wasted time, frustration, and excess costs.

In identifying a service provider it is critical that owners spend time evaluating the types of services provided as well as ask for detailed information on how the project will progress. The dissatisfaction that occurs in many outsourcing arrangements is due to a misunderstanding between the firms involved—spending more time up front can reduce the likelihood of poor outcomes.

Credit Card Processing

The ability to process credit card transactions online is one that has evolved from being a difficult task to a more reasonable service that can be obtained. Initially, Canadian banks were quite hesitant to provide small businesses with **merchant accounts** that were able to accept credit card transactions (e.g., Visa and MasterCard) over the Internet. Due to the new nature of e-commerce, many of the banks required small businesses to establish holding accounts of $5000 to $25 000 in order to ensure that fraudulent transactions would not be defaulted to the bank itself. In addition, some merchant account providers established **holdbacks** of specified amounts, such as 10 percent, that would be held in the holding account for up to six months on a rolling basis. Another major issue at the early stages of e-commerce and still at issue with some merchant card providers is the high **discount rate** applied to online merchant transaction accounts. The discount rate is the amount that the merchant account provider takes as a percentage of sales conducted through credit cards and normally would be less than 4 percent; however, early online entrepreneurs were sometimes faced with up to 15 percent fees, due to the high perceived risk. The result of these complexities for small businesses was a major reduction in cash flow and a deterrent to becoming involved in e-commerce.

> **MERCHANT ACCOUNT:** account held by businesses in order to collect payment through credit cards.
>
> **HOLDBACK:** amount that credit card companies keep in escrow to reduce the risk of bad debts and fraudulent credit card use.
>
> **DISCOUNT RATE:** the amount that the merchant account provider takes as a percentage of sales conducted through credit cards.

Customized services were developed that cater to small business payment processing over the past several years. One example of such a service is Internet Secure, a leading Internet credit card processor, which established itself as an important alternative for small businesses during the period when it was very difficult to obtain an online merchant account. Internet Secure allows its customers to join its service by paying an enrollment fee starting at approximately $300 and guarantees that you receive merchant account status without dealing with banks or other service providers. The company looks after all payment processing and offers various methods of approving transactions such as integrated, online approval. Users of the Internet Secure service can choose from a number of packages that offer Canadian and/or U.S. currency support and pay a discount fee to Internet Secure, similar to other merchant account providers. Numerous other payment service providers have developed services similar to those offered by Internet Secure that simplify the process of accepting payments but may or may

Internet Secure
www.internetsecure.com

not be preferable to dealing with a standard bank/merchant account provider, depending upon the services required.

The pressure mounted upon banks from small businesses and other lobby groups and has since led to major improvements in merchant accounts. Most of the major banks now offer merchant accounts that allow Internet transactions with little or no holding amounts involved, as well as provide additional services. For example, CIBC has partnered with Global Payments/Payway to provide small businesses, web businesses, and large businesses with the ability to accept credit cards online (see Figure 12.8). In this partnership, CIBC is the merchant account provider and banking solution, while Global Payments offers the technology that allows businesses to integrate their e-commerce solution with a secure payment processing technology. This is a common method by which businesses establish their e-commerce systems and allows a company that specializes in transaction processing to handle that end of payment processing.

The growth of e-commerce and demand for payment-processing mechanisms has given way to a wide variety of services being developed. The important features for small businesses to consider in selecting a payment-processing system are ease of integration, currency, and security. If the site is being outsourced or

Figure 12.8   CIBC's Internet Payment Service

CIBC's business services include the ability for merchants to accept credit cards online through its affiliation with Global Payments.

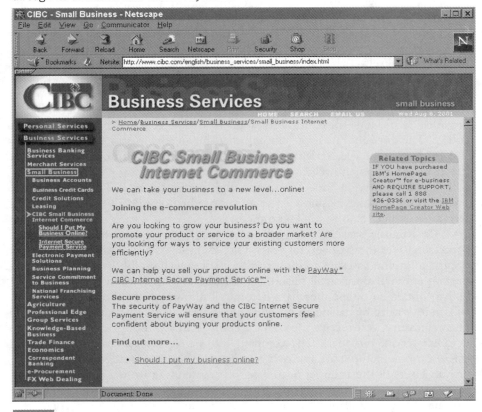

SOURCE: "CIBC Small Business Internet Commerce." *Canadian Imperial Bank of Commerce.* <http://www.cibc.com/english/business_services/small_business/index.html>. August 2001. Reprinted with permission.

developed in-house, it is important that the payment mechanism can be easily integrated with the shopping cart or purchasing mechanism the website uses. Some services, such as the Canada Post eParcel solution for small businesses, provide an easily integrated shopping cart technology. The Canada Post service is provided in partnership with Clic.net and allows web designers to simply cut and paste customized HTML codes into their website to integrate the shopping cart and payment process. Services such as this allow even novice web designers to create powerful, integrated sites.

The ability to deal in multiple currencies can be of importance to online retailers operating in global markets. It is not necessary to deal in foreign currencies, but some Canadian businesses have found that allowing U.S. customers to make purchases with the American dollar resulted in improved sales success. For this reason it is important when establishing a merchant account to give consideration to the currencies that will be accepted and how they will be handled. As evidenced by the discussion here, although credit card processing is only one small component of an e-commerce presence, it is one that is of critical importance and should be fully considered as an e-strategy is being developed. The time involved in establishing a merchant account can also be several weeks for many businesses and therefore this process should be commenced early.

Marketing

The marketing efforts required by small businesses can capitalize on many of the tools available on the Internet. Chapter 11 identified and described many of the marketing and online advertising approaches that can be valuable to small and large businesses. The difficulties small businesses may encounter will include search engine optimization, developing a community, and reaching new markets. The promise of global markets through e-commerce is not untrue, but is commonly misunderstood—since the "build it and they will come" approach doesn't work on the Internet, where billions of websites exist. Whereas large organizations may have employees and automated tools monitoring such issues as search engine placement, many small businesses will need to outsource their website redesign or have fewer resources available. Developing an understanding of how major search engines work will help the company draw traffic to its site.

The approaches to marketing will include the use of traditional media and advertising efforts. Many small businesses now include their website address on business cards, packaging, and on brochures that customers may see. The Internet allows small businesses to be innovative in their approach to developing existing customer relationships as well as in attracting new customers.

Training

The implementation of an e-commerce initiative may also require training for employees. The amount and type of training that will be required will vary by organization according to its size, the type of strategy being pursued, the level of internal expertise required, and the owner-manager's commitment. The implementation of any e-commerce activities should at least be accompanied by basic training sessions that provide employees with an understanding of how the company's own website works, what it offers, and the impact on internal processes so they can effectively deal with customers. In many circumstances it is also beneficial to offer employees general Internet training as well, so they may evaluate competitors, understand the industry, and possibly make useful suggestions. The necessity for Internet training is declining as the use of the Internet increases but is still of benefit within many organizations.

Training efforts may also be necessitated by the adoption of e-commerce depending upon the technologies being utilized and the level of outsourcing being used. For example, a business may decide to outsource initial website development but train employees to maintain the site and make minor modifications. In this instance an employee or a few employees may be trained in basic website design principles using the HTML editor that the firm will use. The key to training efforts is to ensure that employees are comfortable with and understand the technologies being employed *and* understand the business processes related to the e-commerce initiative.

Application Service Providers

The explosive growth of Internet-based products and services has included the development of application service providers (ASPs) with solutions aimed particularly at small businesses. These ASPs offer services such as accounting systems, website tools, payroll applications, and many others. The benefits of utilizing an ASP include reduced need for internal expertise, software upgrades, and administration.

Figure 12.9   Illustration of a Small Business ASP

The Oracle Small Business tools allow small businesses to maintain a powerful set of financial records and develop sophisticated e-commerce capabilities with reasonable costs and relative ease.

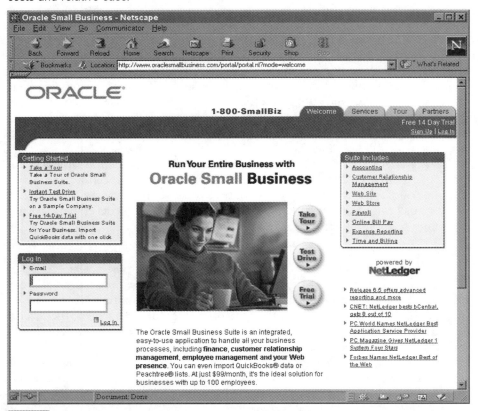

SOURCE: "Home Page." *Oracle Small Business.com*. <http://www.oraclesmallbusiness.com>. December 2001. Reprinted by permission of NetLedger Inc. All rights reserved.

One notable ASP that has targeted the small business sector is Oracle Small Business (originally known as Netledger), which provides an integrated suite of products that handle accounting/finance, customer relationship management, employee management, and your web presence (see Figure 12.9).[11] The Oracle ASP costs small businesses approximately US$100 per month, depending upon the modules it uses, and provides a system that is extremely powerful, fully web-integrated, and relatively hassle-free. The integration with the Web allows small organizations to provide customers with the option to review their account on-line, pay bills, and submit orders—a service that many may find valuable. In addition, the integration allows a custom Webstore to be designed using information from the accounting system to control inventory, pricing, and other issues.

Oracle Small Business Suite
www.oraclesmallbusiness.com

Trading Exchanges and Marketplaces

Internet-based trading exchanges and marketplaces represent an important area where small businesses can market and sell their products or services. Trading exchanges represent a growing market that allows B2B commerce to take place efficiently and effectively online. They are an important trend that small businesses can use to have their products listed as options along with large organizations and other small competitors. The key to the use of trading exchanges for small businesses will be in identifying a strategy for implementation that fits the overall business objectives.

Small businesses that offer numerous products may look to trading exchanges as a means of selling excess products or may use it as a day-to-day sales channel. The key to effective use is to choose a strategy that the business can support and implementing that strategy well—with a focus on customer service and profitability. The use of trading exchanges can also be of benefit to service-based businesses as a marketing channel and can result in important sales leads being generated. Upon devising a strategy for the use of a trading exchange, the company must first determine which exchanges (and how many) they should utilize and then register and become familiar with how the operations work. The exchanges need to be monitored on an ongoing basis, similar to any other sales channel, to determine what is working and what is not.

E-Procurement

The purchase of goods and services online by small businesses represents another important aspect for an e-strategy. The number of firms, both large and small, that are targeting goods and services to small businesses through their own websites as well as through trading exchanges, affiliate sites, and other means, has grown substantially as the Internet evolved. This growth has resulted in a reasonable amount of competition in many areas, thus leading to cost reductions and opportunities for the small business owner.

Small businesses can acquire a wide range of products and services online, from office supplies and computers to Internet services like web design and hosting. The key to the use of e-procurement in small business is to evaluate the market and at least use the options provided to negotiate prices with local suppliers if they are preferred. For example, Staples.ca (and many other firms) offers many office supply products online, where the small business can review the prices easily and demand lower prices from an existing local supplier. Other savings, especially in time, can also be achieved by using e-procurement to acquire goods through the Internet, by creating electronic processes and using technological tools to speed up the entire process. Many unique types of services have been developed that cater to small businesses through partnerships of large organizations as well. For example, CIBC and Staples formed a partnership to provide small businesses with low-cost banking, time savings, and small business knowledge through bizSmart.com. See the Canadian Snapshots box for a discussion of the services offered through this partnership.

CANADIAN SNAPSHOTS

Low Costs at bizSmart.com

bizSmart is described as a unique offering of services designed to save Canadian small business owners and entrepreneurs both time and money. The services are offered as a partnership between CIBC and Business Depot/Staples, along with other contributing members and affiliates who provide discounted products/services and low prices. The bizSmart site also offers free access to the Knowledge Centre, its library of information for the small business owner.

The bizSmart effort targets the small office/home office (SOHO) entrepreneurs in Canada—providing no-fee daily business banking as well as guaranteed low prices on purchases. The banking/financial services end of the partnership is a major selling point of the service, which claims to be able to save many SOHO businesses $2000 per year in unnecessary costs. Online banking can be carried out 24/7 through the service, and ATMs can be used at no cost at all CIBC locations.

Representing nearly 80 percent of the estimated 2 million small businesses in Canada, the SOHO market is an important and growing contingent. The Canada NewsWire reported that bizSmart offers

registered small business members the following specific products and services:

- A suite of no-fee financial services including:
  - a business-operating account with no-fee daily business banking;
  - unlimited free chequing;
  - no-fee set-up for a business line of credit with approvals determined in seconds for up to $100 000 in unsecured credit;
  - a new approach to qualifying startup businesses by taking into account entrepreneurial and management attributes and by changing the definition of an existing business, from the minimum operating history of two years, traditionally used by the financial industry, to one year;
  - a bizSmart Visa card with no annual fee to be available to members; and
  - a business savings account offering high daily interest.
  - Convenient one-stop shopping at bizSmart.com:
  - guaranteed lowest local area rates, plus discounts, on long-distance and cellular telephone services with bizSmart's

SmartRate Service provided by Innofone;
- everyday low prices on Business Depot's full range of office products and free delivery on all orders over $50;
- quick online incorporation services from e-Incorp;
- help in evaluating, choosing, and installing the right Dell desktop, notebook, workstation, and server hardware;
- business books through the customized bizSmart members Chapters.ca book store;
- convenient FedEx domestic and international shipping, ordering, and tracking;
- simplified accounting with QuickBooks software supporting downloads directly from bizSmart business banking accounts; and
- discounts and free shipping on customized NEBS business forms, stationery, and logo wear.
- Free member access to The Knowledge Centre. The Knowledge Centre offers information on over 50 small business management topics, quick tips for saving time and money, interactive presentations, ready-to-use financial

(Continued)

tools and templates, interactive online tutorials, and weekly e-bulletins on a wide variety of subjects.

BizSmart is one of many online service providers looking to capture the important small business market. Several other international players such as American Express and other financial institutions are quickly moving to enter the same or similar markets.

Questions

1. Why can bizSmart offer these valuable services to small businesses at discount prices?
2. Is the business model of bizSmart sustainable? Why?
3. What concerns must bizSmart address as foreign competition enters the market?

SOURCES: www.bizsmart.com; www.newswire.ca/releases/October2000/18/c3897.html.

The use of online procurement by small businesses has led to the development of many small business portals aiming to create their own niche in the marketplace by assisting others to keep costs down. For example, Equalfooting.com is a marketplace that focuses on small businesses within the manufacturing industry. Equalfooting provides the ability to buy products, sell products, and arrange financing through its site. In becoming a member of this site, small businesses are able to purchase goods at pre-negotiated discounts from numerous suppliers. In addition, this site and others provide small businesses with the opportunity to create "Request for Quotations" that are distributed to available suppliers through Equalfooting's network. Service providers like Equalfooting exist for many specific industries and also across multiple industries, and can provide a valuable market for both buying and selling.

Chapter Summary

KEY TERMS

merchant accounts
holdbacks
discount rate

E-commerce represents a significant opportunity for small businesses. Not only does the Internet allow small businesses to increase market reach, but it can provide them with an opportunity to gather a wealth of valuable information. In addition, the use of the Internet to conduct operational processes such as procurement and billing represents an opportunity for small businesses to reduce their costs.

Developing a strategy for small business e-commerce requires planning and analysis similar to any other business decision. The small business must determine what opportunities exist, what costs need to be incurred, and what level of management's involvement will be required. The major issues that small businesses may have to address include overcoming technical weaknesses and ensuring that the costs involved are justified by expected outcomes.

Small businesses may use the Internet to gather competitive intelligence and other useful data or for other purposes. For example, the number of services available to small businesses is expanding rapidly and they can "rent" applications from application service providers or take advantage of other online tools. The Internet has assisted in reducing the in-house technical requirements for many small businesses by converting much software into simple point-and-click usage.

The e-commerce strategy and presence for a small business can take numerous forms. The website can be a simple "brochureware" page or within reasonable costs can become a fully transactional online presence. The small business must determine which strategy is most appropriate for its industry and customer base. The level of e-commerce use by small businesses will continue to grow as the use of the Internet by individuals and businesses becomes more commonplace.

Tools for Online Learning

To help you master the material in this chapter and stay up to date with new developments in e-business, visit www.pearsoned.ca/trites . Resources include:

> Review Questions and Exercises

> Problems for Discussion

> Recommended Readings

> Updates to Boxes, Case Studies and textual material

> Links to demonstration tools related to course topics including sample Web sites

> Streaming CBC Videos with Cases

Endnotes

1. InnovaQuest, "The State of Electronic Commerce in Atlantic Canada," Atlantic Canada Opportunities Agency, March 2000.
2. Carroll, J. and R. Broadhead, *Small Business Online.* Prentice Hall, 1998.
3. Davis, J., "Mom and Pop Go Online," *InfoWorld,* Framingham, May 28, 2001.
4. Carroll, J. and R. Broadhead.
5. Ibid.
6. McCue, S., "Small firms and the Internet: Force or Farce?" International Trade Forum, Geneva, 1999.
7. Carroll, J. and R. Broadhead, p. 180.
8. InnovaQuest.
9. Hunter, G., M. Diochon, D. Pugsley, and B. Wright, "Small Business Adoption of Information Technology: Unique Challenges," Proceedings of the Information Resources Management Association 2001 Conference.
10. InnovaQuest.
11. www.oraclesmallbusiness.com.

Privacy, Legal, and Taxation Issues in E-Commerce

learning objectives

When you complete this chapter you should be able to:

1. Explain the importance of law and taxation in the context of e-commerce and the Internet.

2. Identify and describe the major issues surrounding privacy online.

3. Discuss how organizations can comply with Canadian privacy legislation.

4. Describe how intellectual property issues impact e-commerce.

5. Identify the major legal issues that companies need to be concerned with on the Internet.

6. Discuss the taxation issues that e-commerce has created.

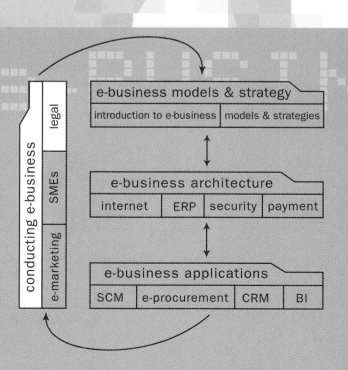

Introduction

The rapid growth in e-commerce and increase in globalization over the past several years has given rise to several new issues in the areas of law and taxation. The legal and tax systems of Canada and most countries worldwide were not designed for the complications of commerce conducted through electronic means. While the existing legal system had previously addressed many similar issues to those raised by e-commerce, the legislation and legal infrastructure have numerous areas where the concerns over e-commerce are not well addressed. Substantial effort has been directed at legal and taxation issues related to e-commerce in the past few years, and progress has been made; however, there remains a great deal of change to be made in the future. This chapter will review the issues, progress, and remaining challenges of the law and e-commerce.

The concerns over e-commerce legal issues have perhaps been brought to the forefront by the Napster case, although it focuses on only one major area of concern—intellectual property. The Napster service has been nearly brought to a halt by the rulings of the court system, which stated that the music copying application violated the intellectual property rights of musical artists by allowing the illegal copying of MP3 files. As an important and developing area, intellectual property issues such as copyright, trademarks, domain names, and patents are all being addressed by the legal systems within countries worldwide.

The improvements in technology and e-commerce applications have given rise to serious concerns over privacy on the Internet. The tracking of users and potential identification of individuals through technology threatens the right to privacy of all Internet users and thus is a growing area of importance. The Canadian government has begun to address the issue of privacy through new legislation, as discussed in more detail below. Other countries and international organizations are also monitoring issues with regards to privacy and many have adopted similar legislation and guidelines that both consumers and businesses need to be aware of.

The legal system is also addressing numerous other issues with regard to e-commerce. Some of the principal concerns are in relation to jurisdictional issues, which also impact taxation. In addition, electronic contracts, enforcement, liability, and unfair competition issues all arise as the use of the Internet and globalization of commerce change the competitive landscape of business. These issues will be discussed throughout this chapter with an aim to highlight areas of importance for management of e-businesses—in specific cases, it is important to consult professional legal counsel.

Internet Privacy

The concerns over privacy have grown immensely as e-commerce has developed and consumers and businesses provide a growing amount of information to often-unknown sources. The major concerns in this regard are wide-ranging, since many types of private information could impact employment, personal finances, and other aspects of life. For example, medical information is a key privacy concern. Imagine if an individual's medical records became available to a potential employer when that individual had a serious illness—the individual could be turned down for a job based on what should be confidential information. In less serious cases of privacy infringement, advertisers may gather details about an individual and flood that person with ads and other information—a serious annoyance. Despite the severity of the issue, one thing is for sure—individuals have a right to privacy and the Internet has changed the landscape for which privacy must be protected.

Information of a personal nature can be gathered through numerous means over the Internet. For example, while surfing the Web, users' movements can be tracked by the use of cookies, web bugs, and other tracking tools, as described earlier in this book. Other data/information can be collected or revealed about an individual through chat groups, news boards, or e-mail. The number of potential sources of information available makes it quite possible that a person's privacy can be inappropriately handled through the Internet. The ability of online businesses to gather data has also been complicated by the issue of merging the online data with offline data, as was the case with DoubleClick (see the New Business Models box on page 214 in Chapter 11). DoubleClick was essentially given the approval to merge data—with the exception of medical and financial information—as long as users are made aware of the use and have the ability to opt-out.

The increasing concerns over privacy have led to the development of legislation within Canada and abroad. The Canadian government developed the **Personal Information Protection and Electronic Documents Act** (originally Bill C-54 and later introduced and approved as Bill C-6) as a component of Canada's Electronic Commerce Strategy. The strategy recognized that one important component of assisting Canada to become a world leader in e-commerce was to instil confidence in the Internet through legislation and other means.[1] The Personal Information Protection and Electronic Documents Act (PIPEDA) provides privacy protection for personal information, and came partially into effect on January 1, 2001.

The PIPEDA is federal legislation that applies initially to federally regulated organizations including airlines, banks, telephone companies, and broadcasting companies. In addition, all businesses in Nunavut, the Yukon, and the Northwest Territories are subject to the act as of January 1, 2001. The second phase of implementation for PIPEDA is January 1, 2002, when all organizations that collect, use, or disclose personal health information come under the legislation. The final phase of implementation is January 1, 2004, when the act becomes applicable to all commercial activity.[2] The implementation of PIPEDA is confused partially by the governmental structure of Canada, whereby the provincial governments are responsible for the issues in this legislation. As such the PIPEDA includes clauses that allow provincial legislation to supersede the act if the legislation is substantially similar to the federal legislation—an attempt by the federal government to encourage harmonization within Canada.

The PIPEDA is designed to protect any personal information that is collected, used, or disclosed within the private sector. The privacy rights of Canadians are protected by the Privacy Act (1983) with regard to the personal information collected, used, or disclosed by federal governmental organizations. Most of the provinces have similar legislation in effect with regard to provincial government organizations. **Personal information** is defined within the act as:

- name, age, weight, height
- medical records
- income, purchases and spending habits
- race, ethnic origin and colour
- blood type, DNA code, fingerprints
- marital status and religion
- education
- home address and phone number.[3]

PERSONAL INFORMATION PROTECTION AND ELECTRONIC DOCUMENTS ACT (PIPEDA): Canadian legislation that provides privacy protection for personal information and comes into effect over the period of January 1, 2001, to 2004.

PERSONAL INFORMATION: information that could identify an individual and could potentially be used to discriminate against or invade an individual's privacy.

The definition of personal information covers each of these specific items in order to ensure that individuals' privacy is respected and not used inappropriately. The misuse of this information can lead to inappropriate business practices, identity theft, and discrimination and is, therefore, of critical importance.

The privacy principles within the PIPEDA are based upon the 1996 standards established by the Canadian Standards Association (CSA) in its "Model Code for the Protection of Personal Information." This code, similar to the new legislation, establishes the rights of individuals to access personal information about themselves held by organizations and to have that information corrected if it is incorrect.

The 10 principles included in the CSA Model Code are as follows:

1. *Accountability.* Organizations are responsible for all personal information under their control and shall establish procedures to ensure that the organization complies with all of the 10 principles.

2. *Identifying purposes.* Organizations will identify the purpose for which they are collecting personal information to individuals prior to or at the time that the information is collected.

3. *Consent.* The individual must give consent to the collection, use, or disclosure of their personal information.

4. *Limiting collection.* All information must be collected by fair and legal means and should be limited to information deemed necessary by the organization for the purposes outlined to the individual.

5. *Limiting use, disclosure, and retention.* The use of personal information should be limited to the purposes outlined to the individual at the time of collection unless further consent is obtained and information should only be retained for as long as deemed necessary by the terms outlined.

6. *Accuracy.* Organizations shall keep personal information accurate, complete, and up to date.

7. *Safeguards.* Appropriate security and internal controls should be in place to protect personal information.

8. *Openness.* Organizations should make their policies readily available to individuals with regard to the handling of personal information.

9. *Individual access.* Individuals have the right to request whether information about them exists and to request the ability to review that information and challenge its accuracy and completeness.

10. *Challenging compliance.* Individuals are able to address their concerns over compliance with the above principles to a designated individual or individuals. In the Canadian context this principle now leads ultimately to the Privacy Commissioner, who has the right to investigate concerns where individuals do not receive satisfaction from the company or organization itself.[4]

The principles set out in the CSA code are, of course, only a set of guidelines that can be interpreted differently by different organizations and individuals. The PIPEDA legislation aims to give the Privacy Commissioner the authority to handle complaints related to privacy whereby individuals are not satisfied with the outcomes of their discussions with an organization. One example of the type of issue that can arise within the legislation that is subject to interpretation is the Toysmart issue that arose in early 2001. Toysmart had filed for bankruptcy protection and the receivers were considering the sale of customer lists and marketing data as one means of recovering funds owed to creditors. The concern that arose was that Toysmart's collection of information had indicated that personal information would not be disclosed to other parties without the express consent of the individual—now that information was potentially going to be sold. The Toysmart case focused around principle five in that use should be limited to that which was identified at the time the information was collected. A court decision was not reached in the case as Walt Disney Co., a major shareholder, bought the list and destroyed it to deal with the issue quickly.[5] This case illustrates how privacy issues can be an ongoing concern and how illegitimate use could have an adverse effect on e-commerce.

Establishing a Privacy Policy

The enactment of PIPEDA has led to the need for many organizations to establish a privacy policy that can be disclosed and communicated to Internet users and customers. In order to comply with the principles in the act and to provide customers with relevant information, the web pages of many businesses now include a "Privacy Policy" link that leads to a full disclosure of the company's policy. For example, MTT is the telecom services provider in Nova Scotia and is a wholly owned subsidiary of Aliant Telecom and Aliant Telecom/MTT. As a federally regulated organization, Aliant and Aliant MTT must comply with PIPEDA and have established a privacy policy and other disclosures on their website (see Figure 13.1). Included in the privacy policy is a discussion of the types of information collected by MTT, the companies that may share the information (related parties), and an opt-out clause to prevent sharing with other subsidiary firms. The privacy policy also discusses the company's use of cookies, the PIPEDA, and discloses how customers may direct their concerns both inside and outside the company (e.g., the Privacy Commissioner's office).

Other Privacy Legislation

The development of legislation in Canada and other countries has been somewhat pressured by the lead taken with regard to privacy in Europe. The European Union's Privacy Directive went into effect in 1998 and established relatively strong privacy regulations for members of the European Union (EU). In addition, the legislation restricts the flow of personal information outside the EU by permitting its transfer only to countries that provide an "adequate" level of privacy protection. Prior to PIPEDA Canada had little protection for privacy, and other countries like the United States were primarily using policies of self-regulation. The EU's approach led to extended negotiations with Canada, the U.S., and many other countries in an effort to establish what has become known as "safe harbour" provisions.[6] The safe harbour provisions would essentially designate specific companies as complying with the EU requirements by becoming certified so that U.S. companies could conduct business in the EU nations. By March 2000 the U.S. government and the EU had nearly reached an agreement, but since that time the EU has voiced concerns over numerous privacy policies in other countries. The Canadian PIPEDA has been criticized for being too slow to be applied to all organizations, Australian policies are criticized for lacking in application, and the U.S. policies of self-regulation were constantly criticized by EU privacy advocates.[7]

Another major issue of concern in the privacy area is the protection of privacy for children. The Internet is an open network and the growth in its use has

Figure 13.1   Example of an Organization's Online Privacy Policy

MTT's website includes detailed information about its privacy policy to users and discusses the means by which users may address their complaints or concerns.

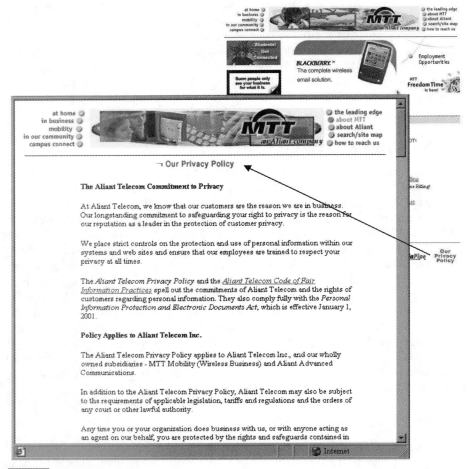

SOURCE: "Our Privacy Policy." *Aliant Telecom/MTT Inc.* <http://www.mtt.ca/AboutMTT/Privacy/privacy.html>. December 2001. Reprinted by permission Aliant Telecom Inc. All rights reserved.

brought many children to become avid users. While children can often learn to use the Internet quite quickly, they are less likely to understand the risks and concerns over privacy protection than adults are. The United States established the Children's On-line Privacy Protection Act, which establishes privacy requirements for websites that target children. The Children's On-line Privacy Protection Act applies not only to U.S. sites but to any website that is perceived to be targeting U.S. children and, therefore, can have wide-reaching effects on the operation of any website in Canada or elsewhere. For example, a toy company established in Canada may decide to sell into the United States to expand its market. If that company's Website could conceivably be used by children and aims to sell to that market the company must be aware of the Children's On-line Privacy Protection Act and its implications on information collection and use. The growth in concerns over privacy protection will continue to give rise to legislation and policies that businesses must consider as they operate outside their own country's boundaries through the Internet.

Privacy and Wireless Devices

The increasing use of wireless technologies is bringing additional privacy concerns to the forefront. Users of cellular phones, PDAs, and other wireless devices may be subject to all of the concerns over Internet privacy but may also be subject to additional concerns. The use of wireless technology can potentially allow a user's exact location and movements to be tracked, in addition to websites visited, telephone calls placed, and other information transferred. These issues are of critical importance as an individual's location and activities are very private information that needs to be protected from misuse.

The use of wireless technologies also brings with it concerns over security. The security of Internet access through telephone, cable, and other access methods has been developing for several years, and just as users are beginning to feel comfortable with these systems, wireless adds a new dimension. Consider the use of a PDA to conduct financial transactions through a bank—requiring the user's password and other personal information to be transmitted. This information is now transmitted through the airwaves and therefore can be much more susceptible to theft or misuse if appropriate security mechanisms are not in place.

The risks of misuse of wireless technologies and infringement of privacy need to be balanced with what may be considered useful to the individual. For example, some advertisers hope to be able to deliver discounts to wireless devices in the appropriate location, such as in a specific mall. If a wireless user walks into the West Edmonton Mall and receives a list of discounts for various stores in the mall, the advertiser has potentially delivered a valuable service. On the other hand, that delivery indicates that the individual's movements are being tracked by at least one organization (wireless service provider) and the information could be passed to advertisers or other organizations, potentially compromising the individual's privacy and freedom of movement. These types of privacy concerns will continue to evolve but represent important issues for individual consumers to investigate fully and for organizations to develop policies around.

Privacy and Technologies

The concerns over privacy on the Internet have stimulated some entrepreneurs to develop software and applications designed to assist users to avoid privacy issues. David Sobel, general counsel for the Washington, DC-based Electronic Privacy Information Center (epic.org) stated, "Technologies that facilitate anonymous use of the Internet are really critical to the survival of the Internet as an open and democratic forum."[8] The technologies that can be used to protect an individual's privacy online are many but most attempt to accomplish a similar goal—to make the user an anonymous web surfer.

**Electronic Privacy
Information Center**
www.epic.org

The programs that can reduce privacy issues include Freedom (Zero-Knowledge Systems Inc.), Anonymizer, SafeWeb, IDzap, Somebody, and several others. Freedom, for example, allows users to surf anonymously by removing information regarding the user's IP address and other identifying information. Freedom routes requests from users through its Montreal-based network servers and provides users with an alias so that they are not tracked by other websites. Users can also release information to trusted parties by asking to unmask some information in order to complete a purchase or fill out a particular form online. See the New Business Models box for a discussion of the privacy protection issue and some of the concerns it raises.

Anonymizer
www.anonymizer.com

NEW BUSINESS MODELS

Privacy Fighting at Anonymizer

The technologies of the Internet bring both positive and negative changes to the world. One of the most serious concerns in recent history has been the protection of privacy and the rights of individuals to use the Web without being tracked and monitored. One of the leading applications for protecting one's privacy online is Anonymizer.com.

The ability for employers to track employee use of the Internet while at work is an issue that has led to much debate. With no clear legal ruling on the issue, companies like Anonymizer have developed a business model that aids web users in "masking" their identity from employers, governments, ISPs, and even the websites they visit. Anonymizer essentially masks your Internet IP address and allows users to visit sites that may be banned or a controversial subject.

The use of anonymous surfing technologies has led to concerns by those who seek to protect specific groups from material on the Internet. Few would disagree with schools aiming to block children from reaching pornographic material online, but tools like Anonymizer

can allow web-savvy students to circumvent the protective controls if those sites themselves are not blocked. Anonymizer has a variety of services, including private surfing, e-mail, chat, and telephony, with the fee for service depending upon the options chosen. Some of its competitors offer similar services—some for free.

Other uses of monitoring and blocking tools online however are much more controversial. Many countries and governments severely restrict the use of the Internet for citizens and monitor their usage. For example, Saudi Arabia restricts its citizens from accessing material that is pornographic or contrary to the state system by routing all Internet traffic through a central server with filter mechanisms. Other countries such as China severely restrict Internet use by requiring ISPs to block sites of Western media, Taiwan and Hong Kong newspapers, and human rights groups. From a Western perspective these practices seem questionable, but tools like Anonymizer can allow web users in these countries to circumvent the rules—at least until the government catches up.

The use of Anonymizer and SafeWeb has created much concern for governments in some countries. Essentially, these tools make it appear to the government filters that the user is visiting the IP address of Anonymizer, even if the user actually accesses pornography or other banned materials. Anonymizer simply encrypts the material and uses a framing mechanism to display the user's destination. Attempting to prevent use of these tools, governments have attempted to block access to Anonymizer's IP address. Anonymizer however, feels that the Internet should be an open forum, and to allow users to continue to use its services, it cycles through various domain names and IP addresses so that users effectively stay one step ahead of their governments.

Some governments and employers are likely very upset with applications like Anonymizer, since their ability to control and monitor use of the Internet is diminished. Privacy advocates, however, congratulate such services on protecting the rights of individuals and keeping the Internet an open medium.

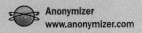

Anonymizer
www.anonymizer.com

Questions

1. Does Anonymizer appear to be providing a valuable service?
2. Should this service be provided to individuals in countries where the government controls Internet use?
3. Should Anonymizer restrict the sites that its users can access, such as forbidding access to pornography, since its tool allows web surfers to waste time at work?

SOURCES: Lee, J., "Punching Holes in Internet Walls," *The New York Times*, April 26, 2001; Van Horn, R., "The Crazy Business of Internet Peeping, Privacy, and Anonymity," *Phi Delta Kappan*, Bloomington, November 2000; www.anonymizer.com.

The use of technologies to protect privacy can take numerous forms. Some applications allow users to control cookies and web bugs while surfing the Internet. Other programs such as Webwasher and AdSubtract can be used to block out banner ads to reduce the amount of advertising one is subjected to. The growing concern over advertising and privacy has led a relatively small percentage of people to sign up for services such as these. Jupiter Media Metrix reported that only about 5 percent of online users were using anonymity tools, although lack of awareness could be one of the major reasons for the limited use.[9]

The technological tools that are designed to protect privacy don't come without their costs and complications. Many of these tools can impede the speed of web usage, since information must pass through a specific server and be rerouted to the user. In addition, the tools can require service fees to be paid depending upon the services selected. Cookie management applications can result in the inability to use some websites and limit the capability to use personalization tools and other aspects of some sites. You can see the impact of cookie management by altering the settings within your web browser to "Do not accept cookies" or "Confirm cookies" and surfing through some sites. The use of privacy protection tools comes with its disadvantages, as described here, and is one reason privacy advocates are pushing for stronger legislative controls to automatically protect user's privacy.

Intellectual Property

The Internet's environment, full of "free" resources and the sharing of information, has led to a great deal of confusion and controversy surrounding intellectual property. **Intellectual property** is a creation of the mind such as an invention, artistic work, symbol, name, image, or design used in commerce. Intellectual property can be divided into two primary categories—copyright and industrial property. **Copyright** includes literary and artistic works such as books, poems, films, and musical works. **Industrial property** includes patents, trademarks, and other industrial designs.[10] Most countries have dealt with intellectual property law for many years and established laws that have become well interpreted. The Internet has changed the circumstances by complicating the issues around intellectual property. See the E-Strategy box for a strategy by an Internet startup to aid businesses in addressing intellectual property issues.

The issues surrounding intellectual property on the Internet have much wider range than just illegal copying of music files. In fact, there are issues with regard to patents, trademarks, books, and most other forms of intellectual property—both copyright and industrial property.

INTELLECTUAL PROPERTY: a creation of the mind such as an invention, artistic work, symbol, name, image, or design used in commerce.

COPYRIGHT: category of intellectual property that includes literary and artistic works such as books, poems, films, and musical works.

INDUSTRIAL PROPERTY: category of intellectual property that includes patents, trademarks, and other industrial designs.

Metatags

The dispute between former rivals Chapters Online Inc. and Indigo Online Inc. provides a good example of the types of issues that can arise on the Internet as competitors strive to gain a captive audience. Chapters had inserted the term "Indigo" within its metatags on its website so that users searching for that term would see the Chapters site listed. The metatags are sets of keywords in the source code of an HTML page that help search engines to categorize sites. Once Indigo discovered that Chapters had used its trademarked name in the metatags, it threatened to sue, and Chapters quickly removed the term from its site.[11] Ironically, these two companies had almost fully merged by 2001 and had combined

E-STRATEGY

Online Monitoring at Cyveillance.com

The cost to build a strong brand image can be very high and, in the world of the Internet and e-commerce, that cost can skyrocket. The technologies of today, however, make it increasingly easy for that brand image to be compromised through the piracy of software, misuse of brand names, and copyright abuse to name a few of the issues. Two young entrepreneurs recognized this issue in 1996 and began developing software that could help businesses protect their brand.

The Cyveillance tools can search millions of web pages per day for trademarks, logos, keywords, graphics, software, music, and videos that may be displayed on sites that don't have approval. The misuses of these items can cost companies tremendous amounts in lost sales, and Cyveillance has signed on major clients like Ford Motor Company, Bell, and Levi Strauss to assist them in their online efforts.

Cyveillance describes their services as enabling "businesses to capture revenue by taking control of their online brand identity, digital assets and corporate reputation." The application can even search out sites that are defamatory in nature and protest sites, and then assist clients to address issues in the best manner possible. Much of the concern clients express involves loss of sales due to misuse of corporate assets. For example, Cyveillance located numerous sites that were using the Dell brand name and/or image to sell their own products, which Dell estimates was costing it millions in lost sales.

Another example of the use of Cyveillance was for the *Washington Post*, where it was discovered that numerous websites were copying stories directly from the company to develop their own content. While Cyveillance doesn't specifically address the legal issues in court, the company's technologies enable businesses to gather the evidence they need to pursue legal action or out-of-court settlements.

Online brand protection can be a major concern for often-criticized large corporations like Nike and Microsoft. The Cyveillance tool allows these businesses to monitor what is being said online and, where possible, to develop methods of counteracting negative publicity.

Questions

1. Why would these large firms hire Cyveillance to conduct the web searching rather than perform the analysis in-house?
2. What rights should businesses have in protecting their brand name online?
3. Should upset consumers be legally entitled to establish complaint sites that criticize corporations?

SOURCES: www.cyveillance.com; "Marketing: Helpline service," *Marketing*, London, June 21, 2001.

---

their affiliate programs and advertising efforts. The issue of metatags has not been completely dealt with in all courts of law, but indications can be drawn from cases completed to date. It appears that the use of any trademarked name in an attempt to draw traffic to a site for commercial purposes is inappropriate. The U.S. court system has ruled on several occasions that use of a trademark within metatags for commercial purposes is copyright infringement.

Some recent cases have begun to provide guidance as to what is acceptable use of trademarks in metatags within Canada and abroad. For example, in early 2001 a British Columbia court ruled that the use of the trademarked names "British Columbia Automobile Association" within the metatags of a criticism and protest site did not constitute copyright infringement. Also at issue in the case was the use of the letters BCAA within the domain name of BCAAonstrike.com. The union in the case had been on strike and had established websites to provide public information related to their concerns. The court found that the use of the trademarked terms did not infringe on copyright, primarily based upon three key factors:

1. The domain name was not identical to the trademark and should not create confusion.

2. The union was providing public information and not competing with the BCAA and, therefore, not attempting to take business directly from the trademark owner.

3. The union's site displayed a disclaimer that clearly indicated that the site was not a BCAA site, and the court liked that the disclaimer clearly removed any confusion over the identity of the site owner.[12]

This case appears to give site owners, social activists, and critics the right to use trademarks to attract visitors, as long as the public is not confused as to who the owner is and the content of the site is not defamatory in nature. The right of free speech has been upheld here and provides some guidance for the future.

The results of this case also provide some guidance to commercial enterprises. The use of a domain name that causes confusion, use of a trademark to lure business away from another, and lack of a disclaimer for discussion of a trademark are all risk factors for commercial enterprises. In general, domain names should not be closely related to another's trademark (as will be discussed shortly) and metatags should not include the trademark of another firm where the nature of the website in question is commercial.

Trademarks

The previous section considered some of the issues related to trademark use with regard to metatags; however, trademark issues can arise on numerous occasions online. Another major area where trademark issues arise is in relation to domain names, which will be discussed further in the following section. In addition to trademark infringements from metatag and domain name use, the legal community has recently demonstrated that trademark use for content or product promotion purposes is also inappropriate.

The issues surrounding trademark law are complex but some scenarios have demonstrated that many of the traditional rules continue to apply online. A small Canadian software developer from Waterloo, Ontario, Pro-C Ltd., filed a suit against U.S. retail giant Computer City for trademark infringement. Pro-C had purchased a rival product in 1994, Wingen, and held all rights to the trademark in North America. In 1997, Computer City launched a new computer product named Wingen and promoted the product online as well as in the traditional media to U.S. consumers. Pro-C was impacted by this use of its trademark due to loss of its control, and in addition its website, Wingen.com was flooded with e-mail and questions that impacted its own customers. The company's site actually crashed due to the demand and interrupted service to Pro-C clients.

Computer City did cease use of the trademark after repeated requests by Pro-C, but the damage had been done. Pro-C filed a trademark infringement suit in Ontario and was awarded approximately $1.2 million in damages. The ruling indicates that trademark infringement online is as serious as through traditional channels. The jurisdiction of the case was also dealt with in this case since the Canadian court ruled that the web-based advertising was sufficient to allow a Canadian court the authority to rule.[13] (Jurisdictional issues are discussed further later in this chapter.) The Pro-C case indicates that trademark infringement is a serious matter and that all companies dealing online must take sufficient measures to ensure that they are not inappropriately using trademarks registered in any country to which they could potentially be selling.

Domain Names

The controversies over domain name use have become commonplace over the past several years. The phenomenon of cybersquatting, registering a domain name and using it in bad-faith, has caused numerous legal disputes and given rise to both legislation and dispute resolution mechanisms within North America and internationally. The vast number of registrations of the leading domains such as *.com*, *.net*, *.org*, and *.ca* in Canada have led to increased competition and controversy over domain name policies.

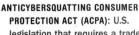

TRADEMARK: a distinguishable feature such as a word, symbol, picture, logo, or design that can be used to identify the products or services of a specific individual or organization.

The legal system's early attempts to deal with domain name disputes made use of trademark law as a major portion of the decisions made. The use of trademark law to deal with domain disputes, however, has resulted in many complications, since the two concepts can be closely related but are quite distinct. A **trademark** is a distinguishable feature such as a word, symbol, picture, logo, or design that can be used to identify the products or services of a specific individual or organization. A trademark provides the owner with the exclusive right to use the mark within the jurisdiction of the appropriate governing body.[14] Trademarks, however, are limited in availability and not all words or marks are available to be registered—this is the key difference between trademarks and domain names. Domain names are by nature unique, can only be held by one owner, and do not need to conform to trademark legislation, as they can take any form (subject to the registrar's rules for length, characters allowed, etc.). For example, surnames such as *Smith* and general descriptive words such as coffee are not able to be registered as trademarks under the Canada Trademarks Act; however, an individual or organization could register the associated domain names—smith.com, smith.ca, coffee.com, coffee.ca, and so on. This distinction gave rise to complexity for the legal system to apply trademark law in settling all domain name issues. The complications in dealing with domain name disputes gave rise to new legislation in the United States to reduce the difficulty in settling them. The first piece of legislation to address the issue was the Trademark Dilution Act, which aimed to reduce the requirements to prove that a domain name infringed on a trademark. Prior to this act, a complainant would need to prove that the domain name was using a trademark for commercial purposes and the use was in competition with the trademark owner. This did not adequately allow trademark owners to recover domain names where the use of the domain was not in competition with the owner. For example, under these rules it would be possible to register cokeclassic.com as a domain and use the website to sell t-shirts without "infringing" on the trademark, since the company would not be in competition with Coca Cola. Noting that this type of use could inhibit the growth of e-commerce and is contrary to the intention of trademark law, the U.S. government enacted the Trademark Dilution Act, effectively removing the requirement to show that the domain holder was in competition with the trademark owner.

The U.S. Congress later enacted a second piece of legislation to further reduce the requirements for trademark holders to prove infringement—the **Anticybersquatting Consumer Protection Act (ACPA)**. The ACPA reduces the trademark holder requirements to simply demonstrating that a domain name has

ANTICYBERSQUATTING CONSUMER PROTECTION ACT (ACPA): U.S. legislation that requires a trademark holder to simply demonstrate that a domain name has been registered in bad faith and that it has been used in an attempt to make a profit.

been registered in bad faith and that it has been used in an attempt to make a profit. The Canadian legal system had not made specific amendments or enacted new legislation by late 2001 but was attempting to address many of the same issues with respect to domain names as the U.S. system had. The domain dispute process has been partially assisted by the establishment of dispute resolution mechanisms in many areas. The most influential domain name registrar is the **Internet Corporation for Assigned Names and Numbers (ICANN)**, which holds control over the primary top-level domains. ICANN is a non-profit organization that describes its own responsibilities as "to oversee the management of only those specific technical managerial and policy development tasks that require central coordination: the assignment of the Internet's unique name and number identifiers."[15]

INTERNET CORPORATION FOR ASSIGNED NAMES AND NUMBERS (ICANN): domain name registrar that holds control over the primary top-level domains.

Copyright

Copyright has become one of the important issues in law with regard to digital media and the use of the Internet. Copyright law is designed to protect many different things such as books, computer programs, music, website content, art, and movies. While it is often assumed that copyright protects ideas, it aims only to protect the embodiment of ideas—that is, their form and presentation. The major means by which copyright can be violated include plagiarism, piracy, bootlegging, and counterfeiting.[16] Each of these violations results in the inappropriate use of another's work for commercial or other purposes. The Canadian Snapshots box gives an example of copyright infringement on the Internet.

The Canadian Copyright Act was first written in 1921 and changed substantially in 1988. The increased concern over copyright due to technologies such as photocopiers, fax machines, and computers led to the modifications to the act in 1988. The Copyright Act provides copyright owners with the "sole and exclusive right to reproduce, perform or publish a work." In general, any original creation is afforded protection under the act and that protection lasts for fifty years after the death of the final author or creator. Canadian laws provide protection in over 140 countries worldwide, as well as through the application of international agreements.

The complexity of copyright law has been brought to the forefront through the Napster case. The creation of a technology that could easily allow millions of individuals to share and distribute copyrighted music files over the Internet led to lawsuits that had far-reaching effects on the music industry and many others. The major defence offered in the Napster case was that the software did not result in Napster actually distributing the music files but merely helping music lovers to find each other. The opponents contended that the Napster application provided a tool that used the Internet to distribute copyrighted material and, therefore, facilitated inappropriate activities online. (The Napster case is discussed in more detail on the website accompanying this text. See www.pearsoned.ca/trites.) The importance of the Napster case has been to bring attention to the issues of copyright online and to encourage the legal community and governments to revisit legislation that was primarily written prior to the Internet.

The issues that can arise with respect to copyright online are many and can include piracy, plagiarism, linking concerns, and even website framing issues. The piracy and plagiarism concerns are similar in many ways to the copyright issues that have existed since the creation of the printing press—protected materials being copied and misused without the owner's permission. These issues have become

CANADIAN SNAPSHOTS

Rebroadcasting at iCraveTV and JumpTV

In November 1999, iCraveTV.com began retransmitting both Canadian and U.S. television signals onto the Web. The Toronto-based company aimed to build a large viewing audience and build a successful online strategy. The ability to legally retransmit television signals within Canada seemed to be provided by the Copyright Act, and iCraveTV felt that its model would be successful.

The Canadian Radio-television and Telecommunications Commission (CRTC) is the regulator of broadcasting in Canada and in 1999 had specifically exempted Internet-based companies from the Broadcasting Act. The exemption was designed to encourage the developing online economy and seemingly to reduce the burden on the CRTC of attempting to regulate this growing medium. This exemption combined with the Canadian Copyright Act's provision for retransmission of television signals seemed to pave the way for iCraveTV.

As one might expect, however, iCraveTV soon drew the attention of major broadcasters in Canada and in the United States who were concerned over what they alleged was piracy and illegal activity. The Motion Picture Association of America, National Football League, and National Basketball Association filed suit against iCraveTV and a Pennsylvania court granted an injunction against distribution of the U.S. content. While iCraveTV intended to utilize technology to limit its retransmission to Canadian viewers, it never successfully came back online, and by late 2001 the website was completely inaccessible.

The application of the U.S. court ruling left an opening for JumpTV Canada Inc. to try where iCraveTV had failed. In attempting to limit its signal to Canada, iCraveTV had required users to enter their postal code—however, any Canadian postal code would allow users worldwide to access the service. JumpTV claims to have developed technology that will limit the use of the service to users truly from Canada.

JumpTV has also attempted to address the issues over legally rebroadcasting signals by aiming to negotiate royalty payments with the appropriate parties. The Copyright Act requires the payment of any applicable royalties to be made in order to comply but the only rates established apply to cable and satellite operations. Despite JumpTV's attempts, however, the broadcasting community appears to prefer to allow JumpTV to operate without tariffs—but only for the short run, as a lengthy review process with government and the broadcasting community may begin to settle the dispute.

The Copyright Act could be amended to deal with the issues according to Industry Canada representatives, although experts argue that specific changes related to the Internet could lead the legislation to become outdated quickly. The CRTC could also reverse its decision to take a hands-off approach to the issue but that may lead to extensive requirements for reviewing the activities of online businesses. The future of Internet retransmission is unclear, but these two Canadian companies are trying their best to gain the legal right and make a profit at the same time.

Questions

1. Why wasn't the iCraveTV use of postal codes to limit use to Canada sufficient? Many other sites ask users to confirm they are of legal age to view material (e.g., beer advertisers). How is this different?

2. Does JumpTV's use of technological tools to determine the location of individuals raise any issues that you are concerned about?

3. Should the Canadian government be spending tax dollars evaluating these types of issues when the U.S. regulations seem to override Canadian law? Why?

Sources: Brethour, P. and H. Scoffield, "Net Rebroadcasts to Be Targeted by Ottawa," *The Globe and Mail*, May 31, 2001; Bonisteel, S., "JumpTV Poised to Launch iCraveTV-like Service—Really," *Newsbytes*, May 1, 2001; Geist, M., "Get Ready for Reruns in Battle over Online TV," *The Globe and Mail*, March 15, 2001.

much more serious, however, with the evolution of the Internet where much material is considered free.

The concept of deep linking is one that has caused difficulty for businesses and the courts in applying existing copyright law. **Deep linking** is the creation of a link on one website to a specific part or page (not the homepage) of another website. The concern over deep linking is understandable since huge investments in web design have been made by businesses in relation to advertising, CRM, and business intelligence efforts. Deep linking can effectively wipe out the effectiveness of these efforts by moving users directly to a specific part of a website. Some out-of-court settlements with regard to linking indicate that linking to the homepage of another site is acceptable, but obtaining permission of the site owner should precede linking to deeper pages.[17] In considering these issues, e-businesses need to closely consider their objectives and the concerns that may be raised by others.

A young Canadian e-business owner, Jean-Pierre Bazinet, has experienced firsthand the difficulties that can arise through the issue of copyright and deep linking. Bazinet's website, Movie-List.com, provides information about movies and links to trailers and promotional information online. In 1999 Bazinet received a request from Universal Pictures to remove all copyrighted materials from his site and later to remove all "deep links" to trailers, with the threat of legal action.[18] Having little ability to fight the case in court, Movie-List.com removed all links to Universal's trailers but left the issue in an overall state of confusion. Linking is one of the major applications of the Internet; however, its use must be related back to issues of copyright concerns.

The issue of deep linking is one that may or may not continue to cause difficulties within the legal system. In considering the issues that deep linking causes, it is interesting to think of how links are established by search engines. The issue of deep linking and some out-of-court settlements seem to indicate that it may be inappropriate; however, search engines also direct individuals to specific sites below the corporate homepage of sites. This would seemingly be a similar concern since many search engines create their own database of sites without the permission of the content owners, due to the use of spiders and other web-crawling tools.

Copyright issues have also been raised with respect to databases, a vital component of many e-businesses. The concern over databases is in determining whether it is original or not—since databases determined not to be original are not protected by copyright. For example, a Canadian court ruled that the Yellow Pages telephone listings was not protected by Canadian copyright laws since it did not meet the criteria of originality required for protection.[19] Organizations such as the WIPO and others have called for extending the scope of protection for databases internationally, since they are the lifeblood of many organizations despite the "originality" aspect. The cost to develop and gather the data can be substantial and often the benefits obtained from the data are only realized after extensive data analysis. The issues around database protection continue to develop as e-commerce grows and the legal community and court systems address the concerns that arise.

The issue of website framing is another that has resulted in lawsuits. **Website framing** is the use of HTML and browser technology to split a page into segments, which is useful for facilitating ease of use and building impressive websites. The issue that can arise with regard to copyright and website framing occurs when one site links the material or web pages of another organization into its own frame. For example, Figure 13.2 illustrates how a page might be framed with material from another company that could result in copyright issues.

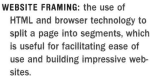

Figure 13.2   Illustration of Web Framing

The display of information in a website frame can lead to legal issues—designers need to be fully aware of copyright concerns in this regard.

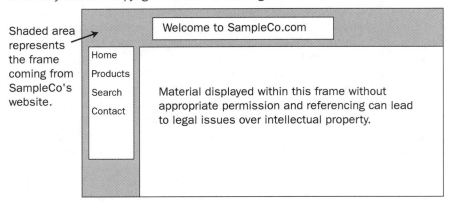

Shaded area represents the frame coming from SampleCo's website.

Welcome to SampleCo.com

Home
Products
Search
Contact

Material displayed within this frame without appropriate permission and referencing can lead to legal issues over intellectual property.

The website framing issue arose in a case between Imax Corporation and Showmax Inc. of Montreal that was decided in early 2000. The issues in this case involved both offline copyright and trademark concerns as well as online issues related to framing and linking. In its arguments, IMAX stated:

> The defendant's internet website uses linking and framing technology such that viewers of the Showmax website see the IMAX mark juxtaposed with the SHOWMAX mark in a manner likely to foster the mistaken belief that the two companies are related.[20]

The use of framing was resulting in confusion for consumers that the two companies may be related and, therefore, had some validity for the court over the issue of trademark. In addition, the reproduction of materials created by IMAX on the Showmax site resulted in a reasonable argument that Showmax was infringing on the copyright materials of IMAX under the Copyright Act. The court ruled in favour of IMAX, stating that although no measurable profits or costs could be determined, the use of IMAX materials by Showmax was inappropriate.[21]

Site designers must take the website framing issue into consideration as the increasing concerns over copyright issues can result in costly legal battles and negative publicity. In designing any framed sites in particular, it is preferred that any materials not owned by the organization be opened within a new browser window so that users are clearly aware that the material is from another location. If the material is to be viewed within a frame, it may be best to seek permission from the copyright owner to avoid concerns. The framing of copyrighted or trademark materials may not cause difficulties if it is evident to users that the material comes from another source; however, caution should be taken in judging what "evident to users" might mean, since a court may have the final decision.

Since the invention of the printing press, the legal system has attempted to deal with issues of copyright infringement. The Internet may have reduced the difficulty with which copyright is violated but it has not simplified the methods for dealing with the problem. The increased efforts to deal with copyright issues in many countries and the recognition that international standards are increasingly necessary will help in the ongoing development of workable copyright solutions.

Patents

Patents are documents issued by the government that grant an inventor or patent owner the right to make and use an invention for 20 years after the patent is filed.[22] The issue of patents has recently become a concern for e-commerce and e-business because "processes" are covered as inventions that may be protected by patents. For example, Amazon.com developed the 1-Click process for its online purchasing system that allows users to easily make purchases by speeding up the checkout process. This process was patented by Amazon, and in late 1999 the company filed suit against Barnesandnoble.com for infringing upon its patent through the use of "Express Lane" technology. Amazon claimed that Express Lane was copying its patented process and therefore was illegal use. The court ruled in December 1999 that the use was infringing upon the patent and granted an injunction.[23] Ongoing issues such as the Amazon 1-Click patent process are very important to businesses that seek to maintain a competitive advantage in the online world.

PATENTS: documents issued by the government that grant an inventor or patent owner the right to make and use an invention for 20 years after the patent is filed.

Jurisdiction

The issue of jurisdiction arises in numerous occasions on the Internet—the global medium of communication and e-commerce. Many of the areas of law discussed in this chapter can be of concern such as copyright, trademark, privacy, and electronic contracts. The World Intellectual Property Organization (WIPO) categorizes the major complexities of jurisdiction into three main issues:

- jurisdiction to adjudicate a dispute at a particular location, known as the **forum**;
- the appropriate law applicable to the dispute (also known as choice of law); and
- the recognition and enforcement of judgements within foreign jurisdictions.[24]

FORUM: legal term that identifies which jurisdiction has the claim on a particular case.

The complications that arise due to these issues have been seen on numerous occasions in the courts within Canada, the United States, and throughout the world.

The jurisdictional issues call into question many business practices as well as actions of individuals online. For example, individuals who create personal websites could be at odds with issues of obscenity, hate speech, or slander worldwide if appropriate jurisdictional issues are not in place and enforced. The U.S. has much stronger protection of free speech than many countries, which complicates many matters. Their constitution prevents the courts from pursuing many issues of free speech that other countries would consider inappropriate. In addition to individual websites, businesses must be concerned with jurisdictional issues that can question the practices carried out online.

Perhaps the best-known issue with regard to free speech in 2001 was the case involving Yahoo France and the sale of Nazi memorabilia within its auctions. A French court ordered the company to block access within France to Nazi materials. (See the E-Business in Global Perspective box for a more detailed discussion of this case.) In early 2001, the company eliminated the sale of all such memorabilia worldwide but went on to pursue legal action in the U.S. court system to overrule the French courts.[25] This case illustrates the difficult balance to be made over the Internet as various international laws, customs, and business practices result in disputes.

In attempting to deal with the issues over jurisdiction, the courts in the United States and Canada have applied a standard that has become known as the

E-BUSINESS IN GLOBAL PERSPECTIVE

Jurisdiction at Yahoo!

The decision of a French judge in November 2000 has made it a possibility that you may not find *The Diary of Anne Frank* on a Yahoo! auction. The decision required Yahoo! to block access to all illegal memorabilia (in particular Nazi materials) from any French web surfers. The effect of the decision, however, resulted in Yahoo! removing all such materials from its auction site in order to comply, since it cannot guarantee that technological tools will block the materials to all users in France. The blocking could even restrict items with keywords deemed inappropriate (e.g., Nazi) from showing up, so the story of Anne Frank could be excluded from some searches.

The concern that Yahoo! appropriately raised was that its French subsidiary was complying in full with the rules and laws in France. However, the French court ruled that the presence of the materials on U.S. servers that could not appropriately be blocked from the country was illegal. The First Amendment in the U.S. gives citizens a right to free speech that would not limit the distribution of materials such as those ruled upon in this case.

The French ruling may not even be enforceable over Yahoo!, but the company decided to comply and restricted the trade of such materials from its website to avoid concern over paying fines of over US$10 000 per day for failure to comply. The company did not, however, require its subsidiary Geocities to restrict comments and discussion online, since that site is dedicated to user communities where individual members may discuss any topic. After having complied with what company owners thought was an unreasonable request, a further surprise devel-oped—the Yahoo! CEO, Tim Koogle, was accused of "justifying war crimes and crimes against humanity" for not ensuring that 100 percent of Nazi materials were removed from all of its sites and subsidiaries.

The French decision aimed to ensure that even listings of the Nazi-related merchandise would not show up on the Yahoo! site. The decision in this case calls into question a number of concerns over national versus international rights. Whether the materials in this case are controversial is not the case according to free speech advocates—the issue is that a foreign country is dictating that its own laws apply to the World Wide Web. Further moves in this direction could lead to geographic boundaries being erected in the online world—something that would significantly change the Internet as we know it.

Questions

1. Do you feel that the French court should have had any right to rule on material on a U.S. web server?
2. How should the Internet balance free speech and hate material regulation?
3. Would this issue differ if the products sold were illegal items in the U.S., such as drugs that were not illegal in the selling country?

SOURCES: Stross, R., "Pardon My French—If it's a World Wide Web, Why is France Censoring Yahoo!?" *U.S. News & World Report*, Washington, February 12, 2001; "Business: Vive la liberté!" *The Economist*, London, November 25, 2000.

PASSIVE VERSUS ACTIVE TEST: standard that attempts to place online businesses along a continuum dependent upon the interactivity of the website to determine if operations within a jurisdiction were planned.

passive versus active test. The **passive versus active test** attempts to place online businesses along a continuum dependent upon the interactivity of the website to determine if operations within a jurisdiction were planned. The test may determine, for instance, that a Canadian firm's website that provides information about its products and manufacturing process is "passive" and, therefore, would not give a U.S. court the right to govern the issue. A site that resulted in online sales within an area and gathered personal information to complete the transaction, however, would be ruled to be "active," and courts within the reach of the website (globally) could attempt to claim jurisdiction. The grey area in between active and passive has been the subject of much debate and many cases that have been considered in court have used considerably different approaches in making a decision.[26]

The difficulties with the passive versus active test are many and have led to calls by some to create improved mechanisms for jurisdictional decision-making. Most notably, Internet law expert Michael Geist argues that the constant change of technology means that the "passive versus active test has not aged well."[27] Giving consideration to the changes in websites from 1995 to present the level of "active" has changed dramatically—requiring courts to constantly reconsider the issue without reliance on many outdated precedents. This has resulted in many cases in the courts overriding the passive–active test. For example, in the Pro-C case that was discussed earlier in the chapter, the Computer City website was ruled to be passive by the court, but Computer City was still ruled to be operating within Canada due to using its online advertising as an integral part of its advertising campaign.[28]

The uncertainty over the application of law and jurisdiction will become a major threat to electronic commerce if it is not handled in the near future. Some countries such as the U.S. have even created legislation that claims to provide rights to govern internationally. Notably, the Children's On-line Privacy Protection Act is written to apply to both U.S. websites as well as any website in the world where a firm is targeting children from the United States. Many other cases have resulted in countries claiming jurisdiction over issues in foreign states, with little concern for the passive versus active test as well. The Alberta Securities Commission took legal action against the World Stock Exchange (of Antigua/Cayman Islands), an online exchange, in a Canadian court after it was ruled that the impact of the site substantially impacted Alberta.[29]

The issues over jurisdiction continue to complicate e-commerce transactions but some steps may assist businesses in addressing jurisdiction. For example, many companies now include "choice of laws" clauses within their contracts to allow trading partners to agree in writing to the legal jurisdiction. This practice is common among B2B partners but should be used carefully when dealing with B2C. Simply including the forum for jurisdiction in an e-contract is subject to the same constraints with other e-contract issues. In the case of *Mendoza vs. AOL*, an American court ruled that AOL's claim to dismiss a case brought against the company in a state outside of Virginia, where the agreement indicated, was overruled. The judge found that "it would be unfair and unreasonable because the clause in question was not negotiated at arm's length, was contained in a standard form contract, and was not readily identifiable by the plaintiff due to the small text and location of the clause at the conclusion of the agreement."[30]

Individuals must also ensure that they are aware of the legal issues they may encounter by dealing with companies in certain countries or making agreements to adhere to another area's laws. Signing an agreement that the choice of laws is in Texas, for instance, may require an individual to incur travel costs and excessive legal costs to address legal issues. Addressing these types of concerns for both businesses and individuals is of extreme importance to the future growth of online business. For now, the passive versus active test is still common, but as additional cases are reviewed the jurisdictional issues are likely to evolve to a more complex analysis.

E-Contracts

In order to conduct business effectively, it is necessary for contracts to be completed in an appropriate manner. The completion of contracts has evolved extensively from the original "handshake" approach to "pen and paper" and now "digital or e-contracts." The issue for e-commerce with respect to contracting is the need for recognition of electronic contracts to ensure enforceability equal to that of more traditional contracting approaches. The governments of many countries, including Canada, have responded to the need for recognition of electronic contracts and created legislation. For example, the Canadian Personal Information Protection and Electronic Documents Act gives legitimacy to e-contracts as described below:

> The purpose of this Part [of the Act] is to provide for the use of electronic alternatives in the manner provided ... where federal laws contemplate the use of paper to record or communicate information or transactions.[31]

Many of the provinces have also enacted legislation to address these issues at the provincial level as well. The recognition of e-contracts through legislation allows the court system to more appropriately deal with electronic contracts than was previously possible.

The United Nations Commission on International Trade Law (UNCITRAL) developed the Model Law on Electronic Commerce in 1996 to address issues such as e-contracting. The UNCITRAL Model Law attempts to guide governments in creating legislation that will stimulate international trade and lead to a harmonization of legal systems. The e-contract issue concerns such factors as the form of communication, acknowledgement of receipt, and acknowledgement of acceptance.[32] Similar to using paper-based contracts, it is necessary for e-contracts to be recognized as fluid mechanisms that can be received but unsigned at stages of the negotiations. Efforts of international organizations such as the United Nations have assisted in stimulating many countries to address these issues.

The creation of e-commerce legislation has led to litigation over contract issues throughout the world. As a leader in e-commerce and a litigant country, the United States has addressed many of the concerns over contracting in its court systems. Michael Geist of the University of Ottawa states that two issues arising from U.S. court rulings are the key to properly dealing with e-contracts:

1. Form of assent. It is necessary for users to indicate by some active means that they agree to the terms and conditions found within the contract. This issue calls into question many of the standard-form contracts that we see every day and in the online world is increasingly difficult to prove.

2. *Reasonableness of contract terms.* The court systems are as likely to rule that a contract is invalid in the online world as they are in the offline world if the terms are not reasonable. The *Mendoza vs. AOL* case mentioned earlier was an example where the court ruled that expecting a customer to come to a specific state to deal with a complaint was unreasonable.[33]

The concerns over issues of the form of assent have led to the development of more online jargon—**clickwrap agreements**. Clickwrap agreements are the online equivalent of the standard agreements included within the shrink-wrap of software bought in physical locations. Increasingly, e-tailers are requiring users to scroll through the terms of contracts and click on "I Agree" or some similar button to ensure that the form of assent criteria is being met. In *Ticketmaster vs. Tickets.com,* a U.S. court concluded that the terms in the contract could not be enforced since users were not required to click "I Agree" to acknowledge reading

CLICKWRAP AGREEMENTS: the online equivalent of the standard agreements included within the shrink-wrap of software bought in physical locations.

the terms.[34] This issue requires website design to provide clearly the terms of a contract and acknowledgement by the user through an active mechanism such as a button or link.

Taxation

Internet taxation is another area of e-commerce and e-business that is complex and has caused considerable difficulty for the legal system and legislators. The issues encompass both income taxation and sales taxes, the two major forms of taxation. The complexity of taxation in the bricks-and-mortar world is more than enough for lawyers, accountants, and legislators to deal with—adding the Internet to the mix has added numerous issues that need to be addressed.

The issue of jurisdiction as discussed above also causes problems for taxation in the global economy. One of the major issues focuses around where a business is located for tax purposes—known as **permanent establishment** in Canada or **physical presence** in the United States. The permanent establishment of an online company can be very difficult to determine since it could be the location of the vendor's head office, the location of the website's ISP, the physical location of the server, or some other location such as the branch closest to the customer. This difficulty in establishing jurisdiction results in extreme difficulties in determining the appropriateness of collecting sales taxes and can also add complications to the subject of income taxation.

PERMANENT ESTABLISHMENT: definition in law that determines where a business is located for tax purposes.

PHYSICAL PRESENCE: definition in law that determines where a business is located for tax purposes.

The Canadian sales tax system has a number of mechanisms in place to encourage compliance, but the concept of self-assessment is likely to fail in the online world equally as it has in the offline world. Sales taxes are supposed to be paid in the province where the good is consumed—the complexity arises, of course, when the vendor and customer reside in different locations. Assume that a student from Winnipeg goes online to purchase a new computer system from a New Brunswick business. The transaction should result in Manitoba sales tax being applied; however, the New Brunswick business is not likely registered as a tax collector for Manitoba. The student should self-assess the sales tax but there is very little likelihood that the transaction will be investigated by Manitoba and, therefore, collection is unknown. The complexity of this transaction grows as you throw a foreign country into the transaction and issues of tax, duty, and customs add to the scenario. These jurisdictional issues will continue to cause difficulties in the Canadian and international systems until increased harmonization occurs.

The risks of tax revenue declines as identified above have led some governments to take action, but whether the actions taken are appropriate is another question. For example, British Columbia amended its legislation in March 2000 to require "persons located outside the province that in the ordinary course of business solicit persons in British Columbia for orders to purchase tangible personal property"[35] to register and collect sales tax for the province. Some analysts claim that the legislation would not be able to force out-of-province businesses to register, since the B.C. courts don't have jurisdiction, but the intention is still controversial. While this legislation may benefit the province's tax collection, it could discourage electronic commerce. If every Canadian province and territory followed suit, online businesses would need to register and periodically file 13 sales tax forms. If each of the states in the U.S. follows suit, businesses could be required to register in over 60 separate jurisdictions. Estimates of international taxation methods reach nearly 7500—any requirements to conform to these numbers of systems would simply fail but the number illustrates the extent of the problem.[36] Harmonization sounds like a simple solution to this problem, but encouraging international and even provincial governments to reach a consensus on appropriate taxation methods is unlikely to occur quickly.

The United States has developed legislation to impose a moratorium on Internet taxation—the Internet Tax Freedom Act. This legislation does not remove online sales taxes; it simply provides that no new Internet-based sales taxes be developed that could slow the growth of e-commerce. The act also created ongoing committees that will continue to review the issue of Internet taxation and make recommendations to the U.S. Congress.[37] The issue of taxation will continue to develop over time, since the existing legislation in most countries is unclear on Internet transactions.

The issue of the type of income is another that e-commerce has brought attention to. The digitization of products calls into question whether the sale is a product or a service. The purchase of a software package in a retail store would clearly be a product but downloading that same software from an online store is less clear—is it now a product or a service? The distinction may seem unimportant but in many jurisdictions the tax laws vary between the two and therefore it is necessary to make a choice. For items such as music, the issue over the digital delivery leads to confusion over the type of revenue earned—is it sales, license fees, or royalties? The issue of product type, like many other tax and legal issues, is one where experts need to be consulted.

The taxation issues on the Internet must be addressed by legislators and the legal system. To reduce uncertainty and encourage compliance, the system needs to be understandable and where possible harmonized. The lack of appropriate standards may encourage non-compliance (deliberate or not) and the development of inappropriate regulations may only lead to hasty decisions and more complexity. The evolution of taxation on the Internet may take several years but one thing is for sure—we will all continue to pay taxes in some form or another, but where?

KEY TERMS

Personal Information Protection and Electronic Documents Act (PIPEDA)

personal information

intellectual property

copyright

industrial property

trademark

Anticybersquatting Consumer Protection Act

Internet Corporation for Assigned Names and Numbers

deep linking

website framing

patents

forum

passive versus active test

clickwrap agreements

permanent establishment

physical presence

Chapter Summary

The Internet's global reach has created numerous legal issues for e-businesses to be aware of. In addition, the power of technology to capture and analyze data has caused concern over individuals' right to privacy. These developing issues require the attention of managers of e-businesses to ensure that appropriate actions are taken to mitigate risks and operate in a socially responsible manner.

Privacy can be compromised through the inappropriate use of personal information about an individual. The gathering of personal information in Canada is coming under the scope of new legislation known as the Personal Information Protection and Electronic Documents Act over a three-year period. This legislation aims to protect individuals' rights to privacy and stimulate the growth of e-commerce. To comply with the act, businesses must inform users of the information they collect and the purpose—often done through a privacy policy on the company's website.

The ease of use of the Internet has also resulted in ease of "theft" of copyright materials, trademarks, and patents. These concerns over intellectual property require organizations to consider their own use of others' material as well as the protection of intangible assets owned. Activities such as linking to other sites and website design have resulted in legal cases due to inappropriate use of copyright materials, requiring managers to give thought to the legal implications of various activities.

The many disputes over domain names and trademarks have led to established processes known as dispute resolution mechanisms. While trademarks are unique in many ways, they differ from domain names in that they cannot be general in nature. The unique aspect of domain names has led to court cases whereby outcomes can be unpredictable.

The taxation of online transactions is closely related to the issue of jurisdiction on the Internet. Determining where a company is located is complex in the Internet age and creates uncertainty over which laws apply and what taxation mechanisms should be in place. E-businesses must examine their operations and through legal and governmental consultation ensure that they are complying with the appropriate rules and regulations in order to limit their risk.

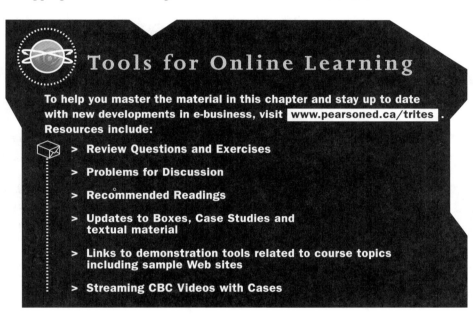

Tools for Online Learning

To help you master the material in this chapter and stay up to date with new developments in e-business, visit www.pearsoned.ca/trites. Resources include:

> Review Questions and Exercises

> Problems for Discussion

> Recommended Readings

> Updates to Boxes, Case Studies and textual material

> Links to demonstration tools related to course topics including sample Web sites

> Streaming CBC Videos with Cases

Endnotes

1. ecom.ic.gc.ca/english/60.html.

2. www.privcom.gc.ca/fs-fi/fs2001-02_e.asp.

3. www.privcom.gc.ca.

4. www.privcom.gc.ca/fs-fi/fs2001-02_e.asp.

5. Geist, M., "Lots of Legal Challenges When Dot Coms Die," *The Globe and Mail,* March 30, 2001.

6. WIPO, "Primer on Electronic Commerce and Intellectual Property Issues," WIPO.org.

7. Geist, M., "Battles Brew as Online Privacy Policies Diverge," *The Globe and Mail,* May 3, 2001.

8. "On-line, privacy fears heightened," *The Globe and Mail,* March 18, 2001.

9. Ibid.

10. WIPO, "Primer on Electronic Commerce and Intellectual Property Issues," WIPO.org.

11. Geist, M. "H is for Hackers: An A to Z Guide to Cyberlaw in 1999," *The Globe and Mail,* December 28, 1999.

12. Geist, M., "B.C. Court shores Up Protection for Anticorporate Protest Sites," *The Globe and Mail,* February 15, 2001.

13. Geist, M., "Trademark Confusion Creeps into Web Site Content," *The Globe and Mail,* September 7, 2000.

14. Harris, L., *Canadian Copyright Law,* 3rd ed., McGraw Hill, 2001.

15. www.icann.org/general/fact-sheet.htm.

16. Harris, L., *Canadian Copyright Law,* 3rd ed., McGraw Hill, 2001.

17. Ibid.

18. Kaplan, C., "Is Linking Always Legal? The Experts Aren't Sure," *The New York Times,* August 6, 1999.

19. Harris, L., *Canadian Copyright Law,* 3rd ed., McGraw Hill, 2001, p. 20.

20. www.fja.gc.ca/fc/2000/ori/2000fc25888.html.

21. www.fja.gc.ca/fc/2000/ori/2000fc25888.html.

22. Harris, L., *Canadian Copyright Law,* 3rd ed., McGraw Hill, 2001, p. 3.

23. news.cnet.com/news/0-1007-200-1476392.html.

24. WIPO, "Primer on Electronic Commerce and Intellectual Property Issues," WIPO.org.

25. Geist, M. "Everybody Wants to Rule the Web," *The Globe and Mail,* January 18, 2001.

26. Ogilvy Renault, "Jurisdiction and the Internet: Are Traditional Rules Enough?" Uniform Law Conference of Canada, July 1998.

27. Geist, M., "Long Arm of the Law Needs New Guidelines for the Internet," *The Globe and Mail, August 9, 2001.*

28. Geist, M., "Trademark Confusion Creeps into Web Site Content," *The Globe and Mail,* September 7, 2000.

29. www.albertasecurities.com/DATA/items/press_rel/0000000059/ ReasonsforDecisionWSE.pdf.

30. Geist, M., "All Electronic Contracts Are Not Created Equal," *The Globe and Mail,* Friday, May 25, 2001.

31. www.parl.gc.ca/36/2/parlbus/chambus/house/bills/government/C-6/C-6_1/ 90052b-2E.html#18.

32. UNCITRAL, "Model Law on Electronic Commerce," United Nations, 1996.

33. Geist, M., "All Electronic Contracts Are Not Created Equal," *The Globe and Mail,* Friday, May 25, 2001.

34. Ibid.

35. Lewandowski, R., "The Net Tax Nightmare," *CA Magazine,* March 2001, p. 21.

36. Deitel, H. M. et al., *e-Business & e-Commerce for Managers.* Prentice Hall, 2001, p. 326.

37. Ibid.

Cars4U.com Ltd.

History

Carriage Automotive Group Inc. has been in the automotive industry for over 30 years. They have seen the industry change many times in the past but knew that there would be many additional changes ahead. As Internet technologies increased, consumers were demanding more from industry retailers. Consumers were shifting towards online purchases due to its convenience. Carriage understood that with so much emphasis being placed on technology prior to the new millennium, there would be potential for more risk associated with e-commerce in terms of competition. The reasoning behind this risk was the fact that businesses were investing in more sophisticated technologies. These new technologies allow car dealerships easier access to e-commerce capabilities, enabling them to compete in a method that wasn't thought of years before. Carriage Automotive Group Inc. believed that manufacturers were going to help drive e-commerce in the automotive industry by being able to deal directly with the consumer through the Internet, and in turn, being able to reduce costs and increase savings for the consumer.

Carriage Automotive Group Inc. knew that they would have to be able to change their business in order to compete with the changing industry and the changing demands of consumers. As a result of these changes, Carriage decided that they would need to be able to offer their products or services online. They felt that it wasn't enough for a dealership to simply have a website. Consumers who were able to reach them via the Internet would want the opportunity to use this medium for the whole purchasing process. Following Carriage's strategic decision to enter the e-business market, the business chose to change its name to Cars4U.com Ltd.

When Cars4U.com launched its website on September 6, 2000, it became the first online car dealership in Canada that allowed consumers the opportunity to purchase or lease a vehicle online at a competitive price. All necessary actions could be handled online, from research (prices, features, etc.) to payment and delivery. The site, although accessible worldwide, only offered online purchases to the Ontario region. Since its launch, Cars4U.com has had over one million hits, and received over 200 orders within the first nine months of operation,

SOURCE: This case was prepared by Myra Cholmondeley, April Wells, and Yves Leblond under the supervision of Professor David Pugsley for the sole purpose of providing material for classroom discussion. The authors do not intend to illustrate either effective or ineffective handling of a managerial situation.

putting them on track to exceed the annual volume of the average Canadian dealership.

The Process

One of the issues faced in e-commerce is making the site attractive, and allowing the site to be easily navigated by consumers. Even more importantly, if customers are serious about a purchase, they usually want to complete transactions quickly and without any inconvenience.

Cars4u.com's website is simple as well as appealing. When searching for a car, the consumer has three options. They can either search for a specific make and model, search for a car that meets specific characteristics, or they can begin their search through a workbook. The purpose of a workbook is to allow consumers a secure area to save personal vehicle profiles, which makes it easier to compare prices and features each time they visit the site.

Once the consumer indicates the make and model or price they are looking for, the site automatically lists and displays the vehicles currently available. To compensate for models that are currently unavailable, they have a section called "coming soon," which talks about the new models that will be available at Cars4U.com in the near future. Once the vehicle is chosen, the individual can then configure it by simply browsing a list of options and checking those they wish to include on their vehicle. The vehicle is then priced automatically, where every component of the final price, including Canadian taxes, appears on the left side of the screen. The right side, which holds both lease and finance calculators, gives consumers the opportunity to compare the two payment options, as well as try out different terms, rates, and down payments.

Cars4U.com offers financing through four to five financial institutions. The calculators automatically offer the most attractive terms available from this collection of lenders. This provides less hassle for the consumer, because the price customers see is the price they will get. This also avoids any dreaded negotiations that often take place at the usual dealer locations. After clicking the cash, the finance, or the lease button on the bottom of the pricing page, the consumer puts down a refundable $350 deposit using their credit card, which completes the loan application. There is also a real-time chat room available at this point where buying customers can get quick answers to any questions or concerns. Cars4U.com then locates the vehicle and contacts the buyer for purchase verification and approval. Once the buyer gives the go-ahead, the deposit becomes nonrefundable. Consumers can take delivery either at the dealership or at their home or office.

Supply Chain Management

In order for Cars4U.com to be able to offer consumers the opportunity to purchase online, without any problems, they need full participation from their supplier. To accomplish a close-knit relationship with its suppliers, Cars4U.com has purchased several physical dealerships. These dealerships allow them to maintain good relations with the manufacturer, which is necessary in allowing them to offer consumers the best possible price.

Cars4U.com owns Chrysler, Acura, and Honda dealerships within Ontario. They also have various other affiliate dealerships that provide them with particular makes and models not available at these dealerships. Cars4U.com has established a close relationship with their affiliate dealers through a trade-off.

Currently, they allow these dealers to become a part of Cars4U.com free of charge. At the same time, Cars4U.com gets a percentage of the profit from each sale. This way, each dealer gets more exposure on the Web, which increases both affiliate dealers and Cars4U.com's revenues.

The Business Model

Cars4U.com online follows a model that allows the customer to be in control, by providing comfort, convenience, and choice. Cars4U.com Ltd. found that clients feel they are not in control in a traditional dealer environment, but are rather at the mercy of the seller. "For the first time in automotive dealing in Canada, the consumer has control over a process they never had control over before," said Barry Shafran, Cars4U.com's CEO. Lilly Buchwitz, the very first customer of Cars4U.com certainly agreed. She knew she wanted a new Volkswagen. But she had neither the time, nor the inclination, to visit a dealer and haggle over price. "I don't believe anyone enjoys haggling over a car," she said. "It just really fills you with dread."

Cars4U.com is also able to increase sales opportunities by giving consumers the chance to shop 24 hours a day, seven days a week, all year long. Over the holiday season, Canadians took advantage of the fact that the Cars4U.com's e-dealer never closes, which meant more customer convenience. As many orders were placed with Cars4U.com in December and January as there were in the previous three months. This growth was even more striking given that December and January are typically the slowest months of the year for automotive retailing. As well, marketing spending in these two months was substantially reduced from previous levels.

In addition to providing customers with the opportunity to shop around the clock, they have also improved the efficiency of their internal business processes. The whole process of ordering a vehicle now takes just a few minutes and delivery takes only a little longer than a week if the specific vehicle is available in the manufacturer's inventory.

In the long term, as they continue to develop their business model, it may also allow Cars4U.com to develop greater cost effectiveness by reducing concessions. For instance, by reducing costs, Cars4U.com may eventually be able to afford more extensive delivery for consumers. Large numbers of orders would make neighbourhood truck delivery possible, straight from the factory to personal homes. However, their current model is to be a new distribution centre, which aims not to replace traditional car dealerships but rather to develop new sales channels online. This can be accomplished by targeting those customers who are looking for more comfort, convenience, and choice and are willing to shop online.

Strategy

Cars4U.com Ltd. is moving from a 30-year old bricks-and-mortar company to a complete clicks-and-mortar organization. As a result, their corporate name changed to incorporate the famous, ".com" ending, which is commonly used in businesses–making them easily found on the Internet. To financing for growth, the company went public on the TSE in May 2000.

The corporate strategy chosen by Cars4u.com online was "launch and learn." In order to be the first online car dealership in Canada, Cars4U.com's management chose to launch an incomplete site on September 6, 2000, although it was not totally integrated. However, this launch and learn strategy allowed Cars4U.com to avoid being the second online car dealer based in Canada. This decision was influenced by such competitors as Carpoint.ca, the little brother of Carpoint owned by Microsoft, and Megawheel.com, which was also in the starting blocks of this type of e-commerce. As a result, Cars4U.com hoped to create a larger awareness of this type of business. Cars4U.com felt this would benefit them by being the original automotive e-business in Canada. They hoped this would influence customers in perceiving them as being the most experienced leader in the industry.

Cars4U.com Ltd.'s divisions, both bricks-and-mortar and online, aim to satisfy consumers in their automotive investments through both quality products and services. Cars4U.com realized that although both of its divisions share the same goals, both follow very separate strategies in achieving these goals. Their bricks-and-mortar strategy involves expanding their physical dealership network to further satisfy consumers who are not comfortable with the e-business concept. On the other hand, Cars4U.com's online strategy is to offer customers more comfort and efficiency by enabling them to make their choices in the comfort of their own home or office, while avoiding any haggling.

Cars4U.com decided they had to maintain and continue to expand their bricks-and-mortar business. The purpose of this decision was to maintain customer loyalty with those consumers who enjoy the experience of visiting and buying from new car dealerships. For instance, their Acura dealership was only acquired in November 1999. This was only a few months before launching their e-business division.

The pricing structure online follows a different strategy than pricing in their traditional dealerships. Cars4U.com stresses that the customer is in control because they do not have to worry about haggling and pricing when shopping online. The price they see is the price they get. As indicated by Lilly Buchwitz, their price was $700 cheaper than the lowest price quoted by any traditional dealer she visited. How does Cars4U.com make money, offering such discounts? It's a matter of perception. This firm gives customers a fixed price, unlike traditional car dealers, where staff members "structure" sales according to how much they think they can get.

Advertising and Promotion

Another major issue facing Cars4U.com was that of advertising and promotion. Since they have two separate business models for each of their divisions, they needed to develop a strategy that would promote their new online store while not giving a negative return to their physical dealerships. Advertising and promotion strategy was designed to centre around being Canada's first ever e-dealer. During the first quarter of 2001, Cars4U.com invested $450 000 on advertising. Because of this investment, they experienced a $212 000 loss compared to their $68 353 net earnings during the first quarter of 2000. Cars4U.com plans to continue advertising but feels they must develop a marketing strategy that will result in an overall profit for the Cars4U.com's online and bricks-and-mortar divisions.

Privacy and Security

When trying to tackle the issues that are relevant to consumers, Cars4U.com had to spend a significant amount of effort on security and privacy concerns. Due to the issues of fraud and hacking, it is in the best interest of the consumer to be sure that they shop only on secure sites. Cars4U.com has outlined several areas where they have taken precautionary steps to help make their site more secure and trust-worthy, through the use of a privacy statement.

All financial information is kept completely confidential. Only information that is necessary in processing the customer's order will be made available to additional parties. These parties may include the alliance dealership that supplies the customer's vehicle, the credit card company, or the institution that finances or leases their new vehicle purchase.

When you place an order, Cars4U.com requires the customer's name, e-mail address, mailing address, and phone number so that they can contact them regarding their order and delivery. This information ensures that the customer is located in an area that Cars4U.com can service. Unfortunately, Cars4U.com does not service areas outside of Ontario. After the customer has placed an order, Cars4U.com will require the customer's driver's licence number, insurance company, and policy number.

While Cars4U.com does indicate that they may provide aggregate statistics about their customers, sales, traffic patterns, and related site information to reputable third-party vendors, they ensure that no personally identifying or financially sensitive information will be passed on.

When a consumer places an order or accesses their account information, Cars4U.com uses a secure server to transfer the data back to them. The secure server software is designed to provide encrypted communications on the Internet.

All information a consumer sends through the Internet is encrypted before it is sent to Cars4U.com to reduce the likelihood of unauthorized access. Cars4U.com maintains secure data networks protected by industry-standard back-ups, such as firewalls and password-protection systems. These software investments protect against the loss, misuse, and alteration of the information.

Conclusion

Barry Shafram, the CEO of Cars4U.com, was quite pleased with the progress of their new online division. He knew, however, that there were many challenges ahead to gain a strong position in the market. For example, the company has been criticized for expanding its "bricks" operations as it expands online. In addition, increasing competition from U.S. sites like Carpoint, which were well financed and growing quickly, were causing some concerns over growth and market share. Barry Shafram needs some innovative ideas on how to strengthen Cars4U.com's e-business.

Discussion Questions

1. Does the continued growth of Cars4U's "bricks" presence make sense for an online company?
2. What alternatives could Cars4U pursue instead of increasing its dealership network?
3. What can Cars4U do to fight off competition from U.S. competitors?
4. How can the company develop an advertising strategy that builds on both the online and offline divisions?

5. Cars4U would like to expand its operations. Should the company expand nationally or provincially and why? What about global or U.S. opportunities?

References

www.cars4u.com

"Cars4u.com sells 200 cars online in nine months." *Canadian Driver*, <http://www.canadiandriver.com/news/010530-2.htm> accessed February 13, 2002.

Neil Faba: "Online car sales skyrocket for Canadian e-dealer." <http://www.canadacomputes.com/v3/story/1,1017,6730,00.htm?tag=81&sb=121> posted May 30, 2001, accessed February 13, 2002.

"Canadian Start-up Pursues eDealer Strategy: Cars4U.com seizes the first-mover advantage." <http://www.autosite.com/iautonews/archive/Canadian12-1.asp> posted December 1, 2000, accessed February 13, 2002.

Monster.com

It was almost midnight on January 31, 2001, the eve of Monster.com's quarterly board meeting, and Chief Executive Officer Jeff Taylor continued to wrestle with what position he would present to the board in less than twelve hours. Monster, the flagship brand of the Interactive Division of TMP Worldwide Inc, sat at a momentous point in its six-year existence. Over the past several months, user levels had reached record highs, due in large part to the massive advertising efforts as well as numerous strategic partnerships with major online portals and expansion into new parts of the globe. Taylor had been the driving force behind these efforts to generate awareness and was now confident that he had achieved these objectives well beyond what he had expected.

Taylor had spent the past two weeks preparing two different proposals for the upcoming meeting, one of which he would present to the board. Which one, however, would be a last minute decision. Taylor saw Monster as being at a crossroads in its life. Since its inception, like most Internet companies, Monster had operated at a loss, focused on its long-term growth. This successful stage led him to assert that perhaps 2001 would be the year to cut back on its expansion plans and focus on turning a profit. On the other hand, however, Taylor saw more potential for untapped markets and further advertising initiatives and considered that maybe now was not the time to put a halt to this operating strategy. He decided that he would examine all relevant evidence one more time and then arrive at a decision.

The Arrival of Online Recruiting

Monster.com is the flagship brand of the Interactive Division of TMP Worldwide Inc. Founded in 1967, TMP Worldwide Inc., with more than 6400 employees in 25 countries in March of 2001, is the online recruitment leader, the world's largest recruitment advertising agency network, and one of the world's largest search and selection agencies. TMP Worldwide Inc., headquartered in New York, is also the world's largest yellow page advertising agency and a provider of direct marketing services. The company's clients include more than 90 of the Fortune 100 and more than 400 of the Fortune 500 companies.

Based in Maynard, Massachusetts, and Indianapolis, Indiana, Monster.com is the leading global careers website with 10.1 million unique visits per month,

SOURCE: This case was prepared by James Blackburn, Maher Markabi, and Arlene Pino under the supervision of Professor David Pugsley for the sole purpose of providing material for classroom discussion. The authors do not intend to illustrate either effective or ineffective handling of a managerial situation.

attracting nearly three times as many visitors per month as its chief competitor, HotJobs.com. It is a global online recruiting network, connecting worldwide companies with various interested employees.

Monster was retooled in January of 1999 as a result of a merger of The Monster Board, (www.monster.com) and Online Career Center (www.occ.com), founded in 1994 and 1993 respectively. The Monster.com global network consists of local content and language sites in 15 countries including the United States, United Kingdom, Australia, Canada, the Netherlands, Singapore, and France.

HotJobs.com: Monster's Direct Competitor

HotJobs.com is a leading career search site on the Web. It earns revenues through monthly subscription fees from its 8000-plus business users, and the company is looking to boost the software-based services it offers to allow companies to manage the recruitment process from the desktop. HotJobs possesses global career portals in the United States, Canada, and Australia. The home page has links for 26 career channels, including entry-level jobs, positions with startups, and a new channel for job seekers fresh out of college. HotJobs expects that positive results are imminent with the implementation of a new headhunter database as well as general improvements to the site itself in late 2001. HotJobs is also quick to call attention to the fact that their clientele is not merely Internet companies but also major international corporate players, including 80 of the Fortune 100.

Like many other dot-com companies, HotJobs relies on the importance of offline advertising with Super Bowl ads constituting a major portion of their ad budget. Approximately US$2.4 million was spent for three pre-game spots and one during the Super Bowl XXXV game itself. It projected its advertising expenses to be approximately US$40 million in 2001, the same as the previous year.

Managers at HotJobs.com believe that they could strengthen their company's credibility and acknowledgment through strong offline advertising and growing word-of-mouth support. They also clearly understand the perpetual power of television. Like Monster.com, New York-based HotJobs.com targets an array of job seekers. Right now, HotJobs.com's outdoor and print campaign reflects its new, optimistic tagline: "Onward, upward." However, Marc Karasu, director of advertising at HotJobs.com, believes that television slots are key for developing an overall brand. "Outdoor ads work in conjunction with the television campaign," says Karasu.

HotJobs is also trying to target a great number of university and college students, as it kicked off a 75-campus campaign late in January of 2001. Under a partnership with Student Advantage, HotJobs has established a presence at big campus events, such as homecoming day.

A continuous objective of HotJobs is to improve its site by adding new and innovative services that would provide more convenience to its customers. Shopping carts and company blocking are just a couple of additional services that were included to target more customer expediency.

A driving force behind the success of online recruiting companies, like Monster and HotJobs, is their ability to offer more than the traditional offline recruiting services, such as newspapers, as well as operate with much lower expenses. This has allowed HotJobs to construct profitability forecasts with greater accuracy. Recently HotJobs announced that, in an effort to streamline operations and attain greater profits, they plan to cut approximately 15 percent of their workforce, or about 100 people.

Making a Name for Itself: Advertising Strategy

As a result of the increasing number of dot-com failures, online companies are giving way to a more sane approach to online advertising. Leaders in online advertising continue to achieve customer loyalty and solid brand awareness by delivering superior services to their clients and customers, encouraging repeat purchases of goods and services. According to a report published in 2000 by the Internet Advertising Bureau (IAB), Internet advertising is continually growing with revenues up 8.8 percent in the second quarter and that this US$2.1 billion in revenue was 127.3 percent of the same quarter in 1999. For online recruiting firms, Monster clearly appears to be the market leader. In March 2001, "Monster.com maintained its strong-hold, with a reach of 5.7 percent, an average of 38.6 pages viewed per user, and a power ranking (1) of 220."[1] This ranking is five times that of its closest competitor. Monster has a 44 percent quarterly revenue growth rate and currently accounts for 12 percent of TMP's revenue. As well, Monster.com is the 82nd most visited domain on the Internet.

Over the past several years, the method of Internet advertising has remained relatively constant. Banner ads account for 50 percent of online ads while e-mail ads capture only about 2 percent of online advertising. Online companies are beginning to realize the importance of offline advertising as well, moving to television advertising and other methods. As the most widely viewed annual event, the National Football League's Super Bowl is considered a powerful advertising tool. CBS reported that approximately 135 million people viewed the event this past January. But because airtime costs US$2 million per 30-second spot, advertisers must make sure that their marketing campaign generates a return on their investment. The most important thing for Super Bowl advertisers was to make sure that it's really your company that is talked about, and not just a catchy ad. It's easy to be caught up in the entertainment and lose sight of brand recognition. Often, there are many great ads during the Super Bowl, but people do not remember what they were for the next day. The number of dot-com advertisers dropped from 17 to just 3 from Super Bowl XXXIV to Super Bowl XXXV. This year, both Monster and HotJobs spent millions on 30-second ads during the broadcast in the hopes of attracting new clients to their electronic resumes. For Monster, advertising during the Super Bowl paid off. Traffic peaked in the 24 hours following the Super Bowl, as 2.2 million job searches were conducted, up from half a million the week before. And about 40 000 job-seekers posted their resumes on Monster.com the week after.

Monster's advertising division has proposed an advertising budget of US$200 million in 2001 year on their advertising campaign, centred on five TV spots, doubling the US$100 million spent last year. A move to spend US$200 million would contradict other dot-com's strategies to pull back from ad spending. Monster's strategic advertising plan focuses on the positive impact that work can have on your life. All of the commercials are skits that highlight work life and how it corresponds with life overall–an attempt to attract to Monster newly laid-off dot-com workers expected to be looking for jobs in the coming months. The underlying punch line is that when work is good, your life is good.

These advertising spots will also bring "Trump," the company's colourful signature monster to the forefront. Previously, he ran across the screen at the end of Monster.com spots. Now, he is going to be a signature signoff, intended to strengthen brand name. Trump was developed by United Virtualities in New York, and was dubbed "Shoshkeles," which is a new technology featuring animation or photography that works across all platforms and requires no plug-ins. Unlike static banner ads, at the top or bottom of a page, Shoshkeles remains in the viewer's sight even when he or she scrolls around the page. Yet it only stays on the page for a few seconds, an important selling point for people who may leave the site if they feel annoyed by advertising.

New advertising plans this year will be visits by the Monster.com "ground crew" at college football games and tailgating parties in the five key markets starting in the second quarter. Monster intends to continue its year-old relationship with AOL and the Monster Show, a 30-second direct response TV effort. Rounding out its advertising efforts this year include an e-mail push to 11 million MyMonster.com members and a direct mail to 50 000 companies in its job bank, in hopes of continuing service with Monster. As for future plans, Monster.com has signed on to sponsor the 2002 Olympic Games in Salt Lake City and the 2004 Olympics in Athens.

Monster has an effective marketing strategy through combining both online and offline advertising in order to attract clientele. They have built strong brand awareness encouraging customer loyalty by delivering quality services. As online recruiting firms continue to be on the rise, Monster has become the standard and leader in this industry.

Expanding Audiences: Monster's Alliances

The advent of mergers, strategic partnerships, and high-profile deals between Web companies is a phenomenon that has taken the e-commerce arena by storm yet, at the same time, leaves much of the corporate community confused. The intangible, virtual nature of the deals inked by online enterprise executives often leaves many to wonder what it is exactly that these giants are actually exchanging and what impact the agreements will really have on their bottom lines and the competitive Internet landscape altogether. These alliances materialize in a variety of forms: fixed sum arrangements, revenue-sharing agreements, "pay as you go" deals through methods such as per-click or per-sale compensation, barter arrangements where one company will trade advertising space with another, and the out-and-out acquisition of one company by another.

While many may believe that the benefits of these deals are immeasurable and thus often quantified inaccurately, this is rarely the case. "'The contracts for these deals often have built-in performance guarantees,' says Bryan Rutberg, director of the Internet investment group at an investment bank that regularly advises Web companies in these matters, 'And the companies have tracking mechanisms to make sure they're met.'"[2] These online collaborations have proved indispensable as they open companies to new markets that otherwise would likely not have been reached.

On December 2, 1999, Taylor inked a four-year US$100 million deal with America Online after a painstaking five years of negotiations. The agreement provided Monster with a contextual integration into AOL sites made available to over

19 million members. Taylor saw this partnership as a major breakthrough toward the assurance of long-run prosperity for Monster. Prior to this Monster's aggressive offline marketing campaign had been the primary method of generating awareness. This arrangement would allow it to reach a new key demographic: online users who are merely a click away from accessing Monster.

Advice and services from Monster.com would be featured daily on the AOL properties, including the heavily trafficked main screen of the WorkPlace Channel (AOL Keyword: WorkPlace). Content from Monster.com also would be featured in the Channel's industry areas, where professionals in a variety of fields meet, trade, and conduct research online.

While AOL is certainly Monster's most significant partner in terms of user span, Monster has aligned itself with several other key portals that allow it to target a wider variety of audiences. Links through major portals such as iWon.com, ESPN, AT&T Worldnet, and World Pages provide the company with increased avenues for traffic and collectively constitute a major portion of its visitors.

The Ultimate Decision

While both alternatives offered their attractive implications, Taylor knew that he had to commit to one with conviction. Was Monster due for a positive bottom line in the eyes of the market? Did it have enough of an edge on the competition to stay dominant if advertising were cut back? Are there more potential partners on the Internet that Monster could benefit from? Is there still a need for more offline advertising? He would conduct one more thorough analysis of all significant factors in arriving at a definitive conclusion.

Discussion Questions

1. What impact do you think the history of TMP Worldwide may have had on the development of Monster as an online competitor?

2. What benefits are there to being a "global online recruiting network"?

3. The main competitor of Monster appears to be HotJobs. If HotJobs has 80 of the Fortune 100 companies as clients, does it seem worthwhile to spend large amounts of money on television advertising campaigns? Why or why not?

4. What is the benefit of advertising during the Super Bowl?

5. Will further advertising initiatives ensure Monster an improved brand image and/or market share? What advertising initiatives would likely be most beneficial at the current stage of the company's development?

Endnotes

1. TMP Worldwide Inc. "Monster.com Continues to Lead the Online Careers Industry," <www.corporate-ir.net/ireye/ir_site.zhtml?ticker=tmpw&script=410&layout=-6&item_id=125262>, March 31, 2001.

2. Blaise Zerega, "Web Deals Are Different," <www.redherring.com/index.asp?layout=story_generic&doc_id=RH190013219>, March 31, 2001.

References

"Red Herring Online." *Red Herring Magazine.* <http://www.redherring.com/index.asp?layout=story_generic&;doc_id=RH190013219>, accessed February 13, 2002.

EoExchange. <http://www.eoexchange.com/home/news.html> accessed February 13, 2002.

Cosima Marriner: "Monster.com Pulls its Head In; Starts Going For Profit." *Sidney MorningHerald.* <http://globalarchive.ft.com/globalarchive/article.html?id=010202000113&query=Monster.com>, posted February 2, 2001, accessed February 13, 2002.

"About HotJobs: Company Profile." <http://www.hotjobs.com/htdocs/about/index.html>, accessed Frebruary 13, 2002.

Nicole St-Pierre: "As Online Job Searching Booms, a Merger Wave Builds." *Business Week Online.* <http://www.businessweek.com/bwdaily/dnflash/aug2000/nf20000823_182.htm>, posted August 23, 2000, accessed February 13, 2002.

Stuart McKie: "Ensuring the E-Customer is Always Right." *Business Finance Mag.com.* <http://www.businessfinancemag.com/archives/appfiles/Article.cfm?IssueID=306&ArticleID=13227>, posted December 1999, accessed February 13, 2002.

Sarah J. Heim: "Hire Minds." *Brandweek Online.* <http://www.findarticles.com/cf_0/m0BDW/43_41/67160395/p1/article.jhtml?term= monster.com>, posted November 6, 2000, accessed February 13, 2002.

Kenneth Hein: "The Monster Roars." *Brandweek Online.* <http://www.findarticles.com/cf_0/m0BDW/2_42/69238865/p1/article.jhtml?term=monster.com>, posted January 8, 2001, accessed February 13, 2002.

Kenneth Hein: "Hotjobs.com Downloads Tactical Ads, Campus Events for 'Better Job Search.'" *Brandweek Online.* <http://www.findarticles.com/cf_0/m0BDW/1_42/68965333/p1/article.jhtml?term=hotjobs.com>, posted January 1, 2001, accessed February 13, 2002.

Karen Epper Hoffman: "Recruitment Sites Changing Their Focus." *Internet World.* <http://www.findarticles.com/cf_0/m0DXS/10_5/59810447/p1/article.jhtml?term=hotjobs.com>, posted March 15, 1999, accessed February 13, 2002.

Louis Rosenfeld: "Deconstructing...HotJobs—Clement Mok." *Internet World.* <http://www.findarticles.com/cf_0/m0DXS/3_5/54558193/p1/article.jhtml?term=hotjobs.com>, posted January 18, 1999, accessed February 13, 2002.

Stephanie Kirchgaessner: "Companies and Finance the Americas: HotJobs to Reduce Workforce." *Financial Times.* <http://globalarchive.ft.com/globalarchive/article.html?id=010328001132&query= hotjobs.com>, posted March 28, 2001, accessed February 14, 2002.

"Advertising." *New York Times.* <http://globalarchive.ft.com/globalarchive/article.html?id=010131003973&query=monster.com>, posted January 31, 2001, accessed February 14, 2002.

"IDC Research: Monster Leads Global Online Recruiting Market." *NUA.* <http://www.nua.ie/surveys/?f=VS&art_id=905356580&rel=true>, posted March 22, 2001, accessed February 14 2002.

Mountain Equipment Co-op

In January, 2001, Geoff Campbell, President and Chairman of the board at Mountain Equipment Cooperative (a firm based in Vancouver, British Columbia, specializing in outdoor recreation and the sale of sporting equipment), sat at his office desk and contemplated the feasibility of establishing an online website. Over the past two years Campbell had been pleased with the performance of the organization reaching annual sales of $500 000,[1] but due to lack of exposure he felt that there were other markets that were not being reached. Campbell was beginning to question if a website was just what his organization needed to get global exposure.

Although his other job kept him from committing 100 percent of his time to researching this potential opportunity, he did have an entrusted committee supporting this prospective endeavour. Everyone respected Campbell and together they all wanted to see MEC grow globally as well as economically.

Company Background

Mountain Equipment Co-op was spawned by a lack of mountaineering stores in Vancouver in the late 1960s. At that time, most mountaineers in need of gear would make pilgrimages to REI, which was based in Seattle. Although this provided adequate service, problems arising with Canadian Customs produced a need for a similar facility north of the border. Therefore, in the spring of 1970 a group of six Canadians began to organize what would later be known in 1971 as the Mountain Equipment Cooperative (MEC).

In the beginning the decision was made to restrict business to the selling of good-quality equipment for mountaineering, rock climbing, ski mountaineering, touring, and hiking. The organization later expanded to include paddling and bicycle touring due to popular demand. The first store was created in Vancouver, and since then the organization has expanded eastward into five different locations. The Vancouver store would also accommodate the head office.

Four years after the introduction of the Vancouver store another was opened in Calgary to represent the Prairie provinces. The Calgary store established an initial presence out of a U-Haul trailer full of gear driven out from Vancouver. Since then, the Calgary storeroom has seen the likes of a cramped office space above a record store and most recently an independent building downtown. The new

SOURCE: This case was prepared by Steve Benvie and Michael Halliday under the supervision of Professor Gerald Trites for the sole purpose of providing material for classroom discussion. The authors do not intend to illustrate either effective or ineffective handling of a managerial situation.

Calgary store was the second store (after Vancouver) to employ environmentally friendly building features, such as a higher-efficiency heating, ventilation, and air-conditioning systems, as well as low-consumption water fixtures.

The next step in the expansion project was an extension to central Canada with the creation of a Toronto store in 1985. However, on March 31, 1998, a new location was needed to accommodate the high traffic volumes and the diverse product offerings. The new facility was 42 000 square feet and was committed to environmental sustainability. The four Rs–reduce, reuse, recycle, and reclaim–guided design and construction. This was truly a step towards building credibility among the Toronto community.

Due to high demand, a second store was needed to serve the Ontario market. Thus in 1992 the first Ottawa store was built in the shell of an old movie theatre. This store became renowned because of its location in the capital of Canada and immediate sales were phenomenal. Yet again MEC quickly discovered that the same volume problems that plagued the Toronto store were also an issue in Ottawa, and a larger location became crucial. (In June of 2000, the Ottawa store moved to a marvellously reconditioned building, which solved the problem with ease, and operations once again continued.)

Then in May of 1998, a team of market analysis determined that Edmonton, Alberta, would be a profitable location for their fifth store as it would help to expose their company to northern Alberta and even into the Territories. By converting a vacant Safeway store, MEC has become a part of a changing shopping district in the neighbourhood of Old Glenora. The building is a good example of MEC's core value to respecting and protecting the natural environment. An attractive and functional facility provided the ascetics to draw in customers and once again the sophisticated equipment and design kept with their objective of significantly reducing the impact on the surrounding neighbourhood.

Throughout the first 30 years, MEC has changed both in size of store (from closet to aircraft hangar) and hours (Wednesday through Friday evenings to seven days a week). This has been directly correlated to the growth of the membership and the future is looking better than ever. To continue this trend, MEC plans to open their sixth store in Halifax, Nova Scotia, in the summer of 2001.

Market Analysis

The market for outdoor sporting equipment consists of several overlapping groups, primarily young adults and sporting enthusiasts. Changing demographics were causing MEC to think in terms of a broader market, particularly families, surrounding businesses, and, to a smaller extent, senior citizens.

Mr. Campbell identified five major market segments:

1. **Young adults.** This group consists of individuals aged 18 to 35. The majority of this group are single male and female sport enthusiasts who enjoy weekend excursions and other adventurous activities to get away from the city life and the related stress.

2. **Elderly.** These are similar to the young adults only they are retired and enjoy weekend outings as well as vacations in a nature setting. Although retired, many of them are financially stable and enjoy spending money for premium products.

3. **Families.** They search for opportunities to escape from the city life and spend time together in nature's wonders. They purchase camping

Exhibit 3.1   Geographic Locations of the MEC Stores.

The dots indicate geographically where the stores located.

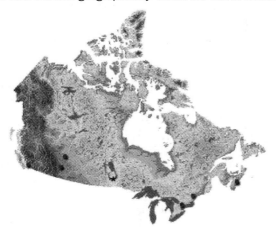

      equipment such as sleeping bags, tents, and outerwear in multiples in order to accommodate all family members.

4. **Businesses.** These are individuals in the workplace that share the same interests but are competitive with one another and desire top-of-the-line products. For example, if someone buys MEC equipment, they convince their co-workers that it is a premium product and, in turn, it stimulates referral purchases.

5. **Gift buyers.** This group consists of parents purchasing equipment for their sons or daughters at Christmas, birthdays, graduations, etc. For that reason, this market is aggressively pursued in and around holidays.

    There are also groups interested in this equipment for more specialized purposes, such as outdoor adventure groups who provide outdoor nature expeditions. Interest was shown all over Canada because the trends toward more active lifestyles were becoming of great interest to Canadians. Head office in Vancouver was receiving high volumes of letters from people who were interested in finding out more about MEC's products and because of their location they didn't have the option of visiting one of the stores. In order to visualize MEC's current exposure, present and future store locations can be seen in Exhibit 3.1. Potential customers were being lost because they were either unaware of MEC or they didn't want to go through the hassle of giving their credit card and personal information on the phone and have to wait six to eight weeks to receive their products. Therefore, MEC was losing sales because customers in the industry were forced to buy cheaper subsidiary products from indirect competition.

    Mr. Campbell and the rest of the board realized that there was a potential to reach 19 5002 Canadians. However, with their current operations they could not reach a majority of this market, so a change was necessary to accommodate the demand.

Competitive Analysis

MEC's equipment essentially served two customer functions. They could be used as gifts for family or friends, or for those who showed great interest in rafting, canoeing, rock climbing, camping, or any other outdoor events that required top-quality gear.

Competition came from all other sporting equipment stores but most of the competition was solely based on cheaper prices for lower-quality gear. The main direct competition is traditional retail chain stores like Sport Chek and Cleves that can provide similar gear that still satisfies consumer needs, but at an exceptionally low price. However, trends began to indicate that many of these customers were beginning to become unhappy with the quality, but the accessibility made up for any losses. They found that they were constantly replacing and returning their equipment because it was simply not durable enough for the terrain they were using it for. Interestingly enough, most purchasers of these cheaper imitations were aware of MEC's product line and did buy some of their equipment from MEC through mail order catalogues. However, most found this to be a huge inconvenience because they did not want to wait for the product to come in the mail. In regards to the indirect portion, a thorough analysis suggested that this portion was comprised of equipment recyclers like Play-It-Again-Sports who go one step further than the traditional outlet by offering second-hand, mediocre equipment at extreme discounted prices.

In a survey conducted by MEC to their members it was asked if, by improving the attainability of their gear, would they increase their purchases at MEC. The response was that close to 85 percent preferred MEC gear to the competition and would increase their purchases of the gear if it was made easily accessible to them. Basically this helped to confirm what was generally thought all along, which was that business could be lost to the competition if accessibility was not improved immediately.

Finances

Before determining how to solve their exposure problems, Mr. Campbell and the rest of the board decided to review their earnings for 1999 and evaluate the feasibility of expanding their operations, either online or through traditional bricks-and-mortar establishments. In examining the costs associated with opening more store locations as opposed to setting up a website, the board decided to produce a cost benefit analysis of the two that can be reviewed in Exhibit 3.2. Although opening more stores would be a good way to increase sales, the cost and time associated with opening more locations was extremely high. With a website the start-up costs were not even close to those of opening a new location, and Mr. Campbell was positive that it would be a success. He also felt that by having a website MEC customers could share their experiences with one another. The only problem with a website is that some people may not feel comfortable with giving their credit card number online, so Mr. Campbell felt they would have to address this issue carefully to ensure the confidentiality of all their customers.

Distribution

Now that the decision to implement a website has been made, Mr. Campbell and the rest of the board have the task of implementing several other activities that will aid in the success of their new website. The first of these considerations is to determine how to expand their supply chain logistics in order to facilitate the extra business that will inevitability occur. As it is now, their mail order catalogue as well

Exhibit 3.2   Mountain Equipment Cooperative

Cost benefit analysis of opening a store or implementing a website.

In order to take advantage of some sensitivity analysis, we will include several alternatives with regards to the sales increases.

(1). Assuming sales increases of 5 percent due to the introduction of a seventh store.

Sales:	$525 000.00
Costs:	$250 000.00
	0.48

Based on this, for every dollar in sales, half would go towards covering the start-up costs.

This is a rough figure developed with the help of the customer service centre. This figure includes the cost of renting, renovating, and moving in to a property.

(2). Assuming the same sales increase for the proposed website:

Sales:	$525 000.00
Costs:	$ 25 000.00
	0.05

Based on this, for every dollar earned in sales, 5 cents would go toward covering the start-up costs.

This is also a rough figure developed with the help of MEC's head office and includes all equipment purchases and maintenance of the system needed in order to initiate an e-commerce solution.

as their telephone service requires an extensive delivery system that transfers the product to each individual purchaser upon receipt of their payment. With the proposed website on the horizon, it is inevitable that customer orders will increase and necessitate a more comprehensive delivery system. Therefore, nurturing their already existent relationship with FedEx is mandatory, as success will ultimately depend on the combined effort of all involved. To make this matter even more difficult, Mr. Campbell feels that his organization should also focus on reducing the amount of time it takes to deliver on orders.

Conclusion

MEC has made a significant commitment to their Canadian customers and developing a website will increase their quality of service and allow continued growth in their market. Although the company realized that it was capable of expanding the number of store locations, they felt that it was unnecessary and even harmful to their operations. Even though the corporate R& D department of MEC continued to research additional market share, the company needed to do a better job of forecasting its long-term opportunities.

As Mr. Campbell sat back in his chair, he felt confident and satisfied with his decision to implement a website because of the low investment needed to receive a high payoff. Even if the performance of the website isn't up to expectations, the initial investment that it necessitates will be minimal, which will protect the organization from incurring great financial losses that would have been needed if they had choosen to implement a new store.

Discussion Questions

1. How should the different market segments impact the website and e-commerce strategy?

2. Would start-up costs for an e-commerce strategy necessarily be lower than opening an additional bricks-and-mortar store?

3. What factors should be considered in deciding between an investment in a bricks-and-mortar store versus a website?

4. What supply chain management concerns must MEC overcome?

5. What types of integration between bricks and clicks should be made in terms of supply chain management?

6. Does the cost-benefit analysis appear reasonable? Support you conclusion.

SOURCE: This case was prepared by Steve Benvie and Michael Halliday under the supervision of Professor Gerald Trites for the sole purpose of providing material for classroom discussion. The authors do not intend to illustrate either effective or ineffective handling of a managerial situation.

Endnotes

1. Based on Mountain Equipment Cooperative's 1999 Income Statement.

2. Statistics Canada, www.statcan,ca/english/census96/canprov.htm.

Starbucks: An E-Commerce Case Study

Starbucks Corporation has greatly expanded over the past 20 years. Growing from a small coffee shop in Seattle, Washington, to one of the most recognized coffee chains in the world, Starbucks has experienced extreme success. However, as the new millennium brings forth a rapid growth in e-commerce, Starbucks is attempting to expand their strategy of growth and branding via the digital world in an attempt to add further value to their customers.

The Company

Starbucks Corporation purchases and roasts high-quality whole coffee beans then sells them, along with fresh brewed coffee, Italian-style espresso beverages, cold blended beverages, a variety of pastries and confections, coffee-related accessories and equipment, a line of premium teas, and music compilations. These items are primarily sold through Starbucks company-operated retail stores. In addition to retail stores, Starbucks sells coffee and tea products through other channels of distribution, including their website. Starbucks, through its joint venture partnerships with Pepsi Cola and Dreyer's Ice Cream, also produces and sells bottled Frappuccino (coffee drink) and a line of premium ice creams.

The company's objective is to establish Starbucks as the most recognized and respected brand in the world. To achieve this goal, Starbucks plans to continue its rapid expansion of retail operations, grow its specialty operations, and selectively pursue other opportunities to leverage the Starbucks brand through the introduction of new products and the development of new distribution channels.

Starbucks retail goal is to become the leading retailer and brand of coffee in each of its target markets by selling the finest quality coffee and related products and by providing superior customer service, and hence building a high degree of customer loyalty.

Starbucks' strategy for expanding its specialty operation is to reach customers where they work, travel, shop, and dine by establishing relationships with prominent third parties who share Starbucks value and commitment to quality. These relationships take form through such outlets as retail store licensing, whole-

SOURCE: This case was prepared by Heather Shillington and Laura MacDonald under the supervision of Professor Gerald Trites for the sole purpose of providing material for classroom discussion. The authors do not intend to illustrate either effective or ineffective handling of a managerial situation.

sale accounts, and through specialty operations such as direct-to-consumer marketing channels.

Company Background

1971 marked the opening of the first Starbucks store in Seattle, Washington. In 1982, now-chairman Howard Schultz joined the team of founders as director of retail operations. After travelling to Italy, Schultz was impressed with the popularity of espresso bars in the country and the huge potential to develop a similar coffee bar structure in Seattle. In 1984, upon return home, Schutlz convinced the founders of Starbucks to test the coffee bar concept in a new location in downtown Seattle. With the success of the coffee bar concept, Schultz founds his own coffee company, 11 Giomale. This coffee bar proved to be successful and took over the Starbucks in 1985 and hence, 11 Giomale changed its name to Starbucks. In 1987, Starbucks expanded out of Seattle into Chicago and Vancouver, with year-end stores totalling 17. All Starbucks stores are company owned and not franchised.

In 1991 Starbucks made an unusual move by becoming the first U.S. privately owned company to offer a stock option that includes part-time employees. Starbucks relies heavily on part-time employees and believes that they should benefit from stock options just as much as full-time employees. Through this pioneering concept, Starbucks is recognized around the world for their job responsibility and benefits. In 1991 Starbucks also ventured into international development and relief programs. A relationship with CARE, the international relief and development organization, led to the introduction of CARE coffee. Rapid growth soon followed as Starbucks formed many alliances and partnerships, and was granted several accounts in the 1990s (see Exhibit 4.1). These accounts included Nordstrom, Starwood Hotels, and Canadian Airlines. Starbucks also integrated into various products through the acquisition of several companies, including Tazo Tea and Hear Music.

Expansion into foreign markets transpired into enormous growth in the 1990s. Starbucks Coffee International opened stores in Japan, the Philippines, Taiwan, and New Zealand among other domestic and overseas locations (see Exhibit 4.2). Expansion via cyberspace took place in 1998 with the launching of Starbucks.com. This site provided an online shopping venue and allowed curious consumers to access company information.

Starbucks Inc. entered the new millennium with a change in executive power as Schultz assumed the role of chairman and chief global strategist. Orin Smith assumed the role of new president and CEO of Starbucks. Under Smith, a partnership with an on-demand Internet-to-door delivery service, kozmo.com, was formed, as well as an alliance with Trans Fair USA to market and sell Fair Trade certified coffee. By the end of the year 2000 there were 3300 stores worldwide.

Industry Overview

Starbucks coffee and coffee products compete directly against specialty coffees sold through retail locations and other distribution channels including all restaurant and beverage outlets that serve coffee, espresso stands, carts, and stores. The specialty coffee segment has become increasingly competitive. All Starbucks products compete indirectly against all other coffee-related products on the market. Starbucks believes that its customers chose retailers primarily on the basis of quality and convenience and, to a lesser extent, price.

Exhibit 4.1   Timeline of Alliances, Agreements, Partnerships and Acquisitions

1990	Awarded the Horizon Air Account
1991	Establishes relationship with CARE, the international relief and development organization.
	Opens first licensed airport location with HMS Host at Sea-Tac International Airport.
1992	Awarded Nordstrom Account.
1993	Begins Barnes & Noble relationship.
1994	Awarded ITT/Sheraton (now Starwood Hotel) account.
1995	Awarded United Airlines account.
	Alliance with Canadian bookstore Chapters Inc.
	Forms joint venture with SAZABY Inc. to develop Starbucks coffeehouses in Asia.
1996	Awarded Westin (now Starwood Hotel) account.
	Partnership with Dreyer's Grand Ice Cream (Starbucks Ice Cream and Starbucks Ice Cream bars).
	Partnership with Pepsi-Cola Company (bottled Frappuccino blended beverages).
1997	Awarded Canadian Airlines account.
	Forms alliance with eight companies to provide the gift of books to children.
1998	Acquires Seattle Coffee Company in the U.K. with more than 60 retail locations.
	Acquires Pasqua Inc., a San Francisco-based coffee retailer.
	Joint Venture with Earvin "Magic" Johnson's Johnson Development Corp., to develop Starbucks Coffee locations in under-served, urban neighbourhoods throughout the U.S.
	Licensing agreement with Kraft Foods Inc. to extend brand into grocery channels across the U.S.
	Partnership with Organic to create and launch commerce-focused site.
1999	Acquires Tazo, a Portland, Oregon-based tea company.
	Forms the "Out of the Park, Into the Books" partnership with Mark McGwire.
	Partnership with Conservation International to promote environmentally sound methods of growing coffee.
	Agreement with Albertson's Inc. to open locations in their supermarkets in the year 2000.
2000	Partnership with Kozmo.com, an on-demand Internet-to-door delivery service.
	Alliance with Trans Fair USA to market and sell Fair Trade certified coffee.
	Agreement with Host Marriott International.

Image

Multinational corporations (MNCs) have a bad reputation. A person in a small-town in Illinois made the following statement: "We don't need more corporate owned chains on the street." There are "street" names for Starbucks like "Big Bucks" and "Corporation Coffee." People would rather support small, locally owned businesses because they feel that they add more value to the community.

Exhibit 4.2   **Timeline of Expansion into Foreign Markets of Starbucks Coffee International.**

1987	British Columbia
1996	Japan, Hawaii, Singapore, and Ontario
1997	The Philippines
1998	Taiwan, Thailand, New Zealand, and Malaysia
1999	China, Kuwait, Korea, Lebanon, and Saskatchewan
2000	Dubai, Hong Kong, and Shanghai

As well, bad multinational reputations have spawned from big names such as Nestle and Levi's, as they have been accused of taking advantage of natives in developing countries. Another issue is that many MNCs are known for the promotion of land wastage and clear cuts for the growth of their multinational crops. This image problem has led to the boycotting of many companies, including Starbucks, and has lead to many anti-Starbuck campaigns such as the Ihatestarbucks.com site. Starbucks does very little advertising over television or radio; most of their promotions are in-house or through their numerous partnerships. What can be done to solve Starbucks' "uncaring Multinational Corporation" image problem?

Partnerships/Acquisitions

Currently, Starbucks has six types of relationships that they nurture:

1. Environmental/social programs
2. Airlines
3. Retail outlets
4. Hotels
5. Coffee
6. Technological programs

Environmentalism/Social Programs

"Contributing positively to our communities and our environment" is a critical principle in Starbucks' mission statement and is the foundation for their involvement in countries that grow and harvest coffee beans, as well as their commitment to environmental practices. Their goal is to help sustain the people and places that produce Starbucks coffees. Purchases of organic, shade-grown coffee, and fair trade coffee create a difference in these developing countries. Starbucks also makes long-term investments in social infrastructures such as funding literacy programs in schools. Starbucks is involved with Conservation International, and through this partnership they promote biodiversity conservation and improve the welfare of coffee-growing families. An association with CARE brings literacy and education programs to coffee-growing regions of Indonesia, Ethiopia, Kenya, and Guatemala.

Starbucks is a "green" company. They have environmental purchasing policies in place, and they buy environmentally friendly products from suppliers that share the same policies. These guidelines address post-consumer recycled materials, unbleached fibre content, and lead-free ink for paper purchases. They also address energy efficiency, certified forest products, and minimal packaging. Starbucks is part of the Climate Wise organization, which is dedicated to reducing greenhouse gas emissions. Waste reduction through "reduce, reuse, and recycle," energy conservation, and education about environmental concerns are also part of Starbucks' commitment to society and mother earth.

Retail/Hotels/Airlines

Starbucks has partnerships with three international airline companies. In 1990, Starbucks was awarded the Horizon Air account, in 1995 United Airlines, and in 1997 they created a partnership with Canadian Airlines. All of these airlines offer domestic and international flights. These partnerships allow Starbucks coffee to be served to customers during their in-flight experience. Starbucks coffee is offered to patrons (specialty drinks and confections are not available), which is served in Starbucks paper cups. Any Starbucks outlets in the airports are arranged with the airport and not with the airlines.

Starbucks incorporates "being available where people shop, travel, etc." into its mission statement. And it does this by creating partnerships with retail outlets in North America. 1992 marked the first retail partnership with Nordstrom, allowing the coffee shop to set up outlets in the store. 1993 marked the start of the ever-trendy bookstore/coffee shop combo with a Barnes and Noble partnership. This combination was very successful for Starbucks as it allowed people to browse books from the store, with the enjoyment of Starbucks darkly roasted coffee. With the start of this partnership, a new culture was born in North America, as people flocked to Barnes and Noble, to have coffee, relax, and buy books. Because of this huge success, Starbucks expanded this idea internationally and fostered a partnership with Canadian book retailer Chapters Inc. in 1995. This partnership proved very successful, and now Indigo's acquisition of Chapters Inc. has included the Indigo bookstore with the Starbucks partnership.

Partnerships with hotels expand Starbucks' mission to be available in all aspects of people's lives, especially travel. The first partnership was made with Sheraton (which is now Starwood) in 1994. This was followed by partnerships with other prominent hotel names: Westin in 1996, Marriott in 2000, and Hyatt in 2001. The latest partnership puts Starbucks coffee in all Hyatt properties, including restaurants, room service, catering, and Hyatt-branded lobby stores. This expands the promotion of Starbucks coffee to the 119 Hyatt hotels and resorts around the world. Marriott, Westin, and Sheraton have numbers very similar to Hyatt's; therefore, Starbucks coffee is accessible to a large number of travellers, and it's becoming the leading retailer of coffee in their target "travel" market.

Starbucks has fostered partnerships with a number of prominent companies in North America. The companies that Starbucks chooses must fit with Starbucks' commitments. Starbucks wants to become the leading retailer and brand of coffee by selling the finest quality coffee and related products and by providing superior customer service to build a high degree of customer loyalty. The companies that they partner with must share these ideas for their own company. The airline stewards must serve Starbucks coffee with a smile, and Starbucks coffee can only be served by quality hotels that share the "good service" value and commitment to customer service.

Starbucks has successfully partnered with very powerful allies in the business world. But these partnerships, although they exist over intranets, do not hold a presence on the World Wide Web. When one goes on the Starbucks website, or any of their numerous partners, there is no link or text (other than what's deep inside the company files) that explains the significance of these partnerships to the average customer. How can Starbucks further enhance the knowledge of these partnerships over the Web? And can they use these partnerships to their advantage through advertising on the Web?

Coffee

Starbucks has acquired a number of coffee and coffee-related companies in its more than 20 years of existence. The first acquisition was during the formation of the company in 1985, when Howard Schultz founded his company, 11 Giomale, and successfully took over the Starbucks Corporation, keeping the Starbucks name. Nineteen ninety-eight marked another takeover from Starbucks. They acquired a Pasqua Inc. in San Francisco, which was a small coffee retailer, and then the small Seattle Coffee Company in the United Kingdom. The following year they acquired Tazo Tea Company, based in Portland Oregon. Tazo Tea had a strong name, and a strong product. Starbucks kept the name and expanded the outreach of the product by acquiring the company to include it in their retail Starbucks outlets.

Technology

The introduction of the Internet has changed the interface of business. E-business and m-business (mobile business) has changed the overall business model of most organizations. Companies must embrace this change, and make it a part of their organization. But how does Starbucks, a company that sells coffee and specialty drinks, embrace the wonder of the Internet? They have done this through supply chain management. Starbucks has a vertically integrated supply chain that requires an investment in top-of-the-line systems, people, and talent. The company uses automated manufacturing systems (Oracle GEMMS) to accomplish distribution and MRP. When it comes to business-to-business embracement of technology, Starbucks passes with flying colours. But how can they use technology and the Internet to further expand their business to consumer relationships?

Starbucks sells not just coffee and specialty drinks and confections, they sell the "Starbucks experience." The experience involves going to the retail store, sitting down in the atmospheric surroundings, receiving exceptional customer service, and enjoying a Frappuccino or latte. After many comments regarding the enjoyment of the in-store music, Starbucks was prompted to create their own CDs through their company Hear Music Ltd. The question, then, is: How can these and other integrated products be sold over the Internet? Moreover, how can the Starbucks experience be sold over the Web?

M-business is an up and coming way to do business. It means that customers can conduct business using their wireless gadgets like cell phones and palm pads. Starbucks is embracing m-business in a unique way. Under a joint development and installation agreement with Microsoft, Richardson, and wireless Internet provider MobileStar Network Corp., Starbucks has considered installing a fixed wireless broadband network deployment in 70 stores. Starbucks' customers could have free access to the wireless network through a "Starbucks/MSN welcome mat" provided through Microsoft's MSN online service. Microsoft could also provide unique content and services to the Starbucks network via MSN. The new technology could help Starbucks spread their business out more evenly through-out the day, as currently their heaviest business occurs during the morning rush. Should Starbucks embrace this facet of m-business, or would it detract from the overall Starbucks experience?

Discussion Questions

1. Does a partnership with an online delivery company like Kozmo make sense for a large organization like Starbucks? Why?

2. How should Starbucks address "anti" sites on the Internet? Are there legal actions that should be taken?

3. Are there risks in forming numerous partnerships with other companies in terms of branding and marketing?

4. How can corporate partnerships assist in the e-commerce strategy of Starbucks?

5. How should Starbucks incorporate both B2B and B2C into its e-commerce strategy?

6. Does selling coffee online potentially cannibalize the sales at Starbucks retail operations? Why?

7. How should Starbucks address m-business?

The Chapters-Trilogy Saga

Overview

The big-business, money-driven corporate world of the twenty-first century can be cutthroat. There are gains to be had, and shareholders of equity-based firms are directly in the middle of the commercial mix. If there is a glitch, another firm can capitalize by accumulating enough voting shares to assume control of operations. These takeover tactics are risky and expensive; however, the potential for larger gains down the road drives such a strategy.

Few businessmen are better at the corporate takeover than Canada's own Gerald Schwartz. He has made a fortune by assuming control of low-achieving firms and reversing company direction. Says Schwartz, "[Takeovers] are my milieu. This is what I do. This is what I get paid for." He recently made waves in the press by partnering with his wife, Heather Reisman, C.E.O. of Indigo Books, with a takeover attempt of Canada's largest bookseller, Chapters Incorporated. Under their partnership known as Trilogy Retail Enterprises L.P. (Trilogy), Reisman's goal was to assume operational control of her much larger competitor. The entire ordeal is an interesting story about corporate Canada and the opportunity for future earnings through hostile tactics. The technologically charged business environment further fuelled the fire, as both Chapters and Indigo were attempting to capture the lucrative online book industry, which Reisman herself describes as a "money pit" (McKlem, 2000). Capturing a strong online following is essential to the modern-day bookseller. The future of buying books is via the Web; therefore, a business strategy must be implemented that focuses on this purchasing trend.

The Story Behind Indigo

Heather Reisman was CEO of Chapters' main rival, Indigo Books & Music Inc. She had built the company from scratch in 1997 through a $70 million fundraising initiative, headed by herself and her husband. Reisman had always been a fan of the arts, and she wished to develop a store that could be considered "a cultural smorgasbord centered around books" (Eichler, 2000). Indigo had yet to post a profit, due in large part to the market share taken up by rival Chapters. Regardless, stores continued to be built, and the total reached 15 by the year 2000. Reisman's

SOURCE: This case was prepared by Trevor Johnson and Kevin Casey under the supervision of Professor David Pugsley for the sole purpose of providing material for classroom discussion. The authors do not intend to illustrate either effective or ineffective handling of a managerial situation.

unique spin on the book-buying environment was a distinct competency offered by Indigo, which drew in a wide mix of patrons.

Adding to the diversity of Indigo was the launch of their official website, Indigo.ca–which was described as the world's first virtual cultural department store and a 100 percent Canadian online book retailer. Formally launched in July of 1999, Indigo.ca is "committed to the time-pressed, convenience-oriented consumer who wants to shop online and doesn't want to compromise quality. The team at Indigo.ca is committed to connecting booklovers to the people and things that inspire them: the authors, thinkers and provocateurs behind the books, music and more that they care about" (Internet Business News, 2000). Indigo's degree of customer relations doesn't only mean the adoption of an online merchant ... it also encompasses overall learning development. Reisman wishes to offer online courses as well as educational programs through the Indigo home page. "The notion of life-long learning is really going to take root as we move forward," says Reisman, who trusts that connecting through a digital means is good business, due in large part to the universal accessibility of websites (Eichler, 2000). Reisman analyzed her primary competitor Chapters, and came to the conclusion that it would be in both her own, as well as Indigo's, best interest to make a bid on Chapters' shares and attempt to garner control. "I could see that there were real vulnerabilities because they had grown so quickly," said Reisman. "In particular, I felt that they had just too many stores close together" (Eichler, 2001).

A Vulnerable Giant

Chapters may in fact have strung themselves too thin. They ran 77 superstores throughout Canada, as well as another 40 traditional bookstores under the Coles, SmithBooks, and Book Company banners. Sales for the fiscal year ended March 31, 2000, were $770 million, with an EBITDA (earnings before interest, taxes, depreciation, and amortization) of $60.8 million. Profits were up 22.4 percent. Financially, the company was starting to prosper; however, the real appeal of Chapters would rest in the wide range of titles their stores had to offer. The average Chapters store holds between 100 000 and 150 000 titles, whereas the industry standard is only 10 000 titles. The ability to cover a wide range of reader interests was a huge benefit for Chapters, and contributed to their business setting of "an inviting, but low-key environment–a cross between the family room and the study" (Chapters.ca).

A Valuable Asset

Also attractive to Reisman was the online version of Chapters, found at Chapters.ca. The e-merchant was owned by Chapters Inc.; however, it was a separate entity, traded on the Toronto Stock Exchange (TSE) after a 1999 I.P.O. that yielded close to $50 million in proceeds. Chapters Inc. retained 72 percent of ownership in the online segment, which houses more than 2.5 million titles, and serves 262 000 customers. Chapters.ca is dedicated to buyer satisfaction, and is a well-known brand name, both of which help online selling. Their first half-year of sales amounted to $11 million, and were expected to grow vastly. Despite being such a new project, Chapters.ca had lofty ambitions, and joined forces with Canada's public broadcaster, the Canadian Broadcasting Corporation (CBC), in early 2000. This agreement allowed the two firms to exchange business and develop a joint web-presence. "The valuable content provided by CBC.ca helps our customers with their purchasing decisions, enriching the overall experience. At the same time, we are drawing additional attention to our country's leading authors and up-and-coming writers," noted David Hairline, executive vice-president, marketing and merchandising, of Chapters.ca (Business Notes, *Maclean's*, 2001). Canadian publishers and writers were particularly concerned with fairness in the bookselling industry in order to maintain a profitable line of work. Publisher relations with corporate booksellers is a close bond that must stay intact in order for each to complement one another, and jointly prosper.

Chapters Inc. was using their website as a serious marketing tool. An endeavour with Microsoft, which involved the implementation of a book reader, had also just been finished, also adding value to the online business. Using the valuable commodity of a website is a modern way for Chapters to expand, which is good business by the book giant.

The Saga Begins...

More people are using the Internet to conduct business, and with Chapters Inc. comes Chapters Online. Thus Heather Reisman saw an opportunity to merge operations and open up massive opportunities with a takeover. Supply-chain management, integration issues, and the elimination of dual business functions would all be issues to address following a takeover, the story of which will now be told.

On December 14, 2000, Trilogy made an unsolicited bid for Chapters Inc., with the idea of merging Canada's two largest bookstore chains and their online units. Reisman and Schwartz offered $13 per share for the 4.9 million outstanding securities. If Trilogy were to obtain these shares they would lay stake to 50.1 percent of Chapters ownership, thus assuming corporate control. Says Schwartz of the offer, "Given the shareholding in Indigo of Trilogy's principals, Trilogy is the only party able to facilitate the mergers, which are expected to result in significant cost savings and efficiencies, and to enhance shareholder value. The mergers will also create an opportunity to improve the financial condition of Canadian publishers, which has been the subject of recent public comment" (Eichler, 2001). Schwartz knew that with an unsolicited bid comes public scrutiny. He also recognized that in order to keep existing as well as future operations running smoothly, harmony must be maintained with the many Canadian publishers. They help to drive both Indigo's and Chapters' sales; therefore, Trilogy must stay close with the Association of Canadian Publishers, which is difficult to do when attempting a hostile takeover. Similarly, the media eats up conflict, and in this case Chapters Ltd. appeared as the "damsel in distress" as one headline had it; consequently, Trilogy was forced to try to keep a clean image in order for Reisman's Indigo to remain prosperous and not lose its wholesome bookstore relationships.

Reaction to the Bid

Chapters' disgruntled board of directors, led by C.E.O. Larry Stevenson, reacted to the $13 offer, calling it "totally inadequate and unacceptable" (Eichler, 2001). The board pointed out that Chapter's 52-week high on the TSE was $23.50, well above the $13 Trilogy offer. Stevenson also raised questions about Trilogy's financial condition and their apparent lack of disclosure on this topic. He felt that Chapters' own position in the market was superior, and therefore shareholders should reject the offer. Clearly the executives at Chapters didn't appreciate being taken over, especially by a smaller competitor, and they wished for a similar response from their shareholders.

The news of the planned merger would have to be addressed by the Canadian Competition Bureau, in order to guarantee that the industry as a whole wouldn't suffer from an Indigo-Chapters amalgamation. In particular, ensuring fairness for those smaller bookstores that don't have the budget to compete with a mega-corporation would have to be tackled. "If the bureau intends to approve the merger, we trust they will set out conditions that will ensure a level playing field to all the players in the bookselling industry," said Sheryl McKeen, executive director of the Canadian Bookseller's Association (Eichler, 2001).

Not everyone was worried by the potential concentration. Nicholas Hoare, owner of a small Toronto bookstore, felt that this merger was a positive move. "We're very keen on it–it's a masterstroke in terms of business decision. It's an intelligent move and it is probably an overdue move. From our point of view as Canadians, it keeps the Americans out, which is salutary. This is a wonderful development in the sense of better the devil you know than the devil you don't." Hoare continues, "I saw this ship [Chapters] as floundering and I had visions of people knocking on the government doors to bail out a collective problem to do with publishers that would sink along with the rest of the ship. This represents, if it goes through, a really good promissory note for the future for both the publishing industry and the bookstores" (Eichler, 2001). The people within the trade realized how much pull Chapters and Indigo have on the overall market for books; therefore, it is crucial for these two to succeed in order to secure industry stability. Even the "little-guys" understand that they would be much better off against a large Canadian retail chain than an American one. It really didn't matter to the bulk of small merchants who assumed control of Chapters, so long as it remained a Canadian business.

An Unexpected Restructuring

One week after the initial cash offering, Chapters Inc. announced that a major restructuring plan they had in the works would make the company more profitable. Despite the timing of the announcement, C.E.O. Larry Stevenson stressed that it had nothing to do with the Trilogy bid. A key ingredient in the plan was the buyback of the 31 percent of Chapters Online that the company had sold only three years earlier. Pegasus, one of Chapter's primary wholesalers, was also part of the buyback design. "By bringing Chapters Online and Pegasus Wholesale in-house, we will benefit from significant cost reductions, but more importantly, will be able to further build Chapters Inc.," said Stevenson (Eichler, 2001). Replied Schwartz, "this transaction uses up all of Chapters Online's cash reserves, requires a further $4 million investment by Chapters Inc., and exposes Chapters Inc. shareholders directly to the ongoing risks of Chapters attempt to turn around this business" (Eichler, 2001). These harsh words were used by Schwartz in order to further sway those shareholders who hadn't yet made a decision on whether or not to sell to Trilogy. Schwartz and Reisman desperately wanted the venture to be triumphant.

Trilogy had accumulated only 11 percent of Chapters when they announced that they were extending their deadline for the bid on Chapters until January 24, 2001. Trilogy claimed that the additional time was needed for the removal of Chapters' poison pill plan, whereas Chapters president Harry Yanowith thought differently. "Clearly, there is little enthusiasm from Chapters' shareholders for Trilogy's bid" asserted the executive.

Chapters Finds a White Knight

Much to the happiness of Chapters executives, Future Shop Limited, Canadian retailer and e-tailer of consumer electronics products raised the bar and offered $16.80 per share for 100 percent of Chapters. Chapters' shareholders would be able to receive the cash compensation, or else two shares in Future Shop in exchange for their stake in the bookseller. The deal was set to close in March 2001. "The chance to create a powerful Canadian retailer like this doesn't come along very often," says Kevin Layden, president of Future Shop Ltd (Canadian Press Release, 2001). "Future Shop and Chapters are outstanding, well established, strong Canadian retail companies. Acquiring Chapters fits into our business model and our strategic plan, which calls for reaching $5 billion in sales in five years," says the president. Future Shop had grand short-term goals, and acquiring 100 percent of Chapters was a big step that undoubtedly would increase company awareness and translate to augmented sales. Future Shop had 88 superstores, five Computer City stores, and an online electronics store found at www.futureshop.ca.

"This is a terrific deal for Chapters shareholders," said Larry Stevenson. "Both companies are strong, profitable retailers; both are successful online retailers; and their products complement one another. This deal will boost our buying power and allow us to add new products." Stevenson was excited by the prospects of what Future Shop had to offer. They provide a different product line and a thriving website, both of which would be embraced by Chapters. Best of all though, the firm wouldn't be taken over by a competitor, and existing company directors wouldn't have to worry about being replaced by Indigo staff. Stevenson further addressed the media, and had the following to say: "We are very confident recommending to our shareholders that they accept the offer from Future Shop. Their strong financial results are a big plus in evaluating this deal, considering the potential for Chapters' shareholders to have a stake in Future Shop after the acquisition. Unlike the Trilogy offer, Chapters' shareholders have a full and complete offer from Future Shop, and the chance to invest in an established, profitable company with real potential for growth."

The Future

Chapters' shareholders who had already tendered their shares to Trilogy would have until January 22 to withdraw and sell to Future Shop. Reisman needed to decide what Trilogy's next step would be. Should they up the Future Shop offer and make another bid, or should she forget the Chapters opportunity and focus on Indigo growth? Regardless of Trilogy's plans, what would be in the best interest for Chapters? Management pushed for the Future Shop deal, but this can be attributed in large part to their disdain for Reisman and Trilogy after their takeover ambitions were known. The Canadian publishers, as well as the bookselling industry as a whole, generally accepted the Indigo deal. It allowed operations to stay solely in Canada, and with Reisman in charge, the industry has someone genuinely devoted to the love of books. On the other hand, a meshing with Future Shop creates a whole new clientele and assortment of products. They are a powerful Canadian retailer, and merging Chapters' selection of books with Future Shop's own inventory is a novel idea that may just work. What would be the best route for Chapters and how will operations change with either the Trilogy of Future Shop bid? How does this impact the Canadian bookselling industry, and would this industry as a whole be better off with new ownership at Chapters?

Discussion Questions

1. What are the strengths and weaknesses of the Trilogy and Future Shop bids from the perspective of Chapters Online?

2. How does the pending merger impact the Canadian bookselling industry, and would this industry as a whole be better off with new ownership at Chapters?

3. If the Trilogy offer is successful, what steps will be necessary to integrate the two companies in both online and offline operations?

4. Indigo has operated an e-commerce presence for several years. Would it be beneficial to merge the e-commerce aspects of the merged companies? Why or why not?

5. If the Future Shop bid was successful, what e-commerce integration and synergies could be capitalized on?

References

Eichler, Leah. "Chapters Online teams up with CBC." *Publishers Weekly*, May 1, 2000.

Eichler, Leah. "Chapters realigns as takeover battle continues." *Publishers Weekly*, December 18, 2000.

Eichler, Leah. "Trilogy extends offer deadline for Chapters." *Publishers Weekly*, January 8, 2001.

Eichler, Leah. "Chapters get electronic white knight" *Publishers Weekly*, January 22, 2001.

Eichler and Millot. "Trilogy ups offer in battle for Chapters." *Publishers Weekly*, January 29, 2000.

Eichler, Leah. "Reisman plans Indigo merger, store closings." *Publishers Weekly*, February 12, 2001.

Eichler, Leah. "Chapters' plans for Chapters Online murky." *Publishers Weekly*, March 5, 2001.

MacKlem, Katherine. "The Book Lady." *Maclean's*, February 26, 2001.

Millot, Jim. "Chapters' results benefit from online investment." *Publishers Weekly*, November 15, 1999.

Sheppard, Robert. "Thinking outside the (big) box." *Maclean's*, January

GLOSSARY

Ad-hoc query: the ability for users to generate any type of query or report they wish within the system.

Affiliate programs: agreements between website operators whereby delivery of customers or prospective customers to another company's site results in compensation becoming due.

Animated Graphic Interchange Format (GIF): a file that consists of a series of frames that are shown in a particular sequence.

Anticybersquatting Consumer Protection Act (ACPA): U.S. legislation that requires a trademark holder to simply demonstrate that a domain name has been registered in bad faith and that it has been used in an attempt to make a profit.

Asynchronous transfer mode (ATM): a switching technology that organizes digital data into 53-byte cell units and transmits them using digital signalling technology. A cell is processed asynchronously relative to other related cells.

ATM/debit card: bank card used for bank transactions at ATM machines and for purchases from retail outlets where payments are made directly from the user's bank account.

Authentication: the property that confirms that a particular person or server is, in fact, the person or server that is identified in a transaction.

Automated teller machines (ATMs): user-friendly computers, usually located in bank branches, that enable bank customers to carry out their own banking transactions online.

Balanced scorecard: a multi-dimensional measurement tool aimed to capture performance measures related to accounting/ finance, human resources, internal processes, and customers.

Bank Internet Payment System (BIPS): facility offered by banks under which their customers can make payments on the Internet by logging onto a special interface set up by the bank

Banner ads: small icons containing advertising messages that, when clicked, take the user to the site of the advertiser.

Brochureware phase: an early stage of the Internet's development where commercial enterprises primarily put existing marketing brochures in digital format.

Brokerage sites: sites that bring together buyers and sellers in order to facilitate business transactions on the Web.

Business continuity: the plans that are directed to ensuring that a business can continue in operation after a major disaster or other event occurs that could otherwise disable the computer systems for a lengthy period of time.

Business intelligence: the environment that supports analysis of data from any source (internal or external) to provide valuable information for making operating, tactical, or strategic decisions.

Business process reengineering: fundamental rethinking and radical redesign of existing business processes to add value or prepare for new technologies.

Buy-side: the purchasing end of the supply chain, which consists of suppliers and the processes that connect with them.

Cash-to-cash cycle: the length of time from purchasing materials until a product is manufactured.

Certificate authorities (CAs): organizations that issue digital certificates and sign them with digital signatures to establish the authenticity of the certificates.

Channel conflict: situation in which various sales channels for a single organization operate in competition with each other.

Check digits: redundant digits added to a set of digits that enables the accuracy of other characters in the set to be checked.

Click-stream analysis: a method by which a user's path through a website can be tracked and analyzed.

Click-through counts: the number of times that users have clicked on a banner ad to take them to the website to which it refers.

Clickwrap agreements: the online equivalent of the standard agreements included within the shrink-wrap of software bought in physical locations.

Client-server systems: network configurations that evolved from networks built around central computers (servers) to provide computing power to the users on their own desktop computers (clients).

Client-side OLAP: processing where the data warehouse passes the data from the server to the client machine, where the majority of the processing occurs.

Client: a computer that is used by a network user to gain access to and operate applications on the network.

Collaborative commerce: the application of technologies to allow trading partners to synchronize and optimize their partnerships; performed in collaboration.

Collaborative systems: information systems that work between enterprises to enable them to work together on common business initiatives and ventures.

Common Gateway Interface (CGI): a method used by a web server to pass a user's request that has come over the Internet to an application program and receive data that can be sent back to the user.

Computer telephony integration (CTI): a technology that allows telephone systems to integrate with computer systems to aid in customer service and data capture.

Computer telephony integration (CTI): a technology that allows telephone systems to integrate with computer systems to aid in customer service and data capture.

Controls: preventive and corrective measures that are designed to reduce the risk of fraud or error to an acceptable level.

Cookies: small text files stored by a website on individual computers that allow the site to track the movements of a visitor.

Copyright: category of intellectual property that includes literary and artistic works such as books, poems, films, and musical works.

Core technologies: those technologies that provide the basic infrastructure for business intelligence.

Cost per thousand (CPM): standard measure of impressions. Charges are set for each thousand users who visit the site or see an advertisement.

Cross-sell: the process of encouraging customers to purchase complementary or additional products or services from the firm.

Customer intelligence: the use of CRM applications to explore the data to identify relevant customer information.

Customer Relationship management (CRM): the use of technologies to establish, develop, maintain, and optimize relationships with customers by focusing on understanding needs and desires.

Cybersquatting: registering of domain names with the intention to use the name for financial gain without legal rights to its use.

Data cubes: multidimensional database structures that allow quick drill-down and reformatting of data.

Data elements: those pieces of primary information used in a business, like customer name, sales invoice number, and payment amount for a transaction.

Data mart: data repository that is dedicated to specific user groups and is often integrated into the data warehouse.

Data mining: the analysis of data for relationships that may not have previously been known.

Data warehouse: a central data repository utilized to organize, store, analyze, and report upon data for decision-making purposes.

Daughter windows: another name for interstitials or pop-up windows on the Internet.

Deep linking: the creation of a link on one website to a specific part or page (not the homepage) of another website.

Digital certificates: electronic documents that contain the identity of a person or server and the related public key. They are used for purposes of authentication.

Digital signatures: encrypted appendages to documents and data transmissions that utilize combinations of private and public keys to establish the authenticity of the signature. They fill the same role as manual signatures on paper documents.

Disaster recovery plan: detailed plan of action that enables an information system to be recovered after a major disaster has made it inoperable.

Discount rate: the amount that the merchant account provider takes as a percentage of sales conducted through credit cards.

Disintermediation: a change in the supply chain where the provider and consumer interact directly with each other, thereby eliminating the need for an intermediary.

Dutch auction: auction that uses a descending price format, whereby the auctioneer begins with a high price and buyers can bid on specific quantities of inventory as the price falls.

Dynamic pricing: the use of market-based, negotiated prices for transactions.

E-marketing: the utilization of Internet and electronic technologies to assist in the creation, implementation, and evaluation of marketing strategy.

E-procurement: the complete business process of acquiring goods through electronic means, from requisition through to fulfillment and payment.

E-wallets: software that holds information about a purchaser, such as name, billing, and shipment addresses and other information needed by a seller such as credit card information, and, upon request, submits this information automatically to a website to complete a transaction.

Electronic data interchange (EDI): a form of conducting transactions, including payment transactions, in electronic form. It is based on the use of widely accepted standards for formatting data in EDI transmissions.

Enabling technologies: technologies that provide the ability of the BI applications to interact and perform tasks within the core technologies, such as the data warehouse.

Encryption: the process of scrambling data by applying an encryption algorithm to it. A key to the algorithm is provided to recipients of the data to enable them to unscramble it and read it.

English auction: auction in which the bidding occurs through an ascending price process when buyers gather in a common location (physical or digital) during specified periods of time.

Enterprise-wide systems: any software systems used throughout an enterprise with the intention of enabling a consistent type of functionality as well as enterprise-wide access to the same data.

Error: an unintentional act or omission that leads to missing, improper, or incorrect information.

Extensible Markup Language (XML): markup language similar to HTML in that they both contain symbols to describe the contents of a page or file, but while HTML describes the content only in terms of how it is to be displayed and interacted with, XML describes the content in terms of what data is being included.

Extraction, transformation, and loading (ETL): the process of gathering data from a system, such as an ERP system, which can be simplified and stored within the data warehouse.

Extranets: computer networks that make use of Internet technology and include users from outside the organization as well as inside.

Fibre optic: the transmission of information as light impulses along a glass or plastic wire or fibre. Fibre optic media carries more data than conventional copper media and is less subject to electromagnetic interference. Most telephone company long-distance lines are now fibre optic.

Firewall: a high-security computer system that acts as the entry point into a network from the Internet. It includes sophisticated security features as well as encryption capabilities to render the data unreadable by unauthorized persons. A firewall also includes security-related policies and procedures that make it effective as a secure entry point.

Forum: legal term that identifies which jurisdiction has the claim on a particular case.

Fraud: an intentional act or omission that leads to missing, improper, or incorrect information.

General controls: controls that are not unique to a particular application or applications.

Holdback: amount that credit card companies keep in escrow to reduce the risk of bad debts and fraudulent credit card use.

Horizontal trading exchanges: trading exchanges that have a product or service focus, such as computers or office equipment, and do not target any specific industry.

Hybrid OLAP: forms that combine various other formats, such as ROLAP and MOLAP.

HyperText Markup Language (HTML): the essential programming language used to create web pages.

HyperText Transfer Protocol (HTTP): an applications protocol or set of rules that is used for exchanging files (text, graphic images, sound, video, and other multimedia) on the World Wide Web.

Industrial property: category of intellectual property that includes patents, trademarks, and other industrial designs.

Input masks: established formats for input areas in a screen that allow certain numbers of characters and/or digits to be entered.

Intellectual property: a creation of the mind such as an invention, artistic work, symbol, name, image, or design used in commerce.

Intelligent agent: a program designed to assist users on the Web to carry out tasks such as searching for information or automate tasks.

Interactive phase: stage of the Internet's development when websites began to allow two-way communication through e-mail and web forms.

Internet backbone: an organized and managed communications system, often based on fibre-optic cables, that forms the central connection for a section of the Internet.

Internet Corporation for Assigned Names and Numbers (ICANN): domain name registrar that holds control over the primary top-level domains.

Internet Protocol (IP): protocol that uses a set of rules to send and receive messages at the Internet address level. Every computer connected to the Internet has an IP address for this purpose.

Internet Service Providers (ISPs): companies that offer Internet access and related services to individuals and businesses for a fee. Connections are offered through telephone lines or direct connection.

Interoperability: the ability of two or more systems to conduct operations processes with each other.

Interstitials: web-based windows created that pop up as a user enters an Internet site, aiming to catch the user's attention.

Intranets: computer networks within an enterprise that make use of Internet technology.

ISDN: integrated services digital network. This is a form of communications line that conveys data in digital rather than analogue format. Digital format means that the data is being converted into bits and bytes, similar to any computer data, while analogue format means that the data is in the form of sound waves.

Java: a programming language that was originally invented for the purpose of enhancing web pages and is used to create animations and moveable, interactive icons. Since its inception, its use has grown markedly beyond web pages to include many business and e-business applications.

Key performance indicators: important measures that a company measures its performance against in relation to goals, competitors, and the industry.

Log file analysis: the process of analyzing information with regards to the movements of users throughout a site based upon data captured in server log files.

Log files: data source that can be used to capture and analyze information online.

Logical access controls: controls that are included in software. Accordingly, logical controls are sometimes referred to as "software controls."

Market segment: a group of customers who share common needs and/or characteristics the selling firm may be able to satisfy.

Maverick buying: the unauthorized purchasing of goods by employees through non-routine and poorly controlled means, such as acquiring office supplies with petty cash.

Megabits per second (Mbps): a measure of speed for data transmission. It means a million bits per second, and states the number of data bits that are transmitted per second on a particular medium.

Merchant account: account held by businesses in order to collect payment through credit cards.

Metadata: a structured definition of data; it is data about data.

Metatags: identifiers within HTML code that indicate the content of the website.

Middleware: software installed to link different systems together so as to make them work together. Middleware is often used to enable an ERP system to pass data back and forth between it and a legacy system.

Moment of truth: the critical moment in a service transaction when the customer's expectations are met, exceeded, or disappointed.

Mondex card: card containing a computer chip that enables it to retain data that can be used for conducting transactions with stores that are equipped to read Mondex cards. Because of their memory capabilities, they are sometimes referred to as "smart cards."

Multidimensional OLAP (MOLAP): applications that make use of data cubes to perform analysis on multidimensional databases.

Online analytical processing (OLAP): process that provides the ability for users to perform detailed, summary, or trend analysis on data and allows for drill-down into that data.

Online transaction processing (OLTP): a program that facilitates and manages transaction-oriented applications, typically for data entry and retrieval transactions across a network.

Order fulfillment: process that consists of many procedures, grouped into the main areas of order processing, warehousing, and shipping and transportation planning.

Packet switching: a method of transmitting data by breaking it up into small segments or packets and sending the packets individually in a stream. The packets are not necessarily sent together, but rather are disassembled, transmitted separately, and then reassembled when they arrive at their destination.

Paperless Exchange and Settlement (PACES): process for settling cheques within the banking system by using electronic images of the cheques captured at the first bank where they are presented

Passive versus active test: standard that attempts to place online businesses along a continuum dependent upon the interactivity of the website to determine if operations within a jurisdiction were planned.

Permanent establishment: definition in law that determines where a business is located for tax purposes.

Permission marketing: the process of marketing only to potential customers who have agreed to receive information on products, new offers, and sales.

Personal Information Protection and Electronic Documents Act (PIPEDA): Canadian legislation that provides privacy protection for personal information and comes into effect over the period of January 1, 2001, to 2004.

Personalization phase: stage in the Internet's development when sites began to develop one-to-one marketing techniques through the use of cookies and other tracking tools.

Physical controls: measures taken to secure the physical safety of a resource (for example, fences, security guards, and locks on doors).

Physical presence: definition in law that determines where a business is located for tax purposes.

Point-of-presence (POP): an access point to the Internet that has a unique IP address. An Internet service provider (ISP), which is an organization that sells access to the Internet, has at least one point-of-presence on the Internet.

Primary data: information that is gathered in an effort to better make a specific decision.

Private exchange: trading exchange that limits participation to specific buyers and sellers,Ä"normally related to the exchange provider's supply chain.

Private key: a set of data used to encrypt and decrypt data transmissions that is known to only one person.

Protocol: a special set of rules that the sending and receiving points in a telecommunication connection use when they communicate. Protocols exist at several levels, including hardware and software. Both end points must recognize and observe a protocol to be able to understand the contents of transmissions. Protocols are often described in an industry or international standard.

Public exchanges: trading exchanges in which buyers and sellers register to join, and there are few limitations to joining.

Public key infrastructure (PKI): a system that stores and delivers keys and certificates as needed and also provides privacy, security, integrity, authentication, and non-repudiation support for various technological and e-business applications and transactions.

Public key: a set of data used to encrypt and decrypt data transmissions that can be shared with anyone.

Pull system: supply chain in which the production of suppliers is determined by the needs of customers who request or order goods necessitating production.

Push system: supply chain in which suppliers produce goods based upon their efficiencies and push them to customers rather than rely on demand to determine production.

Reintermediation: process by which companies constantly reinvent themselves in order to survive by entering a market as a new intermediary.

Relational database systems: logical database model that relates data in different tables within the database by sharing a common data element (or field) between them. The common data element can serve as a reference point in the tables to other data elements in a data record.

Relational database: database that uses numerous tables and can relate fields or tables within the database to one another and can easily be reorganized or extended.

Relational OLAP (ROLAP): applications that allow multi-dimensional analysis within a relational database. The data processing may take place either at the server, intermediary, or client level.

Request for proposal (RFP): the first stage in a procurement process whereby the buyer communicates its needs to potential suppliers, who will then submit tenders based on the requirements.

Reverse auction: auction that uses a descending price format, but in this case the buyer creates the auction to receive bids from potential suppliers. Suppliers must bid lower than the most recent bid in order to gain the sale.

Reverse logistics: the process through which customers can return items purchased either for a refund or for warranty/repair.

Risk: the probability of an event occurring that leads to missing, improper, or incorrect information in an information system.

Sales force automation (SFA): the process of simplifying sales in the field and the integration of sales activity into the corporate information structure.

Scalability: the ability of a system to adapt or be adapted to changing sizing requirements. A system that can easily be expanded to accommodate a growing business is referred to as scalable.

Sealed-bid auction: auction form often used for products/services where price is only one consideration to the decision. For example, construction contracts often go through a sealed-bid process, as the buyer will consider capabilities, product quality, timelines, and past experience of the contractor before awarding the contract.

Secondary data: data that has not been developed specifically for the task at hand but may be useful for decision-making.

Secure Electronic Transaction (SET) protocol: a method of securing credit card transactions that makes use of encryption and authentication technology.

Secure Hypertext Transfer Protocol (HTTPS): a secure form of HTTP. It is a web protocol built into Netscape Navigator that encrypts (scrambles) and decrypts (unscrambles) transmissions between the user and the web server.

Secure HyperText Transfer Protocol (S-HTTP): a security protocol that works with HTTP to wrap transmissions in a secure "envelope" created with encryption technology.

Secure Socket Layer (SSL) Protocol: a security protocol associated with TCP/IP that establishes a secure communications channel between web clients and servers.

Sell-side: the selling end of the supply chain, which consists of customers and the processes that connect with them.

Server: a computer that forms the nucleus of a network, and contains the network operating system, as well as case-specific networkbased applications.

Shipping and transportation planning (STP): the process of getting the finished goods to the consumer quickly and efficiently.

Site stickiness: term to describe the amount of time and likelihood that users will stay on a particular website.

Sniffing: the use of electronic devices attached to transmission lines that can detect and capture data transmissions on those lines. Newer models of sniffing devices can work on wireless transmissions as well.

Source code: the format in which a program is written that can be read by humans and that is converted into a different format that the computer can recognize.

Spam: the name given to the unsolicited sending of e-mail to individuals in an attempt to gain commercial advantage.

Stress testing: process consisting of high-volume entry, processing, and output of test data designed to determine whether the system has the capacity to handle the volumes that will be required of it.

Superstitials©: Internet advertisement spots that load into a user's browser while the Internet connection is idle and then launch as a daughter window showing a short, TV-like advertisement.

Supply chain management (SCM): a business technique involving strategic decisions enabled through the application of technologies.

Supply chain: the set of processes that encompasses raw materials or resource purchases through to final delivery of a product/service to the end consumer.

Systems sizing: process of assessing the volume and processing requirements that will be placed on a new information system and thereby determining the size of system required, including hardware and software.

Threats: conditions or forces that exist to increase the risk of fraud or error.

Trademark: a distinguishable feature such as a word, symbol, picture, logo, or design that can be used to identify the products or services of a specific individual or organization.

Trading exchange: an online marketplace, usually on a website, that enables suppliers and customers to carry out their business electronically, often using auctioning techniques.

Transmission Control Protocol (TCP): protocol that uses a set of rules to exchange messages with other Internet points at the data packet level.

Transmission Control Protocol/Internet Protocol (TCP/IP): the communications protocol of the Internet. In order for any computer to use the Internet, it must be equipped with the program that enables this protocol.

Trust: the confidence in another party (business or individual) to meet its end of a bargain that is established through a relationship over time.

Tunnelling: process under which data packets are transmitted over the Internet by including an additional header that establishes its route through the Internet. This adds some assurance and security to the transmission process because it is known where the data are and where they are going at all times. The route to be followed by the data is called a tunnel.

Uniform Resource Locator (URL): the address of a resource on the World Wide Web. The URL contains the name of the required protocol followed by a colon (normally http:), an identification that a web server is the target (such as //www), and a domain name that identifies a specific web server followed by a slash (e.g., gm.com/), and perhaps a specific file name (such as index.html) to make http://www.gm.com/index.html. Increasingly, the letters www are no longer required as web servers are assumed unless otherwise specified. Index pages are often assumed as well.

Universal Description, Discovery and Integration (UDDI) initiative: a collaborative effort that aims to improve the ability of businesses to carry out electronic transactions with each other.

Up-sell: the process of encouraging customers to purchase higher-priced products or services.

Value added networks (VANs): privately owned networks that are rented to users, along with a package of related services, to operate their EDI systems by providing an environment within which they can work and by connecting them to their customers and suppliers.

Vendor-managed inventory (VMI): the process by which suppliers take over the monitoring of inventory levels through the use of technology and are responsible for replenishment of stock.

Vertical trading exchanges: trading exchanges that have an industry or specific market focus, such as healthcare or energy products and services.

Vickrey auction: auction using an ascending price format in which the highest bidder wins the auction but must pay the price submitted by the second place bidder.

Virtual private network (VPN): a secure and encrypted connection between two points across the Internet.

Viruses: computer programs that are inserted into computer systems on an unauthorized basis, unknown to the system owner or user and with an intent to take some action on that computer that can be mischievous or malicious.

Voice over Internet Protocol (VoIP): the use of an Internet telephony protocol that relays voice signals across the Internet, whether in a computer-to-phone call or a computer-to-computer call.

Web browser: software with a user-friendly interface that enables users to connect to and navigate on the Internet.

Web bugs (clear GIFs): image files embedded into a web page that can track user movements without the user knowing.

Web server: a server attached to a network that is dedicated to specific applications that must be run on the World Wide Web, or used by web users, or interface very closely with the Web.

Website framing: the use of HTML and browser technology to split a page into segments, which is useful for facilitating ease of use and building impressive websites.

World Wide Web: the user-friendly, graphics-capable component of the Internet.

Y2K: term referring to the year 2000. Y2K was a common abbreviation to identify the computer glitches that were widely predicted to take place when the calendar turned to the year 2000.

Yankee auction: auction format similar to an English auction except that multiple items are sold by price, quantity, and earliest bid time. This form of auction can be used by businesses that are buying products where price is not the only factor to consider and quantity available is a key consideration.

INDEX